Jean-Paul Sartre

Jean-Paul Sartre

Contemporary Approaches to His Philosophy

Edited by
Hugh J. Silverman *and* Frederick A. Elliston

DUQUESNE UNIVERSITY PRESS
PITTSBURGH

Copyright © *1980 Duquesne University Press*

*All rights reserved. Printed in the United States of America.
No part of this book may be used or reproduced in any
manner whatsoever without written permission except in
the case of brief quotations for use in critical articles
and reviews.*

*Published by Duquesne University Press, 600 Forbes Avenue,
Pittsburgh, PA 15219.*

*Distributed by Humanities Press, Atlantic Highlands,
New Jersey 07716*

First Edition

Library of Congress Cataloging in Publication Data
Main entry under title:

Jean-Paul Sartre — contemporary approaches to his philo-
    sophy.

    Bibliography: p.
    1. Sartre, Jean Paul, 1905-   — Addresses, essays,
lectures. I. Silverman, Hugh J. II. Elliston,
Frederick.
B2430.S34J38   194   80-17724
ISBN 0-391-01634-2
ISBN 0-391-01635-0 (pbk.)

In Memoriam

JEAN-PAUL SARTRE

Contents

Preface

Jean-Paul Sartre's philosophy has been the subject of a varied reception. Readings of his work diverge because of basic differences in what counts as viable philosophical activity. Phenomenologists, analytic philosophers, Marxists, structuralists, and historians of philosophy each offer distinctive accounts of his thought. The reader of this book will find not only a coherent treatment of Sartre the philosopher but also an example of contemporary philosophical styles in operation.

Our task is to interpret Sartre's philosophy at the turn of another decade. The essays as a whole reexamine the achievement of his early work of the nineteen-thirties and forties—in and around *Being and Nothingness* (1943). They recount its development and transformation into the fifties and sixties—clustering around the *Critique of Dialectical Reason* (1960). And they indicate its subsequent elaboration in relation to both the life of Flaubert and Sartre's reflections on his own enterprise during the seventies. We have sought to accomplish what Sartre himself has attempted throughout his life—to situate a philosophy in its context by identifying its orientation and its place in contemporary thought.

In his autobiography, *The Words* (1963), Sartre announces a radical break in his own passage from reading to writing. His insertion into writing arose out of a free choice and has continued to serve as his fundamental project. From his childhood imitations of magazine short stories to the publication of his first novel, *Nausea* (1938), he endeavored to put his original choice into practice. Once achieved, he turned his project into a philosophy.

Sartre's existential phenomenology is one of several versions that acquired dominance among French intellectuals during and after the Second World War. On the one hand, the narratives, plays, and essays of Albert Camus stressed the absurdity of life. On the other hand, Maurice Merleau-Ponty's rigorous philosophical writings highlighted the primacy of perception and the significance of human embodiment. As a third alternative, Sartre ranged from fiction to philosophy in order to elaborate and communicate his various themes of bad faith, the body, concrete relations with others, and freedom.

In order to continue his protean project, he developed his thoughts on the indistinguishability of good and evil in his play *The Devil and the Good Lord* (1951) and again in his mammoth biographical account of Jean Genet's self-creating enterprise (1952). Then came the years when he sought to assess the meaning of communism, demonstrating that his previous studies of Baudelaire and literature (1947), Genet and play-acting (1952) did not adequately account for the potential dynamics of social structures. This reorientation led him to refuse not only Camus's absurdist variety of existentialism but also Merleau-Ponty's less committed account of dialectic. To mark the divergence even more clearly, Merleau-Ponty turned in a direction similar to that outlined by Heidegger's later thought, while Sartre concerned himself more extensively with the social dimensions of scarcity and need.

In English-speaking countries during the fifties, Sartre's existentialism was under attack. Anglo-American philosophers such as A. J. Ayer found ample ground to satirize the identification of freedom with nothingness. While they were busy dubbing the Sartrian philosophy of the forties as fuzzy-minded, Sartre himself had moved on to problems related to what he viewed as the misadventures of dialectical reason. When the English translation of *Being and Nothingness* finally appeared in 1956, Sartre was writing his preface to the *Critique of Dialectical Reason*, now known as *Search for a Method*. Hence, philosophers writing primarily in the analytic style even in the early sixties still associated Sartre almost exclusively with his earlier existential phenomenology.

In France the situation was rather different. *The Words* (1963) told the story of Sartre's youth. It explained why he did not need Freudian psychoanalysis (since he had no superego) and why his own brand of existential psychoanalysis was a much more suitable basis for self-analysis. In his autobiography he elaborates how his particular historical situation served as the context for his fundamental project as a writer. How Sartre would reconcile this type of individual self-analysis with his commitment to the Communist Party and to Marxism as the philosophy of our time was demonstrated by his situation in May 1968. Sartre, the singular universal (as he called Kierkegaard), spoke before workers and students, but by that time they had already put his philosophy into action.

Godard's film *Tout Va Bien* ("everything's fine" — or is it?) characterized the atmosphere among left-wing intellectuals for several years after the events of May–June 1968. Sartre undertook his detailed study of Flaubert at that time. He finished three volumes — reviewing only a portion of this nineteenth-century petit bourgeois's self-transformation from poet to artist — and, as with so many other projects, he would not allow it to become a finished product. The Maoist cause occupied his attention and he offered his name to the movement.

By the early seventies, particularly in America, analytic philosophers such as Arthur Danto began to find serious philosophy in *Being and Nothingness*. They sought to make sense out of such Sartrian themes as bad faith, human action, and relations between the in-itself and the for-itself. Meanwhile, phenomenologists and existential philosophers in English-speaking countries had been elaborating the importance of Sartre's theories for more than two decades. They developed his notions of freedom, responsibility, and authenticity with their implications in existential psychology, psychoanalysis, literary criticism, and even aesthetic practice. Historians of recent French philosophy also expounded the principal doctrines long before their assessments could be checked against an English translation of the text.

Similarly, the English translation of the *Critique of Dialectical Reason* appeared (in 1976) sixteen years after its original French publication. Even though its appeal and subsequent praxis in the Events of May 1968 cannot be retrieved — (as Gillan, Knecht, and Dufrenne attest in this volume) — the philosophical significance of the *Critique* certainly persists beyond its immediate social and historical circumstances. Full-scale studies of the *Critique* began to appear in English in the mid-sixties, viz. Laing and Cooper (1964), Desan (1965), Sheridan (1969), Lawler (1976), Craib (1976), Aron in translation from the French (1975), and Chiodi in translation from the Italian (1976). The earliest were largely expository in character, but because of the intricately tortuous style of the 755 page tome, without a knowledge of the original its concepts are not readily available in succinct summaries. Its notions of seriality, collective, group-in-fusion, and institution require careful examination and consideration in order to indicate their paramount importance for the understanding of dialectical thought.

What effect will the lag in producing a translation of Sartre's three volume study of Flaubert (1971–72) have on English-speaking readers? Just as *Saint Genet* (published in 1952 and translated in 1963) remains one of Sartre's most compelling and insightful inquiries into the possibilities of human achievement, *The Idiot of the Family* will continue to demonstrate the significance of personalization and constitution within the comprehension of an historical context. Literary critics have already been hard at work introducing its perennial message to the Anglo-American context. Furthermore, the interviews with Sartre like the one in this volume and those in *Politics and Literature* (1973), *Between Existentialism and Marxism* (1974) and *Life/Situations* (1976) have informed readers of his more recent philosophical orientations including his studies of Flaubert. Nevertheless, because of its overt literary topic, *The Idiot of the Family* will probably not occupy an important place in the considerations of American and English philosophers. They will doubtless still respond to Sartre's existential phenomenology. Even the *Critique* should receive more attention, not only by students of Sartre's thought but also by those committed to the recent emphasis on social thought by philosophers in America such as John Rawls and Robert Nozick. Our hope is that what might have been misunderstood or overlooked in Sartre's philosophy can be rectified by the relevant essays in this volume. Its contents and organization should provide a context for further discussion and a challenge for future inquiry.

Since the mid-sixties, structuralism and post-structuralism have dominated French thought as Sartrian existentialism did in the late forties and fifties. The eclipse of the Sartrian enterprise was practically total for almost a decade. The two French philosophers writing in this volume, Michel Haar (treating the early Sartre) and Mikel Dufrenne (stressing the *Critique* and its foundations), indicate that Sartre had fallen out of currency in French circles. Exceptions can of course be found, but for the most part it was deemed inappropriate to take a Sartrian view of the world and human experience. Only recently have structuralist and even post-structuralist readings of Sartrian texts become fashionable in the French context. A. Helbo's *L'Enjeu du discours: Lecture de Sartre* (Brussels, 1978) is one example. Furthermore, the recent study by François George, *Sur Sartre* (1978), the special issue of *Obliques* on Sartre, and particularly the 1979 "Sartre Aujourd'hui" conference, lasting ten days at Cerisy-la-Salle (Normandy, France), indicate a renewed interest in Sartre. They demonstrate that a reassessment of Sartre's writings is beginning to take place in France.

For English-speaking readers, the situation is different. Sartrian philosophy was always foreign—except for those who were already committed to French thought in general. Thus, even when analytic philosophers begin to take up problems raised in Sartre's early work, they do so with the same ease that they enter into the domains of Descartes, Hume, and Kant. Although the form—reading a text in order to show the versatility of the analytic method—is similar to certain varieties of structuralist readings, the result is not the same. Analytic philosophers develop distinctions that highlight the validity, soundness, consistency, and logical entailment of an argument and hence qualify the problem at hand, while structuralists bring out the signs, structures, and systems, in short, the elements and their interrelationships at work within Sartrian texts—particularly the literary ones. Furthermore, structuralist readings have the memory of what they have overthrown, as Zeus remembered his father, Cronus. For the analytic philosopher, it is the victor learning from the vanquished, as Rome learned from Athens.

The prospects of Sartre's philosophy remain at least as multiform as the current styles of philosophizing that engage it. The Sartrian enterprise cannot be overlooked or ignored. It has entered into the texture of twentieth-century thought—not simply as a historical document, but even more as an articulation of the failure and achievement, memory and hope, orientation and prospect of our own thought. It cannot be ignored and we can only benefit from its lessons by knowing it better.

H.J.S.

F.A.E.

General Introduction

This volume grew out of the recognition that among the many books written on the philosophy of Jean-Paul Sartre, none brings together various contemporary styles of philosophizing in a systematic and comprehensive way. The framework for the interpretation of Sartre's philosophy offered here includes a synchronic reading, a diachronic-synchronic study, and a comparative assessment that presumes the first two. For the first part of the book, we solicited essays on *Being and Nothingness* (1943) that stress both its argumentation and position within the context of European philosophical thinking. The second part is diachronic-synchronic in that it brings out the various stages of Sartre's philosophy, from the earliest work to the most recent. The last section interrelates his positions with the formulations of other philosophers commonly cited as having a major influence on his views. An interview with Sartre himself rounds out the assessment of his philosophical achievement.

The first part treats the principal themes of *Being and Nothingness* — the single work that consolidates Sartre's early existential phenomenological outlook. By considering these essays in sequence, the reader will be able to follow in-depth treatments of the dominant concerns of Sartre's phenomenological ontology in its methodological, epistemological, psychological, and ethical aspects. More specifically, the essays provide a careful and sustained examination of the phenomenological reduction, the concept of bad faith, the notion of the body, and the problem of free human action. The style of each of these four studies, however, is different. They reflect our conviction that philosophical texts as rich as Sartre's should be available to a variety of perspectives and approaches. The wide range of philosophical styles stretch from Busch's phenomenological reinterpretation of the Husserlian methodology at work in Sartre's early writings, through Morris's juxtaposition of Sartre's notion of bad faith alongside Freudian and contemporary Anglo-American accounts of self-deception, to Monasterio's Merleau-Pontean reading of Sartre's theory of the human body, and conclude with Atwell's analytic study of Sartre as an action theorist.

1

The second part emphasizes some general philosophical problems and demonstrates how Sartre has dealt with them over the full course of his philosophical itinerary from the 1930s though the 1970s. The essays cover topics in areas including the theory of language, philosophical psychology, aesthetics, and historiography. Silverman's piece delineates three different formulations in the relation between the self and language. Flynn shows how the three-volume *The Idiot of the Family* (1971-72) can be considered as a sequel to *The Psychology of the Imagination* (1940), and examines Sartre's alternative versions of the imaginary in the interim. Kaelin offers an account of Sartre's aesthetic theory by focusing on the question of "meaning" as it is articulated in the whole gamut of Sartre's writings. He also introduces some polemic with a recent study by Flynn on the role of the imagination. This part concludes with Gillan's critical assessment of Sartre's conception of historiography as it relates to Lukács and to current work in France by Foucault and Braudel. As a whole this part seeks to provide a picture of the scope of Sartre's thought, from its literary and psychological aspects to its aesthetic and historical considerations.

The third part shows how Sartre's philosophy both repeats and differs from that of four major figures in continental thought. Elliston offers an account of the Husserlian notion of intersubjectivity and Sartre's critique of it. Haar demonstrates in meticulous detail the distinctive features of Sartre's and Heidegger's pronouncements on questions such as consciousness, nothingness, anxiety, death, and existentialism in general. Both Elliston and Haar emphasize links with Sartre's early writings, particularly *Being and Nothingness* (1943), while Knecht, in a style associated with that of Klaus Hartmann in Germany, focuses on the relationships between Marx's thought and Sartre's more recent *Critique of Dialectical Reason* (1960). Finally, Dufrenne situates his contemporaries Sartre and Merleau-Ponty in their own social and intellectual context. This piece is of especial importance in filling out the volume as a whole and in indicating Sartre's status alongside Merleau-Ponty, the two dominant French phenomenologists of the past half century. This third part distinguishes Sartre from the philosophers who influenced him and how his work stands as a unique contribution to contemporary philosophical understanding.

In a concluding interview conducted by Leo Fretz in 1976, Sartre looks back over his philosophical career and highlights its major features. Fretz's thematization of major issues helps to guide and elaborate Sartre's own assessment of the relationships between the various aspects of his work from his early conception of the individual to a projected book to be entitled *Power and Freedom*.

I.

Sartre's early writings are replete with references to the work of Edmund Husserl, the generally acknowledged founder of the tradition known as phenomenology. Initially preoccupied with arithmetic, mathematics, and logic, Husserl's questions concerning the nature of numbers and the foundations of inference eventually led him into a general theory of knowledge. Sartre appropriates Husserl's tools and orientation for his own study of various psychological processes, such as imagination and feeling. In his early magnum opus, *Being and Nothingness*, Sartre takes up the existential question posed by Kierkegaard and Nietzsche, and pursued more rigorously by Heidegger: What does it mean for me to be? He subtitles this work "An Essay in Phenomenological Ontology," thereby acknowledging his allegiance to Husserl. But the extent and strength of this allegiance is problematic: What is the relationship between existentialism and phenomenology, and what is the basis for Sartre's own existential phenomenology?

To answer these questions fully would require a careful analysis of many issues: the egological conception of consciousness, the notion of intentionality, the role of imagination, the primacy of action over knowledge, and the debate between realism and idealism. In part one of this volume, Thomas Busch examines Sartre's use of one of the techniques essential to the phenomenological method — the transcendental reduction.

Much misunderstanding of *Being and Nothingness* is based upon a failure to appreciate Sartre's appropriation of phenomenology, particularly the phenomenological reduction. An awareness of Sartre's phenomenological view is necessary in order to recognize the limited scope of *Being and Nothingness*, a book that was never intended to treat human existence in its entirety.

Sartre's work prior to *Being and Nothingness* attempted to provide a phenomenological foundation for humanistic psychology, with the ultimate intention of working out an ethic. The basic Sartrian themes of pre-reflective and reflective consciousness, freedom, bad faith, and facticity are all present in the early work. *Being and Nothingness* takes up these themes but focuses on what Heidegger called inauthenticity — what motivates it and how it may be overcome. Here Sartre develops an ontological study of the relationship of consciousness (being-for-itself) to each phenomenon (being-in-itself). The relationship between these two modes of being grounds the psychological impulse toward absolute being. Once this pre-reflective impulse is thematized, the significance of Sartre's appropriation of the phenomenological reduction emerges as the possibility to "disconnect" our reflective life from its natural impulse. Reading *Being and Nothingness* in this light makes sense out of certain fundamental, but much misinterpreted, texts within the book itself — particularly the notion of bad faith.

As a kind of self-deception, bad faith involves the paradox that in the capacity of deceiver one must know what one cannot know in order to be simultaneously the one deceived. Phyllis Morris grapples with this paradox as both a moral and epistemological dilemma, drawing instructive parallels with the writings of analytic philosophers such as Fingarette and Rorty and the psychoanalytic tradition of Freud.

Fingarette's account of self-deception is acknowledged by the author to parallel Sartre's. But Morris shows it to be considerably more dependent than Fingarette indicates. Specifically in his account of the central role of spelling-out or reflection, the notion of the self is represented as a community disavowal and the purposive nature of self-deception. Amelie Rorty credits Sartre (as well as John Austin) for adding noncognitive elements to our concept of belief and for identifying the interest in personal identity as distinguishing self-deceptive beliefs from other forms of erroneous belief. But Rorty fails to see that Sartre's account of self-deception hinges on distinguishing multiple senses of the term *self*, a particularly surprising omission, since it appears to be important in Rorty's own attempt to resolve the paradox of self-deception.

Sartre's criticisms of Freud are inadequate, according to Morris, in that they apply primarily to Freud's early mechanistic account of the ego's activity in keeping itself unconscious. When we look at Hamlyn's rendering of Freud's later notion of the unconscious as purposive selective attention, however, it does not appear to be incompatible with Sartre's account of different levels of awareness. Assuming that Freud might have rejected Hamlyn's interpretation of the concept of the unconscious, and might have insisted that what is unconscious is not in any sense known, Sartre could then revive one of his criticisms of Freud's earlier view: that Freud did away with self-deception.

To the recurrent criticism that Sartre's view of self-deception is based on the model of other-deception, Morris answers that Sartre turns the tables by showing this to be precisely one of Freud's errors. The most important criticisms of Sartre's view are that his account ends in an unacceptable paradox and makes it logically impossible to get out of self-deception. Morris's reply to the critics shows how Sartre's distinctions between prereflective and reflective consciousness, the past, present, and future aspects of the self, and the first- and third-person perspectives enable him to offer a complex, interesting, and nonparadoxical account of self-deception, and, by implication, of authenticity. To identify falsely with one aspect of the self, or to deny any aspect of the self is to enter self-deception.

The dialogue Morris initiates between continental and analytic style philosophies is continued in John Atwell's analysis of free action—a topic much discussed in the secondary literature on Sartre but seldom from an analytic perspective. According to Atwell, Sartre's view of free will aligns him neither with the strict determinists, for whom each event (including human actions) has an antecedent cause, nor with the libertarians, who deny that human actions are caused in any sense. Rather, Sartre's emphasis on finite freedom places him closer to action theorists, who maintain that actions are not caused or predetermined but limited and intelligible in terms of their context. Both distinguish actions from nonactions in terms of intentionality, but Sartre claims this difference is not immediately or intuitively known. Atwell offers a novel interpretation of the relationship in Sartre between intention and action: the former neither logically entails the latter nor temporally causes it; rather, my intention is to be inferred in terms of a pattern among my actions, a "fundamental project."

Most interpreters of Sartre accept a Cartesian dualism, in which intentions are mental acts. Xavier Monasterio examines the comparatively neglected opposite pole of this dualism — the body. Following Sartre, he first distinguishes the body as subject — the center of a perceptual and pragmatic field — and then the body as object — as it exists for others, for their use. But he advances beyond Sartre by developing the notion of the body as thing — initially the correlate of the coefficient of adversity that characterizes physical things, but extended beyond this affective domain into the body with genuine needs of its own. This body as thing is escaped by the *epoché*, whereby a disinterested philosophical viewpoint is achieved. Consequently, for Monasterio the *epoché* becomes a fall into bad faith rather than the basis for good faith, as Busch suggests. The compatibility of the two interpretations indicates the ambiguous status of the *epoché* in Sartre's thinking.

II.

The status of the self is the central concern of Sartre's first philosophical work, *The Transcendence of the Ego* (1936). Hugh Silverman broaches the problem of the self by considering its formulation in relation to language. Like the other issues discussed in part two, this relation extends beyond Sartre's early existential-phenomenological writings discussed in part one to his middle and later periods — or what Silverman calls *epistemes*. Each *episteme* can be characterized in terms of alternative views of the relation between the self and language.

During the first *episteme* — which extends from *The Transcendence of the Ego* and various works on the emotions and imagination through *Nausea* to *Being and Nothingness*, *The Flies*, and *No Exit* — the relation is conceived as external: the self exists without appeal to language and independent of the ways it is addressed. During the second *episteme*, marked at one extreme by *What Is Literature?* and at the other by *Saint Genet*, the relation is internal for some — such as writers, thieves, and homosexuals: the words that label them create their social reality. In his third *episteme* characterized by *Search for a Method*, *Critique of Dialectical Reason*, and *The Words* — the restrictions are removed: the self is both what is signified and the very process of signifying, construed as a dialectical social process. According to this mature view, as Silverman summarizes, "Sartre's words *on* the self have become words *of* the self."

Like the themes of selfhood and language, the notion of reality runs the gamut of Sartre's philosophy, both logically and chronologically. Thomas

Flynn makes its meaning concrete through a series of incisive contrasts focused mainly on Sartre's extensive study of Flaubert, *The Idiot of the Family*. The practical/unreal emerges as the central dyad from Flynn's list of twelve, which progress from the epistemological (true/false) and psychological (perceptual/imaginary) to the ontological (possible/probable) and sociological (person/personage) and culminate in the ideological. The unreal occurs as the imaginary arises from a derealization, whereby one is disengaged from everyday praxis. All art—whether it be acting, music, poetry, or prose—because it feeds on this derealization, has an ambivalent value: it serves both as an instrument of the real—the naturalistic—and as a flight from reality—the symbolic. It is a weapon in the hands of Sartre the moralizer and a consolation for Flaubert, the imaginary man.

Though imagination is central to art, Eugene Kaelin rejects the contention in Sartre's aesthetic theory that it suffices for an explanation of all our aesthetic experiences. He admits the difficulty of determining just what counts as an aesthetic theory for Sartre, since he never wrote one. Interpretations will differ according to whether one draws on the earlier Husserlian-inspired essays or the later Heideggerian ones. In the former the phenomenology of imagination dominates, and in the latter Sartre's doctrine of existential psychoanalysis prevails.

After rehearsing Sartre's use of the Husserlian eidetic description of aesthetic objects found in the conclusion of *The Psychology of the Imagination*, Kaelin compares it with Husserl's analysis of an Albrecht Dürer etching. He then goes on to provide his own phenomenologically eidetic account of the experience of aesthetic objects, indicating the centrality of the context of expression and the structures of the constitutive "counters." For him the critical question is: Are nonobjective works of art "imaginative," and if so, in what sense? His answer is partly couched in Sartrian terms, which he carefully distinguishes: *sense*, the gestalt property of works of art; *signification*, the semantic meaning of a sign; and *presence*, mistakenly interpreted as the "organic unity" of a work. The last, he argues, is systematically ambiguous and thus theoretically dysfunctional.

Contrary to Sartre, Kaelin argues that our appreciation of figurative works is both perceptual and imaginative: our perception of an aesthetic surface motivates the appearance of an image that as an object can only be present in its absence—that is, in its nonadherence within the structures of the real world of that moment. In nonfigurative works, on the other hand, Kaelin contends that the experience is entirely perceptual, a behavioral pattern of our conscious bodily experiences of objects actually present in the same world. The trick for any figurative artist is to evoke the image on the basis of surface manipulations. Sartre errs, Kaelin maintains, in his exclusive appeal to imagination for an explanation of all our aesthetic experiences.

The fourth contribution to part two, by Garth Gillan, addresses the question of history. His essay has three parts: first it locates the problem of history within the Marxist tradition; then it analyzes Sartre's conception of the foundation of historical understanding; and finally it criticizes praxis as a starting point of history in the light of *Les Annales* historiography.

The analytic tool used in the analysis of Sartre's conception of history is the concept of problematic as developed in relation to phenomenology and structuralism. For the Marxist tradition the question of history involves both historiography and politics—as can be seen in *The German Ideology* and in Lukács's *History and Class Consciousness*. According to Gillan, the failure of Lukács to involve a concrete conception of nature or labor in his conception leads to the necessity of locating the recovery of the dialectical understanding of history on new terrain.

In Gillan's view, the project of the *Critique* is to locate—on the terrain of praxis—the recovery of the dialectic from transcendental materialism. The understanding of the dialectical sense of historical events and processes takes place in the concept of totalization. The concept of totalization rests upon an understanding of praxis as a totalizing activity. Thus, Gillan shows how the methodology of history rests upon the starting point of individual praxis. Intersubjectivity is suppressed.

Contemporary historiography and anthropology contest the primacy of subjectivity in the development of historical methodology. Subjectivity does not operate as an explanatory concept, but as what is to be explained. The weight of explanation rests upon what is exterior to subjectivity and focuses upon the requirements of the *exposition* (writing) of history. Both points indicate what Gillan takes to be the failure of the Sartrian project: to found historical understanding upon the transparence of praxis to itself. Nevertheless, Gillan credits Sartre with locating an issue that others ignore: the problem of mediations.

III.

Whereas part one focuses on existential phenomenological themes, especially in Sartre's early writings, and part two emphasizes more general themes spanning much of Sartre's career, part three treats Sartre's relation to major figures in recent Continental philosophy—Husserl, Heidegger, Marx, and Merleau-Ponty. Though this list of philosophies is hardly exhaustive and the magnitude of the debt is variable, the role of these figures in Sartre's thinking is pervasive and consequential.

Frederick Elliston discusses the philosopher who dominates Sartre's early philosophy perhaps more than any other—Edmund Husserl. Though much has been written on Sartre's commitment to Husserlian phenomenology, Elliston emphasizes a point of comparison that has received relatively little attention—intersubjectivity.

Elliston argues that Husserl's analysis in the Fifth Cartesian Meditation is

fundamentally sound and methodologically fruitful. Husserl discloses the
foundation for all of the self's experiences of others by carrying out a new
kind of *epoché* that strips the world of all direct or indirect reference to
others—in short, of all social meaning. What remains is the sphere of ownness, a field of sensations directly tied to my body, termed the *animate organism*. Through pairing with bodies that look and act as mine would if I
were there, the sense *alter ego* is constituted.

In order to establish the relation between self and others, in opposition
to all such forms of rationality, Husserl appeals to apperception as a single
(albeit mediated and complex) act, whereas Sartre invokes emotions such
as pride and shame. Likewise, both emphasize the internal and reciprocal
character of interpersonal relationships: the self is defined in terms of the
other, and vice versa. Moreover, both reject any Kantian conception of others as noumenal entities in favor of the other as encountered within lived
experiences. They differ significantly, however, on the interpretation of the
other's otherness: for Sartre the other's subjectivity is experienced as my objectivity, ultimately because consciousness as *néant* is polarized into a nihilating for-itself and a nihilated in-itself; for Husserl, however, the lack of
immediacy or privileged access that makes it impossible for me to feel your
pain as you do prevents the other from collapsing into a mirror image of
myself.

Sartre charges that Husserl is inconsistent in his appeal to an intuition of
another's presence when his mental life is (and can be) only indirectly
given, and that he fails to account for one's unshakable confidence that
others exist. In defense of Husserl, Elliston argues that Sartre has misinterpreted intuition by construing it as the completion of a process of evidence
or of imaginative variation, rather than as direct apprehension. Moreover,
others as objects are also problematic for Sartre: only the existence of the
other as subject is absolutely certain. But such an other is a curious entity—
without fixed locus, sex, or identity. And the indubitability of others' existence is emotional not cognitive, felt rather than proven.

Next to Husserl, Heidegger is perhaps the most important thinker for
Sartre's early philosophy. The statement that existence precedes essence in
Existentialism Is a Humanism seems to align Sartre with a fundamental
tenet of *Being and Time*. But Michel Haar contends that this apparent
agreement is misleading for the two philosophers are diametrically opposed
on several basic themes—consciousness, nothingness, anxiety, others, and
death.

As Sartre notes, the word *consciousness* is conspicuously absent from *Being and Time*. But whereas Sartre takes this omission as a shortcoming,
Haar takes it as an accomplishment. Heidegger's alternative notion, *Dasein,*
undercuts the Cartesian dualism that has plagued Western metaphysics
and restores the integrity of human existence. Sartrian consciousness is a
nothingness that, through reflection, is discovered to be synonymous with

our freedom. For Heidegger, on the other hand, this nothingness is not a feature of the self; it appears on the side of the world and does not originate with the world. For Sartre anxiety reveals this nothingness, or freedom, whereas for Heidegger it appears as the meaning of mundane things and dissolves, revealing the structure, the worldhood of the world. Sartre's consciousness of the other in the look is dialectically polarized so that society means struggle. Heidegger's *Mitsein* signifies coexistence rather than conflict, a mistake according to Sartre but a virtue according to Haar. For Heidegger the confrontation with our human mortality marks the transition to authentic existence, whereas for Sartre death is meaningless and absurd, not so much a possibility but a probability that never quite convinces us.

In Heideggerian fashion Haar traces these differences back to competing conceptions of Being and Time. Whereas Heidegger emphasizes the future, Sartre emphasizes a present-at-hand that serves the ideology of domination and masks a radical nihilism.

Much as Husserl and Heidegger dominate Sartre's early philosophy, Marx dominates the later. Ingbert Knecht examines Sartre's commitment to Marxism in terms of alienation. For Marx alienation was attributable to the fetishism of the capitalist mode of production—the fact that workers were forced to specialize in meaningless, repetitive jobs, selling themselves to those who owned the means of production and hence the fruits of their labor. Writing a century later, Sartre is confronted with the incongruous fact that alienation has continued into postcapitalist, socialist society. To save Marxism he relocates the ground of this new phenomenon, social alienation, in features of the group rather than in the private ownership of the means of production.

As in Marx, alienation still derives from a system of relations that forms an independent power against those who once created the system and who continue to participate in it. But whereas Marx restricted himself to the economic system, Sartre's genius is to generalize beyond it to any competitive and discordant system to which atomized individuals find themselves subjugated. His simple paradigm is the series in which isolated individuals are brought together by a common goal, but only externally and anonymously united, unable unilaterally or concertedly to alter the very situation they have created. As such groups increase in dimension, fragmentation, and dispersion, their members become ever more helpless and alienated. Collaboration becomes impossible because of the dialectical contradictions that mediate our relations—scarcity, powerlessness, and conflict.

Despite these parallels, Knecht notes several divergences between Sartre and Marx. Sartre's anthropology is based on a plurality of irreducible subjectivities, whereas Marx's persons are merely instantiations of economic categories. For Sartre, one is alienated from oneself because one is divorced from one's projects, as they are continually modified by the actions of others and by the unintended results one is powerless to control; for Marx,

individuals are cut off from themselves because of a failure to possess the
product in which they have objectified themselves and the specialization
that diminishes the fullness of the person. Marx's solution is an economic
revolution by the proletariat in which private ownership of the means of
production is abolished. Sartre seeks authentic mutuality within new social
situations that enable individuals to carry out their projects without the
counterfinality of the practico-inert and anonymous others. He claims that
his theory simply draws out the full theoretical consequences of what was
restricted to a historical concrete object in Marx's theory of capitalist economy. Knecht contends that Sartre had violated the commandment of
Marxist ideology that alienation exists only under conditions of class struggle and the division of labor in capitalist society. He has thereby abandoned
Marxism.

Mikel Dufrenne, an accomplished philosopher in his own right, also
stresses Sartre's later work by situating it within the context of the earlier
writings and by comparing him with another major figure in our epoch—
his contemporary, collaborator, and former friend, Maurice Merleau-
Ponty. They both attended the École Normale, where Sartre was three
years his senior. They fought in the same war, Sartre as an enlisted man in
the meteorological unit and Merleau-Ponty as a junior officer in the infan-
try. They joined Socialism and Liberty, a short-lived resistance group that
lasted just long enough to renew their friendship. And after the war they
served as coeditors, in all but name, of *Les Temps modernes* until a minor
dispute, which Sartre called "idiotic," terminated their formal collaboration and cooled their friendship. Politically they were strongly divided by
Merleau-Ponty's refusal of allegiance to the Communist Party, which Sartre in *The Communists and Peace* deemed necessary for uniting the atomized, "massified" workers into a cohesive political force, the proletariat.

Philosophically, Dufrenne stresses their commonality—in Heideggerian
terms, as two be ıgs-in-the-world they opened up the transcendental field
and its ambiguities. As complementary rather than conflicting philosophers, Sartre plummets the social world, Merleau-Ponty the natural. Each
recognizes the tension between our finite perspectives and the world's un-
ending horizons. Dufrenne locates their differences more in their existential
choices than in partisan doctrines. Sartre's Kantian project is to seek the
conditions for intelligibility within the social, where totalization is the key—
accomplished through perception in *Being and Nothingness* and by work in
the *Critique of Dialectical Reason*. The product of this totalization undergoes a dialectical reversal: ends are perverted when we inevitably dirty our
hands and the fruits of our labors confront us as an alien power. Through
this process, history is generated as that which man has made and that to
which he must submit. More so than Merleau-Ponty, Sartre accepts a debt
to this dialectic as the spring of history and the source of its intelligibility.
But this difference is not so much a matter of right and wrong for Dufrenne

as an orientation of sympathies—a tendency that also guides Dufrenne's own thought.

IV.

We complete the volume with an interview conducted by Leo Fretz in 1976. Since the occurrence of almost complete blindness, Sartre has granted a number of interviews as an avenue for his ongoing philosophical enterprise. We are fortunate to have Fretz's probing questions and framework for establishing in terms of Sartre's own evaluation the links between Sartre's earlier and later philosophies. Fretz poses the problem of what Bacheland and Althusser have called "an epistemological break." It has also been termed the question of a "radical conversion" between Sartre's existential phenomenology and his subsequent Marxism. In effect, Sartre affirms a uniformity to his thought but allows for the revision of former misjudgments.

Most of these essays were commissioned specifically for this volume. None has been published previously; only the interview has appeared recently, in Dutch. As such, the book is a group project whose praxis can be assessed only by the totalization that it produces (to employ the language of Sartre's more recent position). As editors, we have attempted to bring together in a coherent framework a variety of contemporary styles of philosophizing drawn from both North American and European contexts. Practically all of the contributors have published significant books or articles on Sartre. As philosophers themselves, the contributors bring their own perspectives to the exposition, analysis, interpretation, and critique of perhaps the most important thinker and writer of our century.

The current status of Sartre's philosophy is not without debate. Because of his versatility and effectiveness in a wide variety of areas (including philosophy, the novel, theater, biography, autobiography, political theory, and criticism), he has been called the most significant writer of our times.

Some claim that he is the most notable recent addition to a long line of philosophers in the Western tradition beginning with Plato. Others emphasize that his philosophy is essential to the development of recent trends in humanistic and existential psychology, in theories of morality, and in aesthetics. Some point to the fact that his theses concerning contemporary philosophical problems are at last becoming recognized as worthy of analytic scrutiny by the Anglo-American philosophical world. It has been asserted that his early existential positions are still viable studies of human experience, that his more recent political writings are accurate descriptions of present-day scarcity and need, and that his novels and plays are the most perspicacious of those produced in the post–World War II period.

By contrast, some have argued that Sartre's importance has waned with the decline of existential phenomenology and his brand of existential Marxism in European intellectual circles. Still others dismiss Sartre as an insignificant philosopher when placed alongside Husserl, Heidegger, and Merleau-Ponty, because he depends too heavily on the philosophical tradition that he reinterprets into his own language.

Despite this controversy, there is no doubt that Sartre's work needs to be read, studied, and evaluated in order to be understood, fully. The present volume is our contribution to that enterprise. By producing a book that represents the variety and conflict of interpretations as well as the substance and significance of Sartre's philosophy, we hope to supply scholars, students, and general readers with insight into the work of a philosopher who will not be forgotten — a writer who has become immortal in his own lifetime.

Key To Abbreviations

AS   *Anti-Semite and Jew*. Translated by George J. Becker. New York: Schocken Books, 1965.

B   *Baudelaire*. Translated by Martin Turnell. New York: New Directions, 1967.

BN   *Being and Nothingness*. Translated by Hazel E. Barnes. New York: Philosophical Library, 1956.

BT   *Between Existentialism and Marxism*. Translated by John Mathews. New York: William Morrow and Company, 1974.

CA   *The Condemned of Altona*. Translated by Sylvia Leeson and George Leeson. New York: Knopf, Vintage Books, 1963.

CDR   *Critique of Dialectical Reason*. Translated by Alan Sheridan-Smith and edited by Jonathan Rée. London: New Left Books, 1976.

DH   *Dirty Hands*. Translated by Lionel Abel. In *No Exit and Three Other Plays*. New York: Knopf, Vintage Books, 1955.

EA   *Essays in Aesthetics*. Translated by Wade Baskin. New York: Washington Square Press, 1966.

EE   *Essays in Existentialism*. Edited by Wade Baskin. New York: Citadel Press, 1965.

EM   *Emotions: Outline of a Theory*. Translated by Bernard Frechtman. New York: Citadel Press, 1971.

EX   *Existentialism*. Translated by Bernard Frechtman. New York: Philosophical Library, 1947.

FL   *The Flies*. Translated by Stuart Gilbert. In *No Exit and Three Other Plays*. New York: Knopf, Vintage Books, 1947.

IM   *Imagination*. Translated by Forrest Williams. Ann Arbor: University of Michigan Press, Ann Arbor Paperback, 1972.

LP   *Literary and Philosophical Essays.* Translated by Annette Michelson. New York: Collier, 1962.

LS   *Life/Situations.* Translated by Paul Auster and Lydia Davis. New York: Random House, Vintage Books, 1978.

N   *Nausea.* Translated by Lloyd Alexander. New York: New Directions, 1950.

PJ   *The Philosophy of Jean-Paul Sartre.* Edited by Robert D. Cumming. New York: Random House, Vintage Books, 1965.

PS   *The Psychology of Imagination.* Translated by Bernard Frechtman. New York: Citadel, 1961.

SG   *Saint Genet: Comedian and Martyr.* Translated by Bernard Frechtman. New York: New American Library, 1963.

SM   *Search for a Method.* Translated by Hazel E. Barnes. New York: Knopf, Vintage Books, 1963.

ST   *Sartre on Theatre.* Translated by Frank Jellinek. New York: Random House, Pantheon Books, 1976.

TE   *The Transcendence of the Ego.* Translated by Forrest Williams and Robert Kirkpatrick. New York: Noonday Press, 1957.

W   *The Words.* Translated by Bernard Frechtman. Greenwich, Conn.: Fawcett, 1964.

WA   *The Wall.* Translated by Lloyd Alexander. New York: New Directions, 1948.

WL   *What Is Literature?* Translated by Bernard Frechtman. New York: Harper & Row, Colophon Books, 1965.

PART ONE

Existential Phenomenological Themes

Thomas W. Busch

1. *Sartre's Use of the Reduction:* Being and Nothingness *Reconsidered*

The publication of *Being and Nothingness* (BN)[1] in June 1943 was scarcely noted. The initial apathy that greeted the "essay on phenomenological ontology" was succeeded in time by a series of misunderstandings and misinterpretations that, unfortunately, continue up to the present.

There are many reasons for the misunderstandings. The book's very length can easily conceal its essentially limited character. Then, Sartre's use of Hegelian and Heideggerian language has led many critics to assume that he meant to adopt the basic positions of these men. The dramatic statements "man is a useless passion,"[2] human relationships form a hellish "circle,"[3] and "all human activities are equivalent"[4] have distracted critics into tirades against Sartre's supposed pessimism and antihumanism. Of course a good deal of the misunderstanding can be attributed to Sartre himself, who gives the reader only scanty references (sometimes couched in footnotes) as to what he is about. He presupposes that the reader is more than familiar with his earlier work and aware that his principal inspiration is Husserl's phenomenology. Despite the important suggestions offered some time ago by Simone de Beauvoir[5] and Francis Jeanson[6] that it is necessary to read Sartre as working within a phenomenological perspective, influential commentary on and criticism of Sartre has insisted upon stressing his differences from Husserl or simply ignoring his phenomenology.[7]

1. *L'Être et le néant* (Paris: Gallimard, 1943). The English translation that I use in this paper is that of Hazel E. Barnes, *Being and Nothingness* (New York: Philosophical Library, 1956), hereafter abbreviated as BN.

2. Barnes, trans., *Being and Nothingness*, p. 615; Fr., p. 708.

3. Ibid., p. 412; Fr., p. 486.

4. Ibid., p. 627; Fr., p. 721.

5. Simone de Beauvoir, *The Prime of Life*, trans. Peter Green (New York: Lancer, 1971), pp. 161–162, 223–224. See also her *The Ethics of Ambiguity*, trans. B. Frechtman (New York: Citadel, 1964), p. 14.

6. Francis Jeanson, *Le problème moral et la pensée de Sartre* (Paris: Éditions du Myrte, 1947).

7. According to Herbert Spiegelberg, *The Phenomenological Movement*, vol. 2 (The Hague: Nijhoff, 1960), p. 478: "The phenomenological reduction is not very prominent in

We intend to offer a reading of BN that discloses its partial character —
the fact that it was never intended to render intelligible the full range of
human activity — and to demonstrate that this partial character can be understood only within the context of Sartre's use of the phenomenological reduction. Finally, we will suggest that Sartre's philosophy can be seen as an
extension of Husserl's programmatic.

I. Sartre's Use of the Reduction prior to BN

We disagree with Klaus Hartmann when he states in the preface to his
Sartre's Ontology, "it is not essential to us that a certain form of phenomenology precede *L'Être et le néant* in Sartre's intellectual development."[8] It
is essential to situate BN within the context of the early work, for the ontology addresses itself to a problem rising directly from the early work: the motivation for adopting the natural attitude. However, before we examine
Sartre's use of the reduction, it will be helpful to consider the Husserlian
phenomenological reduction.[9]

Husserl contrasts the phenomenological viewpoint, gained by the reduction, with the natural attitude — "our first outlook upon life." In this natural attitude one confronts a "spatio-temporal fact world" as well as a *"world
of values*, a *world of goods*, a *practical world*,*"* which are taken in uncritical
fashion "to be out there" just as they give themselves, as having being "out
there."[10]

For the purpose of establishing a scientific, critical philosophy, this nat-

---

L'Être et le neant." Wilfred Desan, *The Tragic Finale* (New York: Anchor Books, 1960), p. 5,
holds that "Heidegger and Sartre have abolished the reductions." Maurice Natanson, *A Critique of Jean-Paul Sartre's Ontology* (Lincoln: University of Nebraska Press, 1951), p. 70,
claims: "Our basic criticism of this analysis of Being is that whatever its merits or insights, it is
not a phenomenological analysis. Quite to the contrary, the Husserlian method is put aside as
inadequate. To begin with, no *epoché* or reduction has been performed." In a recent interview on a reissue of Natanson's book, A. G. Pleydell-Pearce, although taking issue with certain of his views, states: "Natanson correctly points out that Sartre found no role in his philosophical method for that central feature of Husserlian phenomenology — the epoché." *The
Journal of the British Society for Phenomenology*, vol. 5 (January 1974), p. 86. Robert Solomon, in *Phenomenology and Existentialism* (New York: Harper & Row, 1972), p. 20, holds:
"Sartre and Heidegger explicitly reject the reduction in all its forms." In his recent *Commentary on Jean-Paul Sartre's Being and Nothingness* (New York: Harper & Row, 1974), Joseph
Catalano writes, p. 8: "He (Sartre) rejects Husserl's phenomenological reduction." Richard
Bernstein, in his fine *Praxis and Action* (Philadelphia: University of Pennsylvania Press,
1971), unfortunately ignores Sartre's phenomenology, with the result of confusing bad faith
and authenticity.

   8. Klaus Hartmann, *Sartre's Ontology* (Evanston: Northwestern University Press, 1966),
p. xvii.

   9. By "reduction" we refer to the transcendental reduction, as shall be explained. The
"eidetic" reduction, accepted by Sartre, is not at issue here.

   10. Edmund Husserl, *Ideen zu einer reinen Phänomenologie und phänomenologischen
Philosophie. Volume I: Allgemeine Einführung in die reine Phänomenologie*, edit. W. Biemel
(The Hague: Nijhoff, 1950). The English translation cited here is that of W. R. Boyce Gibson,
Ideas: General Introduction to Pure Phenomenology (New York: Collier, 1962), pp. 93-96.

ural attitude must be suspended, "bracketed," "put out of action." In this way what is actually given to consciousness can be dissociated from various theses about the given. This *epoche* permits a disinterested reflective posture toward conscious life "with all the pure subjective processes making this up, and everything meant in them purely as meant in them: the universe of 'phenomena.' . . ."[11] This marks the transcendental moment of the reduction through which objects intended by consciousness are grasped in their essential correlation with the intending acts of consciousness. Objects, thus reduced to the status of meanings *for* consciousness, are further grasped as constituted *by* the meaning-giving acts of consciousness: "Reality and world are just the titles for certain valid *unities of meaning* . . . related to certain organizations of pure absolute consciousness which dispense meaning . . . in certain essentially fixed, specific ways."[12] Conscious life, under the exercise of reduction, comprises a field of study for phenomenology in two directions: there is the *noema*, or object exactly as meant, and the *noesis*, or intending, meaning-giving act of consciousness.

In *The Transcendence of the Ego* (TE),[13] his first philosophical work, Sartre proposes to determine the structure of consciousness. He distinguishes unreflective and reflective consciousness. Unreflective consciousness intends or posits an object other than itself and is simultaneously nonpositionally self-aware. This latter dimension, self-consciousness, precludes an unconscious consciousness and allows for the possibility of reflective knowledge. Reflective consciousness intends or posits an object, but in its case the object is another act of consciousness. The reflective consciousness is also non-positionally self-aware (allowing for the possibility of knowing it). The basic structure of consciousness, in either case, is the same: awareness of an object and simultaneous awareness of being aware of the object. Unreflective consciousness is given "ontological priority"[14] over reflective consciousness, since the latter requires the former for its existence. Additionally, unreflective consciousness is considered an "autonomous" region having its own intelligibility. On the level of unreflected consciousness,

Everything happens as if we lived in a world whose objects, in addition to their qualities of warmth, odor, shape, etc., had the qualities of repulsive, attractive, delightful, useful, etc., and as if these qualities were forces having a certain power over us. . . . In fact, I am plunged into the world of objects; it is

11. Edmund Husserl, *Cartesianische Meditionen, Husserliana I* (The Hague: Nijhoff, 1950). English translation by Dorion Cairns, *Cartesian Meditations* (The Hague: Nijhoff, 1960), p. 20.

12. Gibson, trans., *Ideas*, p. 153.

13. *La Transcendance de l'ego:* esquisse d'une description phénoménologique, introduction, notes, and appendices by Sylvie Le Bon (Paris: Vrin, 1972). The English translation that I cite in this section is by Forrest Williams and Robert Kirkpatrick, *The Transcendence of the Ego* (New York: Noonday, 1957).

14. Williams and Kirkpatrick, trans., *Transcendence*, p. 58; Fr., p. 41.

they which constitute the unity of my consciousness; it is they which present themselves with values, with attractive and repellent qualities—but *me*, I have disappeared.[15]

Reflection "poisons" this unreflected situation, because through it consciousness pulls itself back from its absorption in objects and their qualities:

> On the unreflected level I bring Peter help because Peter is "having to be helped." But if my state is suddenly transformed into a reflected state then I am watching myself act. . . . It is no longer Peter, who attracts me, it is my helpful consciousness which appears to me as having to be perpetuated.[16]

To the distinction between the unreflected and the reflective must be added the distinction between two different types of reflection: pure and impure. We have observed that on the unreflected level objects and qualities can appear as "forces having a certain power over us." On this level consciousness is aware of itself only nonpositionally, or marginally; it does not *know* itself directly. A reflection (impure) can occur that grasps consciousness in such a way as to prolong this state of the power of objects over us. A reflection (pure), which is phenomenological, can occur that grasps the true being of consciousness. In this case subjectivity, which was aware of itself only non-positionally, is recovered and known, with the consequence that objects no longer persist with force over us. In the previous example of helping Peter, the transition from unreflected to reflected is seen to cast upon reflective consciousness the burden of ethical responsibility: the helpful consciousness must be "perpetuated" and is not a victim of external control.

Purifying reflection also allows us to grasp the constitution of the ego. Sartre notes that "the consciousness which says *I think* is precisely not the consciousness which thinks."[17] Husserl, for whom consciousness was egological, is accused of harboring the "thesis" of the ego, of taking a product of consciousness for a real part of consciousness. Sartre traces the ego's constitution: "*really* consciousnesses are first; through these are constituted states; and then, through the latter, the ego is constituted."[18] Impure reflection (the natural attitude) reverses this process: "the order is reversed by a consciousness which imprisons itself in the world in order to flee from itself; consciousnesses are given as emanating from states and states as produced by the ego."[19] Through impure reflection consciousness is reified, made worldly and subjected to worldly forces (heteronomy). It is only on "the pure reflective level" that consciousness is seen to maintain (constitute) the

15. Ibid., pp. 58, 49; Fr., pp. 41–42, 52.
16. Ibid., p. 59; Fr., p. 42.
17. Ibid., p. 45; Fr., p. 28.
18. Ibid., p. 81; Fr., p. 63.
19. Ibid.

ego outside by a "continued creation." Since what Sartre means by "ego" is synonymous with essence, moral identity, TE offers an argument for moral autonomy and must be considered the foundational work for "an ethics and a politics."[20] Access to this ethics and politics can be had only through the reduction "the *epoche* is no longer . . . an intellectual method, an erudite procedure: it is an anxiety. . . ."[21]

The themes of unreflected and reflected consciousness, pure and impure reflection reappear in Sartre's short work on the emotions, the only fragment published of the larger work *La Psyché*.[22]

As an unreflected experience, emotional consciousness is world- or object-centered: "emotion returns to the object at every moment and is fed there." Sartre calls emotional consciousness a magical transformation of the real world that occurs when the latter becomes too difficult to live in. Emotional consciousness is an escape into the magical world that it constitutes, all the while believing in this magical world. Because emotional consciousness does not know that it constitutes its world (it is only non-positionally self-aware), it is "caught in its own trap. . . . The objects are captivating, enchaining: they seize upon consciousness." The spell can be broken by "a reflective activity of reduction. . . . Freedom [moral] must come from a purifying reflection or total disappearance of the affecting situation."[23] Unfortunately, we usually direct upon consciousness "an accessory reflection which perceives consciousness as consciousness, but insofar as it is motivated by the object."[24]

Notice that both TE and the work on emotions indicate the possibility of various levels of exploration—one bearing upon the description of the world as unreflectedly lived, one bearing upon impure or accessory reflection, and one bearing upon reflective (pure) consciousness insofar as it recovers itself as constituter of the world.

Nausea (N)[25] is a work that touches upon all of these levels. Roquentin's journal traces the experience of living through the reduction. Roquentin can no longer live "normally" (naively). His direct immersion in the "life-

20. Ibid., p. 106; Fr., p. 87.

21. Ibid., p. 103; Fr., p. 84.

22. "Meanwhile Sartre was writing a treatise on phenomenological psychology which he entitled *La Psyché*, and of which in the end he published an extract only calling it *Esquisse d'une théorie phénoménologique des émotions*. Here he developed his theory of 'psychic objectivity' which had been sketched out in the essay on *The Transcendence of the Ego*. But to his way of thinking this was little more than an exercise, and after writing four hundred pages he broke off to complete his collection of stories." Simone de Beauvoir, *The Prime of Life*, pp. 383–384.

23. *Esquisse d'une théorie des émotions* (Paris: Hermann, 1939), p. 53. The English translation is by B. Frechtman, *The Emotions: Outline of a Theory* (New York: Philosophical Library, 1939), pp. 78–79.

24. Frechtman, trans., *Emotions*, p. 91; Fr., pp. 60–61.

25. *La Nausée* (Paris: Gallimard, 1938). The English translation cited in this section is that of Lloyd Alexander, *Nausea* (New York: New Directions, 1964).

world" (the world of meaning and value) is suspended ("Something has happened to me . . . things have lost their usual look").[26] At length he comes—for example, through reduction of use-objects and words—to discover the constitution of the life-world: "Of these relations (which I insisted on maintaining in order to delay the crumbling of the human world . . .) *I felt myself to be the arbitrator; they no longer had their teeth in things."*[27] The life-world does not have its being "out there." The very method Sartre uses —such as scrambling metaphors, offering fantastic contingencies—to show that the life-world is relative, dependent, and constituted is quite similar to Husserl's proposal, in *Ideas* I, of the "nullifying of the world," an experiment whereby "we mentally destroy the objectivity of things."[28] Husserl used the nullification of the world to display the residuum of absolute consciousness. In N, Roquentin discovers a different residuum—existence, "the very paste of things,"[29] at the very basis of the world and of the subject. If TE established that Husserl had not gone far enough with the reduction, N argues that, in a certain way, he went too far. Specifically, for Sartre employment of the reduction reveals that there are *limits* to the constitutive activity of consciousness.

In *The Psychology of Imagination* Sartre addresses precisely this question of limits:

> After the phenomenological reduction we find ourselves in the presence of the transcendental consciousness which unveils itself to our reflective descriptions. We can thus fix by concepts the result of our eidetic intuition of the essence "consciousness." Now phenomenological descriptions can discover, for instance, that the very structure of the transcendental consciousness implies that this consciousness is constitutive *of a world*. But it is evident that they will not teach us that consciousness must be constitutive *of* such a world, that is, exactly the one where we are, with its earth, its animals, its men and the story of these men. We are here in the presence of a primary and irreducible fact which presents itself as a contingent and irrational specification of the noematic essence of the *world*.[30]

Phenomenology, in other words, can account through transcendental subjectivity for the appearance of objects and the world *in general*, but not for the fact of this object and world.[31] For Sartre, consciousness is meaning-giving (primarily in a practical or cultural way) and objects and world are

26. Alexander, trans., *Nausea*, p. 4; Fr., p. 16.

27. Ibid., p. 128; emphasis added.

28. Gibson, trans., *Ideas*, p. 133.

29. Alexander, trans., *Nausea*, p. 127; Fr., p. 162.

30. Jean-Paul Sartre, *L'Imaginaire* (Paris: Gallimard, 1940), p. 227. The English translation is by B. Frechtman, *The Psychology of Imagination* (New York: Washington Square Press, 1966), p. 233.

31. The same criticism is leveled at Husserl from a non-Sartrian perspective by Robert Sokolowski, *The Formation of Husserl's Concept of Constitution* (The Hague; Martinus Nijhoff,

grasped as meant (the life-world), but lurking in the process, unnoticed by the naive consciousness, is the irrational facticity he alludes to as *existence*.

Furthermore, since existence is depicted as "paste" and "stuff," a comparison to Husserl's use of *hyle* is suggested. In explaining how objects are constituted, Husserl at first employed a matter-form theory whereby the intentional act animated (gave reference to) certain immanent sensible contents (*hyle*). In themselves, the *hyle* were meaningless and were distinguished from the noema or meant-objects. The *hyle* never appeared in the intending of noema, but could be grasped only when the normal intentional process was interrupted. In N, Sartre's famous example of the chestnut tree is an instance of the breakdown of normally functioning intentionality into an experience of existence. The "tree" becomes a "mass" when intentionality breaks down. Roquentin's vision is of the disappearance of the life-world in favor of "masses, all in disorder."[32] Existence, as senseless stuff, can be interpreted as Husserl's *hyle*, ejected from the status of being immanent to consciousness. Additionally, for Sartre the intentional functioning of the subject (the act itself) can also break down, resulting in the apprehension of the real subject's own "meaningless stuff" — as when the intending body becomes flesh — "an inert datum."[33]

In N, existence appears, upon exercise of the reduction, as "irrational stuff," normally grasped (naively, in the natural attitude) as meaningful, but given sense by intentional activity. Roquentin has always been "like the others" and has not noticed existence, neither his own nor that of things. He comes to utilize a reduction that leads to the separation of the constituted and the nonconstituted, of meaning and existence. Toward the end of the novel he suggests that there was a deep-seated motivation not to effect such a reduction: he wanted to hide his contingent existence in favor of trying to *be* absolutely. This realization brings about a catharsis: at the very end of the book he must *decide* what to do with his life.

II. The Reduction in BN

The difficult question of determining the exact relationship between N and BN will not be taken up here. It is sufficient for our purposes to note that both books attempt to sort out the constituted and nonconstituted, with *Being*, of course, belonging to the latter category.[34]

1964), p. 218: "In providing only subjectivity as a condition of possibility, Husserl is left with the content of constitution as an unexplained residuum, a pure facticity which escapes the principles of his philsophy."

32. Alexander, trans., *Nausea*, p. 126; Fr., p. 162.

33. See the passages in which Roquentin's face becomes a "lunar world" (pp. 16–17; Fr., pp. 30–31) and his hand a "crab" (pp. 98–99; Fr., pp. 127–128; also in BN, the treatment of the body in the phenomenon of desire (pp. 388–392; Fr., pp. 458–462).

34. There are serious ambiguities in Sartre's use of the terms *transcendent* and *being-in-*

The introduction to BN stresses the ontological primacy of prereflective experience. Sartre's presentation appears very much influenced by *Ideas*, particularly sections 34 through 42, wherein, under the heading of a "Psychological Phenomenological" inquiry into the essence of consciousness, Husserl distinguishes (eidetically) between the fundamentally distinct ways of being — consciousness and reality. Sartre, however, will not accept what is s ated under the exercise of phenomenological reduction, from section 50 on, namely that "Reality . . . is, absolutely speaking, nothing at all . . . is *only* intentional, *only* known. . . ."[35] — if by "reality" is meant "being." On the other hand, Sartre does agree with Husserl that consciousness dispenses meaning (section 55), so that the "world" for both becomes a unity of meaning related to certain organizations of consciousness. For Sartre being-in-itself is "the condition of all revelation."

To understand BN properly — particularly to see the relationship of ontology to the ethics and politics — it is essential to note that being-for-itself is identified as "the being of the pre-reflective cogito"[36] and *Erlebnis*.[37] We recall that for pre-reflective consciousness objects have a weight or force, they are attractive, horrible, useful, and so forth. Since pre-reflective consciousness is only non-positionally self-aware, it is lost in the objects before it. They are dominating:

> Thus in what we shall call the world of the immediate, which delivers itself to our unreflective consciousness, we do not first appear to ourselves, to be thrown subsequently into our enterprises. Our being is immediately "in situation"; that is, it arises in enterprises and knows itself first insofar as it is reflected in those enterprises. We discover ourselves then in a world peopled with demands, in the heart of projects "in the course of realization." I write. I am going to smoke. I have an appointment this evening with Pierre. I must not forget to reply to Simon.[38]

---

itself in BN. For example, each profile of a thing "is already in itself alone a transcendent being" (p. lxi; Fr., p. 28); "A great joy which I hope for, a grief which I dread acquire . . . transcendence in immanence" (p. lxi; Fr., p. 71). Motives also have this curious "transcendence in immanence" (p. 34; Fr., p. 71); "The Ego appears to consciousness as a transcendent in-itself . . ." (p. 103; Fr., p. 147); "The past is the in-itself which I am . . ." (p. 118; Fr., p. 162); the look of the other fixes me as "in-itself" (p. 262; Fr., p. 320); the body of the other is given to me "as the pure in-itself of his being" (p. 343; Fr., p. 409). In the chapter on "Being and Doing: Freedom" the in-itself is referred to as "brute being" (p. 488; Fr., p. 568), "material things" (p. 456; Fr., p. 533), "real things" (p. 483; Fr., p. 563). At times being-in-itself is ascribed to all objectivities and at times to perceptual objects. The "ontological proof," however, does not identify being-in-itself as any particular object but as the *ground* of all objectivity, the foundation on which the for-itself surpasses itself toward both real and unreal worlds.

35. Gibson, trans., *Ideas*, p. 139.
36. Barnes, trans., *Being and Nothingness*, p. lxiii; Fr., p. 31.
37. Ibid., p. 95; Fr., p. 139.
38. Ibid., p. 39; Fr., pp. 76-77.

In the concluding remarks of the very first chapter, "The Origin of Negation," Sartre tells us that it is possible to achieve a reflective apprehension of our consciousness as it constitutes the meaning of the world.

> But as soon as the enterprise is held at a distance from me, as soon as I am referred to myself because I must await myself in the future, then I discover myself suddenly as the one who gives meaning to the alarm clock, the one who by a signboard forbids himself to walk on a flowerbed or on the lawn, the one from whom the boss's order borrows its urgency, the one who decides the interest of the book which he is writing, the one finally who makes the values exist in order to determine his action by their demands. . . . It is I who sustain values in being.[39]

We can readily see here the anguishing passage from immediacy to the morally autonomous consciousness and ethics. Ethics becomes possible only when reflective consciousness can hold the immediate at a distance, which occurs by means of the reduction "only reflective consciousness can be dissociated from what is posited by the consciousness reflected on. It is on the reflective level only that we can attempt an Ἐποχή, a putting between parentheses, only there that we can refuse what Husserl calls the *Mitmachen*."[40] At the same time Sartre indicates the possibility of what was referred to in the early work as impure reflection: "it still remains possible for me to maintain various types of conduct with respect to my own anguish — in particular, patterns of flight."[41] It is crucial to note that having introduced the reduction as the foundation of ethics, Sartre, in BN, does not proceed to discuss the recovery of responsibility or the constitution of values consequent upon reduction, but instead proceeds to discuss impure reflection. Flight is presented as bad faith or seriousness; an attempt is made to account for the prevalence of flight (Sartre's literature is witness to his belief that most people are in bad faith) by offering a motive for it (the passion to be). Then the possibility is offered, through existential psychoanalysis, of interpreting our lives in terms of the passion to be, and, one hopes, of using this knowledge as "a means of deliverance."[42] Sartre explicitly informs us, prior to taking up these matters, that the "transcendence" of the immediate available to us through purifying reflection needs "separate study."[43] This "separate study" is repeated several times throughout the remainder of the book and hinges on a new use of the reduction:

---

39. Ibid.
40. Ibid., p. 75; Fr., p. 117.
41. Ibid., p. 40; Fr., p. 78.
42. Ibid., p. 627; Fr., p. 721.
43. Ibid., p. 44; Fr., p. 82.

1. In the footnote that closes the discussion of bad faith, Sartre mentions the possibility of radically escaping bad faith. He writes:

    > But this pre-supposes a self-recovery of being which was previously corrupted. This self-recovery we shall call authenticity, the description of which *has no place here*.[44]

    In authenticity, reached by a self-recovery, which is the reduction, the aim of being a thing (the aim of bad and good faith) is bracketed and refused as a goal by moral consciousness.

2. In the footnote that concludes the discussion of bad-faith relationships with "the other" in "Concrete Relations with Others," Sartre refers to the "possibility of an ethics of deliverance and salvation. But this can be achieved only after a radical conversion *which we cannot discuss here*."[45] The radical conversion is the employment of the reduction to effect a suspension by pure or moral reflection of the ideal value haunting the for-itself. Sartre thus reserves his treatment of authentic human relationships for separate study.

3. In the discussion of play and seriousness Sartre informs us that play, unlike seriousness, "strips the real of its reality" and "releases subjectivity."[46] The serious man attributes more reality to the world than to himself, thereby overlooking constitution. Play aims at "the absolute freedom which is the very being of the person."[47] He continues:

    > This particular type of conduct, which has freedom for its foundation and its goal, *deserves a special study* [emphasis added]. It is radically different from all others in that it aims at a radically different type of being. It would be necessary to explain in full detail its relations with the project of being God, which has appeared to us as the deep-seated structure of human reality. But such a study *cannot be made here* [emphasis added]; it belongs to an *Ethics* and it supposes that there has been a preliminary definition of *nature and the role of purifying reflection (our descriptions have hitherto aimed only at accessory reflection)* [emphasis added]; it supposes in addition taking a position which can be *moral* only in the face of values which haunt the for-itself.[48]

    These "values" that haunt the for-itself become thematic via the reduction and then questionable. As long as the for-itself is plunged into immediacy, it is a victim of "nature" (the passion to be) and is not autonomous. Play is the symbol of an autonomy that can be gained through effecting the reduction.

4. In the conclusion of BN, in the section "Ethical Implications," Sartre suggests the use of existential psychoanalysis as a method of delivering us from seriousness. "Freedom will become conscious of itself"[49] and the possibility arises for freedom "to turn its back" on the ideal value of in-itself-for-itself. However, this refers us "to a pure and not an accessory reflection," which

---

44. Ibid., emphasis added; Fr., p. 111, n. 1.
45. Ibid., p. 412, emphasis added; Fr., p. 484.
46. Ibid., p. 580; Fr., p. 669.
47. Ibid., p. 581; Fr., p. 670.
48. Ibid.
49. Ibid., p. 627; Fr., p. 722.

puts us "on the ethical plane." This other "fundamental attitude" will be treated in a "future work." This reference to freedom becoming conscious of itself is, of course, directed to a thematic consciousness gained by reduction. Through reduction it is revealed to man *"that he is the being by whom values exist,"*[50] that "freedom is the unique source of value and the nothingness by which the *world* exists."[51] The spirit of seriousness is overcome, that attitude whereby consciousness "considers values as transcendent givens independent of human subjectivity."[52]

BN, then, despite its size, is evidently a deliberately incomplete account of human activity. We have suggested that its incompleteness is intelligible in the light of Sartre's peculiar use of the reduction. Actually, three different uses of the reduction are discernible in those works we examined: 1) the reduction applied to psychic life resulting in an ontologically free impersonal consciousness; 2) a reduction applied to the life-world, resulting in the distinction between meaning and existence; and 3) a reduction applied to the ideal value of absolute being, which haunts pre-reflective consciousness, resulting in the refusal of that value by moral consciousness. This last use of the reduction is crucial to understanding BN. The pre-reflective is a lost or naive consciousness (recall Sartre's use of the term "nature" in the discussion of play), since it loses itself in favor of objects. Sartre tells us: "It is not then through inauthenticity that human reality loses itself in the world. For human reality being-in-the-world means radically to lose oneself in the world through the very revelation which causes there to be a world."[53] Bad faith, seriousness, impure reflection are merely accomplices to this original loss. "The world's belonging to the *person* is never posited on the level of the pre-reflective cogito"[54] That marks the limits of BN.

One can sympathize with those critics who insist that Sartre does not follow Husserl's use of the reduction with respect to the issue of "existence." However, to claim, as so many critics do, that there are no reductions in Sartre eclipses the fact that he employs the reduction with respect to *meaning* and *value* in order to achieve a morally autonomous consciousness. Ethics would involve a study of pure reflective consciousness in relation to existence and would require a theory of value constitution.

III. Sartre and Husserl

Ian Alexander, in his article "The Phenomenological Philosophy in France," likens the impact of Husserl on French thought to that of Wittgen-

50. Ibid.
51. Ibid.
52. Ibid., p. 626; Fr., p. 721.
53. Ibid., p. 200; Fr., p. 251.
54. Ibid., p. 104; Fr., p. 149.

stein on British thought: "the result in both cases has been to revolutionize the philosophical perspective."[55] When he goes on to assess individual philosophers, his judgment is that "of French phenomenologists Marcel and Merleau-Ponty come closest to its essential aim." This type of evaluation is commonplace. Husserl's work is seen to issue into existentialism via his emphasis, particularly in his last work, on the pretheoretical life-world. Sartre once made an interesting comment on his relationship to Merleau-Ponty on the question of phenomenology: "Alone, each of us was too easily persuaded of having understood the idea of phenomenology. Together, we were, for each other, the incarnation of its ambiguity."[56] The ambiguity of phenomenology is its emphasis, on the one hand, upon the *cogito*, reflection, and constitution, and on the other, upon description, lived experience, and the life-world. In moving toward the *cogito*, Sartre developed phenomenology in a direction different from both Heidegger and Merleau-Ponty. To judge who was more faithful to Husserl is another issue, which raises a host of questions not the least of which involves a final assessment of Husserl's work. If one is convinced, as I am, that Husserl consistently adopted the viewpoint of the *cogito*, transcendental consciousness, and constitution, then it is easy to say that Sartre was the more observant of Husserl's programmatic. Sartre's entire thought, not just the work up to and including BN,[57] is animated by the phenomenological viewpoint: the reduction, intentionality, constitution. To be sure, he employs these tools in a unique manner, not simply copying Husserl in every respect.

It may appear absurd to compare the German academician favorably with the philosopher of the café. But perhaps the validity of the comparison will emerge if we disclose the deep *humanism* underlying their thinking. This humanism appears in those writings of Husserl that discuss his work — and it appears with a sharp sense of urgency.

In 1911, in "Philosophy as a Rigorous Science," Husserl wrote that philosophy is a vocation whose task it is "to teach us how to carry on the eternal work of humanity."[58] Philosophy *bears directly upon culture*, and thus values. That is why Husserl writes out of "the conviction that the highest interests of human culture demand the development of a rigorously scientific

---

55. Ian Alexander, "The Phenomenological Philosophy in France: An Analysis of Its Themes, Significance and Implications," in *Currents of Thought in French Literature: Essays in Memory of G. T. Claxton* (Oxford: Blackwell, 1966).

56. "Merleau-Ponty Vivant," *Les Temps modernes* (October 1961). "Merleau-Ponty," in *Situations*, trans. B. Eisler (Greenwich: Fawcett, 1965), p. 159.

57. On this point see Thomas W. Busch, "Sartre: From Phenomenology to Marxism," *Research in Phenomenology*, vol. 2, 1972, and "Sartre: The Phenomenological Reduction and Human Relationships," *The Journal of the British Society for Phenomenology* (January 1975), pp. 55-61.

58. Edmund Husserl, "Philosophie als strenge Wissenschaft," *Logos* (1910-1911). The English cited here is that of Quentin Lauer from his *Husserl: Phenomenology and the Crisis of Philosophy* (New York: Harper & Row, 1965), pp. 72-73.

philosophy."[59] Consequently, a tremendous burden of social *responsibility* falls on the philosopher: "we remain aware of the responsibility we have in regard to humanity."[60] Husserl's attack on psychologism, naturalism, and historicism can be read as an attempt to extricate reason from an alienated state that is responsible for what he called at the end of his life "Europe's sickness." In *The Crisis of European Sciences and Transcendental Phenomenology*,[61] he advises his readers that his work touches directly upon the questions "of the meaning and meaninglessness of the whole of human existence. . . .

> In the final analysis [these questions] concern man as a *free, self-determining* being in his behavior toward the human and extra-human surrounding world and free in regard to his *capacities for rationally shaping himself and his surrounding world*.[62]

These remarks cast a moral and political significance upon Husserl's treatment of the life-world. Man must move from naive acceptance to active shaping of his identity and world. Husserl perceives

> . . . a far-reaching transformation of the whole praxis of human existence, i.e., the whole of cultural life: henceforth it must receive its norms not from the naive experience and tradition of everyday life but from objective truth.[63]

The reduction ultimately brings the life-world within the scope of human constitution and evaluation. Through this recovery of the life-world by consciousness Husserl envisions the beginning "of a new human epoch—the epoch of mankind which now seeks to live, and only can live, in the free shaping of its existence, its historical life, through ideas of reason, through infinite tasks."[64] Is it not just such a society, a materialization of the city of ends, that the revolutionary Sartre envisions in *What Is Literature?*?[65]

What Sartre shares with Husserl is this use of phenomenological tools— in particular the reduction—to recover from an alienated state our individual lives and social institutions, and return them to the human.

---

59. Lauer, Husserl, p. 78.
60. Ibid., p. 141.
61. Edmund Husserl, *Die Krisis der europäischen Wissenschaften und die transzendentale Phänomenologie*, edit. W. Biemel (The Hague: Nijhoff, 1954). The English translation is by David Carr, *The Crisis of European Sciences and Transcendental Phenomenology* (Evanston: Northwestern University Press, 1970).
62. Carr, trans., *Crisis*, p. 6.
63. Ibid., p. 287.
64. Ibid., p. 64.
65. "Qu'est-ce que la littérature?," in *Situations*, vol. 2 (Paris: Gallimard, 1948). The English translation is by B. Frechtman, *What Is Literature?* (New York: Harper & Row, 1965).

Phyllis Sutton Morris

2. Self-deception: Sartre's Resolution of the Paradox[1]

Most of the discussion of self-deception among contemporary analytic philosophers has originated from an apparent paradox in that concept, which was set forth by Sartre in *Being and Nothingness*.[2] To my knowledge, there has been virtually no direct discussion of Sartre's attempted resolution of that paradox, even though some of the discussions appear to have borrowed, sometimes heavily, from Sartre. The most common assumption, in fact, has been that Sartre ends, as well as begins, with an intellectually unacceptable paradox.[3] An additional criticism of Sartre that recurs is that he treats self-deception on the model of other-deception.[4]

The main point of the present article will be to show that Sartre provides

---

1. Research for this paper, and notes for the first draft, were undertaken while I attended a summer seminar under the auspices of the National Endowment for the Humanities in 1974. I wish to express my gratitude to N.E.H., to members of the seminar who assisted me by their comments, and to the late Professor Theodore Mischel, leader of that seminar, whose detailed criticisms were especially helpful.

That section of the paper which directly sets forth Sartre's resolution of the paradox of self-deception was presented at Union College (Schenectady) in February 1976; at the Pacific Division meeting of the American Philosophical Association in March 1976; and at the University of Dayton Colloquium in Philosophy on the Thought of Jean-Paul Sartre in October 1976. I have benefited greatly from comments and criticisms made by persons who heard the paper on those occasions.

In addition, I have profited by the suggestions of Professors Frederick Elliston and Hugh J. Silverman, and have been assisted by colleagues at Kirkland and Hamilton colleges who heard the short version presented informally.

2. Jean-Paul Sartre, *Being and Nothingness*, trans. Hazel E. Barnes (New York: Philosophical Library, 1956); hereafter abbreviated in the text as "BN." Except where otherwise indicated, present discussion is based on Sartre's account of bad faith, pp. 47-70. References to *L'Être et le néant* (Paris: Librairie Gallimard, 1949) are given as "Fr."

3. See Herbert Fingarette, *Self-deception* (London: Routledge & Kegan Paul, 1969), p. 92. Fingarette is otherwise sympathetic to Sartre, and points out that his own position "parallels" Sartre's very closely at certain points, p. 7. Also see Amelie Oksenberg Rorty, "Belief and Self-deception," *Inquiry* 15: 399. Rorty misconstrues Sartre as claiming that it is logically impossible to get out of self-deception.

4. John V. Canfield and Don F. Gustavson, "Self-deception," *Analysis* 23, no. 2 (December 1962): 32-33. Also Fingarette, *Self-deception*, p. 21.

a complex and interesting resolution of the paradox of self-deception. It will be seen that one of the main elements of Sartre's critique of Freud is that the latter mistakenly treats self-deception on the model of other-deception. Several analytic philosophers will be discussed in order to answer their criticisms of Sartre and to show some parallels between their handling of the paradox and Sartre's treatment of the subject. An account of the necessary conditions of authenticity will be reconstructed from Sartre's position, in reply to Rorty's claim that Sartre makes it logically impossible to get out of self-deception.

I. Sartre's Initial Statement of the Paradox

As Sartre sees it, the apparent paradox arises in the following manner. Bad faith, or self-deception, is often construed as a kind of lie. If we construe self-deception on the model of lying to others, however, we seem to arrive at a paradox. Let us look at this more closely. If I deceive someone else, the assumption is that I mislead the other in some fashion, perhaps to believe p, which I know to be false, or to believe that I know p when I don't know it. Lying or deception with respect to others may take many forms, but in each case a liar is in possession of a truth that he hides from the other. The paradox that arises if self-deception is construed on the model of other-deception, says Sartre, is that "I must know in my capacity as deceiver the truth which is hidden from me in my capacity as the one deceived." (BN, p. 49; Fr., p. 87)

II. Sartre's Rejection of the Model of Other-deception

One solution, Sartre notes, has been to adopt the Freudian account of the unconscious mind. Sartre's discussion and critique of Freud's notion of the unconscious, as it bears on the concept of self-deception, can be explained in the following manner.[5] To say that one deceives oneself means that the liar and the lied to are the same; in order to explain this odd fact, the individual must be, in some sense, both a unity and a duality. However, Freud's attempt to account for self-deception treats it on the model of other-deception in the sense that his distinction between id and ego effectively cuts "the psychic whole into two." (BN, p. 50; Fr., p. 89) The "line of demarcation" here is the censor; the person can say, then, that "I *am* the ego but I *am not* the *id*." (BN, p. 50; Fr., p. 89) Since I have no more access to my id than I do to the consciousness of another person, I can be deceived by that other, the id.

---

5. As I will show later, Sartre's critique is inadequate in that it does not sufficiently take account of Freud's later view of repression as a form of ego activity.

The first problem, says Sartre, is that that total inaccessibility of the id's wishes and desires makes it seem very odd to speak of *self*-deception; it seems to be much more like a case of ordinary other-deception. Perhaps it is not even that, Sartre suggests, for in the case of another person, we can at least observe his actions and utterances over a period of time, and compare some with others, take note of his facial expressions, find out whether his actions match his utterances in this situation, etc.

One might be tempted to think of the id as a nonperson, in the sense that it resembles a natural object, such as a volcano, which sends out occasional eruptions, not in response to provocations, but without meaning. But this temptation would lead us astray also, Sartre points out; a thing like a volcano is indifferent when we come close to it, whereas Freud reports resistance when psychoanalysis approaches the truth.

The difficulty is in trying to understand that resistance, which is objectively observable in the patient's refusal to speak, his show of defiance, his threat or decision to cease treatment, and so on. What part of the self can resist? It cannot be the ego (qua consciousness, which is the only form of ego functioning considered by Sartre in this context), since the ego is perceived by Freud as having an outsider's view of the meaning of his own reactions. If one were to construe resistance as conscious pretense, there would be no need to resort to the unconscious to explain self-deception, since there would not even *be* deception of self involved. Nor can the complex itself be construed as the source of resistance, since, according to Freud, the complex tries to disguise itself in order to get past the barrier into consciousness.

The censor alone can understand the danger of the psychoanalyst's questions, for it alone knows what it is repressing, and it must be able to identify lawful impulses and needs in order to let them pass through. This is not a mechanistic process, Sartre points out; the censor must in fact be conscious of the forbidden drive *in order not* to be conscious of it.

Sartre concludes that Freud's attempt to resolve the apparent paradox of self-deception, by using the model of other-deception, does not work. Either no self-deception is involved at all, or Freud ends up with a single entity anyway, instead of the ego/id duo. This single entity, the censor, must both know and not know what it knows. Sartre says that Freud simply leads us back, then, to the paradox.

Further discussion of Sartre's treatment of Freud will be postponed until Sartre's account of self-deception has been spelled out. Sartre's discussion thus far can be faulted for its failure to acknowledge that in Freud's later intentionalistic accounts the ego's activities were not always conscious but were sometimes unconscious, and could thus provide a basis for an account of self-deception within the ego. However, it should be clear from this discussion that Sartre's critics are mistaken in thinking that Sartre adopts other-deception as a model for self-deception. There are more serious criticisms of Sartre, and many of these are offered by Herbert Fingarette.

III. Fingarette's Resolution of the Paradox and Criticisms of Sartre

In his little volume *Self-deception*, Fingarette reviewed the analytic discussion of the paradox of self-deception that had developed since 1960,
when Raphael Demos's article, "Lying to Oneself," appeared. In his review
of the literature, Fingarette argues convincingly that prior discussions by
analytic philosophers had either eliminated the paradox by discussing cases
of something other than self-deception, or had introduced variant forms of
the paradox in attempting to resolve it.[6] Fingarette's book is an attempt to
resolve the paradox while still talking about genuine cases of self-deception.
I want to show that Fingarette (who admits his "parallelism" to Sartre's position) is considerably more dependent on Sartre than he realizes. I want
also to show some of the ways in which he misconstrues Sartre and fails to
see some forms of self-deception described by Sartre.

The basic problem that Fingarette finds in his predecessors' approach to
the problem is that they have characterized self-deception, following Sartre's lead, in terms of the language of knowledge and belief, and have not
given attention to the concept of personal identity, which Fingarette sees as
more central. Fingarette includes Sartre (mistakenly, as I will show) among
those who have concentrated on self-deception as arising primarily within a
cognitive context. Fingarette accuses Sartre of having ended in a "deadend
of paradox," just as the analytic philosophers later did, as a result of this incorrect starting point.[7] Sartre's actual position will be clarified shortly, but
it will be helpful first to summarize some of the main elements in Fingarette's treatment of self-deception, insofar as it bears on the present discussion of Sartre's view.

Fingarette's basic move in his attempt to resolve the paradox of self-
deception is to shift attention from the context of belief and knowledge,
and to treat self-deception as part of the " 'volition-action' family."[8] Fingarette begins by rejecting an older model of consciousness as both passive
and modeled on vision. Instead, says Fingarette, consciousness should be
seen as active and as more similar to linguistic activity than to vision. What
is of special importance to the discussion of self-deception is the skill of becoming explicitly conscious of what we are doing or experiencing. This
skill, "spelling-out," is akin to linguistic activity, and is the essential means
by which self-deception occurs. Fingarette acknowledges that his concept of
"spelling-out" is borrowed from Sartre's concept of reflection, but he claims
that Sartre "never makes . . . explicit" or "capitalizes on" the possibility of
refusing to reflect.[9] These are misinterpretations of Sartre, as we will see.

The importance of the skill of spelling-out is that Fingarette sees self-

---

6. Fingarette, *Self-deception*, p. 13.
7. Ibid., p. 92.
8. Ibid., p. 34.
9. Ibid., pp. 96, 98–99.

deception as an intentional activity that has, as its point, the protection of the self-deceiver's personal identity. Ordinarily we are engaged in activities that we have no reason to spell out, or to become explicitly conscious of. Fingarette treats the self as a "community" of engagements.[10] Sometimes we have an "overriding reason" *not* to spell out, or make explicit, a particular form of activity in which we engage.[11] Where we exercise our skill in order to avoid spelling out this activity, we disavow this engagement as being part of our genuine self. For Fingarette, self-deception is inauthentic disavowal of one of our regular forms of activity.[12] He notes that persons have a "special authority" in spelling out, or making explicit, their own activities, an authority traditionally connected with the "supposed 'privileged access' to the contents of one's own consciousness afforded by introspection."[13] Fingarette says nothing to cast doubt on that tradition.

As noted earlier, Fingarette thinks that Sartre treats self-deception as a cognitive notion, rather than connecting it to personal identity. In addition, he accuses Sartre of losing sight of the intentional aspect of putting oneself in self-deception.[14] These points, combined with the serious criticism mentioned earlier (that Sartre ends in paradox), are misrepresentations of Sartre's position, as I will now try to show.

It should be emphasized that Fingarette acknowledges a clear debt to Sartre in that his own account of self-deception "parallels" Sartre's account.[15] I want to show, however, that he is more heavily indebted to Sartre than he realizes, specifically in the way Fingarette handles the role of spelling-out, or reflection, and in his accounts of the self as a synthesis, or community, of engagements, disavowal, and the purposive nature of self-deception. All of these are central to Fingarette's account, and — although Fingarette denies most of these points — all are equally important to Sartre's account.

Fingarette's brief characterization and criticisms of Sartre's position can be seen to be mistaken if we turn now more directly to Sartre's account of self-deception.

IV. Sartre's Resolution of the Paradox of Self-deception

Sartre's resolution of the apparent paradox of self-deception is one that begins, as we noted, by rejecting other-deception as its model. It is based, rather, on certain distinctions that need to be made with respect to the indi-

10. Ibid., pp. 81, 85. Fingarette acknowledges his debt to A. Murphy in particular and to the philosophical tradition, but apparently fails to see that for Sartre, also, the self is a synthesis.

11. Ibid., p. 43.

12. Ibid., p. 72.

13. Ibid.

14. Ibid., p. 94.

15. Ibid., p. 7.

vidual conscious human being. The concepts and distinctions relevant to Sartre's treatment of self-deception are as follows: 1) the pre-reflective versus reflective levels of consciousness; 2) past, present, and future aspects of the self within the temporal synthesis of consciousness; and 3) being-for-itself versus being-for-others (or, more simply, the first-person perspective versus a third-person perspective). Each of these distinctions can be elucidated and discussed in turn.[16] (For simplicity in the ensuing discussion, "aspect of the self" will often be discussed as "self.")

While all self-deception has as its point the evasion of responsibility by escaping oneself, it will become apparent that there are many possible patterns of evasion for Sartre. (BN, p. 66; Fr., p. 106)

In distinguishing between the pre-reflective and the reflective levels of consciousness, Sartre calls attention to the important fact that we can be directly engaged in activities in the world of our concerns, as we are most of the time, but we can also take those activities themselves as the direct object of our attention, as we do in reflection. (BN, pp. 160-170; Fr., pp. 208-218) To be able to reflect is a distinctively human activity, one that needs to be explained and one that requires practice to be performed well. For Sartre, as for Fingarette, one may fail to give this kind of explicit attention to one's own activities, and this neglect or refusal opens the door to some forms of self-deception. (BN, pp. 261-262; Fr., pp. 319-320)

There is another set of distinctions that needs to be made. Sartre suggests that when we use the word *I*, we may mean one of several different aspects of ourselves. In one sense, I am my body. (BN, p. 325; Fr., p. 390) The body (like Strawson's "person") can be the subject of *both* material and conscious properties (states, relations, acts, etc.). Thus we can say, "I am six feet tall," or "I can see the tree," or "I chop down the tree." Sartre's example of the self-deceiving woman who permits her hand to be held by a potential lover, *as if* her hand were solely a material object, is based in part on this point. (BN, p. 358; Fr., p. 426) The body as possessor of spatio-temporal qualities, and as subject of present consciousness, is only one of the structures of the total self, however. (BN, p. 60; Fr., p. 100)

In addition, Sartre notes that we use the term *I* in the context of summarizing certain patterns of past actions and utterances in relation to objects and to other people. If I correctly say of myself, now, that "I am a coward," I am referring to a series of past actions that have taken place within certain kinds of circumstances. Character-trait attributions are one example of this. (BN, p. 166; Fr., p. 213)

In addition to the present and past selves, Sartre speaks of a chosen ideal self, or "fundamental project," which gives our lives and activities an ultimate purpose, structure, and meaning. Sartre has often been interpreted as

---

16. A much fuller account of these distinctions is given in my book *Sartre's Concept of a Person: An Analytic Approach* (Amherst: University of Massachusetts Press, 1976).

a nihilist because of his claim that the human being begins as "nothing." It would be more accurate, I think, to see that Sartre is offering an activist version of the traditional empiricist's "blank tablet" view of man. Sartre does not believe that Hume, for example, could account for the large degree of coherence in the activity and outlook of individual human beings, for Hume constructs the mind from a chaotic array of external and past events. To correct that flaw, Sartre notes that to the extent that we succeed in giving our lives some unity and meaning, it is when we select our actions and shape our utterances in accordance with the future or ideal self we have chosen to become. (BN, p. 480; Fr., p. 559) So long as we remain engaged pre-reflectively, we may not become explicitly aware of that chosen future self.

Many of the forms of bad faith discussed by Sartre are based on a failure to acknowledge that there are connected, but temporally distinguishable, elements of the self. It is this important distinction that underlies his baffling formula: "the condition of the possibility for bad faith is that human reality . . . must be what it is not [i.e., the future self] and not be what it is [the past series of acts]." (BN, p. 67; Fr., p. 108) This formulation, which reflects some of the ambiguity that Sartre claims is implicit in the concept of a person, may be part of what gives rise to some of the common misconceptions among analytic philosophers with respect to the alleged final paradox of self-deception in Sartre's analysis.

In addition to the distinctions between the pre-reflective and reflective levels of consciousness, and the past, present, and future aspects of the person, there is another distinction that needs to be clarified before seeing how Sartre applies these to specific patterns of self-deception. Sartre speaks of being-for-itself and being-for-others. Put in more familiar terminology, Sartre here distinguishes between the first-person and the third-person perspectives on the self and its activities.

To the extent that I engage pre-reflectively in certain kinds of activities, aiming toward those subsidiary ends that can be integrated with my fundamental choice of an ideal self, I am being-for-myself. I see the objects and circumstances that engage my actions, that is, in terms of my own goals.

But my activities do not take place in a social vacuum. Others have observed the ways in which I typically act, and they have applied certain kinds of character predicates to me and to others behaving similarly. These attributions are often based on how my aims and actions help or hinder the goals and activities of others. Sartre points out that when I reflect on my own past acts, and try correctly to assess my social self, I attempt to take an observer's stance with respect to myself and my actions. (BN, p. 274; Fr., p. 333)[17] I have learned from others how to do this, but there is room for self-deception when I fail to do this or do not do this correctly.

---

17. Both Skinner and Wittgenstein agree that others teach us self-knowledge. See B. F. Skinner, *Science and Human Behavior* (New York: Macmillan, 1953), pp. 259–261. Also Ludwig Wittgenstein, *Philosophical Investigations*, trans. G. E. M. Anscombe (New York: Macmillan, 1953), pt. 1, paragraphs 246–249, 253–272, 355, 416–417.

Let us see now how Sartre uses these distinctions in exhibiting some of the various forms of self-deception. According to Sartre, it is when we attempt to achieve a false self-identity by disowning one aspect of our self, or falsely identifying with any one aspect of our self, that we engage in self-deception. (BN, pp. 56, 66–67; Fr., pp. 95, 107) How does this work?

I am deceiving myself if I believe that my own purpose, to maintain the national security, is the only perspective by which my acts of entering a doctor's office and taking records ought to be judged. My acts take place within a social framework; they have an objective element, and they clearly involve a form of behavior that is at cross-purposes with the goals and aims of others. Thus, whatever "privileged access" I may have to my own intentions needs to be supplemented by reflecting on the point of a whole series of my actions to see how others might characterize that series. If I refuse to acknowledge my social self, I deceive myself. But that does not mean, for Sartre, that we are better off if we try to be *only* our social selves. His example of the waiter who tries to be nothing but what others demand of him as a waiter is also an example of self-deception, for this person has tried to identify wholly with his social self, and has thus attempted to refuse responsibility for his own purposes.

Other forms of self-deception involve the temporal elements of the self. For instance, without reflecting on my past series of temper outbursts, I can try to treat my present rage as something isolated, something wholly called forth by that other's present outrageous remark, and wholly isolated from my own past tendency to react violently to small provocations.

On the other hand, I can acknowledge a past series of acts in a self-deceiving manner. This is the kind of point Fingarette overlooks when he treats self-deception as simply a disavowal of some part of ourselves.[18] Sartre gives here the example of someone who is urged by a friend to admit sincerely that he *is* a homosexual, on the strength of his past actions. The man might admit isolated past acts but treat them as unimportant episodes, thus refusing to see the homosexuality as a pattern.

Another, and perhaps subtler, form of self-deception would be if he were to admit with hypersincerity, "Oh yes, I *am* a homosexual!" The element of self-deception in this case would be the attempt to identify solely with the past self, pretending thereby that present choice and one's future self are somehow as closed and finished as what one has done in the past. Such sincere avowals can be a strategy, in other words, to avoid responsibility for one's present and future actions. The drunkard, the coward, perhaps even the upright bank president may all enjoy the comforting self-deception that once they have begun in a certain direction, they can't avoid going in that direction in the future.[19]

18. Hamlyn mistakenly thinks *both* Fingarette and Sartre overlook false avowal as a form of self-deception. D. W. Hamlyn, "Self-deception," *Aristotelian Society Supplementary* 45 (1971): 50–51.

19. Sartre distinguishes sharply between sincerity, which is a form of bad faith, and au-

Another form of self-deception is total identification with the future ideal self. Garcin, in Sartre's play *No Exit*, is an excellent example of this. He wants to claim that he *is* a hero, although this represents only his ideal self, an ideal that Garcin failed to realize in action. His past acts proclaim him, in fact, a coward. Here again, self-deception takes, in part, the form of an avowal, rather than simply Fingarette's disavowal. Garcin's self-deception consists in trying to identify himself with his future ideal self and in denying the relevance of the third-person perspective on acts that seem to observers to be moving in a cowardly direction.

This has been a brief sketch of Sartre's account of self-deception, based on Sartre's three sets of distinctions among 1) the pre-reflective and reflective levels of consciousness; 2) the past, present, and future aspects of the self; and 3) the self as it is for itself and the self as it is for others. These enable him to describe a number of patterns of self-deception, while exhibiting their common goal of avoidance of responsibility for integrating all of the structures of the self. Since there are many aspects of the self that need to be integrated, there is no ultimate unacceptable paradox in Sartre's account of self-deception. Deceiver and deceived are both me, in the sense of being aspects or structures of myself, and also not me, in the sense that no one aspect is all of myself.

At this point it will be fruitful to return to Fingarette's account of self-deception and his critique of Sartre.

V. Fingarette and Sartre

Earlier we claimed that Fingarette's account of self-deception is closer to Sartre's than Fingarette recognizes; more specifically, his position resembles Sartre's in the way Fingarette handles the central role of "spelling-out," or reflection; in his notion of the self as a community, or synthesis; in the importance of disavowal; and in the purposive nature of self-deception. These claims need now to be supported more fully, especially since Fingarette denies or seems to deny the centrality of most of these elements for Sartre.

We also claimed that Fingarette's basic criticisms of Sartre are unjustified. The most important of these is the claim that Sartre's account of self-deception ends in an unacceptable paradox; the answer to this criticism has been developed at some length. Another passing criticism made by Fingarette is that Sartre bases his account of self-deception on the model of other-deception; Sartre's critique of Freud makes it clear that he does not use this model. Two other criticisms of Sartre's position are mentioned: Fingarette claims that Sartre treats self-deception as a cognitive notion, rather than connecting it to personal identity, and he claims that Sartre loses touch

---

thenticity, which is not; the latter will be discussed shortly. See BN, p. 65, 70n.; Fr., p. 106, 111n.

with the intentionality involved in the way we put ourselves into self-deception. The replies to these last points by Fingarette have been touched on, but can be expanded at this point.

To these points it can be added that Fingarette's account, even when it resembles Sartre's, misses some of the more complex and interesting elements in Sartre's account of self-deception.

To begin with, as we noted earlier, Fingarette acknowledges that his concept of spelling-out is borrowed from Sartre's idea of reflection. Fingarette denies, however, that Sartre makes the role of refusal to reflect explicit and that Sartre "capitalizes" on this in his account of self-deception. Our own account of Sartre's position makes it clear that Fingarette is mistaken on both counts.

Fingarette's failure to see how central the pre-reflective/reflective distinction is for Sartre may be owing, in part, to his taking Sartre's discussion of bad faith out of context. Later sections of *Being and Nothingness* develop and expand the concept of reflection that is briefly set forth in Sartre's early section on bad faith. What is of particular interest in the present context is Sartre's attempt to account for the puzzling human capacity for reflection. In his section on the existence of others, Sartre devotes a good bit of attention to a critique of the Cartesian tradition that made self-knowledge certain and unproblematic. Sartre expands on his earlier discussion of bad faith to note that people have a strong tendency to apply double standards; he says that the total pattern of our actions may be even more obvious to others than it is to us, and also points out that it is this total pattern whose correct identification makes possible an accurate judgment about the underlying point of a particular series of actions. We come to be able to reflect accurately on what we have done through the help of others who apply the appropriate predicates to our actions. Sartre would not, of course, deny the relevance of the first-person account of intentions. But he denies that we have privileged access to the point of a whole series of actions, and thus the third-person perspective (offered by others in fact or by ourselves in reflection) is central in accounting for how it is that we can come to have evidence for someone's being in self-deception.

Fingarette misses all of this in Sartre's account. In his own discussion of spelling-out, Fingarette simply refers to the familiar Cartesian claim that a person who exercises this skill has a peculiar authority connected to the traditional privileged access that persons have to their own consciousness. Fingarette does not dissociate himself from that tradition. In failing to do so, Fingarette leaves us in the dark concerning how people can acquire the skill of spelling-out and also how we can have evidence that others may be engaged in self-deception.

Fingarette also misses, I think, the extent to which his concept of the self as a community of engagements resembles Sartre's characterization of the past self as " . . . a series of undertakings . . . the organization, the set of relations that constitute these undertakings."[20] Fingarette treats Sartre's notion of authenticity as rooted in the "coincidence" of acts and projects; he believes that one is authentic as a Sartrian when one's acts "express" the self. Again, Fingarette claims that for Sartre, consciousness is "unified."[21] While these are not wholly inaccurate characterizations of Sartre's position, Fingarette's emphasis on coincidence and unity obscures the degree to which Sartre distinguishes complex structures within the total self. We will discuss Sartre's concept of authenticity later, but it is worth noting in the present context that Fingarette's concept of the self qua community omits some of the important elements included in Sartre's more complex concept: most notably, the role of the body and the social aspect of the self.

I think that Fingarette also omits consideration of that aspect of the self that Sartre calls the ideal self or fundamental project. It may be, however, that when Fingarette makes the rather vague claim that the self-deceiver has an "overriding reason" to avoid spelling out an engagement, his notion of such a reason owes a lot to Sartre's concept of the fundamental project. If so, Fingarette clearly fails to recognize this, for one of his criticisms of Sartre is that the latter omits the intentional element from his account of how we put ourselves into self-deception in the way we go to sleep. What Sartre adds is that "there is no question of a reflective, voluntary decision" when we put ourselves into self-deception. (BN, p. 68; Fr., p. 109) Fingarette's criticism ignores Sartre's distinction between the pre-reflective and the re-flective levels of consciousness, and he fails to note that the point of Sartre's remark is to deny reflective awareness, not to deny purposiveness. In fact, however, our pre-reflective engagements take place, according to Sartre, within a world that is structured by that chosen fundamental project. We may not be explicitly aware of that underlying purpose until we reflect on a series of our actions, Sartre claims, and some of those acts may of course be designed to distract us from that knowledge.

There is another important misconception involved in Fingarette's claim that Sartre loses sight of the intentional nature of self-deception, and this is connected with his point that Sartre poses the problem of bad faith in terms of belief. The latter point is partially correct, but Fingarette is mistaken in thinking that Sartre therefore omits what is purposive. Fingarette tries to move the discussion of self-deception from the belief-knowledge context to the action-volition context. In doing so, he treats cognition and purpose as wholly separate functions.

Sartre would object to this sharp dichotomy. For Sartre, the fundamental project that serves as the ultimate point of our cognitive as well as our affective activities enables us to structure situations in ways that are instru-

20. Jean-Paul Sartre, "Existentialism is a Humanism," trans. Philip Mairet, in *Existentialism from Dostoevsky to Sartre*, ed. Walter Kaufmann (New York: Meridian Books, 1957), p. 301.

21. Fingarette, Self-deception, pp. 94, 96–98.

mental to that project. This is not to deny any objective or cognitive element in those activities, for we cannot climb a rock effectively if we misconstrue its physical properties, or become a physician if we fail to take the steps necessary for getting into a medical school. How we select and classify the properties of objects and situations, and what we set about to know or refuse to know, is for Sartre as much a product of our short- and long-range goals as of our cognitive efforts. There isn't a sharp separation to be made between the cognitive and purposive elements in a situation, and this is why Sartre uses *both* the language of belief and the language of avowal and disavowal in characterizing the problem of self-deception.

Fingarette notes the language of belief in Sartre's analysis, but since Fingarette himself treats knowledge-belief and action-volition as sharply dichotomous functions, he fails to notice that Sartre deals with self-deception as a more complex phenomenon, which includes both cognitive and purposive aspects. Thus Fingarette denies that Sartre's account of self-deception includes reference to its purposive nature, and does not see the extent to which his own account of self-deception as disavowal of one of our engagements can be traced directly to Sartre.

This discussion of Fingarette's position has attempted to answer his criticisms of Sartre, to show some of the ways in which Fingarette's own account of self-deception resembles Sartre's more closely than Fingarette recognizes, and to exhibit some of the interesting elements in Sartre's account that are missed by his critic. At this point it makes sense to turn attention to a more recent discussion of self-deception, since this account also includes some significant resemblances to, and misconceptions of, Sartre's position.

VI. Rorty and Sartre

Amelie Rorty's more recent analysis of self-deception acknowledges some large debts to Sartre, but is in fact more similar to Sartre's position in one major respect than she recognizes. While Rorty has some important insights concerning Sartre, her criticisms include significant misconceptions of Sartre's position. The present concern is not Rorty's analysis, per se, but the ways in which her account resembles and misconceives Sartre's position.

Rorty credits J. L. Austin and Sartre with a new perspective, which permits us to see that sentences that appear to assert facts may also be doing additional work. In particular, Sartre has reminded us of those descriptions of beliefs that purport to be objective descriptions of independent facts but may actually be constituted "by our engagements or avowals."[22] In effect, then, Rorty's beginning point is to refuse to make the sharp dichotomy between cognition and purpose that previous analytic philosophers (including Fingarette, as we showed) have made.

---

22. Rorty, "Belief and Self-deception," p. 337.

Noting that self-deception makes use of most of the same devices that are at work in ordinary belief, Rorty makes several points. For one thing, we may not always know what we believe, and yet these "precritical beliefs" may guide our actions. When faced with a request for justification, we may find good reasons for continuing to hold these formerly implicit beliefs or we may not find good reasons and thus give up these beliefs; but we might also find no good reasons and yet resist giving them up, because important theories or habits of ours are at stake. All belief, she notes, involves certain distortions and selective focus of attention.

Rorty gives credit to Sartre for showing what is distinctive about self-deception. This type of belief involves "deception of the self by the self, about the self, for the sake of the self," and not simply error or conflict.[23] For Rorty, the conditions of being self-deceived are that S believes and does not believe d, and that S recognizes that it is not rational to believe and not believe d, while acknowledging that he does so but mistakenly believing that some strategy enables him to reconcile his believing and not believing d; moreover, S has an interest in claiming that believing and not believing d is rational, such interest being, as Sartre reminded us, the preservation or alteration of personal identity.

The expansion of belief to include noncognitive elements enables Rorty to avoid the paradox that many other analytic philosophers have claimed results from saying the self-deceiver both believes and does not believe d. In particular, belief involves behavior and convictions as well as factual assertions, so that one may well believe d at the level of action without believing it at the level of either conviction or factual assertion.

Furthermore, in connection with her point that the self-deceiver has an interest in preserving or altering his identity, Rorty notes that the tradition has overemphasized the unity of personhood. Although she does not spell out this point in connection with her discussion of self-deception, Rorty says that there is no need for *strict* identity of the deceived and the deceiver in self-deception; the connection that she sketches here is apparently intended to be part of a method for resolving the paradox of self-deception.[24] In another article, Rorty exhibits the complexity of criteria for personal identity, noting that there are many possible answers to the question of whether this is the same person, depending on whether body, character, or memory are emphasized; the age of the person; the context; and what a particular set of criteria of personal identity is designed to do.[25]

In addition to noting the ways in which Sartre has influenced Rorty's handling of the problem of self-deception, several points are important in

23. Ibid., pp. 393, 398.
24. Ibid., p. 406.
25. Amelie Oksenberg Rorty, "The Transformations of Persons," *Philosophy* 48, no. 185 (July 1973): 273.

connection with our discussion of Sartre. First, Rorty fails not only to note that Sartre has distinguished among different aspects of the term *self* (past, ideal, social, etc.), but also that he does so for a reason that appears to be similar to Rorty's reason for saying that identity of deceiver and deceived in self-deception need not be strictly the same. One of her criticisms of Sartre, in fact, shows that she wholly misperceives what Sartre is saying on this issue. She says that "avowals and declarations seem to presuppose a self; they cannot, *pace* Sartre, compose one out of nothing."[26] This criticism ignores Sartre's discussion of the body as the continuing subject of acts and experiences, and his claim that the ego, or character, is constructed as a continuing pattern of relations with the world and other people. Since the body would continue even when character changed radically, Sartre is able to answer Rorty's objection as well as show rather precisely some of the ways in which there are (as Rorty herself agrees) multiple senses of the term *self*.

A second criticism Rorty makes of Sartre is that he can't distinguish self-deceptive beliefs about oneself from other beliefs about oneself, and thus self-deception disappears. Her reason for making this curious criticism is that "if everything one says about oneself is constitutive of a choice rather than a description, questions of truth and validity cannot arise at all."[27] The reason this is an especially strange mistake for Rorty to make is that Rorty recognizes, and also apparently accepts, the important point made by existentialists that there is a mutual dependence between awareness of others and self-awareness. For Sartre, it is specifically the role of others to provide us with an objective view of ourselves, and this outside perspective, central to our development of the capacity to reflect on ourselves, is what helps to correct an overemphasis on the possibly biased first-person perspective. Rorty correctly notes that Sartre does not account for self-deception on the model of other-deception, but her criticism suggests that she does not fully recognize the role that Sartre says others must play if we are to make accurate assessments of ourselves.

The most serious objection Rorty makes to Sartre's position also embodies a major misunderstanding of what he says. Rorty claims that Sartre makes it logically impossible to get out of self-deception.[28] Although she does not cite a reference to support this claim, Rorty may have in mind the formula discussed earlier, that consciousness is what it is not, and is not what it is. Since Rorty has made a similar distinction, she might have seen that Sartre is here working with the notions of a past and future self. A more direct answer to Rorty can be given by constructing a set of conditions that enable a Sartrian to achieve authenticity and avoid self-deception.

---

26. Rorty, "Belief and Self-deception," p. 404.
27. Ibid., p. 398.
28. Ibid., pp. 398–399.

VII. Authenticity: A Reconstruction

Although Sartre does not undertake an analysis of "self-recovery," or au-thenticity, he tells us that failure to achieve authenticity occurs when we conflate different senses of the self, attempting to achieve a false self-identity by disowning one aspect of our self or by falsely identifying with just one aspect of our self.

Sartre certainly does claim that sincerity is a form of self-deception, as we noted earlier; perhaps this is part of what led Rorty astray. It is clear from Sartre's examples of sincerity, as in the case of the man who acknowl-edges that he *is* a homosexual, that these involve a false identification with a single aspect of the self. This is why Sartre does not recommend sincerity, but points in the direction of possible "self-recovery," or authenticity. (BN, p. 70; Fr., p. 111)

What conditions would someone have to fulfill in order to be considered authentic by Sartre? Based on the earlier analysis of self-deception, the fol-lowing set of conditions might be formulated. The person who does not deceive him- or herself is 1) one whose moments of reflection on his pre-reflective activities are accurate: he has learned to see his own activities as objectively as an outside observer would, when necessary, while still pre-serving a sense of his own goals; 2) one who not only knows what separate acts he has done in the past, but can see what kind of pattern they form; 3) one who can make the correct connections between past acts and his ideal self—seeing where the acts obstruct, fall short of, or actually tend in the direction of the ideal; and 4) one who does not mistake that connection for a causal connection: he accepts responsibility for the fact that present and/or future acts might follow a somewhat or even wholly different pat-tern from the pattern of his past acts, if he chooses a different ideal; he does not mistake that future self for a predetermined goal.

While it might be difficult for someone to achieve the needed insight, there is surely no reason to think that Rorty is correct when she says Sartre makes it logically impossible to get out of self-deception.

VIII. Another Look at the Unconscious

Given this analysis of Sartre's view of self-deception and authenticity, we need to ask now whether Sartre can handle those phenomena that Freud thought could be explained only by reference to the unconscious mind. To begin with, Sartre's account of self-deception extends rather considerably the range of self-deceptive activities that can be described without referring to unconscious mental processes.

Again, Sartre sounds a brief but tantalizing note when he says that the psychiatrist Stekel found that whenever he was able to carry his research far enough, the "crux of the psychosis was conscious." (BN, p. 54; Fr., p. 93)

Sartre goes on to suggest that when a frigid woman engages in a strategy of distraction, what she does is far better explained by an appeal to an intentional, although not necessarily explicit, consciousness, than by appeal to the blind unconscious mind. Sartre implies by these remarks that Freud may have based his theory of the unconscious on research that was not prolonged enough to exhibit his patients' implicit awareness of their actions.

As we suggested earlier, however, there is a serious difficulty in Sartre's interpretation of Freud, for his criticisms are based primarily on Freud's early account of repression, in which the undifferentiated blocked energy of the unconscious libido might well be described as "blind" and thinglike. Sartre does not address himself to Freud's later account of repression, in which the ego includes unconscious activities as well as conscious ones, and can engage in purposeful construction of defenses against the instinctual processes.[29]

Freud's later work on anxiety, in other words, does not represent repression as a blind force, if "blind" is construed as purposeless. It is, rather, one form of dynamically unconscious defense that the ego actively constructs against anxiety. Not only repression but also other forms of defense have a purpose, namely, "protection of the ego against instinctual demands."[30] In his later work, then, Freud claims intentional status for the ego's efforts to keep itself unconscious of what it is doing to maintain that unawareness.

Sartre apparently does not believe that it makes sense to say that something totally unconscious can have a purpose. One must in *some* sense be conscious of what one is about—implicitly and pre-reflectively, if not explicitly and reflectively—if one's action can be said to have some point, and if we are to be held responsible for that action.

Sartre and Freud appear to be wholly at odds on this issue. But is this really so? Curiously enough, D. W. Hamlyn's analysis of Freud's later account of unconscious ego activity, if correct, suggests some resemblance to Sartre's position. The reason for suggesting this is that Hamlyn never speaks of what is unconscious as being wholly hidden from view. Rather, in ap-

---

29. Freud's early view is found, e.g., in *A General Introduction to Psychoanalysis*, trans. Joan Riviere (New York: Pocket Books, 1953), 25th lecture. For a comparison between the earlier and later views, see S. Freud, *New Introductory Lectures on Psycho-analysis*, Standard Edition of the Complete Psychological Works, trans. James Strachey in collaboration with Anna Freud, vol. 22; especially lecture 32, "Anxiety and Instinctual Life." Also S. Freud. *The Ego and the Id*, trans. Joan Riviere, rev. and ed. James Strachey (New York: W. W. Norton & Co., 1960); Freud here discusses the ego's purposive activity, and speaks of the id, in relation to the ego, as a "second external world," p. 45. See also Anna Freud, *The Ego and the Mechanisms of Defence*, trans. Cecil Baines (London: Leonard and Virginia Woolf at the Hogarth Press and the Institute of Psycho-Analysis, 1937), p. 73. A lucid and illuminating account of Freud's earlier and later views can be found in Theodore Mischel, "Understanding Neurotic Behavior: From 'Mechanism' to 'Intentionality,' " in ed., Theodore Mischel, *Understanding Other Persons* (Oxford: Basil Blackwell, 1974).

30. S. Freud, *The Problem of Anxiety*, trans. Henry Alden Bunker (New York: The Psychoanalytic Quarterly Press and Norton & Co., 1936), p. 111.

pealing to a Freudian view of unconscious mechanisms of defense in his own attempt to resolve the paradox of self-deception, Hamlyn says that Freud distinguishes between *fully* knowing (or being conscious of) what one is doing and "in *some* sense" knowing what one is doing.[31] To be unconscious, then, according to Hamlyn's interpretation of Freud's later view, is "to know" in a sense that is less than full knowledge. But what does this mean?

Hamlyn gives us several clues when he points out that the human capacity for self-deception depends on one's having intentions and a complex awareness of what one is doing. He adds, "the human mind is not capable of giving everything equal attention, and people may be inclined for reasons which may differ from case to case to accept what is most close at hand and most nearly the object of attention."[32] Later Hamlyn adds, "he may prevent that awareness . . . as easily by being too aware of part of the truth as by being inattentive to the truth in general."[33]

Hamlyn denies that the term *unconscious* is to be taken as meaning that what is known is not made explicit, although he acknowledges that Fingarette's model may represent one way of entering self-deception.[34] Hamlyn's concept of the unconscious seems to include two elements, purpose and attention. What Hamlyn *seems* to be saying is that we can be unconscious of an activity by attending to only part of that activity, or not paying attention to "the truth in general" of that activity. Hamlyn's account is somewhat obscure, but perhaps we can attempt to compare it to what Sartre said when he pointed out that we might focus on any one aspect of the self (past acts, future goal, or the isolated present, for example), and that self-deception could arise as a result of refusing to see the whole self. Again, Hamlyn's mention of being "inattentive to the truth in general" — if it makes any sense at all — might fruitfully be compared to Sartre's account of how we become directly engaged in activities without pausing to, or sometimes refusing to, reflect on the total direction those actions have taken.

If being unconscious is to be taken, as Hamlyn suggests, as simply being narrowly attentive for some purpose or being inattentive for some reason, then Sartre would be quite comfortable with Hamlyn's approach to the problem of self-deception. And if Freud's later concept of the unconscious as belonging in part to the ego's defensive activity is accurately reflected in Hamlyn's account of the unconscious, then Sartre could be seen as much closer to Freud than he thinks he is. There might be some reason to doubt whether Hamlyn accurately captures Freud's later view, however.

One reason for raising this question is that at a time when Freud treated the ego as purposive he also insisted that all of our knowledge is bound to

---

31. D. W. Hamlyn, "Unconscious Intentions," *Philosophy* 46, no. 175 (January 1971): 19.
32. Hamlyn, "Self-deception", p. 58.
33. Ibid.
34. Ibid., p. 56.

consciousness. Thus, Freud would probably not agree with Hamlyn's characterization of the unconscious as "in some sense knowing." Another reason for doubting the accuracy of Hamlyn's interpretation of Freud is that the latter explicitly denied that by *unconscious* he meant simply "what is unnoticed"; he attributed this type of interpretation to those thinkers who equate what is mental with what is conscious.[35] To be sure, Hamlyn does not analyze unconscious acts solely in terms of what is unnoticed or not attended to; he adds purpose or intent to the picture. It is unclear, however, that this addition is sufficient, for Freud seems to mean that what is unconscious is hidden or inaccessible, and not simply purposely overlooked. I believe, then, that Sartre's position is not wholly incompatible with that espoused by Hamlyn, in those respects that have been discussed; but both positions probably differ from Freud's later account of unconscious ego activity.

There is another way of attempting to link Sartre and Freud, however. While Freud originally identified the ego with consciousness, in his later work he said that the ego includes both conscious and some unconscious processes. Moreover, the ego is seen as a set of *bodily* functions, Freud said.[36] Sartre sees the conscious body as the necessary condition of all "psychic" or purposive activities, and "it is this . . . which motivates and to some degree justifies psychological theories like that of the unconscious." (BN, p. 338; Fr., p. 404) Sartre could agree, then, if what Freud meant by saying that there is an unconscious mind is that all human activities that are neither conscious nor preconscious are physical processes that are not now accessible to consciousness.

The important difference, I believe, is that whereas Sartre would not deny that there are unconscious processes in this sense, he would deny that they are purposive. (BN, p. 358; Fr., p. 426) They could therefore be of little use in an attempt to show how we intentionally, although not necessarily explicitly, deceive ourselves.

If this does represent an important difference between Sartre and Freud, then we might follow Fingarette's suggestion and seek an answer in those experiments being performed on the two halves of the brain. The evidence already suggests that in the case of a split brain purposive activity can continue in the absence of the ability to describe that activity explicitly. The capacity for reflective awareness is of a sort that seems to be dominated by the left hemisphere; complex, abstract linguistic performances belong to this side. The studies show that the right hemisphere can understand language and respond intelligently even though it does not appear to be directly involved in the use of language.[37] As Fingarette describes it, then, the evidence is compatible with Sartre's claim that ordinary persons enjoy non-

---

35. Freud, *The Ego and the Id*, pp. 6, 9.
36. Ibid., pp. 16, 17.
37. Fingarette, *Self-deception*, pp. 156-157.

positional consciousness of what they are doing even in the absence of explicit awareness of it.

Further brain experimentation might show Sartre to be incorrect, however, in claiming that all purposive activities are at least nonpositionally conscious, if not explicitly so. Future studies might conclusively favor Freud's strong claim that we can engage in purposive activities without in *any* sense knowing what our unconscious intentions are. How serious would this be for Sartre? For one thing, Sartre could revive the criticism he made of Freud's early model, and say that this would be to dissolve self-deception, since the sharp line between what is known and what is not in any sense known reintroduces the model of other-deception as the core of Freud's attempt to explain self-deception.

The other effect, I think, would be to suggest that Sartre's account of self-deception is not exhaustive, that some forms of self-deception might elude his rather complex description. Since, however, Sartre does not claim that he has given an exhaustive analysis of the phenomenon of self-deception, I cannot see that this is a real objection to his position. Even if it were necessary at some point to add new patterns of self-deception, it would not diminish the phenomenological value of his complex and subtle descriptions of a wide range of patterns of self-deception, which can be accounted for without reference to a Freudian unconscious mind.

IX. Summary and Conclusions

This study of Sartre's concept of self-deception has had two major aims. I wanted to show that some of the contemporary analytic discussions could illuminate Sartre's account of self-deception because of interesting similarities, acknowledged or unacknowledged. More important, I wanted to answer some of the more serious criticisms of Sartre that are current among analytic philosophers who discuss self-deception.

In connection with the first aim, I looked briefly at Fingarette's account of self-deception, which was acknowledged by the author to parallel Sartre's discussion. I tried to show that that account was considerably more dependent on Sartre's analysis than Fingarette acknowledged, specifically in his account of the central role of "spelling-out," or reflection, the notion of the self as a community, disavowal, and the purposive nature of self-deception. Amelie Rorty credits Sartre as well as Austin for adding noncognitive elements to our concept of belief; she also points out that Sartre identified the interest in personal identity which she takes as distinguishing self-deceptive beliefs from other forms of erroneous belief. I showed that Rorty failed to see that Sartre's account of self-deception hinges on distinguishing multiple senses of the term *self*, which refer to various aspects of the self. This is a particularly surprising omission, since Rorty's own account of multiple senses of the term *self* appears to be important in her attempt to resolve the paradox of self-deception.

I acknowledged that Sartre's criticisms of Freud were inadequate in that they applied primarily to Freud's early mechanistic account of repression but ignored Freud's later intentionalistic account of the ego's activity in keeping itself unconscious. When, however, we looked at Hamlyn's rendering of Freud's later notion of the unconscious as purposive selective attention, it did not appear to be incompatible with Sartre's own account of different levels of awareness. Assuming that Freud might have rejected Hamlyn's interpretation of the concept of the unconscious, and might have insisted that what is unconscious is not in any sense known, Sartre could then revive one of his criticisms of Freud's earlier view: that Freud did away with self-deception by assimilating it to the model of other-deception.

In connection with the second aim, I showed how Sartre could answer a number of criticisms of his account of self-deception. The criticism that Sartre's view of self-deception was based on the model of other-deception was answered by showing that Sartre thinks one of Freud's errors was to do just that. The most important criticisms of Sartre are that his account of self-deception ends in an unacceptable paradox and that Sartre makes it logically impossible to get out of self-deception. Our reply to the critics was to show how Sartre's distinctions among pre-reflective and reflective consciousness; the past, present, and future aspects of the self; and the first- and third-person perspectives enable him to offer a complex, interesting, and nonparadoxical account of self-deception, and by implication, of authenticity. To falsely identify with one aspect of the self or to falsely deny any aspect of the self is to enter self-deception. Sartre suggests the way out of bad faith, as well as presenting a solid and coherent account of self-deception. Analytic philosophers interested in the concept of self-deception would do well to take another look at Sartre's discussion.

Xavier O. Monasterio

3. *The Body in* Being and Nothingness[1]

Between the analysis of the intentionality of a pure, abstract consciousness, which characterized the phenomenological movement at its beginnings, and the analysis of a body in the world, there is a significant difference — and a significant progress too, at least in my estimation. With a few other existential philosophers, such as Heidegger, Marcel, Merleau-Ponty, and Ricoeur, Sartre contributed to that progress. However, his only systematic treatment of the body appeared in *Being and Nothingness*, which preceded by a number of years his encounter with Marx and dialectical materialism. For good or bad, Sartre's views on the individual and his mode of being in the world underwent a profound transformation owing to that encounter. It is obvious that Sartre would not write *Being and Nothingness* today the way he wrote it some thirty-five years ago, if at all.

This would also apply to the chapter on the body. But would Sartre reject that chapter completely? My bet is that he would not, given the way in which he has evolved since he wrote *Being and Nothingness*. But I am not interested in bets. To put the matter in a more positive way, whatever Sartre's personal opinions may be, I find much that is rich in Sartre's analysis of the body in *Being and Nothingness* and, at the same time, I am profoundly dissatisfied with his analysis. What I propose is to offer an alternative analysis, which attempts to integrate what I find rich in Sartre's and explores certain dimensions that he disregarded. This approach has at least the virtue of moving beyond a merely negative criticism of *Being and Nothingness* to the more challenging and constructive task of improving on what Sartre did.

Significantly, *Being and Nothingness* does not focus initially on the body. In parts one and two Sartre is concerned with the structures of a for-itself, or human reality, which might as well be bodyless. The result is that

1. I express my gratitude to Professor Frederick Elliston for his careful editing and useful criticisms of my earlier draft. I take responsibility for any deficiencies in this version. The first draft of this paper was read at the Seventh Annual Colloquium in Philosophy on "The Thought of Jean-Paul Sartre" at the University of Dayton, October 1-2, 1976.

the body of which Sartre speaks in part three is actually tailored to the measurements of the for-itself previously described. This restriction, however, does not preclude positive insights in Sartre's analysis. And I will start with them.

I. A Bodily Subject

The substantive portion of Sartre's analysis of the body begins with the perspectival structure of perception:

> *For me* this glass is to the left of the decanter and a little behind it; for *Pierre*, it is to the right and a little in front. It is not even conceivable that a consciousness could survey the world in such a way that the glass should be simultaneously given to it at the right and at the left of the decanter, in front of it and behind it. . . . Similarly if the table leg hides the designs in the rug from my sight, . . . it is because a rug which would not be hidden by the table, a rug which would not be either under it or above it or to one side of it, would not have any relation of any kind with the table and would no longer belong to the "world" in which there is the table.[2]

The experiential fact is that the objects I perceive are given to me in an organized structure of which I am the center. I can change my position so that the glass that was previously to the left of the decanter be given to me as being to the right of the decanter. But I cannot change the fact that the objects I perceive are given to me in a perspective of which I am the center. Were I not the center, the glass would remain to the left of the decanter even after I went half a circle around them.

This first approach gains in depth as soon as we realize with Sartre that the perspective in which objects of perception are given to us is not purely contemplative, but practical, instrumental. We are centers of instrumental perspective.

> It is impossible to distinguish "sensation" from "action" . . . reality is presented to us neither as a *thing* nor as an *instrument* but as an instrumental thing. (BN, p. 320; Fr., pp. 383–384)

What does this mean?

> Objects are revealed to us at the heart of a complex of instrumentality in which they occupy a determined *place*. This place is not defined by pure spatial coordinates but in relation to axes of practical reference. "*The glass is* on

---

2. Jean-Paul Sartre, *Being and Nothingness: An Essay in Phenomenological Ontology,* trans. Hazel E. Barnes (New York: Philosophical Library, 1956), pp. 306–307. *L'Etre et le neant* (Paris: Gallimard, 1949), pp. 368–369.

the coffee table"; this means that we must be careful not to upset the glass if we move the table. The package of tobacco *is* on the mantelpiece; this means that we must clear a distance of three yards if we want to go from the pipe to the tobacco while avoiding certain obstacles—endtables, footstools, *etc.*— which are placed between the mantelpiece and the table. In this sense perception is in no way to be distinguished from the practical organization of existents into a *world*. Each instrument refers to other instruments, to those which are its *keys* and to those for which it is the *key*. But these references could not be grasped by a purely contemplative consciousness. For such a consciousness the hammer would not refer to the nails but would be alongside them; furthermore the expression "alongside" loses all its meaning if it does not outline a path which goes from the hammer to the nail and which *must* be cleared. The space which is originally revealed to me is hodological space; it is furrowed with paths and highways; it is instrumental and it is the *location* of tools. (BN, p. 321-322; Fr., pp. 385-386)

Thus, the contemplative perspective of which I am the center is an abstraction. Concretely, perceiving is being the center of an instrumental field of action organized in relation to the perceiver. The perceiver, however, is a body, not a consciousness. The glass is given at the left of the decanter because I am on this side; if I moved around them half a circle, the glass would be given to me at the right of the decanter because I myself would be over there instead of being here. But if I am here and can be over there, then I am a body. A pure consciousness is nowhere, neither in front of the decanter nor behind it. In simpler terms, since a pure consciousness is nowhere, it would perceive nothing. Given the finite character of perception, perceiving is inseparable from being a body. This point becomes even more obvious if we think in terms of action. The field of action of which I am center indicates me as a body, not as a pure consciousness. The hammer is a hammer because I have a hand. To use Sartre's expression, "we can insert ourselves into the field of instrumentality only by being ourselves an instrument," that is, a body. (BN, p. 324; Fr., p. 388)

I am not a pure Cartesian thinking substance, I am a body, a body-subject. For Sartre this means that I am in a situation as the center of the situation. In order to grasp the meaning of the term *situation* some elaboration is needed.

Situation is a term that implies a subject, and *subject* is a term which implies a situation. To use an analogy, these terms exhibit a mutual implication comparable to that between *circumference* and *center*: neither term can be understood except in relation to the other, because they define each other.

If we see a desk lying on its writing surface rather than standing on its legs, we find the desk in the wrong position. *Position*, too, is a term that involves a relationship. The desk is in the wrong position in relation to the ceiling. But then we could as well say that the ceiling is in the wrong position in relation to the desk. Positional relations in Sartre's terminology are "external" to the things related, in that they are established by a witness who *arbitrarily* takes one of the terms involved as center or subject of the relationship. As neither the desk nor the ceiling *is* a center of perspective, either can be taken as the subject of the relationship. What is missing for their relationship to be situational rather than merely positional is something that *is* a center.

However, it would be odd to say in this case that the desk is in the right position, while the ceiling and the floor are in the wrong position. The reason for this oddity is that we are body-centers. And although the floor and the ceiling are correctly oriented toward us, the desk is not. Indeed, we meet them from the standpoint of bodies who use the floor, the ceiling, and the desk. Consequently, the right position of the desk is that which is optimal for the user of the desk. Better yet, because I am this body-center of instrumental perspective, I demand to be taken as center. A description of the situation stating that my body is in the wrong position in relation to the desk would be not only trivial but unacceptable. I am a body that *is* a center, a subject, while the table is not.

At this level of analysis, situation is an instrumental relationship between a body-subject and an environment, characterized by the fact that the elements that constitute the environment are structured around the body as their center. What gives unity to a situation is its center. The body-subject *is* a center in that it alone is a project in relation to which the environment can acquire instrumental character. In the case of the circumference and the center, the center renders the circumference intelligible and the circumference renders the center intelligible. Not so in the case of situation. Though the center of the situation cannot be a center without the environment, and the environment cannot be an environment without the center, the intelligibility of the situation rests on its center, for it is through the instrumental orientation of the elements of the environment toward the body-subject that the situation is a situation.

II. Body-Object

My being body-subject is not, however, the only dimension of my being body. I am also a body-object. Sartre means by *subject* a body that in a situational relationship functions as a center, a body in relation to which the rest is instrumentally oriented. Sartre calls *object* that rest which is instrumentally oriented toward a body-subject. *Things*, in Sartre's view, can be part of a situational relationship only as objects, not as centers, for their mode of being is not that of a body-subject. Things cannot have the world by which they are surrounded as *their* field of action.[3] However, a body that

---

3. Following Sartre's example, I will ignore animals throughout this article. However, I

is a subject can also find him- or herself in a situational relationship as object, that is, as an instrument for *another* body-subject, who in the particular case happens to function as the center of the situation. A body-object is at the other's mercy, passive to the other's initiative. The situation is not *his* anymore, it is the other's situation, for the other is now in control. The other is the center of instrumentality, and among *his* instruments is to be counted this that which I am.

If I were a pure consciousness the other could never use me. The other can use me as he uses things because I am a body. However, even in this case, Sartre would not equate me with a thing, and for good reason. Unlike a thing, a body-object is an "explosive instrument to be handled with care," for at any moment his or her recovery of control can redefine the whole situation. (BN, p. 29F; Fr., p. 358) But for a while, the body-object functions like a thing, as an instrument for the project that another body-subject is. The actions of the body-object, without ceasing to be actions of a human, are responses to a situation defined by another body-subject.

III. Body-thing

In the two preceding sections I have been following Sartre's analysis. It seems to me that the two dimensions of the body he has so far presented are to be retained. My reconstructive task begins at this point. My purpose is to show that we are not only body-subjects and body-objects, as Sartre would have it, but also body-things.

For the early Sartre, of course, such a claim would be anathema. If his being body-object was already felt by him as a form of "alienation" of his freedom, at least he could console himself with the thought that his freedom was limited by another freedom.[4] And this, to the idealistic author of *Being and Nothingness*, still sounded somehow compatible with his views on freedom. But to accept his body as a thing would have forced him to see the impossible freedom he attributed to the for-itself curtailed by the very fact that the for-itself is bodily.[5]

One aspect of our mode of being-in-the-world carefully avoided by Sartre in *Being and Nothingness* is our *passivity to things*. The only concession he feels constrained to make in this regard is that, sometimes, our projects are opposed by a certain "coefficient of adversity" in things.[6] Things are in-

---

want to state that I ignore animals not because I consider them as mere "things" but simply not to complicate inordinately my task and that of my reader.

4. See BN, section three of the chapter on "the body".

5. Characteristic of Sartre's reluctance to identify himself as body-thing are his reflections on "the thing 'leg' " in the introduction to the chapter on "the body," particularly pp. 304-305; Fr., pp. 366-367. Supposedly, if Sartre's "thing 'leg' " had been amputated, Sartre would not have been amputated — not to say anything of what would have happened to Sartre if the "thing 'body' " had been cut from the "thing 'head.' "

6. See BN, p. 324 (Fr., 389), where Sartre introduces this notion.

struments because there are bodies who are users of things, that is, body-subjects. It would seem, therefore, that the body-subject determines the instrumentality of things; but not quite. Sartre is forced to admit that there is in things a certain instrumental quality of their own, which does not depend on the user and to which, consequently, the body-subject is passive. Thus, we can use a hard material to build a house, but we cannot use a soft material for that purpose. We cannot control the hardness or softness of the material as well as its lending or not lending itself to our particular project. This feature of things is what Sartre calls their "coefficient of adversity." And it is the only form of bodily passivity to things explicitly acknowledged by Sartre in *Being and Nothingness*. (BN, p. 482; Fr., p. 562) Moreover, he detracts from the significance of such passivity by interpreting it simply as the form of "facticity" of things that makes possible the realization of our projects:

> . . . the resistance which freedom reveals in the existent, far from being a danger to freedom, results only in enabling it to arise as freedom. There can be a free for-itself only as engaged in a resisting world. (BN, p. 483; Fr., 563)

It is true, then, according to Sartre, that we cannot do anything about the fact that stones are hard and that a house can only be built with hard materials. But the very fact that stones are hard makes it possible for us to realize our project of building houses. So our passivity to things turns to our profit.

I think, on the contrary, that our passivity to things cuts far more deeply than Sartre would have us believe. The "coefficient of adversity" that things present to our projects is only one aspect of our passivity to them, and not the most important or the most threatening. And, if I am not wrong, our passivity to things is far more significant than Sartre makes it sound, for it reveals the body as *thing among things*, not merely as subject among objects and object among subjects.

No less than the other, things sometimes take the initiative. A tornado destroys with the same force trees, houses, and *people*. The brutal power of the torrential river carries us downstream together with branches and rocks. Our being body-subjects does not seem to constitute a good enough excuse to be treated differently from trees and houses and branches and rocks.

Such simple facts constrain us to revise and enlarge the analysis of the body presented in *Being and Nothingness*. Sartre failed to realize that we are as pervious to the activity of things as to that of other bodies. The result is that the body as viewed by Sartre is strangely unlike ours in certain regards. The Sartrian body truly *inter*-acts, that is, entertains a two-directional relationship, with other bodies. It acts on them and is acted upon by them. Thus, it alternatively functions as subject and as object.

But, in Sartre's analysis, the body does not really interact with things, it only acts on things. Its relationship to things is uni-directional, from body-user to thing-instrument. A sort of mysterious transcendence allows the Sartrian body to pursue its purposes by using things without itself being exposed to the action of things, as if it acted on things from above. But we do not act on things from above; we interact with them, at their very level, and sometimes we are completely at their mercy. And if our being at the mercy of the intentional activity of other body-subjects reveals our being body-object, our being at the mercy of things will reveal our being body-thing.

Sometimes we interact with other things as mere things. The torrential river carries us like other things, and we simply go downstream with the other things carried. If we still are conscious and valid, we will try to direct our course toward that rock which emerges over there, where we could wait for help. In this case we still are in a situational relationship. Though not having the full initiative that characterizes the Sartrian body-subject — for we are far from being the masters of the situation — we still have a project in terms of which the river reveals its coefficient of adversity. This fact makes the action of the river appear as a sort of negative instrumentality, a kind of counter-project, as if the river intended to prevent us from reaching the rock where we can wait for help.[7] But our struggle with the river may well come to an end, if we are knocked unconscious. Then there is not the slightest trace of instrumentality left. For, as Sartre rightly points out, what confers to a factual state of affairs the structure of instrumental complex, that is, of "situation," is a project. And the river has no project in carrying us and we have no project in going downstream. Of course, we may regain consciousness, we may even come to be in complete mastery of the situation. As we are "explosive instruments" when used by the other, so we are "explosive things," but we *are* things nonetheless.

In *Being and Nothingness* Sartre reduces our mode of being-in-the-world to being in situation either as subject or as object. As previously indicated, the fundamental characteristic of *situation* is that it has a center, that it is oriented toward a body-subject as its center. But now we have discovered a state of affairs without center of instrumentality, which organizes itself by itself, as it were. Of such a state of affairs we are no less part and parcel than of a situation in which we function either as body-subjects or as body-objects. So we are not merely *in* the world; we are *of* the world. Being *in* suggests a Cartesian possibility of being *out*. Apparently the Sartrian for-itself cannot go to sleep, has to be perpetually vigilant, lest he "cease making the world come into being." (BN, p. 334; Fr., 399) Had Sartre realized his being body-thing, he could have sent his for-itself to sleep. The world *of*

---

7. In the *Critique de la raison dialectique* Sartre thematizes this negative instrumentality of things under the title of the "*practico-inerte*." Even there, however, he does not explicitly rework his theory of the body.

which we are, and our being *of* it, has no exit. We do not escape from it by being unaware of it. We are inescapably *in* it as being *of* it. Like things. There is more to it. Our being body-things is *fundamental* in that it is the very condition of possibility of our being body-subjects and body-objects. Were we not body-things we would be mere objects-of-consciousness-for-the-other, part of his dreams. The other would neither be able to use us for his purposes nor be used by us for our purposes. Only bodies that weigh as things do, that fall as things do, that occupy a place as things do, can be used like instruments and, in their turn, use instruments. Only bodies that can be acted upon as things can "modify the shape of the world" and not simply the shape of their dreams. (BN, p. 433; Fr., p. 508)

IV. Affective Body

This body that I am, so much part of the world that it interacts with other things as a thing, possesses nonetheless the startling characteristic of being affected by what is done to it. I interact with things, that is, I produce changes in things and things produce changes in me. For instance, I make a dent in the table by pushing my pencil too hard when I am writing, and the window suddenly pushed by the wind hits me and makes a dent in my forehead. In this regard the table and the body are similar. But in another regard, the regard of affectivity, they are very different. The table is changed but not affected by the change. For the table, it amounts to the same to be dented or not. Not for my body. I feel my being dented. Feeling does not mean only being conscious. I am conscious of the dent in the table, but I am not affected by the dent in the table because I do not suffer that dent as subject of it. Thus, like things, the body is object of passivity, in that it is changed. But unlike them, the body is also *subject* of passivity in that it is affected by the changes of which it is object.

This capacity to be affected reveals a further dimension of the body. The body-subject was previously characterized by its functioning as center of instrumentality. Now an enlargement of that characterization is called for. The body is not only center of instrumentality but also center of passivity. My being center of instrumentality manifests my ability to manipulate things and other people for my own purposes, my being intentional agent. This is the subject in its active capacity. But this is only one side of my being body-subject. The other side is my being subject in a passive capacity, body toward which the situation is oriented as center affected by what is done to it.

To the affective dimension of the body Sartre is practically blind in *Being and Nothingness*.[8] As an easy illustration of my point, take his views of our concrete relations with others. According to Sartre, any concrete situa-

---

8. Sartre actually concerns himself with affectivity (see BN pp. 330-339; Fr., 394-404). But his analysis differs from mine in at least two significant respects. First, Sartre does not re-

tion of encounter with the other is to be characterized *either* as one in which I am the center of instrumentality (that is, subject), *or* one in which I am not the center of instrumentality (that is, object). In my interpretation of the body, by contrast, in the latter situation I am an object-subject. I am object in that the other has me at his mercy: he can use me as an instrument for his own purposes. But I am subject, too, in that I am consciously affected by what the other does to me. Indeed, this is why Sartre is right in characterizing the body as an "explosive instrument." Things, by contrast, are not "explosive," in Sartre's sense, because they are insensitive to what is done to them, they are not affected by their being used. Things can be used as much as bodies, but they do not mind it, because they are not affected by what is done to them. But I do mind it, because I remain subject, center of affectivity, even when the other is center of instrumentality.[9] And because I remain center of affectivity, I may try to regain the initiative and become master of the situation. Were I as insensitive and hence as invulnerable as things are, I would not be "explosive." Thus, Sartre is right in realizing my explosiveness. But this characteristic of the human who is object for the other remains unintelligible in *Being and Nothingness*, because Sartre ignores the body as affective subject.

Because he ignores the body-center of affectivity, he consequently ignores another important aspect of our mode of being-in-the-world. A body-center of affectivity is born engaged in the world. There is nowhere to go where I could escape my vulnerable exposure to the world. Twenty-four hours a day, even when I am not thinking of the world around me, even when I am doing nothing, even when I am asleep, I belong there because I am exposed. At any moment, without previous notice, I may be recalled to function as what I indeed am: center of affectivity. As such, I belong in the world whether I like it or not. I am rooted to the world.

---

late the affectivity of the body to our passivity to the world. Second, and as a result of the former, Sartre tends to interpret affectivity as a characteristic of a pure consciousness rather than of a *body*. The least one can say is that Sartre's treatment of affectivity is so ambiguous and so loosely related to the rest of the chapter that it is impossible to think that he attributed serious importance to it in the total picture.

9. This seems to open a new alternative to Sartre's treatment of human relations. When I am master of the situation, I undoubtedly can abuse the other by treating him as my instrument. And the other can abuse me when he is master of the situation. These are the only two forms of relation acknowledged by Sartre. From this he draws the conclusion that human relations are necessarily conflictive and condemned to fail. But if, as I have argued, the other remains affective subject even when I master the situation, then the possibility remains open for me to recognize him as such and to be recognized by him as subject who recognizes him as subject. This is truly human reciprocity, encounter between subject and subject. Such an encounter may be difficult, for the *practical* recognition of the other as subject when one can easily use him is indeed difficult. It may even be impossible to a very large extent within societies in which sheer competition is maximized owing to brute material scarcity or to the elevation of production–consumption to the category of an end in itself. But it does not seem to be precluded by the very structure of the human reality, as Sartre would have us believe.

V. Needful Body

I am rooted to the world still more deeply than the preceding section revealed, for I am a needful body, a body who needs the world and who, as an affective body, is affected by the response the world offers to his needs. I am rooted to the world by my need of it as the tree is rooted to the soil by the roots through which it extracts its very life from the soil, as the fetus is rooted by the umbilical cord to the maternal womb from which it lives. I am a body that needs the world in order to be a body. I am a hungry body, and if the world does not respond to my hunger with food I cease to be a body, as the tree ceases to be a tree if the soil becomes barren and as the fetus ceases to be a fetus if the maternal womb ceases to support him. Unlike the tree, I suffer if this happens, for I am an affective body; but like the tree, my mode of being in the world involves vital dependence on the world. Unlike the tree, I can realize what would happen to me if the world stopped producing food. As an affective body, I care about what would happen to me in that case, and as body-center of instrumentality, I do my best to prevent that from happening. But my being dependent on the world in my very being is like the tree's.

My being needful body manifests a sort of intentionality, or directedness to the world. But such intentionality — far from being primarily the rather ethereal directedness of a pure thinking consciousness to an object of thought — is the practical, biological, heavy directedness of a body that depends on the world in relation to the world it vitally needs.

Certain passages of *Being and Nothingness* might suggest that Sartre did not quite ignore this dimension of the body. For instance, he insists that the body is the center of practical, or instrumental, not merely contemplative, perspective, directed to the world as its field of action. And when he studies the structures of the for-itself he explicitly describes its intentionality as that of a lacking to be completed by the world as *lacked*.[10] But the lacks of Sartre's for-itself possess an ideal character in which it is difficult to recognize the weight of our very bodily needs, of our vital dependence on the world as needed. Sartre's for-itself lacks the world in that it cannot realize its projects without acting in the world. This is why Sartre's for-itself fully chooses its own self and is fully responsible for the self it chooses. It has desires and preferences because it decides to desire this and to prefer that, because it freely makes itself desire this and prefer that, but it has no need of this or of that. A being who chooses himself in this way may be absolutely free, as Sartre actually regards the for-itself in *Being and Nothingness*, but it really has *no needs* and consequently his mode of being-in-the-world is radically different from ours.

---

10. See particularly BN sections two and five, chapter one, part two.

Indeed, the needfulness of the body adds a further twist to our mode of being-in-the-world. We simply do not live like the Sartrian for-itself. The latter remains eerily transcendent even after it supposedly becomes bodily in part three of *Being and Nothingness*. It seems to enter the world and disappear from it at will, as Orestes, the hero of *The Flies*, enters the city of Argos at the beginning of the play and leaves it at the end, to go God knows where. From previous steps in our analysis we know that our inherence to the world is far thicker than Sartre imagined. A body-thing does not enter the world; it is *of* the world. A body-center of affectivity does not disappear from the world by forgetting the world; it belongs in the world by its vulnerability to it. A needful body is rooted to the world by its radical dependence on it. The belongingness to the world of an affective, needful body is utterly inescapable. Such a body cannot attempt to minimize his exposure to the world by trying to withdraw from it without, by the same token, maximizing his exposure to the world by becoming *deprived of it*.

Here we touch, I think, at the roots of the problems raised by the famous philosophical *epoche* — be it Cartesian, under the form of doubting, or Husserlian, under the form of suspending the belief in existence. Certainly we are able to reflect on our experience of the world and take in regard to it a purely contemplative attitude. Thereby, we reduce ourselves to subjects of merely contemplative experience. Unsurprisingly, then, we have all the supposedly philosophical problems that certain philosophers have been carefully nurturing since Descartes. Indeed, a subject of purely contemplative experience would be unable to distinguish between dreams and reality. But as we happen not to be in the world as the subject of purely contemplative experience, the world recalls us, whether we like it or not, to our bodily form of existence. For the world as object of need can be momentarily forgotten, but not bracketed. The *epoche* does not cure us from the needs and risks involved in living as humans do. It only creates in us the harmful Platonic illusion that the point of view of the disembodied thinker is *the* point of view from which the truth is, or can be, seen. Thus, for all the good intentions of its practitioners, the *epoche* turns out to be the form of bad faith of those who fancy themselves pure *thinkers*, though they live, like the rest of us, as *bodies*.

VI. In-Itself-For-Itself

Up to this point I have been considering different dimensions of the body. Supposedly, these different dimensions are of *one and the same* body. But are they, really? How can the same body be subject and thing, for-itself and in-itself?

Characteristically, Sartre sees the problem in *Being and Nothingness* in terms of choosing one or the other:

Either it [the body] is a thing among other things, or else it is that by which things are revealed to me. But it cannot be both at the same time. (BN, p. 304; Fr., p. 366)

Needless to say, confronted with such a dilemma, Sartre chooses the body-subject and conveniently forgets the body-thing. For Sartre there is nothing in common between his body as object of study for the physicist or the biologist and his body as lived by him. In much the same way and because of the same radically dichotomous approach, the reductive materialists of all kinds choose the body-thing and deny the body-subject. The question is: Can we accept such a dilemma, given the type of body we are? The answer, it seems to me, is that we simply cannot.

I wake up in the hospital. People tell me that I was knocked down by a car and carried in an ambulance. Unavoidably, I identify myself with the thing that was hit by a car and rushed to the hospital. How come? Notice that I identify myself with *this* thing that was carried to the hospital, not with that other thing, my watch, which was also carried to the hospital with "me." If it were a matter of pure reason, there is no reason in the world why I should identify myself with this body rather than with that watch. But it is not a matter of reason. The simple fact is that I am this body, not that watch.[11] For this body reclaims me in a way in which the watch does not. This body recovers itself as affective subject. It recovers itself to suffer itself. I wish I were the watch, for then I would not suffer. But I am not. I am this body who cannot move the left arm anymore. *It* does not obey *me*. The doctor explains to me that my motor nerves have been severed, and that I will never be able to move my arm again. So I am motor nerves too, though I have never experienced them. All my life I will carry this thing-arm that I am, which I reclaim only to suffer it.

VII. Conclusion

Apart from its obviously sketchy character, the analysis of the body I have presented as an alternative to Sartre's analysis is incomplete. First, we

---

11. By "simple fact" I do not mean that *I happen* to be the subject of this body nor that *I could have been* the subject of the body of a chimpanzee or of another person. This sort of issue is possible only within a dualistic conception of consciousness *and* body. The very point of this section is that our form of life is such that it rejects the neat distinctions of analytic reason. Try as we may, we meet a paradox. Dualism neatly distinguishes the subject from the thing, only to find, as Descartes did, that the pilot and the ship cannot be fully distinguished from each other. Idealistic monism attempts to reduce the body to the consciousness of the body, only to be confronted with the paradox of the passivity of consciousness to the very body it supposedly constitutes. Materialistic monism attempts to reduce the body to the thing-body, only to be confronted with the paradox that the body does not passively accept being treated as a mere thing. There is always a residuum left on which the opposing views find their source of counter-arguments, and the controversy goes on forever. We had better accept the "simple fact"—that is, the ineluctable facticity—of our being for-itself-in-itself.

are not born adults. We grow up. Indeed, we grow so much that we grow old and even end up dying. The dimensions of the body described above would have to be placed in a developmental context of which I have said nothing in this paper. Second, the body we are is born and develops within a group, whose economic, social, and linguistic institutions shape it and with which it interacts in a dialectical relationship. Again, I have not spoken of this institutional context. The result is that my analysis remains profoundly abstract. It represents only a first step.

Nonetheless, the preceding thematization of the different dimensions of the body as well as of their unity seems to have its usefulness, both in that it allows us to discriminate between what is valuable and what is mere wishful thinking in *Being and Nothingness*, and in that it provides us with an orientation for our comprehension of the human praxis.

To zero in on the concrete issue that constitutes the heart of Sartre's thought, not only in *Being and Nothingness* but in his whole work, my analysis of the body allows us to see that the kind of freedom Sartre attributed to us in *Being and Nothingness* has little to do with our reality. As I have repeatedly indicated, the body is too much of the world to be able to transcend the world in the Sartrian manner. But it is only fair to acknowledge that Sartre's views on human freedom have undergone a profound transformation since *Being and Nothingness*. The question is whether the preceding analysis is compatible with any kind of freedom, whether a body of the structure described in this paper can be free at all, and if so, what kind of freedom will it have?

I do not think that this question can be answered seriously without explicit reference to the developmental character of the body and to the economic, social, and linguistic institutions with which it interacts and by which it is undeniably shaped. Thus, all I can do here is express an unsupported personal opinion.

I believe that my analysis of the body is compatible with a view of relative, dynamic (progressive as well as regressive), historical freedom. By this I mean a freedom to be gradually conquered — though never to be possessed in absolute security — by means of a skillful steering of the very material, social, and economic conditions on which we depend as bodily existents. For the conditions that reduce or even do away with our freedom are by the same token *conditions of possibility* for our freedom. Indeed, a body that can grasp one's being conditioned and that by which one is conditioned, as we seem able to do, has the possibility of using those conditions as means to make oneself free.

As I believe that the view of freedom implicit in Sartre's more mature works does not differ much from the one just expressed, this paper may well turn out to be a mere thematization of the view of the body also implicit in Sartre's more mature works.

John E. Atwell

4. *Sartre and Action Theory*

But after all it's what we've done that makes us what we are—Jim Croce

I.

One of the most interesting developments in twentiety-century philosophy is the widespread attention focused on the concept of human action.[1] Prior to the present century, many philosophers referred to human actions, of course—especially in connection with questions of ethics, freedom, and responsibility—but for the most part they took the notion of action to be relatively unproblematic.[2] The massive amount of recent literature on the subject surely attests to the falsity of this assumption. This emphasis on the concept of action has been motivated, I suspect, by the impasse reached in the ancient problem of "free will," or, in more modern terminology, the problem as to whether human actions are free or not. Determinists argue, on the one hand, that all human actions are causally determined to occur just as they do occur owing to the presence of antecedent events or conditions.[3] Libertarians argue, on the other hand, that at least some human actions are not causally determined by antecedent events or conditions, and further that these "free" actions are those for which it is proper to hold the

---

1. A good collection of important papers on human action is Myles Brand, ed., *The Nature of Human Action* (Glenview, Ill.: Scott, Foresman and Co., 1970), which includes a lengthy introductory essay by the editor.

2. "For the most part" is a necessary qualification, since—to say nothing of Aristotle and Aquinas—several past philosophers dealt with the notion of human action in a perceptive way. Cf. G. F. W. Hegel, *Reason in History*, trans. S. Hartman (Indianapolis: Bobbs-Merrill, 1953), pp. 76, 89-90; Arthur Schopenhauer, *The World as Will and Representation*, trans. E. F. J. Payne (New York: Dover Publications, 1966), 1:100-101, as well as elsewhere; and John Stuart Mill, *A System of Logic* (London: Longmans, 1967), p. 35.

3. It is customary to distinguish between "hard" determinism—which holds that since determinism is true, no one is responsible for his actions—and "soft" determinism—which argues that despite the truth of determinism agents are responsible for some of their actions. Although this is no doubt an important distinction, I have no need to observe it for the purposes of this paper.

agent responsible.[4] Though both parties to the dispute bring forth subtle, even ingenious, arguments in support of their respective positions, many of those philosophers not directly involved in this (as they see it) imbroglio entertain little hope of resolving the matter until and unless a good deal more examination is made of such central notions as causation, causal laws, explanation, responsibility (along with blameworthiness and praiseworthiness), and — above all else — human action. If the question is "Are human actions free or not, causally determined or not, causally explainable or not?," then we had better be quite clear on what a human action is. For it may very well turn out — and this is the view "action theorists" have reached — that human actions, by their very nature, are not subject to causal determinism, and cannot possibly be causally explained, that is, explained by appeal to antecedent events or conditions.[5]

My first concern is with the question as to where Jean-Paul Sartre stands with regard to the three positions on human freedom mentioned above, determinism, libertarianism, and action theory. In his anthology *Free Will and Determinism* Bernard Berofsky includes a selection from Sartre's *Being and Nothingness*, which he places in the chapter on libertarianism. But when he comes to introduce Sartre's views on freedom, determinism, and action, Berofsky expresses some doubt about the appropriateness of this classification:

> It would perhaps be better to place Sartre in the next chapter [on action theory] as it certainly sounds as if he is rejecting the possibility that determinism is applicable to human action on the basis of analyses of the concepts of action and determinism. But we shall follow tradition and call him a "libertarian."[6]

Sartre certainly has been called a libertarian traditionally, indeed a radical or extreme libertarian,[7] but perhaps this is because the alternative classification (action theory) did not become popular until several years after the publication of *Being and Nothingness* (1943). So, is Sartre better regarded a libertarian or an action theorist? The question is important if for

    4. Cf. C. A. Campbell, "Is 'Free Will' a Pseudo-Problem?," *Mind*, October 1951, pp. 441–465.

    5. Action theory is suggested, or even explicitly argued for, by the following authors: R. S. Peters, *The Concept of Motivation* (London: Routledge & Kegan Paul, 1958); A. I. Melden, *Free Action* (London: Routledge & Kegan Paul, 1961); G. E. M. Anscombe, *Intention* (Oxford: Basil Blackwell, 1958); Stuart Hampshire, *Thought and Action* (New York: Viking Press, 1960).

    6. Bernard Berofsky, ed., *Free Will and Determinism* (New York: Harper & Row, 1966), p. 112.

    7. Wilfrid Desan, for instance, speaks of Sartre's advocacy of "the most extreme form of freedom the history of philosophy has ever presented," *The Tragic Finale* (New York: Harper Torchbooks, 1960), p. 160. And S. Morgenbesser and James Walsh, eds., *Free Will* (Englewood Cliffs, N.J.: Prentice-Hall, 1962), introduce a selection from Sartre by saying: "It would be hard to find a more radical or eloquent proponent of Libertarianism than Sartre," p. 93.

no other reason than that the proper classification will aid us in understanding Sartre's position on human freedom, including of course his apparently outlandish views on responsibility (man is "responsible for the world and for himself as a way of being")[8] and deserts ("If I am mobilized in a war, this war is *my* war; it is in my image and I deserve it").[9]

Berofsky's second thoughts certainly seem fitting, given his characterizations of the two theories:

> The libertarian, although a bit worried that he might be wrong, denies *in fact* that deterministic accounts can be provided for all actions. The action theorist denies *in principle* the same proposition and is not, therefore, worried. He claims that, given the notion of "deterministic account of *x*" and "*y* is an action," it is conceptually impossible for *x* to be identical with *y*.[10]

An action theorist holds, in other words, that human actions—or at least full-fledged, voluntary human actions—cannot, logically, be understood as causally produced by and contingently related to prior events (or antecedent conditions) in the world of nature or in the agent. Being conceptually immune to causal explanation, human actions can be explained only in a teleological fashion, that is, by appeal to the agent's ends, aims, goals, purposes, reasons, or intentions—none of which, it is claimed, can be regarded as causally connected to actions. Strictly speaking, an action theorist need not also be a teleologist, for one could maintain the negative theory that no action can be accounted for deterministically (action theory) without maintaining the positive theory that actions can be accounted for by appeal to ends, aims, purposes, and so on (teleologism). In effect, this would be to claim that human actions cannot be accounted for or explained at all; but I know of no action theorist who has held this view. In any case, I shall assume an action theorist to maintain: that which explains why a specific individual did a specific action is his goal (etc.), and his goal cannot be thought of as a prior event, contingently and causally connected with the action. For example, "Why did he beat his fist on the table?" "In order to get the attention of Smith." And this goal is not a cause of his action: it is not an occurrence that preceded and causally brought about his action, though it does indeed explain why the agent performed the action.

I believe, and have argued elsewhere,[11] that there is good reason for classifying Sartre as an action theorist with respect to characterizing and explaining human actions; but I believe, equally, and shall argue here, that he is not a normal sort of action theorist. Beginning with an analysis of his basic characterization of actions, I shall proceed to examine how Sartre

---

8. BN, p. 553.
9. Ibid., p. 554.
10. Berofsky, *Free Will and Determinism*, p. x.
11. Cf. my "Sartre's Conception of Action and His Utilization of *Wesensschau*," *Man and World*, May 1972, pp. 143–157.

proposes to distinguish, in actual cases, actions from nonactions, that is, how he applies his conception of action to concrete cases. On this issue, I submit, his procedure differs sharply from the method usually employed by action theorists.

II.

Initial evidence for calling Sartre an action theorist derives from his definitional or perhaps stipulative assertion that "an action is on principle *intentional*."[12] Those philosophers of action in the "analytic" tradition whom we normally classify as action theorists urge the same view, though they usually replace "on principle" with "a priori" or "conceptually," following which they, like Sartre, immediately launch into a discussion of intention.[13] It seems to me, however, that one should first of all explicate the expression "on principle" (or "a priori" or "conceptually"); for one might mean at least two quite different things with this expression, and which of the two one does mean obviously affects the meaning of the entire assertion. One may wish to say, for instance, that every single action is intentional — that is, analytically actions are intentional — from which it follows, on logical grounds, that "an unintentional (or even nonintentional) action" is a self-contradictory expression. On this interpretation, a person may *do* something unintentionally, or without an intention, but it is not possible for a person to *act* unintentionally. This view may then be called the "logical thesis" of the concept of action.

According to the second way of understanding the expression "on principle," the assertion in question amounts to saying this: it belongs to the nature of an action to be intentional, or actions are by their nature intentional. The import of "by their nature" is difficult to spell out, but it is not, I think, a mysterious or unfamiliar notion. It amounts to saying that actions are presumed intentional, such that to regard someone's doing something as an action is to regard it as intentional, until and unless evidence to the contrary is furnished. Quite clearly, this second interpretation — to be called the "conceptual thesis" — does not logically preclude the possibility of there being, even fairly often, unintentional actions; it does not make the expression "unintentional action" self-contradictory. It insists, however, that a necessary condition for there being any actions, as we now conceive actions, is that an action is prima facie intentional, though it allows that there may be numerous unintentional or nonintentional "doings" properly called actions. Actually, the conceptual thesis seems to reflect more accurately our nonphilosophical, or prephilosophical, view. For we often speak of unintentional actions, yet we do so, it is arguable, against the underlying assumption that actions are intentional.

---

12. BN, p. 433.

13. Unlike Sartre, most "analytic" philosophers stress (indeed, overstress) the importance of bodily actions, which are, after all, not the sort of actions we are normally most concerned with.

We may mark the distinction I am attempting to elucidate by saying that some assertions of the form "*A*s are *B*" are analytically or logically true and some are conceptually true.[14] "Bachelors are unmarried" and "kittens are feline" illustrate analytic truths; "promises are sincere," "utterances are meant," and "adult human beings are rational" illustrate conceptual truths. Thus, to say that Peg is a kitten is to imply, on logical grounds, that Peg is feline. But to say that Jones is an adult human being is merely to suggest that he is rational, though strongly enough that if the speaker believes Jones not to be rational—and perhaps therefore not responsible for his behavior—the speaker would be guilty of misleading his listener should he not explicitly state his belief.

Does Sartre maintain, then, that analytically every single action is intentional (the logical thesis), or does he hold that conceptually actions are intentional (the conceptual thesis)? And what does he mean by "intentional"? Though he does not answer these questions directly, he does make a number of relatively straightforward assertions from which we may perhaps judge what his answers would be. To begin with, he writes that "to act is to modify the *shape* of the world; it is to arrange means in view of an end. . . ."[15] If a person carelessly discards a lit cigarette and thereby causes a powder magazine to explode, he has not acted. But if a person obeys the order to dynamite a quarry, and produces the expected explosion, then he has acted, for "he knew what he was doing or, if you prefer, he intentionally realized a conscious project."[16] Sartre refuses to label as an action those "doings" that incorporate into their description unforeseen consequences or unknown side effects of genuine actions. Constantine, for example, created Constantinople —he created "a new residence for emperors in the Orient"; and although this action (describable apparently in two ways) had several unforeseen consequences that we might say Constantine "did," it would be mistaken to say that weakening the Roman Empire was one of Constantine's actions, even though this result did come about. For "he performed an act just in so far as he realized his project of creating a new residence for emperors in the Orient. Equating the result with the intention is here sufficient for us to be able to speak of action."[17]

Sartre, then, appears to be maintaining the logical thesis of action, for he seems to be saying that each and every human action is a doing performed

---

14. What I call "conceptual truths" are similar (I think) to one sort of statement discussed by P. T. Geach, in "Good and Evil," *Analysis*, 1956, p. 39. The sort of statement he discusses is not analytic, nor is it an empirical generalization; and the sort I have in mind is neither analytic nor empirical either. Of course, some assertions of the form "*A*s are *B*" are simply empirically true, e.g., "crows are black."

15. BN, p. 433.

16. Ibid. It seems clear that the careless smoker has acted in discarding a lit cigarette, though it may not be proper to say that he has acted in exploding the powder magazine. Sartre actually says, here: "The careless smoker who has through negligence caused the explosion of a powder magazine has not *acted*."

17. Ibid.

for the sake of effecting a quite definite and fully conscious end or intention: an end or intention that the agent has in mind and could cite at will, as no doubt Constantine could have. Of course, how we describe the person's action will depend on a number of things, above all, on whether or not the end was attained. Sartre does not say much about the matter of properly describing an action, but I believe he would assent to the following account. If a person does X for the sake of effecting Y, and Y does not come about, then we may say only that he did X, or that X was his action (though we might add that the agent attempted to bring about, or do, Y). But if Y is produced by his doing X, then we may also say that he did Y, or that Y was his action. In either case, the person has acted: he did X for the sake of effecting Y. And this is sufficient and necessary for action.[18]

Though apparently quite clear, this picture of Sartre's position is blurred by the fact that he uses the term *intention* so widely that occasionally the agent will not "know" what the intention of his action is, or indeed that what he has done is a genuine action. Sartre will often speak of someone's behavior as a case of intentional action, although most of us, I think, would classify it as unintentional or nonintentional, simply because the agent is believed not to have sought, with full and explicit knowledge, a given end by means of his behavior. Consider, for example, the persons portrayed as behaving in bad faith. Sartre ascribes to such people efforts, aims, attempts, and the like—all of which suggest intentional behavior or action— yet he admits that in some sense these same persons do not explicitly know the ends or intentions of their behavior.[19] Now if such explicit knowledge is deemed necessary for intentional action, then the persons in bad faith cannot be said to be acting, at least in a full-fledged manner. We might, then, judge that Sartre maintains the conceptual thesis of action, therefore allowing for the possibility of unintentional or nonintentional actions.

The main point to keep in mind is that Sartre's conception of action (or intentional behavior) is not nearly as luminous as it may at first appear. Consequently, how he would distinguish actions from mere doings and/or "undergoings" is far from obvious. Even if we were to agree that analytically every action is intentional, we would still encounter great difficulty in distinguishing actions from nonactions. For, in addition to the aforementioned problem of discerning intentions—a problem resolvable only by observing Sartre's crucial distinction between "is conscious of" and "knows"[20]— Sartre ties the intention of an action so closely to the action itself that we

---

18. There are complications. If the agent intends to bring about Y by doing X, and Y is indeed produced by X—though not at all in the manner that the agent meant or expected— then we may feel hesitant to ascribe Y to the agent as a genuine action. And of course not everything an agent might bring about by doing something else can be described as his action, e.g., I may do something with the intention of bringing about an accident, and even though I fully succeed, it cannot be said (in English) that "I have accidented."

19. Cf. BN, pp. 47-70.

20. I briefly explain and apply to the notion of action the distinction between "knowing"

can hardly expect to apprehend the intention independently of the action and then proceed to take it as clear evidence for the agent's acting rather than his merely doing or undergoing something. This problem can be made prominent by contrasting Sartre's version of teleologism with a slightly different version.

III.

As I have defined their position, teleologists contend that intentions (purposes, wants, desires, choices, decisions) are connected a priori with "corresponding" actions. This thesis is urged in the effort to refute the doctrine of "mental causes," which maintains that intentions, and so on, causally produce human actions, especially bodily actions such as raising one's arm. The teleologist's strategy is quite simple: if A is the cause of B, then A and B stand in a contingent relationship, that is to say, it is logically possible for A to occur and B not to occur; however (the teleologist continues), an intention to move one's arm does not stand in a contingent relationship to moving one's arm, hence the intention cannot be the cause of one's arm movement. If we interpret a priori to mean "logically," then the teleologist has to show that it is not logically possible for the intention to occur and the bodily action not to occur. And this is no easy task, since apparently it is sometimes true that a person intends to move his arm, yet his arm does not move. Faced with this problem, the teleologist will introduce the notion of countervailing factors, arguing that an intention can fail to result in an action only if some factor interferes, while a cause can, logically, fail to result in its normal effect even though nothing interferes at all. In other words, claims the teleologist, it is logically true that "if a person intends to move his arm, then ceteris paribus he will move his arm," but it is not logically (only contingently) true that "if water is heated to one hundred degrees centigrade, then ceteris paribus it will boil."

There are various ways of stating the teleologist's thesis: one can, for example, speak of actions other than those consisting of bodily movements, and one can stress the goal (telos) wanted by the agent, but which is attainable only by doing something believed necessary for attaining it. These features occur in Norman Malcolm's formulation of the thesis.

> It could not fail to be true that if a person wanted X and believed Y was necessary for X, and there were absolutely no countervailing factors, he would do Y. This purposive principle is true a priori, not because of its form but because of its meaning — that is, because of the connection of meaning between the words "He wanted X and he realized that Y was necessary for X" and the words "He did Y."[21]

(Sartre's "thetic" consciousness) and "is conscious of" (his "nonthetic" consciousness) in section IV.

21. Norman Malcolm, "The Conceivability of Mechanism," *Philosophical Review*, January 1968, p. 51.

In illustration of this thesis, Malcolm writes as follows: "If a man wants to retrieve his hat and believes this requires him to climb a ladder, he will do so provided there are no countervailing factors." Such factors, he adds, might be the unavailability of a ladder, the fear of climbing ladders or of heights, the belief that someone will remove the ladder, leaving him stranded on the roof, and so on; but "the man's failure to climb a ladder would *not* be a countervailing factor." Now if there were no countervailing factors of any sort whatever, then "if the man did not climb the ladder it would not be true that he *wanted* his hat back, or *intended* to get it back."[22]

When compared with Sartre's mode of expression, it becomes immediately evident that Malcolm's formulation of the teleological thesis is much more "linguistic" — but, despite that, not essentially different.[23] There does seem, however, to be a real and significant difference concerning the matter of countervailing factors. For Sartre contends:

> Our description of freedom, since it does not distinguish between choosing and doing, compels us to abandon at once the distinction between the intention and the act. The intention can no more be separated from the act than thought can be separated from the language which expresses it; and as it happens that our speech informs us of our thought, so our acts will inform us of our intentions. . . .[24]

Coupling this passage, especially the first sentence, with such beliefs that man is not what he conceives himself as being but rather what he wills,[25] and that, there being no reality except in action, man is "nothing else than the ensemble of his acts,"[26] it is reasonable to interpret Sartre to hold: I choose or intend to do act *X* if and only if I do act *X*. As reported above, he maintains that it is impossible to act without intending to act (or indeed without intending to achieve something by acting), but now he appears to assert that it is impossible to intend or choose to act without actually acting. Not only does Sartre seem to regard so-called countervailing factors impossible, he also suggests in some passages that intentions and actions are one and the same thing,[27] though paradoxically the latter are said to "inform us" of the former. But if so, then we cannot use the presence of intention,

---

22. Ibid., p. 48.

23. Sartre, for example, never speaks of "the connection of meaning" between words, as Malcolm does in the passage cited in note 21.

24. BN, p. 484.

25. Sartre, "Existentialism Is a Humanism," Trans. B. Frechtman in *Existentialism* (New York: Philosophical Library, 1947), p. 19.

26. Ibid., p. 38.

27. Cf. BN, pp. 476, 483. The expression "one and the same thing" will have to be clarified, and perhaps qualified, even though Sartre does say, on p. 483, that choice is identical with action.

knowable somehow independent of an action, as a criterion for distinguishing actions from nonactions. So, a host of problems now arise, but they are, I shall argue later, resolvable. Here I have merely tried to point up a possible, and reasonable, interpretation of Sartre's views, but one that will finally turn out to be inaccurate.

Let us consider now the possibility of intentions being interfered with and thus failing to result in actions. That there could be such a failure presupposes a temporal distinction or time lapse between the intention and the action. Charles Taylor, a teleologist, surely makes this presupposition when he writes that "this is part of what we mean by 'intending X' that, in the absence of interfering factors, it is *followed by* doing X."[28] In a formula, Taylor maintains: if a person intends to do X—presumably for the sake of attaining some goal Y—then, in the absence of interfering factors, he will do X. Notably, the intention is said to occur some time prior to the act, and apparently for this reason it is possible for something to happen that prevents the person from doing what he intended to do.

Sartre's view is rather different. For one thing, he seems to deny any time lapse between (what may be called) forming an intention and actually acting. Hence, he does not, and need not, allow for interfering factors. Moreover, since the action, as he puts it, informs us of the intention, there can be no intention in the absence of the action. But this makes a self-contradiction of the statement "I intended to do X, but I didn't." The man who lost his hat (in Malcolm's illustration) might say, upon learning that the ladder's rungs were broken, "I intended to retrieve my hat, but I didn't get it back because the ladder was broken." It seems, in fact, that he would not even have discovered the broken rungs unless he did intend to retrieve his hat, for it was the intention that "motivated" him to fetch the ladder in the first place. More generally, how can there be the obstacles Sartre makes so much of if nothing can interfere with one's intentions? For something becomes an obstacle only if it prevents one from doing what one intends to do, only if it frustrates a chosen end.[29]

Is there any way for Sartre to extricate himself from this apparently untenable position? Perhaps not entirely, but there is, I think, some justification for his denial of factors' interfering with intentions. Like Malcolm and others, Sartre is anxious to draw a fairly sharp distinction between a mere wish and a genuine intention, between a "*representation* which I could choose"[30] and a real choice, between a "dream" and an undertaking. On this score, he writes that "it is necessary . . . to note that the choice, being identical with acting, supposes a commencement of realization in order

---

28. Charles Taylor, *The Explanation of Behaviour* (London: Routledge & Kegan Paul, 1964), p. 33. Italics mine.
29. Cf. BN, pp. 481-489.
30. Ibid., p. 483.

that the choice may be distinguished from the dream and the wish."[31] For, to cite an example, it is only by trying to escape, hence by doing something toward escaping, that the prisoner learns of his own intention (not mere wish) to escape.[32] Sartre does not believe that a person must succeed in doing something X in order to intend to do it, but he must do or succeed in doing something directed toward successfully doing X. The prisoner may not actually escape, of course, even though he fully intends to do so, but he must at least, say, search for loose bars. Otherwise, we would simply say that he would like to be free. So, Sartre only denies the possibility of completely incapacitating interferences to intentions. He certainly does not claim that if a person intends or chooses to do some action (say, escape), then he will do that action; but he must do something (say, seek loose bars) toward carrying out his intended or chosen action. It follows that, contrary to the above interpretation, Sartre's view does not result in making self-contradictory the statement "I intended to do X, but I didn't do it"; it only makes self-contradictory "I intended to do X, but I didn't do anything toward doing (i.e., accomplishing) X." In short, in Sartre's view, if I intend to do X (open the door), then I must do something Y (turn the knob, or at least move my arm) that I take to be instrumental in getting X done; but I may still intend to do X even though X does not get done. For the door may be locked, jammed, or otherwise unopenable, though this does not falsify the statement that I intend to do X. Sartre would therefore deny the need for or appropriateness of adding a "ceteris paribus" clause to the *general thesis* that intending entails acting, that is, that if I intend to do act X, then I shall perform some action (say, Y or Z), though not necessarily act X. Although it is perhaps not obvious, Malcolm agrees entirely — which is not extraordinary, given that both men oppose the doctrine of mental causes and both distinguish mere wishes from genuine wants (Malcolm), intentions, and choices (Sartre).

In response, I would guess, to alleged counter-instances of the thesis that "could not fail to be true" — that is, "if a person wanted X and believed Y was necessary for X, and there were absolutely no countervailing factors, he would do Y" — Malcolm allows an alteration. "This [the thesis] is true," he says, "if we use 'wants X' to mean 'is aiming at X.' But sometimes we may mean no more than 'would like to have X,' which may represent a mere wish."[33] Now, contrary to what Malcolm appears to think, this is not an insignificant qualification. For if a person is aiming at (is trying to get?) X, he must be doing so in some manner or other; and he will doubtless be doing so in the manner he believes is required for getting X. Employing the above illustration, the thesis then becomes: if a person is aiming at (or trying to retrieve) his hat in the manner he believes is required — for example, climbing

---

31. Ibid.
32. Ibid., p. 484.
33. Malcolm, "The Conceivability of Mechanism," p. 51, n. 7.

a ladder, or going for it, or anything else—then he *is doing* (not *will do*) that which he believes is required, and the question of factors' interfering with his doing that action cannot even arise. Whether he actually retrieves his hat is another matter—for the wind may blow it away, or he may suffer a heart attack, just as he reaches for it—but whether he is doing something that he believes is required for retrieving the hat is settled. In brief, "if we use 'wants X' to mean 'is aiming at X,'" then the man who wants X is at the very same moment aiming at X; for, indeed, to want X is to aim at it, and to aim at it is, in this case, to do Y. Hence, there is no possibility that doing Y will be interfered with, once we suppose that the man wants X; and there is no need for a "ceteris paribus" clause with regard to his doing Y. In fact, such a clause becomes wholly superfluous to Malcolm's formulation of the teleological principle.[34]

The interesting point to note is that both Sartre and Malcolm deny the possibility of, let us say, intentions that fail to result in or to be accompanied by some minimal action undertaken for the purpose of fulfilling the intention. Intentions are not pure mental events, standing apart from and causally productive of actions, but are rather integral parts of those human "doings" that are most properly called actions. An intention, says Sartre, is "a choice of the end,"[35] which end does not yet exist and which the action is meant to realize. Should no action be done at all, it would be mistaken to say that the agent had an intention or chose the end. In an older parlance, there is no such thing as a pure "act of will."[36] With regard to explaining why someone did a certain action, it will always be relevant and indeed essential to cite the end he intended to realize by means of the action in question. Why Clovis converted to Christianity, for instance, may be partially explained by citing his end, which was, in Sartre's judgment, to conquer all of Gaul.[37] To choose this end, to have this intention, is—under the conditions obtaining at the time, at least as Clovis saw them—to convert to Christianity. So, again, the choice of the end or the forming of the intention is not to be separated from the performance of the action itself.

Sartre's conception of the relation between intention and action should be clearer now, but nothing said so far really helps much in determining when a person has acted as opposed to when he has merely done something (such as rearranging dust particles by, say, bowing his head) or undergone something (such as suffering a headache). And it is precisely this issue, solely with regard to Sartre's thought, that I wish now to pursue.

---

34. Possibly Malcolm assumes this without clearly stating a different principle, namely, that "if a person intends or tries to do X, then ceteris paribus he will do X." That is to say, a person will indeed do (or succeed in doing) that which he truly intends or tries to do unless something interferes. But this principle seems dubious; for although I intend and try to pocket the nine ball in billiards I may not do it at all, and nothing—literally, at least—interferes.

35. BN, p. 477.

36. Cf. Schopenhauer, *The World as Will and Representation*, 1: 100.

37. BN, p. 446.

IV.

When Sartre claims that our acts inform us of our intentions, he means to put forth a number of distinguishable, but related, propositions: 1) He wants to say that our acts enable us to focus attention on, or "objectify," our intentions rather than merely to "live" them, that is, "to make objects of them instead of limiting us to living them."[38] 2) He emphasizes that our acts alone allow us to differentiate what we really intend from what we merely wish or conceive. And 3), he asserts something very much like Schopenhauer's contention that the character of man is empirical, that is, that "only through experience can one get to know it." "This applies," Schopenhauer adds, "not only to others, but to oneself."[39] I may think, and hope, and even assert, that I am a generous, altruistic sort of person, but only my acts will determine whether or not this is so. Where Schopenhauer speaks of the character, Sartre will speak of one's "fundamental project,"[40] or "original choice,"[41] or even "choice of oneself."[42] But that they agree on the decisive evidence rendered by acts in determining one's character (Schopenhauer) or one's fundamental project (Sartre) is undeniable.[43] Acts, however, are to be understood as intentional doings, so only when we have intentionally done something will this doing reveal the agent's character or fundamental project. On the other hand, only when a person has acted, and indeed has acted in a certain way, will he be informed of his intentions, and ultimately of the sort of person he is. How then does Sartre propose to break out of this obvious circle? That there is a circle is clear, for actions are said to inform us of our intentions, and only when we have intentionally done something may that doing be called an action.

Does one simply know when one has intentionally done something? Is one somehow immediately aware of the distinction between doing something with an intention and merely doing (or even undergoing) something? That Sartre would answer affirmatively to these questions is suggested by Mary Warnock, who writes that, for Sartre, "the difference between the active and the passive, between doing things and having things happen to

---

38. Ibid., p. 484. Intentions are "lived" in being acted out; and although we may not actually focus attention on them, the actions enable or allow us to do so.

39. Arthur Schopenhauer, *Essay on the Freedom of the Will*, trans. K. Kolenda (Indianapolis: Bobbs-Merrill, 1960), p. 50.

40. Cf. e.g., BN, p. 466. On this topic, Anthony Manser writes:

> By talking of a single fundamental project or original choice, Sartre wishes to stress that a person is a unity, possessing a certain "style" or manner of living which can be detected in every one of his actions, even the most trivial; everything that a man does is revealing.

This appears in *Sartre: A Philosophic Study* (New York: Oxford University Press, 1967), p. 121. Support for this interpretation may be found in BN, pp. 436, 457, 463, 563, 568, 570.

41. BN, p. 570.

42. Cf. BN, p. 469, where Sartre speaks of "Adam's choice of himself," and p. 39, where the expression "my choice of myself" is used, as well as numerous other passages.

43. Cf. BN, p. 567, in addition to the passages cited in note 40.

one, is a manifest difference, which can be experienced all the time."[44] Although Warnock is explicitly concerned with the distinction between doing things in an active manner (thus, with genuine actions) and having things happen to a passive individual (thus, with undergoings), she would presumably be willing to extend this distinction to action in contrast to unintentional or nonintentional doings. Thus, she would probably say that the difference between acting and merely doing something can be "experienced" all the time, at least by the individual himself. In this view, one just "knows"[45] when one is moving one's leg and when one's leg is reflexively moving, or when one is flexing a muscle and when one's muscle is twitching. This is not an unreasonable contention, but whether it actually expresses Sartre's view is surely open to question.

If Warnock's interpretation implies that, for Sartre, there is never an instance in which a person can sincerely ask himself whether he is acting or undergoing, then it is not clear to me that Sartre has been correctly understood. Suppose that during a heated argument Jones begins coughing "uncontrollably," and that it is asked whether or not he intentionally did so, say, for the purpose of terminating a debate he believed himself to be losing. Was the coughing something Jones *did* (in a full-fledged sense), or was it something that *happened to him*, something he *underwent?* It was without doubt a doing, for he did cough. But did he cough intentionally or unintentionally? "Only Jones knows for certain," it might be said. But is this really true? And is it Sartre's view? Is it not possible for Jones to ask himself, in all sincerity, whether he intentionally initiated a coughing fit or merely suffered one?[46] And given Sartre's bent for some form of behaviorism,[47] is it not true that an observer stands in much the same position as Jones himself? So, if an observer can sincerely ask the question—which seems obviously true—then apparently Jones can, also. Now if this line of argument is

---

44. Mary Warnock, *The Philosophy of Sartre* (London: Hutchinson University Library, 1965), p. 111. No support from Sartre's writings is given for this interpretation; but the main difficulty is the ambiguity of the term *experienced*, as I shall point out below.

45. As indicated by the quotation marks, I use *knows* advisedly. I suspect, however, that it does reflect Warnock's understanding of Sartre, provided it is used in the manner that G. E. M. Anscombe speaks of "nonobservational knowledge," in her *Intention* (Oxford: Basil Blackwell, 1958), pp. 13–15. I do not say, let it be understood, that Anscombe uses the notion of nonobservational knowledge for the purpose that Mary Warnock apparently ascribes to Sartre, i.e., the purpose of distinguishing intentional doings from other doings or undergoings.

46. In the play *Kean*, trans. Kitty Black in *The Devil and the Good Lord and Two Other Plays* (New York: Vintage, 1960), pp. 152–279, act five, Sartre has the main character ask himself a similar question, and indeed he is not certain of the answer.

47. Sartre is certainly not a behaviorist in the strongest sense, according to which so-called mental things (including choices, desires, intentions, etc.) are "reduced to" physical behavior. But he does seem to hold a weaker and more plausible version of the doctrine, as indicated in the passages on choices being identical with actions and on intentions being inseparable from actions, and by such remarks as: frowns, redness, and so on "do not *express* anger; they *are* the anger" (BN, p. 346). Sartre's main point, in the last passage quoted, is to show that we do not perceive human physical bodies and then infer the presence of mental or emotional states.

sound, it is false to say that the individual "experiences" all the time the difference between acting and merely doing, between the active and the passive.

Sartre, however, maintains that in the hands of a skilled existential psychoanalyst a person may come to recognize explicitly and acknowledge his "original choice" or "fundamental project." But how could he do this unless he were somehow immediately aware of what he had chosen and intended to do on particular occasions? Jones might come to admit, for instance, that he did intentionally begin coughing, for this "uncontrollable," "involuntary" doing turns out to be a genuine manifestation of his "original choice." To admit this, in Sartre's judgment, presupposes that Jones, at the time of the coughing, was "conscious of" coughing intentionally. Hence, in this line of thought, there appears to be some reason for agreeing with Warnock's view that a person "experiences" the difference between acting and merely doing. But, as noted above (concerning the fact that an individual can sincerely wonder whether he acted or merely did something), there appears to be some reason for disagreeing, too.

The main difficulty lies with explaining the meaning of such terms as *knows, is conscious of,* and *experiences.* Sartre does not use the term *experiences* in this connection, and he uses the terms *knows* and *is conscious of* in a technical way. Very briefly, to *know* something is to be explicitly conscious of it, to "posit" it as an object, to direct one's attention toward it; accompanying every such knowledge of an object there is an implicit *consciousness* of knowing the object, and knowing it perhaps in a certain way (say, detesting it), though this implicit consciousness may pass without ever being explicitly known or reflected on.[48] For example: I look at (explicitly know) a figurine that I detest, so I am implicitly conscious of looking at it in a detesting way; but I may not reflect on my looking at it or on my detesting manner of looking at it. Relating this to our topic, I may sometimes do something for the sake of a fully known end, in which case I shall obviously be acting; but I may at other times do something not fully knowing what the end is or even that there is an end, in which case it is not clear whether my "doing" is a genuine action or not. The latter case is illustrated, I am supposing, by the coughing fit.

By what method shall we then determine whether such a "doing" is or is not an action? I suggest the following procedure, which I believe Sartre would endorse. First of all, we should notice that Sartre will not attempt to distinguish, in some general and abstract way, the class of actions from the class of undergoings; he will not say, for instance, that universally moving one's arm is a genuine action, whereas suffering a spasm or upset stomach or coughing fit is an undergoing.[49] The only answerable question is "Is this

---

48. BN, pp. li–lv.
49. Of course, how we describe what someone "did" will often indicate whether we believe

person's doing such-and-such, at this time, an action?" Sometimes coughing will be an action, and sometimes not. But how do we tell?

If we are to distinguish Jones's actions from his undergoings, we must, of
course, start somewhere; and we shall not start with coughs, falling on the
pavement, driving into another car, or even bodily movements. We shall
start with those doings the ends of which Jones will openly state and anyone
can recognize with relative ease. Examples are many and varied: tossing
sand on the icy sidewalk, walking to the drugstore, stepping on the bath-
room scales, brushing one's teeth, firing a rifle, cleaning the keys of one's
typewriter, making a phone call, pocketing the six ball before the seven
ball, and so on. It is easier to recognize and state the ends of some of these
doings than others, but that all such doings have ends — thus are genuine
actions — seems relatively incontestable. (This is not to deny, however, that
circumstances could be imagined such that some of these doings would not
count as actions, say, when the "agent" has been hypnotized against his will
or when he is under the control of a mad scientist.)

Having dealt with so-called clear cases of Jones's intentional doings, or
actions, we can now (and only now) attempt to determine whether his
coughing was an action or merely something he underwent. Sartre suggests,
I think, that no one, including Jones himself, can make this determination
as long as the occurrence in question is attended to in isolation from Jones's
many paradigmatic actions such as those cited in the previous paragraph.
Only in light of a pervasive "pattern" of actions — the discovery of which, in
hard cases, is the existential psychoanalyst's task — can it be said that the
coughing was or was not an action. It will be called an action if it fits into
the Jones pattern, and otherwise not. Sartre does not speak of a "pattern of
actions" or "style of life," but he does regard man as a "totality" that gets expressed in his every action, every attitude, every tendency, and every
mannerism — even in those that appear most insignificant.[50] He even allows
himself to speak of the "choice of an intelligible character," which is "the
transcendent meaning of each concrete, empirical choice."[51] Very briefly,
Sartre portrays a person as a fundamental choice that is the ultimate meaning of every concrete choice the person makes, much in the same way that
the universal redness is expressed in every instance of red,[52] or the "principles of the feudal technique" are expressed in "each individual conduct" of
the feudal period.[53]

Suppose we have learned that Jones invariably initiates competitions

---

the doing to be intentional or not. It someone utters a false statement (a rather "neutral" doing), I may say that "he lied" — indicating intentional action — while you may say that "he mis-
spoke" — indicating unintentional behavior.

    50. — Cf. note 40.
    51. BN, pp. 563–564.
    52. Ibid., pp. xlvi–xlvii.
    53. Ibid., p. 523. For a fuller discussion of this point, cf. my article cited in note 11.

such as chess but quits when he foresees defeat ("I just remembered, I've got to make an appointment"). We shall then conclude that Jones's coughing was fully intentional, hence a genuine action; for, once again, he foresaw defeat. But had Smith been in Jones's place, Smith's coughing would have been labeled a mere undergoing, not an action. For Smith is not the "sort of person" to quit anything, least of all an argument, even though he foresees the peril of defeat ("I'll think of some devastating counter example to his thesis"). The discovery of a person's "original choice," of his general form of intentional behavior, is frequently neither difficult nor unusual. Indeed, its possibility is assumed by every inquiry into a person's character and personality, as we find in requests for character references and letters of recommendation.[54]

But what are we to make of Sartre's apparent view that, for example, Jones can come to admit the intentional nature of his coughing, and that this possibility presupposes his having been "aware of" intentionally doing so at the time? Does this view imply that Jones does have some sort of privileged access to his own intentions, that is, a sort of immediate "awareness," which an outsider can acquire only gradually and inferentially? Sartre holds, on the one hand, that such a person as Jones is the least likely one to determine the proper classification of his doings, for most people actually try to hide from themselves the intentional nature of much of their conduct. Yet Sartre holds, on the other hand, that the attempt to hide one's intentional conduct from oneself reveals one's recognition of the very thing one wishes to conceal. One major point in the section on "bad faith" is that a person is often perfectly "aware of" that which he seems not to — and in a sense does not — "know."[55] So Jones, it may be said, is "aware of" having coughed intentionally, even though, in some sense, he does not "know" that he did.[56]

But what does Sartre mean by claiming, to use our example again, that Jones is aware of intentionally coughing? This is not easy to answer, as it takes us into the entangled maze of bad faith, or self-deception, but the "cash value" of Sartre's claim is simply that Jones can come to know explicitly what his fundamental project is, and that his coughing on that particular occasion was one manifestation of it. Jones may see, when confronted with several examples, that he typically terminates competitions when defeat is feared — this being a central aspect of his fundamental project — and he may see further that the coughing fits into this mode of behavior so neatly

---

54. Cf. the perceptive paper by Richard B. Brandt, "Traits of Character: A Conceptual Analysis," *American Philosophical Quarterly*, January 1970, pp. 23–37; also Maurice Mandelbaum, *The Phenomenology of Moral Experience* (New York: Free Press, 1955).

55. BN, p. 54.

56. Another example of "bad faith" may be this: a middle-aged man begins a program of vigorous physical exercise in order to "prove" — to himself and others — that he is in "the prime of life." If he really believed what he is trying to prove, then he would probably not have begun the program in the first place. I cannot elaborate this suggestion further in this paper.

that a denial of its being intentional, that is, of its signifying his typical mode of behavior, is wholly unwarranted. For he has absolutely no grounds for making the denial.[57]

Prior to raising an obvious objection, I want to summarize the results of the above discussion. First, Sartre rejects the idea that a person has privileged access to his own intentional behavior. Such behavior is public, not private. Only if it were possible for intentions to be separable from conduct, such that, for instance, public conduct referred to private intentions, would the contrary be the case; but since it is not possible, intentional behavior is a public matter. Second, Sartre separates a person's actions from his undergoings or mere doings on the basis of that which manifests his fundamental project and that which does not. Some doings are obviously intentional actions, and starting with these it is possible to discover a person's fundamental project, which in turn is employed to differentiate genuine actions from unintentional doings in nonobvious cases such as coughing, fainting, or getting a severe headache. Third, Sartre's insistence that a person is always "aware of" the difference between acting and undergoing should not be interpreted to mean that a person always "knows" the difference — or even "experiences" it, to use Warnock's ambiguous term — but that he, like a trained and perceptive observer, can come to know when he has acted and when he has merely done or suffered something. And he comes to know this difference by coming to recognize, quite explicitly, his fundamental choice, which his actions do and his undergoings or mere doings do not "signify."

V.

There are many questionable aspects of Sartre's notion of human actions, both with regard to what an action is and with regard to the proper explanation of actions. The main difficulty, which is not surprising, is that Sartre does not provide explicit answers to questions that several philosophers have raised about actions over the past thirty years or so. Is there, for example, only one proper way to describe a person's action? It seems clear that at this moment I am acting, but what exactly my action is might be described in various ways: "writing a paper on Sartre," "typing words on this

---

57. Stephen David Ross has made a *rather similar* point:

> I can accept an act as mine only when I understand myself and how the action follows from what I am, both bodily and spiritually. My slip of the tongue is but a blind and meaningless event until it is made part of me by showing how it is a rational consequence of what I am. My stumbling and clumsiness are but empty errors until it is revealed that they are not merely physical events, but to be understood in terms of my feelings and surreptitious goals. When I discover in myself the source of my acts, then I can genuinely claim them to be mine.

This passage comes from his book *The Nature of Moral Responsibility* (Detroit: Wayne State University Press, 1973), p. 33.

sheet of paper," "moving my fingers," and so on. Is any one of these descriptions the best or correct one? Is there any criterion for correctly describing an action? If so, what is it? Most important perhaps, may I not describe my action such that what might be called its "mental element" is omitted and then subsequently mentioned as the "causal antecedent" of my action? I could say that my action is "typing words on this sheet of paper," and that this action is "motivated," or caused, by the mental desire to write a paper on Sartre. In such a case, the action itself could be said to be caused by the desire that was not referred to in the description of the action. A good many philosophers would claim that this is the proper way to describe and conceive of human actions. So, until we have some guideline for describing actions, the dispute between teleologists (who would tie the desire logically to the action) and determinists (who would make the tie causal) will remain unresolved. At any rate, this brief discussion shows the crucial importance of how to conceive of and properly describe human actions.

Related to this matter, of course, is the problem of how to explain actions. Will my desire to write a paper on Sartre explain my action of typing these words? Or, must I, as Sartre seems to say,[58] make reference finally to my fundamental project? And what is the precise relation between one's fairly concrete actions and one's fundamental project? For those who prefer to explain actions in terms of the agent's character, a similar question arises.

These are surely important questions, but I propose to discuss, in conclusion, only one issue, and indeed the one that appears most prominent in light of the central theme of this paper. We are inclined to think that quite possibly a person will do something that falls into his general pattern of conduct — or that "fits his character," as the saying goes — but which, on a particular occasion, he did not do intentionally: "It is just the sort of thing that he *would* do intentionally." It may be claimed, for example, that Jones's coughing fit falls into the Jones pattern of terminating competitions when defeat is foreseen, but that on this one occasion the coughing fit was something he underwent rather than something he intentionally did. Hence, we may be persuaded of the truth of Jones's statement that "I certainly did not intend to begin coughing so violently." Now, if this view holds true, then Sartre's method of distinguishing actions from undergoings (as I have presented that method, of course) falls apart. For Sartre, I have suggested, has no grounds for allowing that although this particular bit of behavior of Jones's is unintentional, it is typical of Jones's project of terminating competitions when defeat is foreseen. To say that the behavior is typical, or that it reveals one of Jones's central projects, is precisely to say

---

58. BN, pp. 454ff., which asks why a certain hiker falls to the wayside before reaching the planned destination, while his companion, who is equally fatigued, does not.

that it is intentional—so no possibility of its being unintentional remains open. Yet we certainly seem inclined to allow for such a possibility. Our inclination could be wrong, I grant, but it *seems* not to be.

Let us consider the purpose of denying that one did something intentionally. Since there are probably several purposes possible, depending on the setting and the sort of thing that is said to have been done intentionally, let us suppose that Jones himself denies coughing intentionally in the aforementioned illustration. What then is his purpose in disclaiming intentional behavior? Well, one purpose he might have is this: to inform his listener that he is not the sort of person who would do such a thing intentionally.[59] But this is *ex hypothesi* false! For he is just this sort of person, as his general pattern of conduct clearly reveals.[60] (And this is not dependent on whether we speak of habitual ways of behaving or of fundamental projects, nor is it dependent on our method for discerning what these are.) So, if this is Jones's purpose in this particular case, then it is doomed to failure. We shall not be persuaded by his disclaimer. He might just as well accept full responsibility for the coughing fit, for there is no chance that denying responsibility for it will be accepted by his listener.

As I have said, there may be many different reasons or purposes for saying such things as "I did not mean to do X," or "I did not do X intentionally," but one reason is to convince one's listener about the sort of person one is. That Sartre should point to this reason through his insistence that "man is a totality and not a collection"[61] is good; for it draws to our attention the fact that many expressions containing "intentional," "did not mean to," and so on are not properly regarded as reports of internal pulls and pushes, but are rather efforts to say something about the "sorts of persons"[62] we believe ourselves and others to be. There are other ways of doing the same things, but there is this way, too.[63]

---

59. Cf. the following remark by L. Wittgenstein:
    Why do I want to tell him about an intention too, as well as telling him what I did?—Not because the intention was also something which was going on at the time. But because I want to tell him something about *myself*, which goes beyond what happened at that time.
This appears in *Philosophical Investigations*, trans. G. E. M. Anscombe (New York: Macmillan, 1953), par. 659.

60. An analogous, but by no means identical, case is discussed by Sartre, BN, pp. 63-65.

61. BN, p. 568.

62. By "sorts of persons" I mean something as difficult to make precise as "character" or "fundamental choice"; but this much is clear: when asked "What sort of person is so-and-so?," we would answer with such terms as "courageous," "deceitful," "overly ambitious," "humane," "gentle," and not such terms as "short," "left-handed," "thin." Sometimes we would be willing to pick out *one* term that we believe to characterize the individual in question, but usually we would use several different, though consistent, terms. An individual would not be said to be both ruthless and gentle, for instance.

63. For discussing with me some of the ideas in this paper, I am grateful to Ellen Gaskell; and for forcing me to clarify some of my views, I am indebted to Professors Elliston and Silverman.

PART TWO

Philosophical Problems

Hugh J. Silverman

5. *Sartre's Words on the Self*

In Sartre's descriptions of the self, the function of language changes in accordance with alterations in his concept of self. The change in the relationship between the self and verbal expression is a genetic interest that can be restated synchronically by citing three moments along Sartre's way. Each stage indicates a different formulation of this relationship. What I am suggesting is that one can speak of an *episteme* at differing moments within the work of an individual rather than limiting such a consideration to a historical context, as Foucault proposes.[1] Thus Sartre's early writings (1936–44), dealing with the transcendental ego, the ontological restructuring of consciousness without an ego internal to it, presuppose that a particular linguistic determination of the self will not affect the true self in any critical fashion. Yet in *Saint Genet* (1952), as representative of the second *episteme*, the word — a dizzying word — "Thief!" alters Genet's whole experience of himself and who he is. In this context, the self is formed in reaction to words. By the time of *The Words* (1964), the writer's experience of language and the linguistic analogy become the locus of self-expression. I shall examine in turn each of the three self/language binary structures.

---

1. Michel Foucault in *The Order of Things* (New York: Vintage, 1970), originally published as *Les Mots et les choses* (Paris: Gallimard, 1966), speaks of the *episteme* as the conceptual scheme or pattern of knowledge characteristic of different periods within Western thought. Sometimes the term *paradigm*, as employed by Thomas S. Kuhn in *The Structure of Scientific Revolutions* (Chicago: University of Chicago Press, 1962), is substituted for *episteme*. The correlation is suggested by Jean Piaget in his *Que sais-je?* volume on *Structuralism*, trans. C. Maschler (New York: Harper & Row, 1970), p. 132. Kuhn speaks of a paradigm as that model of scientific thought under which ordinary scientists work and out of which the extraordinary scientist must break. Although both Foucault and Kuhn are speaking of epistemological time slices within history, Piaget himself directs his genetic epistemology at stages in child development. That Piaget's work deals with the individual, with personal levels of thought, approximates more closely in this particular respect what I am proposing concerning Sartre's development. Kierkegaard's notion of "stages in life's way" is perhaps also worthy of mention. What I am suggesting by my use of the terms *episteme* and *paradigm* is that in Sartre's work there are different stages of thought in which the relationship between language and the self forms different (but comparable) structures.

I.

The first *episteme*, that of the self without words (*sans paroles*), is most clearly formulated in *The Transcendence of the Ego* (1936) and *Being and Nothingness* (1942), though the point can also be made by an examination of *Nausea* (1938) and some of the plays such as *The Flies* (1943) and *No Exit* (1944). To be *sans paroles* is to affirm the possibility of speaking about the self without the self speaking or being named. In his critique of Husserl's transcendental ego,[2] Sartre proposes a revision in the status of the ego. This revision stems from a difference of opinion as to the nature of consciousness. Husserlian phenomenology asserted that along with the noetic (meaning-giving act) and noematic (meaning-given) elements of consciousness, there is also a transcendental ego that stands behind all acts of consciousness and which serves as the source of intentionality. This transcendental standpoint operates as the subject-pole for the directedness of consciousness. Husserl distinguishes between the transcendental ego and the psychophysical, or empirical, ego, in that the latter is refined (bracketed) methodologically in order to facilitate phenomenological investigation — leaving the transcendental ego inside consciousness.[3] Within the phenomenological field,[4] only the conscious life remains. Though Husserl speaks of consciousness as a whole in terms of "subjectivity," the ego-pole is most appropriately called the self, or even the true self. The psychophysical ego corresponds to the self prior to the phenomenological reduction.

Husserl's establishment of the pure self does not depend upon the individual's recognition or experience of language. Of course, the statement of method is linguistic, but the status of consciousness is not. Similarly, Sartre's critique of the transcendental ego is not founded on linguistic conditions. Sartre claims that the ego cannot rest within the transcendental field. It must be outside consciousness, that is, temporally, it must be the ego that I just reflected upon. Whenever the ego is taken as an object of reflection, it cannot, according to Sartre, be an ego within consciousness. The ego cannot be caught red-handed in the act of reflecting upon itself.[5] It is always experienced cognitively as the self whose act is complete and which is no longer

2. Jean-Paul Sartre, *The Transcendence of the Ego*, trans. R. Kirkpatrick and F. Williams (New York: Noonday, 1957). Original French: *La Transcendance de l'Ego* (Paris: Vrin, 1965).

3. For a more fully developed discussion of Husserl's notion of the self, see my "The Self in Husserl's *Crisis,*" *Journal of the British Society for Phenomenology* 7, no. 1 (January 1976): 24–32.

4. The phenomenological field is referred to as the "transcendental field" by Sartre and is to be distinguished from what Merleau-Ponty calls the "phenomenal field" in *Phenomenology of Perception*, trans. C. Smith (London: Routledge and Kegan Paul, 1962). Merleau-Ponty's conception also includes bodily experience in addition to the Husserlian and Sartrian non-reified consciousness.

5. The expression "catching the ego red-handed" was suggested by Professor Algis Mickunas in "The Concept of Transparency in Husserl," given during the Husserl Circle meetings, April 4–5, 1975, at the State University of New York at Stony Brook.

in consciousness, or as the self that is not yet, but that is projected to be. Whatever self is reflected upon *(réfléchi)* must be an object of an intentional act. All intentional acts have objects (all consciousness is consciousness of something). When the self is reflected upon, it appears as outside consciousness, since it is an object of consciousness. Consciousness therefore must be unreflected *(irréfléchi)*. Meaning can arise only when consciousness is reflective. If consciousness itself is unreflected, then it must not have meaning until it is reflected. When it is reflected, the meaning is a meaning of a past self, a self that is not the self of consciousness. Since consciousness has no meaning when it is unreflected, it cannot have a content. This rejection of the Cartesian *cogito* as nonsubstantial is the basis for Sartre's conclusion that consciousness is empty.

Can we claim, however, that this empty consciousness is the true self? Clearly the projected or past (reflected) self is not the true self—even though, in Sartre's formulation, it is identical with a transcendent ego. If we do not require that the true self be the ego, and there is no reason—except for Cartesian convention—that we should, then the unreflected consciousness would be the most appropriate candidate. Precedent exists for a nonunitary conception of the ego as an alternative to the Cartesian-Husserlian view. One could cite the Freudian self as a tripartite id-ego-superego structure, the Humean self as a bundle of disparate impressions, and the Aristotelian self as a functional unity of body and soul, where each is not associated with a unitary ego. The Sartrian version is somewhat curious, by contrast, for Sartre proposes that the self is a non-self, but an active, individual non-self (unlike the Platonic world-soul or Chinese Tao). Since this self is not an ego and is without content, without a meaning to define it, there is surely no name that characterizes a particular self, no word that will serve as the predicate noun or adjective indicating who the self is. Thus, Sartre does not introduce words for the self. It has no experiential meaning; likewise, no linguistic meaning. The true self (that is, unreflected consciousness) of the first *episteme* is empty and without words. The reality of the self (Corbin's translation of Heidegger's *Dasein* was *la réalité humaine*, which Sartre employs regularly) is distinct from the words necessary to describe it. The self does not associate its experience with the names applied to it.

Non-thetic (or non-positional) consciousness is an epistemological structure. The self's attempts to posit its own ontological status as a participant in and even the center of consciousness is doomed to failure. In seeking to know who the self is, the self exhibits its own incapability: it cannot take itself as the theme of its own experience and still hope to be the self of that experience. The self-knowing act is a self-negating act. As I attempt to know who I am, I find that I am not that which I propose to know. The thetic (noetic) act[6] should give as the meaning of its object the self that is its sub-

---

6. All thetic acts are noetic; but, as Sartre shows, not all noetic acts are thetic.

ject. But the bankrupt character of the traditional subject-object distinction is brought into focus here. The cognitive act that seeks to know its own subjectivity, and which must take that subjectivity as an objectivity, cannot succeed in restoring the subjectivity to a pure state. The subjectivity qua self must always remain other, because it has treated itself as other (that is, as what it is not). In being taken as other than what it is, the self is not the thesis of its own conscious act, for the self is not that other. The self becomes that other only when it is no longer itself. The self loses its identity and becomes an otherness when it cannot grasp itself in its own self-conscious act. Self-consciousness—consciousness (of) self—is non-thetic self-consciousness in that the self's awareness of itself is the denial of making itself other than what it is. When it becomes other, it is no longer the self. When the self refuses to be other—a self outside consciousness—it must be non-thetic.

Self-consciousness is non-self-referential. Even if language were introduced—at least a conception of language as referential (in the Fregean sense)—the self would not be characterized. Since in this sense linguistic meaning (*Sinn*) refers to some referent (*Bedeutung*), the difficulty in the case of the self is that there is a meaning (*Sinn*) but no referent (*Bedeutung*) that corresponds to the *Sinn* in question. But the self is not Pegasus, nor a unicorn. The self exists. Pegasus and unicorns do not exist, though some philosophers, such as Meinong and Russell, have claimed that they subsist. For Sartre, the self *is*, but not as referent of a cognitive or a linguistic act. That the self exists was made quite evident in *Nausea*. Roquentin experiences that which lies behind the veneer of things, that which underlies their essences. But he experiences even more strongly the existence that underlies any values or determinations that he might select for himself. To write a history of the Marquis de Rollebon might be a way of suggesting that this self is a historian, that this self can be referred to as a historian. Roquentin has a title, an essence, a name. The meaning of that essence will be his *self*— the label that he will be able to call his own. This nominalist identification is reassuring to him. The title will comfort him. Yet when he considers whether the appellation *historian* will in fact (-icity) be himself, he experiences nausea. He becomes aware that his self will not be identifiable with the referent *historian*. Nausea, then, is the experienced awareness that the self exists, but that it is not any particular essence. This experienced awareness of being other than essence, other than labels, is frightening to Roquentin. He is confronted with his own existence—the existence of his self, a self that has meaning but no referent. Whenever it is a referent such as *historian*, the label will be different from the self as a meaning (the meaning of the self). The nausea is what one undergoes when confronted with this unusual situation. Undergoing the nausea, as in Nietzsche's *Thus Spoke Zarathustra*, is going under (*untergehen*) in order to overcome (*übergehen*) one's self. For Dostoevski's underground note writer, going underground and being spiteful are the analogues of experiencing nausea. In Sartre's terminology, to be nauseated is to be conscious of one's self and its existence — without linguistic reference.

What is this self that cannot be known thetically or referred to linguistically? Since it exists, its ontological mode must be its manner of being understood. *Being and Nothingness*, which occurs within this same *episteme*, is subtitled "An Essay in Phenomenological Ontology." One of the tasks here is to bring out the being of the self in order to consider it as a phenomenon. What, then, is the meaning qua appearance of the self? There should be "selfness," though there may not be a self that is a reflected object or a referred name. This "selfness," Sartre proposes, is nonsubstantial. It is not an object, in-itself, a thing. A nonreified meaning, however, is not unusual. All phenomenological meanings (*eidoi, noemata*) are not, as such, things. Many such meanings are meanings *of* things, but this is not to suggest that they themselves *are* things. There are also meanings of poems, images, dreams, sounds, and so on. In each of these cases, that of which there is consciousness is other than the consciousness itself. We have already seen that whenever the self is other than the consciousness itself, it is not the same self that has been under investigation. If, however, the self is the same self that is conscious, it must occupy a rather unusual status. What then is the meaning of the self, the "content" of consciousness — the selfness — when the self is the very consciousness itself?

When Sartre claims that this true self is entirely for-itself (*pour-soi*), he means that it cannot be an object for itself and still be itself. So he calls the true self, this being for-itself, *nothingness*. As *nothingness* (*le néant*), the self is a meaning with no referent, an existence with no essence, a consciousness with no object that is other.

This pure unreflected subjectivity is active, always becoming (Kierkegaard's contribution). The flux of the self is its temporality. The future self (who I shall be) and the past self (who I was) are outside consciousness. Such selves cannot be identical with the self that I am. Each must necessarily be in-itself, an object for reflective consciousness, before or after my true self. When Roquentin thinks of his future visit with Anny or when he remembers his past occasions with her, he distinguishes the present self from those other selves. The self who he is can be described temporally as present. Therefore, what is present is the true self, the unreflected consciousness, the for-itself, and existence. Though present, a reflective act attempting to identify its nature will reveal only a "just-having-been," a self that is no longer the present self. Similarly, when a specific future self is projected, this self that is about to be will also distinguish itself from the present. This present is not quite a specious present, but it does clearly distinguish itself from other moments of the temporal flow. It acquires special renown in that the present is the moment of the true self. If the self is present, absence will clarify the character of that presence. Presence differentiates itself from what it is not, whether it be presence of the self or the presence of some object: a chestnut-tree root, Peter in the café, or Orestes for Electra. When the other (thing or person) is absent, then the critical question is whether that absence is present or whether it is simply absent. When Electra in *The Flies* laments the absence of Orestes, his absence prohibits her from effecting revenge and retribution upon her mother, Clytemnestra, and her lover, Aegisthus. Orestes' absence is therefore quite present to Electra. She experiences the nonpresence of her brother. Again, this experience is not formulated as such in terms of words—even when he does appear, she refuses to call him Orestes until she is convinced that he is the brother who will assist her in returning justice to Argos. Even when he tells Electra his name, she does not take the name as identical with the reality. The reality of Orestes is most important to her—his name is only incidental and secondary. Thus, she will attribute the name to him only when she is convinced of the reality of his presence. This de-emphasis on the role of language in the formulation of the self is echoed in Merleau-Ponty's comment that the two lovers in the *Charterhouse of Parma* know the presence of love even before it is named.[7] The name simply confirms the knowledge—and renders it transcendent. In *The Flies*, the present absence of Orestes does not depend upon Orestes' naming himself in order for him to become a present presence. The direct experience is what counts. Electra must experience him as Orestes. The word itself will not suffice.

Sartre outlines a similar movement when he describes the experience of one's self as absent. Here, however, it is not the other who appears as absent, but rather one's very own self. The self appears as an "absent-presence":

> Selfness represents a degree of nihilation carried further than the pure presence to itself of the pre-reflective cogito—in the sense that the possible which I am is not pure presence to the for-itself as reflection to reflecting, but that it is *absent-presence*.[8]

Selfness as an absent-presence is the full appearance of a meaning within consciousness, but a meaning without a referent—hence, a consciousness whose content is the presence of an absence. Consciousness cannot provide an elaboration of selfness as pure presence. The self as absent-presence in-

---

7. Merleau-Ponty writes: "Consider the example in Stendhal's *The Charterhouse of Parma* when the Count fears the first word of love that will confirm the young couple's feelings, which as yet have not been verbally expressed." See Merleau-Ponty, *Consciousness and the Acquisition of Language*, trans. Hugh J. Silverman (Evanston: Northwestern University Press, 1973), pp. 4–5.

8. Jean-Paul Sartre, *Being and Nothingness*, trans. Hazel E. Barnes (New York: Philosophical Library, 1956), p. 103; hereafter incorporated into the main text as BN. Original French edition: *L'Être et le néant* (Paris: Gallimard, 1943), p. 148; hereafter cited with an "Fr.," abbreviation, as in the case of each original French edition.

dicates the emptiness of consciousness in the sense that the self's possibilities are evident though no specific definition can be made available. Once the multiplicity of possibilities has been determined as one particular formulation of the self, the self becomes pure presence. Therefore, the fundamental characteristic of selfness is its possibilities. Sartre's *No Exit* demonstrates quite vividly the absent-presence of selfness in that the three characters occupy an afterworld in which the world is still present to them. They have an openness onto what other people are still saying about them. Language identifies them, but the speakers are not aware that what they say is available to the awareness of those (dead) who are under discussion (i.e., referred to). This awareness is exaggerated in that it is located in the afterlife, and hence inaccessible to the speakers on earth. Nevertheless, the absent-presence is emphasized by the dissociation between the statements about them and the consciousness that perceives their articulation. Garcin, for example, now in this hell, understands how his possibilities are limited. He no longer has the full freedom of possibilties available to the living self. Naturally, in a play, the self speaks. But Sartre does not point out that this is a speaking self. Rather, we are aware that the self's possibilities have been limited only by the situation in which the three characters find themselves. Since they cannot manifest an openness onto the future as we who are alive can, they must continue eternally in their absent-presence. When a full, living human being is in question, the totality of possibilities, which the self is qua "circuit of selfness," "is what the for-itself lacks in order to be itself." (BN, p. 102; Fr., p. 147) By passing through that which is absent, that which is lacking, the specific lack of being becomes evident. The circuit of selfness delineates the structure of the self without requiring that there be something, a content, or an in-itself, within consciousness. The circuit of selfness is the delineation of pure phenomenological meaning.

II.

In 1947-48, Sartre is on the threshold of a new positivity. A new conceptual scheme begins to arise. Sartre writes *What Is Literature?* (1947) and then produces *Dirty Hands* (1948). His epistemological break with an alinguistic ontologization of cognitive experience points to a new view of the self. *What Is Literature?* provides the groundwork in that the concept of the prose writer, as one who ought to be committed to the freedom of other people, becomes the paradigm of the self expressing itself through language. Freedom, which was a well-developed notion in *Being and Nothingness*, serves as the principal feature of the self's contact with language in *What Is Literature?* In the earlier view, freedom was described as the specific character of consciousness in its field of possibilities. The very nihilating quality of consciousness-as-self is its freedom. By negating the objectlike status of the in-itself, consciousness as for-itself makes its projects as free acts in a situation of possibility. In this work on the nature, function, and purpose of literature, Sartre proposes that freedom is intimately bound up with the activity of the writer in relation to his reader:

> The author writes in order to address himself to the freedom of readers, and he requires it in order to make his work exist. But he does not stop there; he also requires that they return this confidence which he has given them, that they recognize his creative freedom, and that they in turn solicit it by a symmetrical and inverse appeal. Here there appears the other dialectical paradox of reading; the more we experience our freedom, the more we recognize that of the other; the more he demands of us, the more we demand of him.[9]

The notion of the self that is founded in its freedom is hereby placed in a linguistic context. The writer must necessarily write in order to be a writer, and the reader must necessarily read in order to be a reader. In both cases, writing and words serve as the medium for the expression of freedom. The dialectic between reader and writer places these particular species of self in direct relationship with words. The free self addresses or is addressed through writing. Thus, the writing functions as a means by which one self communicates with the freedom of another. What does not occur, however, is an identification of the self with the language of writing. Rather, we live within language — as Heidegger claimed, "Language is the house of Being." Language is

> our shell and our antennae; it protects us against others and informs us about them; it is a prolongation of the senses, a third eye which is going to look into our neighbor's heart. We are within language as within our body. We feel it spontaneously while going beyond it toward other ends, as we feel our hands and our feet; we perceive it when it is the other who is using it, as we perceive the limbs of others. There is the word which is lived and the word which is met. But in both cases, it is in the course of an undertaking, either of me acting on others or the other upon me. The word is a certain particular moment of action and has no meaning outside of it. (WL, pp. 14–15; Fr., p. 71)

That words are bound up with action and that the self qua conscious being *is* only in its action indicates the central function of words in the ontology of the self. Sartre even suggests that for the "engaged" writer "words are action." (WL, p. 17; Fr., p. 73) If the self *is* through its action, and words are action, then, in this case of the prose writer, the self can reveal its being through words. Not everyone, however, employs words as a mode of action. The committed writer and his readers are not the only possibilities.

---

9. Jean-Paul Sartre, *What Is Literature?*, trans. B. Frechtman (New York: Harper & Row, Colophon Edition, 1965), p. 45; hereafter incorporated as WL. Original French: "*Qu'est-ce que la littérature?*" in *Situations, II* (Paris: Gallimard, 1948), p. 101.

Picasso's painting of the destruction at Guernica, Merleau-Ponty's conception of gesture, and Camus's rebel are all nonverbal forms of action. In this
respect, Sartre still finds validity in the priority of action over words. He
would agree with Goethe's revision of the Gospel according to John, which
reads: "in the beginning was the Act" (rather than the Word). Not all individuals define themselves in terms of words.

The second *episteme* enters into a living relationship between self and
words, but only for selected selves, only for those involved in a committed
enterprise. Presumably we are all "within language as within our body."
However, only action makes the words of that language significant. Hugo,
in *Dirty Hands*, knows that he talks excessively. He is called a "chatterbox."
Olga tells him that he talks too much, that he talks to make sure he is alive.
The words that he speaks are what confirm his life. Words even seem to define his life — he recounts in acts one through six the events leading up to his
deed. But the deed achieves signification only as Hugo recounts it. Although, as Goethe says, "*Im Anfang war die Tat*," here the deed must be
talked about in order for its meaning to be assessed: "Telling it, that's not
hard; I know it by heart; I recited it to myself every day in prison. But what
it means, that's something else again."[10] Action signifies only as it is given in
words. Language (here: speech) is the mode by which action achieves phenomenological meaning (*Sinn*).

When Hugo killed Hoederer, was it an assassination or a crime of passion? Is Hugo salvageable or not? The resolution of the latter question may
also depend upon history, as in Bukharin's case.[11] He is salvageable if his act
was a crime of passion, if his motive was not political. Since Hoederer has
been reinstated politically and his work must be carried on, his assassin cannot be salvaged (revived, brought out of the junk heap). But if the crime
were committed out of jealousy, then Hugo did not kill Hoederer for politi-
al reasons. In this case, the meaning of the act as recounted to Olga is different. Like Dostoevsky's murderer Raskolnikov, whose name Hugo takes
before the crime, he can be saved. Olga is his Sonya. The life after prison
can be his resurrection. But the difference here is that the meaning of his
deed depends upon what he says to Olga. The meaning of the act depends
upon his words.

Hugo sees that the act establishes his identity and fulfills his reality, but
his identity and reality attain meaning only through words. He must define
himself through his deed. He is called a traitor by those who put him up to
it, and an assassin by Hoederer and Jessica (his wife). But he is also accused
of play-acting as both traitor and assassin. Who is he? What is the meaning

---

10. Jean-Paul Sartre, *Dirty Hands*, trans. Lionel Abel in *No Exit and Three Other Plays*
(New York: Knopf, Vintage Books, 1949), p. 142. Original French: *Les Mains sales* (Paris:
Gallimard, 1948), p. 33.
11. See Maurice Merleau-Ponty, *Humanism and Terror*, trans. J. O'Neill (Boston: Beacon Press, 1969).

of the deed when he does kill Hoederer? Was he in fact an assassin or a traitor? He has acted, but he has not chosen. Only his words two years later will define his deed and hence his being. The words will be his choice. The word that he finally chooses, "unsalvageable," is a commitment to self-destruction. Like Hoederer he will be killed and history as it is written will determine the significance of his life. His own word, "unsalvageable," the last word of the play, will finally be identified with his reality. Hugo will not be open to the charge of play-acting.

In this second *episteme*, tentative corrections are offered between verbal expression and the existing self. Hugo is a case in point. He tries out defining himself as a traitor, then experiments with assassinhood. He acts out of equivocal motives and is deemed a jealous husband by his victim and by society. Only when he calls himself "unsalvageable" does he accept a name for himself. Nevertheless, the clear dichotomy between language and reality is maintained.

In *Saint Genet*, Sartre's view is that instead of the dichotomous relationship between words and reality that is expressed in *Dirty Hands*, words are here identified with reality, play-acting and overt action are associated with appearance. This inversion of the situation in *Dirty Hands* is due to Genet's peculiar circumstances. The difference, however, expresses the same position (by negation). Just as Hugo ends with an identification of his self with a name—his condemnation—Genet begins his life with a similar identification. In both cases, the dialectic between the self and words is in operation.

Genet is orphaned. He knows nothing of his mother or father. At the age of seven, he is taken to the home of Morvan peasants, who give him everything he has. Genet owns nothing; everything is a gift. Hence, when he is caught taking a pair of scissors from the utensil drawer, it is viewed as theft. However, we are told that Genet condemns theft, since it is immoral to steal. Even so, Genet has been stealing all along without realizing it, since he does not distinguish between taking and partaking of what has been made available to him. His verbal condemnation of stealing and his action of stealing remain separate until Genet is "caught in the act."

His hand reaches into the utensil drawer and the look of the other (his foster parents) is translated into the words "You are a thief!" Instead of distinguishing the words from himself, Genet takes them as a specification of who he is. He assumes that because he has been called a thief, he must *be* a thief. A spiritual death occurs. His multifaceted existence has now been given a unitary meaning: "Thief." He has been objectified and made other by his foster parents. His task remains one of determining what to do with his new-found identity (his received self).

Genet decides to be what crime made of him. He takes on the label and begins to activate the evil will that has been attributed to him. Genet is Evil, because decent folk, like his foster parents, are Good. Good folk would not steal, hence Genet is Evil because he is a thief. If Genet is Evil, an in-itself, his for-itself must express itself through a will—in Genet's case, an Evil will. He has been named an outcast by society. Now he must act as other, as alien to everyone in society, as unacceptable to the community of selves.

When introducing *The Thief's Journal,* which Genet wrote in 1949, Sartre spoke of Genet as Narcissus: "Not all who would be are Narcissus. Many who lean over the water see only a vague human figure. Genet sees himself everywhere. . . ."[12] Genet is always someone other than himself for himself. Once he has identified himself with words, he cannot distinguish himself from them. His otherness has been initiated by the verbal self-definition. From then on, his selfhood will always be otherness. Hence, when Genet, like the mythical Narcissus, looks into the water, what appears is not an image of his identity—but rather his very identity. He is the thief, the beggar, the homosexual, the poet, the saint, the double, and so on. Whenever the self seeks to know itself, a word appears and the self is identified with it. "The reflective consciousness must fall back into the immediate consciousness and fade out there. For the reflective consciousness was a flashlight that searched the immediate consciousness with the aim of discovering the Other there. But it failed in its task and could only produce a paltry Ego."[13] Like the attempts of a reflective consciousness to reveal the unreflected in *The Transcendence of the Ego,* the reflective consciousness here is a flashlight that cannot accomplish its task. No light is shown on the self as immediate consciousness. What appears is the "paltry Ego" that bears a name, which *is* the name: *Thief.* He finds the other, it is himself.

Rimbaud wrote: *"Je est un autre"* — I is another. In speaking of Genet, he might have added: and the other is a word. What Sartre says, however, is: I is another and the other is God. But what does it mean to be God here? By being treated as other, Genet can choose to do what he will with the identity that he has been given. Because he is other, he is alienated from himself. Just as Feuerbach claims that man in his self-alienation created God (which was Feuerbach's response to Hegel's thesis that God in his self-alienation created man), Sartre affirms that Genet in his self-alienation is other, is God. Because he is other, Genet is free to exercise his will in whatever fashion he may wish. In this sense he becomes pure freedom, pure will—pure evil will. Because he is pure freedom, he can be God. Since he is alienated from himself, however, he cannot be God, for God has nothing alien within him. Once otherness enters into God, it becomes demonic (according to

---

12. Jean-Paul Sartre, foreword to Jean Genet, *The Thief's Journal,* trans. B. Frechtman (New York: Grove Press, 1964), p. 7. Note that the "foreword" is a word before other words; the other words in this case are those of Genet's autobiography.

13. Jean-Paul Sartre, *Saint Genet,* trans. B. Frechtman (New York: Braziller, 1963), p. 85; hereafter incorporated as SG. Original French: *Saint Genet: comédien et martyr* (Paris: Gallimard, 1952), p. 86.

Sartre). The otherness within Genet makes him a demon. He remains a demon because he has been called evil and because he continues to associate words with his own reality.

Normally, language is an instrument, a tool, a means to the end that is communication. Sometimes words attain a more independent status; they become miraculous, illustrating the power of language over the self. Sartre says that language is Genet's "most inward reality and the most rigorous expression of his exile." (SG, p. 276; Fr., p. 259) His reality has been defined by language. Also, language is the means by which Genet's alienation from decent folk occurred and the means by which Genet continues his exile. Society has taken care of *things*; Genet can do what he wishes with *words*. Genet is a being-toward-prison, to speak in Heideggerian terms, and no matter what he does, society has isolated him. When in prison, it does not matter whether he calls it a prison or a palace; as far as society is concerned, he has been taken care of. "What counts is the word's material presence, which symbolizes the signifying content that, for Genet, is none other than the being of the thing signified." (SG, p. 280; Fr., p. 261) Genet associates the thing signified with the meaning of the word that is symbolized. The association is not, however, a correlation. Rather, it is an identification in which there is no difference. The word takes on the ontological character of the thing.

When Genet enters the bookstore with his rigged briefcase, he asks the bookseller for a rare book. The bookseller makes the normal correlation between the book requested and the words "I would like to see the book." Genet, however, proposes his own words as the thing signified. What he means is: I would like you to leave the open store. His words are the absenting of the bookseller, just as normally a rose is the red flower on the thorny bush. When the bookseller leaves, Genet places the book that really interests him in his special briefcase. The other meaning of the words "I would like to see the book" has been realized.

Similarly, when a policeman stops him (after the theft of the book) and asks him what is in his briefcase, Genet answers, "Nothing." For Genet, the reality is the word *Nothing*, the reality is not what is in the briefcase. As Genet interprets the situation, his *answer* is the thing to which the policeman's question refers. Here language is a tool in that it will dissuade his interrogator from pursuing the investigation. For Genet, what is in fact in his briefcase is an appearance, whereas for the policeman the appearance (which can be deceptive) is Genet's word. If the man does not believe Genet's negation, then Genet's word has broken down like a lawn mower that no longer works. The thing (word) will have failed to operate.

This identification of words with things is an extension of Genet's identification of words with his subjectivity. Genet's gestures are intended to derealize things. "Speech is a gesture and the word is a thing." (SG, p. 392; Fr., p. 364) By speaking, Genet gives life to the self that has become a word.

Since words are things, Genet's self is a thing for himself. Yet when he speaks, he is able to go beyond his self-reification through the language and words that have been given to him. The relationship between words and speech is parallel to that between poetry and prose. This distinction, first expounded in *What Is Literature?*, is reiterated in Genet's case and again for Flaubert.

Genet first writes poetry "in order to be moved." Dante and Petrarch would write of Beatrice or Laura because they were moved by a *visio Dei* or a love for the woman, but Genet creates words that will stimulate his own emotion. The poetic words are written in order to activate the self: "I was twenty years old; a little girl whom I loved had died ten years before, and it was the anniversary of her death. I wrote the verses in order to be moved." (SG, p. 426; Fr., p. 396) This was Genet's first poem. By writing it he would hear himself as another. He reads his own words: they are himself but as an otherness. Because he is other for himself he can be moved emotionally by his own words, and only by writing them does the sense of loss become real.

The poetic act is a gesture. Hence it is a form of speech. The self speaks by creating words. As the words are created, the self is defined, spoken, but only in an isolated form. The poem is not an end-in-itself, rather it is a means to martyrdom. Genet martyrs himself by making the poem other. Since, however, he is already other when he writes, he must perform a double negation in order to martyr himself, that is, to place himself in a position where he has been wronged by others. When he writes "The Condemned Man," he achieves the goal. He has been called a thief by others because he possessed nothing. Now he collects the very words of his poem from other poets: Cocteau, Valéry, Mallarmé, Hugo, Baudelaire, everyone. His poem is a patchwork of phrases written by others. No one would have wanted him to be in a situation where he must steal. Hence he is pitiable. He has been wrongly persecuted and he wants to return this to society—to martyr himself before good people. Genet's poetry is not written so that we will see, since his poetry itself is theft (plagiarism). His poetry is an expression of his own experience in order to observe himself. He is the condemned man, like Villon in "The Ballad of the Hanged Man," who reflects upon his own fate. Poetry, as Sartre pointed out in *What Is Literature?*, is on the side of things, not signs. Poetry is a structure of the external world. When Genet sees himself as the condemned man, the poem serves as a mirror for his own self. In just the same way that the mirror is material, and reflects the image of the visual self, Genet's poetry is a means of placing his life before him. Sartre calls this "poetry-fatality," which has an end. It is determined and inevitable—a clear reflection of the self for itself.

In contrast to poetry-fatality, Sartre refers to "deliberate poetry." Deliberate poetry is founded on choice: choice of words, audience, style, and so forth. Deliberate poetry is written for a purpose. Thus Genet "puts fatality into his poems and his deliberate art into prose." (SG, p. 444; Fr., p. 412)

The deliberate in prose is the presence of choice and freedom in Genet's work. Bound to himself when he writes poetry, in prose he is able to achieve his full martyrdom. He will not only be something alien for himself as he is in his poetry, but he will also be alien to other people who read his prose. Through words, he will reach beyond his personal experience to that of other people.

Writing prose is a departure from the passiveness of poetry. As a creator, Genet writes prose. Prose is factual and participates in a world of facts. But it is also "overdetermined." A multiplicity of meanings fills the prose moment. A metaphorical language appeals to the other and speaks to others with its multi-directionality. Here the artist's consciousness is not simply self-indulgent, but has a purpose, a direction, and an audience. Overdetermined prose is the medium for Genet's full self-expression.

If Genet did not write, he would be just one more thief, one more homosexual, one more person who lives in his own self-enclosed world. Yet he does write. Since *he* is in his poetry, his poetry is Evil. But when he writes prose, the poetry tampers with it — gets in the way — Evil taints the prose, which is Good. Poetry gives the prose false pretenses. The prose is a victim of the poetic activity. What is normally Good (prose) is placed on an Evil base (poetry).

Through the influence of poetry as Evil, Genet in his prose enters the homes of the Good people of society. The work of art is a substitute for crime. The work of art is a type of Apollonian dream that people experience while they are awake, as opposed to the dream of crimes occurring in their homes while they are asleep.

By writing, Genet reaches beyond the walls that have isolated him from society as a whole. Police, magistrates, and prison guards all insulate him from decent people. Society has delegated these individuals to keep selves such as Genet's away from the daily activities of society. When Genet writes, the social character of words allows them to universalize their significations. Words penetrate prison walls and social castes. When uttered, a word is as a subject speaking; but when heard, it takes the form of an object. When Genet writes, he becomes an object for himself in his poetry; and when it is deliberate qua prose, he martyrs himself for others. He presents himself as victim to them. But his victimization is also his betrayal. When he frightens other people, then he achieves the glory he seeks. His victory is verbal in that he restores negativity to his readers. They react against him and hence burn him at the stake. But this is what he wants.

Genet objectifies himself in the language of his autobiographical novels as we do ourselves in our dreams. He makes himself into many different characters, for example, Divine, who is living with Darling. The only way for him to believe in the real existence of Darling is to objectify himself as Divine (the queen). In that way, Genet can be with Darling and believe in him. Genet must see himself in the female role in order to create the existence of Darling. Genet is Divine, whom he has created in words. As an objectification of Genet, Divine is also an object for decent people.

Given an ego, a self, Genet wants to return it to decent people and install it within their daily experience—he wants to throw it back into their laps. Hence his use of *I* in the fictional work. The reader encounters the *I* in the novel and confuses it with his own. In referring to a subjectivity, the *I* is referred to one's own. But that *I* is of course the *I* of a thief and homosexual. In identifying his self with that of the novel, the reader is made uneasy. He is inclined to ask, "What else did I do?" (SG, p. 499; Fr., p. 461) "Genet holds the mirror up to us: we must look at it and see ourselves." (SG, p. 599; Fr., p. 550) His self penetrates into our own through the language of autobiographical fictional prose. We are forced to react because of the uneasy identification. Genet becomes a victim to us and we give him the sainthood that is his victory over us. Through words, Genet brings his self before those who read him. Because he *is* the words he creates, this particular self presents itself to other humans for their unwitting participation. Thus the universalization of the self occurs through the words that the self creates in order to communicate.

III.

The third paradigm is once again a new stage of thought in the development of Sartre's philosophy. No longer is the self simply identified with words—particularly in prose writing—but now the self is articulated directly in linguistic terms. What was an aberration in Genet becomes the *modus vivendi* for the Sartrian man of the 1960s. With the appearance of *Search for a Method* (1957) as an introduction to the *Critique of Dialectical Reason* (1960) and *Words* (1965), Sartre puts forth this new position quite explicitly. A full reformulation of the relationship between the self and language is here achieved.

Only suggested in *Saint Genet*, the position that language is a social phenomenon, that words universalize, is made clear in *Search for a Method*. In emphasizing the role of social structures, Sartre points out that we are not only knowers, but we also appear as known.[14] As known, we are manifestations of the interests of a class engaged in a collective project. Classconsciousness is

> not the simple lived contradiction which objectively characterizes the class considered; it is that contradiction already surpassed by *praxis* and thereby preserved and denied all at once. But it is precisely this revealing negativity,

---

14. Jean-Paul Sartre, *Search for a Method*, trans. H. Barnes (New York: Knopf, Vintage Books, 1963), p. 9; hereafter incorporated as SM. Original French: *Questions de méthode* in *Critique de la raison dialectique* (Paris: Gallimard, 1960), p. 18.

this distance within immediate proximity, which simultaneously constitutes what existentialism calls "consciousness *of* the object" and "nonthetic self-consciousness." (SM, p. 33n; Fr., 31n)

Going beyond the lived contradiction of a given class is the nature of this class consciousness. Praxis is the means by which a class goes beyond its contradictions in order to effect appropriate changes. Thus, praxis is the analogue of the non-thetic self-consciousness that was characteristic of the first *episteme*. But praxis is a social phenomenon — it is what *we* do. My praxis is paired with the praxis of others through reciprocity. We are known through the expression of our common praxis and language is one of the most central forms in which this social self is exhibited.

Sartre explains his position, particularly in footnotes to *Search for a Method*, in the light of semiological formulations. Although de Saussure thought that linguistics was merely a part of the general science of signs, Roland Barthes suggests that, on the contrary, semiology is a part of linguistics.[15] Following Barthes, to speak of the self in semiological terms is to offer a linguistic consideration. Sartre bases his own stance on the shoulders of Hegel and Kierkegaard:

> —for Hegel, the Signifying (*le Signifiant*) (at any moment of history) is the movement of Mind (which will be constituted as the signifying-signified and the signified-signifying; that is, as absolute-subject), the Signified (*le Signifié*) is the living man and his objectification. For Kierkegaard, man is the signifying; he himself produces the significations, and no signification points to him from outside (Abraham does not know whether he is Abraham); man is never the signified (not even by God). (SM, pp. 9-10n; Fr., p. 18n)

That the French *signifiant* can be translated both as "signifying" and as "signifier" must permeate an understanding of Sartre's claim. For Hegel, absolute mind (*Geist*) in its movement is the signifier — that which motivates signification through signifying activity. When *Geist* achieves its fulfillment, it is the signifier-signified and signified-signifier. Sartre refers to this achievement as the absolute subject, which would be analogous to his own being-in-itself-for-itself.

The difference in translation is also worthy of consideration with respect to Kierkegaard. Man is the signifier, in this case. As an individual, he does the signifying and produces the significations. He is never the signified, because he is never an object for himself or for anyone else. But Sartre does not say "object" here. He says "signified," suggesting that a man is never linguistically specified (Genet would be an exception). Man is always linguistically specifying — he specifies what is by giving it names and labels. For

---

15. Roland Barthes, *Elements of Semiology*, trans. A. Lavers and C. Smith (Boston: Beacon Press, 1967), pp. 9-11.

Kierkegaard, the individual never specifies himself, although Sartre characterizes his nature as a signifier or as signifying.

This linguistic formulation of the self in terms of the Hegelian and Kier-
kegaardian views is surpassed in the Sartrian position. Sartre proposes that
the Hegel-Kierkegaard conflict is resolved in that man is neither signified
nor signifying (signifier). Man is *at once* both signified-signifying (signified-
signifier) and signifying-signified (signifier-signified). Sartre states that this
is like the Hegelian absolute subject but in a different sense. (SM, pp. 165-
166n; Fr., p. 103n) In his UNESCO lecture on Kierkegaard (1964),[16] Sartre
characterized this same notion of man as "the singular universal" and as
"the subject-object paradox." But in *Search for a Method*, the semiological
terminology helps to clarify man's situatedness in language. Sartre's move
here is to give the self the status of man, as signified-signifier and signifier-
signified.[17] The self is situated squarely inside language and inside culture.

When the self is inside language, one is inside "a special field of instruments." Language is an "objectification of a class, the reflection of conflicts, latent or declared, and the particular manifestation of alienation."
(SM, p. 113; Fr., p. 75) To be inside language is to be part of the social
structures that characterize one's class and that represent conflicts that
arise out of the presence of need in a field of scarcity. Thus, the conditions
of class consciousness through the activity of praxis in the face of practico-
inert elements are worked out within language.

For this very reason, Sartre can and must, in this third *episteme*, or paradigm, discuss the self in terms of language. Where, in the first stage, the self
could be discussed without reference to language and, in the second, language becomes important only for the committed writer or for one such as
Genet who identifies the self with words, at this third *episteme* the self must
appear within the very words that one uses. Since, in the Marxist formulation, there are only men and real relations among men, these relations also
involve one's particular linguistic structures. Sartre claims that man defines
himself by his project. But in *Search for a Method*, it is a collective project
rather than the individual fundamental project of *Being and Nothingness*.
As the self goes beyond its material conditions, it establishes significations
within its social context.

Significations come from man and from his project, but they are inscribed everywhere in things and in the order of things. Everything at every instant is al-

---

16. Jean-Paul Sartre, "Kierkegaard: The Singular Universal" in *Between Existentialism
and Marxism*, trans. John Mathews (New York: Pantheon, 1974), pp. 141-169. Original
French: "L'Universel singulier" in *Situations, IX* (Paris: Gallimard, 1972), pp. 152-190.

17. For the distinction between *self* and *man*, see Hugh J. Silverman, "Man and the Self as
Identity of Difference," *Philosophy Today* 19, no. 2. (Summer 1975): 131-36. Also see Hugh
J. Silverman, "Sartre and the Structuralists," *International Philosophical Quarterly* 18, no. 3
(September 1978): 341-358, for a study of Sartre's formulation of the Saussurian signifier/
signified relation.

ways signifying and significations reveal to us men and relations among men across the structures of our society. But these significations appear to us only insofar as we ourselves are signifying. (SM, p. 156; Fr., p. 98)

Through signification we participate in the collective activity of our situation. The self signifies through its signification, through its language, from which it cannot extract itself. At most, the self can continue to signify. The self totalizes, as Sartre points out in the *Critique of Dialectical Reason*, through a "dialectical circularity." This dialectical circularity is the first paradigm "circuit of selfness" placed in a social and linguistic context. By means of *need*, the self totalizes itself with other selves through a common praxis. Man mediates things to the same extent that things mediate man. Praxis confronts the practico-inert as much as the practico-inert, the material elements of social life, presents itself to man. The self is caught up in the dialectic and can totalize itself only in a series or group and by its act of signifying—by creating significations.

The self signifies the signified by signifying significations. Although actions signify, so too do words. *The Condemned of Altona* (1960) illustrates this point in that Franz, who has been hiding in his room for thirteen years since the Second World War, still believes that Germany is in ruins. He wants this to be true to such an extent that he says, "I'm making progress. One day the words will come by themselves, and I shall say what I want to."[18] If Franz is successful, his words will not even require a self to make them signify. They will take on the signifying by themselves. In this sense, history will follow its progressive inevitable path, as Marxists claim, and signification will be self-supporting: the self will be a signifier only when there are signifieds to actualize it.

The progressive-regressive method, however, also prescribes that one go back to the family and class conditions that make certain significations inevitable. Franz's incestuous relations with Leni close him off from events. He is unable to express his common praxis with others. Hence he can conceive of the possibility of his words signifying by themselves. As his sister-in-law says, "words don't have the same meaning up there." (CA, p. 102; Fr., p. 220). A regressive consideration will show that this is not possible: words cannot signify by themselves. Franz must leave his room and face the practico-inert or die. He selects the latter. His voice and the words of the tape recorder can only announce that he has been, that he must be responsible for and answer for what does occur among men. Like the view of Sartre's first *episteme*—for example, in *Existentialism Is a Humanism* (1946)—in choosing one chooses for all mankind, but here choice and responsibility

---

18. Jean-Paul Sartre, *The Condemned of Altona*, trans. Sylvia Leeson and George Leeson (New York: Knopf, Vintage Books, 1961), p. 60; hereafter incorporated as CA. Original French: *Les Séquestrés d'Altona* (Paris: Gallimard, 1960), p. 128.

come from a common praxis in view of common practico-inert conditions. In this third paradigm, choices must signify — perhaps they are signification itself — but in any case signifying necessarily implicates a living self (the signifier).

Franz would not deal with his family and the real responsibilities that gave him signification. Sartre takes this to heart and writes his autobiography as an attempt at a self-reflexive progressive-regressive study. He calls it *The Words*. His project: to save himself — "a whole man, composed of all men as good as all of them and no better than any."[19] *The Words* is Sartre's attempt to show that the self must be expressed in terms of words. The self signifies particularly through the language in which it is inscribed.

Sartre writes. What he writes, like his words, is the locus of his projects. Through his books, Sartre projects himself into culture. He recognizes himself in what he writes in that writing is a product of human activity, human praxis. Because he was told by his grandfather, whom he resented, that he would make a good teacher, he decides to select the words that Blanche Picard offers for him. "The child will be a writer," she says. Sartre speaks of it as a "sign on his brow." Through this sign he will achieve signification — the progressive perspective will reveal his being. The status of his grandparents, the early death of his father, the indenture of his mother to her parents, the absence of a requirement that he follow in his father's shoes, all form the regressive elements that contribute to a comprehension of Sartre. The self is its words — first play-acting with them, then taking them as his vocation:

> I took language for the world. To exist was to have an official title somewhere on the infinite Tables of the Word; to write was to engrave new beings upon them or — and this was my most persistent illusion — to catch living things in the trap of phrases: if I combined words ingeniously, the object would get tangled up in the signs, I would have a hold on it. (W, p. 114; Fr., p. 151)

By writing words, Sartre attempted to be like Genet: to identify the words with things. But he knows that the words will signify things and that they will signify the self when it activates the words. This was Roquentin's thought when he contemplated breaking away from history writing and creating a novel. What was a possibility for Roquentin is a necessity for Sartre in his third *episteme*. As Sartre says in *The Words*, "I was Roquentin." Now he must write and create out of the significations of his social context.

Sartre's blindness in later life does not deny him the fulfillment of this third paradigm. He wrote until he could no longer write, but the end of

---

19. Jean-Paul Sartre, *The Words*, trans. B. Frechtman (Greenwich, Conn.: Fawcett Premier, 1964), p. 160; hereafter incorporated as W. Original French: *Les Mots* (Paris: Gallimard, 1964), p. 213.

writing is not the end of the self. There are still the very words of the speaking subject. Although he says that tape recorders are an inadequate substitute for the stylistic formation of words beneath his pen, there are those who continue Sartre's signifying activity through interviews, films and television broadcasts (with Simone de Beauvoir, Pierre Victor, Philippe Gavi, Michel Contat and others).[20]

The view that began with the conviction that the self can exist independent of words, and which turned to an interrelational notion of identity and language, concludes with the necessary role of signification in the formation of the self. With the recognition of the social nature of the self in praxis, Sartre has realized the function of language in the delineation of self-expression. Sartre's words *on* the self have become words *of* the self.

---

20. See Jean-Paul Sartre, *Life/Situations: Essays Written and Spoken*, trans. Paul Auster and Lydia Davis (New York: Pantheon, 1977); and especially "Self-Portrait at Seventy," pp. 4–92. Original French: *Situations, X* (Paris: Gallimard, 1975). See also *On a raison de se révolter,* discussions with Philippe Gavi and Pierre Victor (Paris: Gallimard, 1974). and *Sartre: By Himself*, trans. Richard Seaver, a film directed by Alexandre Astruc and Michel Contat. (New York: Urizen Books, 1978). Original French: *Sartre* (Paris: Gallimard, 1977).

Thomas R. Flynn

6. Sartre-Flaubert and the Real/Unreal

In a good critical work, we will find a good deal of information about the author who is being criticized and some information about the critic. The latter, moreover, is so obscure and blurred that it has to be interpreted in the light of all that we know about him. —Saint Genet[1]

Of the many subjects treated in Sartre's massive study of Flaubert (three volumes to date), none is more pervasive than that of the relation between the real and the unreal. This will surprise no one familiar either with Sartre's prewar writings or with his lengthy introduction to Genet's collected works. In fact, the persistence of his concern with this topic should earn Sartre the title "philosopher of the imaginary"—at least if *imaginary* is roughly equivalent to *unreal*, as Sartre often assumes. By examining a dozen uses of the distinction "real/unreal" in *L'Idiot de la famille*,[2] I hope to establish both their variety and their interrelation. The continuity between this and his early study of the imagination, *The Psychology of Imagination*,[3] should thereby come into focus as well. Finally, Sartre's caveat to the contrary notwithstanding, this critique of Flaubert offers a good deal of information about the critic himself. Limiting ourselves to his understanding of the real/unreal, we shall assess his entire Flaubert enterprise in terms of this distinction.

Accordingly, after a brief summary of the theoretical background in *The Psychology of Imagination* (see I, A) and a short exposition of the general argument of the Flaubert volumes (I, B), I shall construct a typology of the concepts from *L'Idiot* in terms of which this distinction is drawn (II). The goal of this typology and of our essay, as well, is the discovery of a core or primary use around which the others turn; they can then be reread as reflections of this core in varying degrees. Part three will add observations on what the preceding indicates about Sartre's Flaubert as *l'homme imaginaire*

---

1. Jean-Paul Sartre, *Saint Genet: Actor and Martyr*, trans. Bernard Frechtman (New York: Braziller, 1963), p. 563, n.; hereafter abbreviated as SG.

2. Jean-Paul Sartre, *L'Idiot de la famille: Gustave Fleubert de 1821 à 1959*, 3 vols. (Paris: Gallimard, 1971-72). References to this work both in the notes and in the body of the text will be by roman and arabic numerals, referring to volume and page, respectively.

3. Jean-Paul Sartre, *The Psychology of Imagination*, trans. Bernard Frechtman (New York: Citadel, 1961); hereafter abbreviated as PS. Original French: *L'Imaginaire* (Paris: Gallimard, 1940).

and part four will view this complex and paradoxical Flaubert study as revelatory of Sartre himself as *démoralisateur*.

I. Background and Argument

A. L'Idiot *as Sequal to* The Psychology of Imagination. Barring a close reading of the early work, the best introduction to the later one, let us consider three theses from *The Psychology of Imagination* that are basic to *L'Idiot*, namely, the nature of the image, the family of images, and the imagination as paradigmatic of Sartrian consciousness, that is, as the locus of possibility, negativity, and lack.[4]

Sartre defines the image as "an act which intends an absent or nonexistent object in its corporality by means of a physical or psychical content which is given not for its own sake but only as an 'analogical representative' (*analogon*) of the intended object."[5] The image is really an act, imaging consciousness, not a hypostasis. The object it intends is envisaged under the aspect of absence or nonexistence, that is, as *unreal*, Sartre will often write. But it employs something real as an analogue by means of which it constitutes this "unreal" object. Thus, a perceptual object, an actor on a stage, for example, would be "derealized" by the audience for whom he functions as an analogue of the imaginary object Richard III. Richard of flesh and blood would be present but "out of reach." He would be present-absent, Sartre writes, that is, present in the imaginary mode. Moreover, something can serve as analogue of itself, allowing itself to be "derealized" into its own image. Consider, for example, the attitude of the photographer who "composes" natural views. Sartre will exploit this self-derealization of the world throughout *L'Idiot*.

Analogues can be as diverse as markings on a canvas or eye movements and phosphenes, in the case of dreams and hallucinations. They constitute a family of imaginary objects ranging from the aesthetic or fanciful to the oneiric and hallucinatory. But each shares the feature of rendering its object present-absent, that is, present in a derealized state.

Throughout *The Psychology of Imagination* it is implied that the imaginative act is paradigmatic of consciousness in general. The famous "nihilating" function whereby Sartrian consciousness "holds the real at bay" in its very act of constituting the world as phenomenon is revealed to consciousness *only* in the imagining act. (PS, pp. 270–272; Fr., p. 358) Moreover, the imagination is the locus of possibility, of the objects of negation, and of pri-

---

4. For an extended treatment of these theses and of Sartre's theory of the image in general, see my "The Role of the Image in Sartre's Aesthetic," *The Journal of Aesthetics and Art Criticism* 33 (1975): 431–442.

5. PS, p. 26; Fr., p. 45. Substantially the same definition is repeated twice in *L'Idiot*, except that on the first occasion he calls the *analogon* a symbol (I, 662) and on the second he explains "in its corporality" as "just as it was given to our senses" (II, 1941).

vation.[6] Sartre calls it "an essential and transcendental condition of consciousness." (PS, p. 273; Fr., p. 361) It is on these nihilating and derealizing features of imagination that Sartre grounds Flaubert's life project and works.

B. *The Argument of* L'Idiot, I-III. Comprising Sartre's overwhelming response to the question "What can we know about a man in the present state of our knowledge?" (I, 7), these volumes form a compendium of and an object lesson in Sartrian anthropology. This is their intended role in the corpus of Sartre's theoretical writings.[7] By a subtle and exhaustive use of the progressive-regressive method developed in *Search for a Method*,[8] he examines those childhood and family relations that he believes necessarily mediate socioeconomic conditions and individual projects. Indeed, the practical application of this method should prove one of the lasting achievements of this work.

The starting point for his regressive analysis is Flaubert's protohistory, viz., his early childhood and intrafamilial relations. This phase establishes the crucial fact that Flaubert was constituted capable of merely *passive activity*, a phrase from the *Critique* signifying a subject as "reflector" of others' actions and no true agent in his own right. "*From the start* he is deprived of the cardinal categories of *praxis*." (I, 143) Denied his mother's love and his father's preference, young Flaubert develops a self-hatred and resentment that last his entire life. Sartre's Flaubert reads family romance and sibling rivalry in terms of being and nonbeing. If father and family name represent the realm of being, Gustave will distinguish himself from his elder brother "in proportion to the *quantity* of nothingness (*du néant*) he introduces into himself." (I, 1140) So begins the odyssey of Flaubert's self-derealization, in which, in Sartrian fashion, he makes himself into that nonentity that others have prepared and expected him to be—the family idiot.

---

6. See PS, pp. 271-273; Fr., pp. 359-361. Later in characterizing the real as the realm of possibility and chance, I will distinguish "concrete possibility," offered by the imagination *in the service of the real*, from both "abstract possibility," which prescinds from the real/ unreal, and the imaginary in its pure form as other-than-real. Though the imagination figures in all three forms, it is the first form that distinguishes the real from the unreal or purely imaginary. See in essay part II, F, and note 28.

7. See his discussions with Philippe Gavi and Pierre Victor published as *On a raison de se révolter* (Paris: Gallimard, 1974), especially pp. 69 and 77.

8. Jean-Paul Sartre, *Search for a Method*, trans. Hazel E. Barnes (New York: Random House, Vintage Books, 1968). Sartre regards *L'Idiot* as the continuation of *Search for a Method* (see I, 7). The regressive phase of the method requires a detailed analysis of major features of the subject's biography—e.g., Flaubert's passiveness—in order to establish the "objective conditions" of their possibility. The progressive phase then pushes forward in a spiral movement from those conditions toward a totalizing synthesis of the agent, his motives and products (objectifications), to account for that unique phenomenon which is the agent himself as concrete universal, e.g., Flaubert as the author of *Madame Bovary*. This method is first suggested in *Being and Nothingness* in the context of existential psychoanalysis; see *L'Être et le néant* (Paris: Gallimard, 1943), p. 537, or the Hazel Barnes translation (New York: Philosophical Library, 1956), p. 460, hereafter "BN".

A new term appears in Sartre's lexicon, *personalization*, meaning "the surpassing and conserving (inner assumption and negation) at the heart of a totalizing project of what the world has made—and continues to make—of [the individual]." (I, 657)[9] The progressive method now traces four turns in the spiral of Flaubert's personalization: the imaginary child, the actor, the poet, and finally the novelist—all forms of self-derealization wherein his ego remains an alter ego, mirrored off family, friends, and public. Sartre interprets the final turn from poet to novelist as follows: "The *poetic* attitude was only the flight from the real to the imaginary; *artistic* activity consists in devaluing the real by realizing the imaginary." (II, 1488) At last his self-hatred and resentment converge with his project of personalization: in derealizing himself as artist, he will derealize the world.[10] His vocation crystallizes on that traumatic night in late January 1844 near Pont-l'Évêque, when Gustave falls at his brother's feet in symbolic death to rise as artist, *l'homme imaginaire*. Such, in brief, is Sartre's reading of the events in Flaubert's biography.

Two questions must be answered to complete the argument and with it the context for our typology, namely, What is the link between Flaubert's concept of art and his personal neurosis? and How does this concept reflect the general condition of French society in the second quarter of the nineteenth century? These are the existential-psychoanalytic and the Marxist questions, respectively.

In response to the first query, one must assume that the unblinking eye of Sartrian consciousness precludes unconscious motives on Flaubert's part. His neurosis, therefore, is conscious, chosen in the sense that one "chooses" one's meanings/directions (*sens*) by the practical projects one sets for oneself. Flaubert's personalizing project is to be a literary artist, a practitioner of the black art of the "lie" either for its own sake (*l'art pour l'art*) or to tell the truth (realism). If art is derealization, Sartre's Flaubert must derealize himself; if it is a realm of its own, he will be its sovereign, "the Lord of Non-Being" (I, 452); finally, if art employs the real as analogue, Flaubert will "imagine being" itself, viewing everything *sub specie phantasiae* by a sustained adoption of the aesthetic attitude (II, 1932–42). Sartre claims that Flaubert's conception of art *necessarily implies* his neurosis, that it is no mere de facto concomitant: Flaubert chooses the life of a neurotic, *l'homme imaginaire*, in order to be able to write.

Lest we conclude that Flaubert's concept of art as the imagining of being is merely the subjective outpouring of a disturbed mind, however, the last move in Sartre's argument links this concept with the "objective neurosis" of

---

9. Constitution and personalization are reciprocally related in a manner similar to that previously ascribed to facticity and transcendence in BN; see I, 654–659.

10. "To imagine is simultaneously to produce an imaginary object and to make oneself imaginary (*s'imaginariser*); I did not insist on that sufficiently in *The Psychology of Imagination*" (I, 912n.).

French society in the 1830s and '40s, which left its artists no choice but "neurotic art" (*l'art-névrose*), viz., a complex of attitudes that stressed detachment, solitude, derealization, failure (*l'échec*), misanthropy, and nihilism.[11] The French under Louis-Philippe were developing a self-image that was positivist and utilitarian, as personified in Flaubert's father. (See III, 662) Sartre sees the son's choice of neurotic art in the crisis of 1844 both as an anti-utilitarian reaction and as a prophetic anticipation of France's own option for the unreal in the person of Napoleon III, the latter in flight from the dark side of its image as revealed by the massacres of 1848. For Sartre, this is the deep reason for Flaubert's popularity in the Second Empire: the unreal is addressing the unreal.[12] "A man . . . totalizes his age to the precise degree that he is totalized by it." (III, 426) In a manner that we have come to expect from Sartre, biography has broadened into social criticism.

It is in this context, therefore, and armed with the theses of *The Psychology of Imagination* that we begin our classification of the uses of real/unreal in *L'Idiot*.

II. A Typology of the Real/Unreal

John L. Austin has located *real* among those words used only "to rule out the suggestion of some form or all of its recognized antitheses."[13] What follow are the major — though by no means all the uses of the antithesis real/unreal garnered from the first three volumes of *L'Idiot*. Though neither synonyms nor definitions in any strict sense, they are interrelated, as we hope to show, and their consideration, besides being mutually illuminating, will shed cumulative light on Sartre's understanding of real/unreal in his philosophy as a whole. The dozen categories of contrast that we have selected exhibit a certain progression from the epistemological and psychological through the ontological to the sociological. This corresponds roughly to the evolution in Sartre's own use of the distinction. We are offering a typology from *L'Idiot*, however, and not a genetic study from the entire Sartrian corpus.

A. *True or False*. Though *Being and Nothingness* argues that human reality stands in a prejudgmental relationship to being, *L'Idiot* often contrasts the real and the unreal in terms of the latter's being neither true nor false.[14] Unlike the real, which is correlative to true and false judgments (al-

---

11. This is the general theme of volume three of the study. "Neurotic art" refers more to the conduct and attitudes of its artists than to the art works themselves. The impossible demands of society on contemporary artists, Sartre believes, made it necessary for them to become, or at least to act like, neurotics (imaginary men) in order to write; see III, 65–66.

12. "At Pont-l'Évêque a cycle had begun; at Sedan it had terminated" (III, 600).

13. J. L. Austin, "A Plea for Excuses," *Philosophical Papers*, ed. J. O. Urmson and G. J. Warnock, 2nd ed. (Oxford: Oxford University Press, 1970), p. 180.

14. "Let us say that *for Gustave* this *personnage* [*le Garçon*, a role he used to assume in his

beit problematically), the unreal lacks the evidence and consistency that grounds the real. Thus, Flaubert in his battle for the unreal against the real is depicted as robbing the real of its principal weapon, truth: "[Reality] is granted an obtuse material presence . . . ; without truth, the being of the real is only an appearance of being and its cohesion hides an infinite dispersion." (II, 1306)

B. *Knowledge and Belief.* Following upon the foregoing is the contrast of the real/unreal in terms of knowledge and belief or opinion. Flaubert's passive constitution, Sartre claims, inclined him to accept all statements on the authority of others, resting content with *doxa* (opinion), whereas his father and brother forged ahead in the area of scientific knowledge based on (analytic) reason and evidence.[15] Developmentally, Sartre speaks of an "original belief" from one's protohistory becoming the means by which a child as passive agent adapts to the conditions of life.[16] With maturity, a youth's belief normally turns to knowledge as his personal identity is established. Sartre had noted this in his own case in *The Words.*[17] But for Flaubert this did not occur. He remained an imaginary child who, when the occasion arose, chose to become an imaginary adult. For this actor manqué, to be was to be believed (I, 673); it was all the same for him to feel or to imagine that he felt (I, 677). Where knowledge yields to belief, the distinction between the real and the unreal is blurred and tends to disappear.

Without attempting a systematization of Sartre's theory of knowledge, something he has never undertaken himself, it is clear that for him evidence, reciprocity, intuition, praxis, and knowledge are interrelated.[18] Thus, Gustave is said to suffer from "truth sickness" *(une maladie de la Vérité),* in that he lacks the cardinal categories of praxis and vision. Though the relation between praxis and vision has never been worked out in Sartre's own epistemology—that is, he continues to straddle the gap between Marx and Husserl—he now speaks of human truth as "reciprocity of position" between an object and a multiplicity of knowers (III, 12), which relies upon "reduction agents" *(réducteurs),* especially the intuition of evidence, to overcome the subjectivism he identifies with mere belief (I, 163-72). He considers intuition, however, to be "a practical unveiling" (I, 622), and he comes to the point of saying that the true "is praxis itself, a

---

dealings with friends] is neither true nor false; it's unreal, that's all" (II, 1327). Given the ontology of *Being and Nothingness,* however, the real/unreal distinction presupposes both being and nonbeing in the sense of *en-soi* and *pour-soi,* respectively, as does every distinction that one could make in that context.

15. See I, 502, 547, 667, and II, 1813, 1936.

16. Specifically, he speaks of Flaubert's original belief in a parental malediction (see II, 1818-19).

17. Jean-Paul Sartre, *The Words,* trans. Bernard Frechtman (New York: Braziller, 1964), p. 230; hereafter "W". Original French: *Les Mots* (Paris: Gallimard, 1964), p. 193.

18. See my "Praxis and Vision: Elements of a Sartrean Epistemology," *The Philosophical Forum* 8, no. 1 (fall 1976): 21-43.

double and complex relationship of men among themselves via their fashioning of the world and of men to the world via virtual or real reciprocity in human relationships" (I, 166). But Flaubert is incapable of reciprocity. Hence, his epistemological schema will read belief, authority, nonreciprocity, rather than knowledge, evidence, reciprocity. Where belief masquerades as knowledge we have *imitation*, the unreal world of the artist.

The *body* figures more importantly in belief than in knowledge by supplanting "the gentle and irresistible power of evidence . . . by the weight and seriousness of its materiality." (II, 1813) Examples of such "somatization" of ideas whereby the world is transformed with the help of bodily changes center on Flaubert's penchant for autosuggestion, his recurrent seizures, and especially the crisis of 1844.[19] Again, the unreal is a function of belief; the real of knowledge.

C. *Perception and Imagination.* Typical of the sustained dichotomies to which Sartre was given in his predialectical writings is the sharp distinction between perception and imagination in *The Psychology of Imagination.* The former, for example, is never complete but places us in touch with the real through an infinite number of profiles (Husserl's *Abschattungen*). The ideal synthesis of these profiles is the epistemological criterion of the reality of the perceptual object.[20] But the image is always complete — as finished as we care to make it. It is essentially poor, Sartre insists. It teaches us nothing because we find in it only what we have placed there. Moreover, "the real and the imaginary are essentially unable to coexist." (PS, p. 210; Fr., p. 282)

The physical analogue is the point of contact between perception and imagination, the real and the unreal. Though Sartre has still not offered a formal analysis of the crucial concept of analogy, he now speaks more clearly of "imaginative perception" (*imaginer la perception*) and "imagining observation" (II, 1951) in a way similar to Wittgenstein's "seeing as."[21] The original dichotomy now appears more nuanced. Thus, for example, imagining observation "uncovers more features in the object [observed] than

---

19. Sartre had discussed this phenomenon at length in his early study of the emotions, *The Emotions: Outline of a Theory*, trans. Bernard Frechtman (New York: Philosophical Library, 1947), p. 61; original French: *Esquisse d'une théorie des émotions* (1939; reprint ed., Paris: Hermann, 1960). "In the case of emotions, it is the body directed by consciousness which changes its relations with the world in order that the world change its qualities. If emotion is a game, it is a game we believe in" (p. 44). Sartre now contrasts the passive activity of the pseudo agent with the *active passivity* of the organism. *Autosuggestion* is the product of their encounter; see II, 1742. Of autosuggestion Sartre writes: "What one began by willing, one suddenly starts to undergo" (II, 1808). It reveals to Flaubert "the frightful power of his body" (II, 1790).

20. Sartre subsequently articulates his difference from Husserl, who would see in this objective synthesis the *reality* of the perceptual object. Sartre claims that reality is *more* than objectivity; see BN, p. xlvii.

21. Ludwig Wittgenstein, *Philosophical Investigations*, trans. G. E. M. Anscombe, 3rd ed. (New York: Macmillan, 1958), pp. 203ff. Sartre had previously spoken of natural beauty as correlative to imaginative perception: "We sometimes perceive in the manner that one

does practical observation, but it discovers them in order to integrate them into an imaginary whole." (II, 1951) He introduces the term *voyance* to designate this imaginative perception. "A methodical and immediate transmutation of experience," *voyance* overcomes the poverty of the image by the practice of "distancing" whereby one conditions oneself to "see without perceiving." (II, 1970)[22] The richness of the material world, its details, textures, and the like, are thus integrated as analogues for the imagination. *Voyance* affirms the dependence of the imaginary (unreal) on the real, but at the price of compromising the earlier dichotomy; for example, the essential poverty of the image.

D. L'Échec *and the Magical.* We are moving from categories of contrast that are epistemological and psychological to those that are clearly ontological. The present use bears features of both. The real imposes itself by the harsh fact of failure (*l'échec*). Choice of the imaginary — for example, the "magic" of a fainting spell in the face of unavoidable danger — is the major self-defeating activity (*conduite d'échec*) that Sartre discusses throughout his works. The self-derealization demanded of "neurotic art" is a specific form of self-defeating activity. Sartre often speaks of relations within the emotive or the imaginary as magical, that is, as operating contrary to causal laws that mark the real. The imaginary itself is causally inefficacious.[23] The imaginary man dreams and yearns but does not decide or will. (See II, 1689) This contrast of the real as causally productive with the unreal as a childlike world of play, dream, and self-deception pervades the three-volume study. It reaches its climax with the final *échec* of the dreamy militarism of the Second Empire at the hands of a scientific Prussian military machine.[24] Sedan was irrefragable proof to Flaubert that "imagination is in principle powerless." (III, 593)

E. *Praxis and Passive Activity.* No doubt the chief category of the real for Sartre is praxis (roughly, human activity in its material environment).[25] He calls is "the key to the world." (I, 311) Since the *Critique of Dialectical*

---

imagines: we apprehend reality as unreality, being disappears in the presence of its own appearance" (SG, p. 372). But if Sartre is to maintain the dichotomy, he too must face the objection leveled against Wittgenstein, viz., that seeing as is still seeing.

22. "By *voyance* I mean here the contrary of perception. Let us say that in any case he is now capable of grasping the given of experience as analogue of an infinite totality" (II, 1969).

23. In the service of the real the imaginary, of course, shares the efficacy of the real, whose instrument it becomes. But Sartre insists that "the detection of possible [moves] in a practical perspective" is merely a "subordinate function" of the imagination (III, 189). See notes 6 and 26.

24. "These men [the Prussians] are reality; through them it bursts into France" (III, 594; and see 650).

25. *Praxis* is defined as "an organizing project which transcends material conditions towards an end and inscribes itself, through labour, in inorganic matter as a rearrangement of the practical field and a reunification of means in the light of the end." *Critique of Dialectical Reason*, trans. Alan Sheridan-Smith (London: NLB, 1976), p. 734; hereafter CR. Original French: *Critique de la raison dialectique, précédé de question de méthode*, vol. 1, *Théorie des ensembles pratiques* (Paris: Gallimard, 1960), p. 687.

Reason it has enjoyed a primacy in his thought previously reserved for consciousness. He now claims that "the uncovering of the real is a moment of action: to the project which overcomes it, [the real] manifests itself simultaneously as practical field and as constant threat (coefficient of adversity); its being is resistance and possibility. When perception is no longer *practical*, it turns toward the imagination." (I, 666) This is Sartre's assessment of Flaubert's life. Incapable of praxis from childhood, resigned to a life of passive activity, which Sartre aptly characterizes as "gliding" (*vol à voile*), Flaubert slips into the imaginative mode as a denunciation of the real, praxis, which eludes him. (See III, 174-176) But he cannot elude it. With the debacle at Sedan and the billeting of Prussian soldiers in his home, "reality reveals itself to Flaubert as that which is most foreign to him and of which he has greatest abhorrence: pure *praxis*." (III, 594)

F. *Possibility and Chance.* If praxis uncovers the real, it shows it to be a dialectic of necessity/contingency. (See III, 188) "It is the contingency of the fact which is the best mark of its reality." (II, 1377) The real is full of surprises, of opportunities won and lost, and of counterfinalities. It is the realm of facticity and of *concrete* possibility. We say "concrete" possibility to distinguish it both from what could be called "pure" or "abstract" possibility — for instance, Leibniz's intrinsically possible worlds — and especially from the imaginary as an end in itself.[26] This distinction corresponds to one drawn in *Being and Nothingness* between the future (the zone of what we have called "concrete" possibility) and the imaginary as designating respectively a world *beyond* and one simply *apart from* the present world.[27] The former is a function of praxis and the here-and-now the way the latter is not. The "temporal filament," if you will, is preserved in the one case and broken in the other. (This aspect will be developed at our eighth point of contrast, H.) Concrete possibility as a feature of the real is a determination of what Sartre terms the *realizable* (see II, 1816n.), saying that it manifests "the *reality* of the future" (III, 194). The unreal, in contrast, is without concrete possibility. Sartre mentions the "world without possibilities," for example, into which belief plunges us (II, 1814-15). He notes that imagination in its state of free play places us beyond all impossibility and so

---

26. In fact, one can discover a hierarchy of possibilities in Sartre's ontology, which we might rank according to decreasing "reality" as follows: 1) concrete possibility, or the future as possibility; 2) the realizable, "neither real nor unreal *for me*" (II, 1816, n.), though within the field of choices and not mere wishes, should I change my project; 3) the unrealizable, real but external to my project and not interiorized except as unrealizable (see BN, p. 531; Fr., p. 614); 4) pure or abstract possibility (see BN, p. 469; Fr., p. 547); 5) the imaginary as derealization, as total absence of instrumentality and adversity, as the sphere where if everything is "possible" nothing is possible. Of this realm Sartre has written: "If it suffices to conceive of (an object) for it to be possible, I'm thrown into a world similar to that of the dream, where the possible is no longer distinguished from the real" (BN, p. 483; Fr., p. 562). For the existentialist Sartre, if nothing were real nothing would be possible; possibility is a function of actuality, existence "precedes" essence.

27. BN, p. 127; Fr., p. 172. See above note 23.

beyond chance, too. For with the disappearance of the impossible and with
it the real, chance vanishes as well or, better, it collapses into necessity—
that self-imposed inevitability that we have experienced in our dreams. (See
III, 189)

G. *Being-in-the-World*. This Heideggerian category has always con-
noted the real for Sartre. (Correlative to consciousness and intentionality
understood in a vectorial sense, this category is perhaps best understood as
being-*into*-the-world.)[28] To be in-the-world is to be *situated* by space, time,
others, death—all those aspects of the human condition discussed in *Being
and Nothingness* under "Freedom and Facticity." (BN, pp. 481ff.; Fr., p.
561) In *L'Idiot* he introduces the term *anchorage* (l'ancrage) as a touch-
stone of the real roughly equivalent to *facticity*, but with a socioeconomic
connotation.[29] It is defined as "the exterior world as foundation of our inner
reality." (II, 1933) Economic and social *interest*, the "objective reality" of a
particular class for a Marxist, now figure essentially in that exterior world
that grounds our inner reality.[30]

Accordingly, to derealize oneself in this seventh form of the antithesis is
to *desituate* oneself as an imaginer—hence, to break the bonds of space,
time, and especially *interest* that tie one to the real world of one's contemporaries. (II, 1558) This disinterested, detached "spectator attitude" *(conscience de survol)* that the imaginer strives for does not so much deny his
facticity and rootedness as question their importance.[31]

With the loss of situation comes a partial "loss" of world and of the real as
a result. In *The Psychology of Imagination* Sartre writes of one member of
the family of images, the dream, as "a privileged experience which can help
us conceive what consciousness would be like which had lost its 'being-in-
the-world' and by the same token would be deprived of the category of the
real." (PS, p. 229; Fr., p. 340) But it should now be clear that this is true,
mutatis mutandis, of the rest of the family of images as well. To imagine is

---

28. See Sartre's "Intentionality: A Fundamental Idea of Husserl's Phenomenology."
Translated by Joseph P. Fell, *Journal of the British Society for Phenomenology* 1, no. 2 (May
1970): 4–5. Original French: "*Une Idée fondamentale de la phénoménologie de Husserl: l'in-
tentionalité,* in *Situations, I* (Paris: Gallimard, 1947), pp. 29–32.

29. So, for example, he writes of the bourgeois's ignorance of his own class being: "An obscure but constant adherence to self prevents him from discovering in himself his anchorage.
Barring an outside mediation, his class being will remain unrealizable for him" (II, 1352).

30. Sartre has developed this concept of interest in the *Critique*. For example: "Interest is
being-wholly-outside-oneself-in-a-thing insofar as it conditions *praxis* as a categorical imperative"; in other words, "interest is a certain relation between man and thing in a social field"
(CR, p. 197; Fr., p. 261). What he has in mind is the relationship of private property. '

31. In order to "break with the real," Sartre's Flaubert must "lose the ordinary understanding of objects, acts, and words *(paroles)* to the precise degree that absolute negation
obliges him to share common ends no more. [This incomprehension] aims at revealing things
in an estrangement due precisely to the refusal to integrate them into a real system" (III, 142).
Sartre had already introduced the phrase *projet de survol* in *Being and Nothingness* (p. 486;
Fr., p. 566).

to raise one's anchor from the real to some extent, though only the psychotic is completely at sea.

H. *Temporal Ekstases*. Another Heideggerian concept, "ekstatic temporality," is a defining characteristic of existentialist man.[32] He "exists" three heterogeneous temporal ekstases, viz., the future as possibility, the past as facticity, and the present as "presence-to" being. Such, at least, is Sartre's reading of these temporal dimensions. And because time is "the very weft (*trame*) of *praxis*" (II, 1872), it is essential to the real. This grounds our distinction between concrete possibility, on the one hand, and abstract possibility and the imaginary on the other. The former shares in those relations of means and ends that constitute the future as a real possibility for *this* present agent. The latter is off the temporal track either as prescinding from the temporal or as constituting a "time" of its own; for example, the tempo of a nocturne or the sequences in a dream.

Furthermore, time is a basic feature of the real as situation. The process of desituating, therefore, demands a shift in one's relations with the temporal. In fact, Flaubert's project of self-derealization is viewed as "a battle against temporalization," especially against *his* future.[33] On that fateful evening at Pont-l'Évêque, Sartre's Flaubert "changes his life into memory in order to make it the reservoir of the imagination," because "the necessary condition to become an artist is to dream one's memory and imagine one's perception."[34] This is the temporal aspect of Flaubert's metamorphosis into *l'homme imaginaire* and forges the crucial link between his personal neurosis and his concept of art.

I. *Artifice, Laughter, and the Other*. Artifice and laughter emerge from *L'Idiot* as especially revelatory of the unreal in the sense of "appearance" that human reality introduces into being or reality. The ominous presence of "the other," on the contrary, continues to function as sign and source of the real for Sartre.[35] So this apparently psychological contrast is basically an ontological one.

---

32. See *Being and Time*, trans. John Macquarrie and Edward Robinson (New York: Harper & Row, 1962), pt. 1, division 2, "Dasein and Temporality." Sartre's position is developed chiefly in BN, pt. 2, chap. 2, "Temporality."

33. II, 1868. In one swoop Flaubert succeeds in "killing a promising young man and giving birth to a man without a future" (ibid.). Elsewhere, Sartre notes Flaubert's "suppression of the principal temporal ek-stasis, the relation to the future" (II, 1746). If this is Sartre's own view of the role of the future, it marks a significant shift from the position in BN, which claimed a primacy for the present (in "original" time) and for the past (in "psychic" temporality); see BN, pp. 142, 165; Fr., pp. 188, 212.

34. Again, "Flaubert's relationship to art is the key to his neurosis" (II, 2009). This is a basic methodological thesis in Sartre's analysis; see also II, 2057. Of course, *de*situating is effected by imaginatively locating oneself elsewhere spatially, too. On Flaubert's penchant for picturing himself in distant locales, see II, 1558-60.

35. It is no longer the sole source of the real, however. In BN only another freedom could limit freedom-consciousness. Since the *Critique* (1960), the practico-inert plays a clear, limiting role, as well.

Sartre retains his existentialist thesis that we mask the anguish of our freedom by attaching ourselves to dependable regularities (*constantes "sécurisantes"*). When the expected order is upset, when, for example, a fake sugar cube floats instead of sinking in our cup, the tenuousness of our attachment is betrayed and our freedom (anguish) is revealed. (II, 1311-12) The resultant laughter is an attempt on the part of those who are in on the joke to reestablish equilibrium (reason and order). "This instantaneous mini-scandal thus appears as a vaccine against the anguish of existing." (II, 1314)

But the antidote is itself infected, for it fosters another type of unreality, viz., the serial existence of alienated men.[36] "By laughing I valuate seriality because I adopt it or simultaneously accentuate it as an instrument of defense adopted by the group to which I pretend to belong." (I, 822) By unmasking false seriousness in the victim, the laughers defend "true" seriousness (e.g., the serial state of conformism), thereby evading the genuine — that is, Sartrian — insight that *all* seriousness is false. Their laughter erroneously implies that "nothing is real which is not serious nor serious which is not real." (I, 826) On the contrary, Sartre claims, laughter is the sign of separation and thus a token of the unreal in the valuational sense that we shall analyze as our eleventh contrast, in section K.

On the other hand, it is ultimately the other who manifests the real. Just as in *Being and Nothingness* the other "robbed" me of freedom by his look and constituted a new dimension of my being, viz., being-for-others, so in *L'Idiot*:

> It is the *existence of the Other* which in the long run succeeds in ruining every attempt at derealization. If you can't escape the real, it is because you are *re-alized* by the Other, whatever you do: it is because man is the existence through whom being-an-object comes to man. At once (*du coup*) to imagine is to deliver oneself to the Other, to place oneself at his mercy. (III, 585)

By leaving himself vulnerable to objectification by the other, the imaginer has "opted for the triumph of reality" that the other constitutes. (Ibid.)

J. *Person and* Personnage. *Person* is repeatedly distinguished from the French *personnage* ("stage character, role") in these volumes as the real from the imaginary (unreal). *Person* has already been described in *Being and Nothingness* as a "transcendent, psychic unity," an ideal synthesis of psychological states, qualities, and acts (BN, p. 162; Fr., p. 209) As such, it is an object for reflective consciousness, as real as anything empirical psy-

---

36. The series is a social relation in exteriority, which excludes reciprocity. It is thus "unreal" in the evaluative sense. By arguing that laughter and the comic are "serializing" phenomena, Sartre is claiming that they actually separate those whom they seem to unite; see I, 816. Thus, two major and related forms of alienation in CR, seriality and passive activity, reappear in *L'Idiot*.

chology may study. This concept now figures in *L'Idiot* via those spirals of personalization that trace the path of Flaubert's biography. It signifies "the abstract and endlessly revised product of personalization, the only real, that is, *lived* activity of the living being." (I, 656) *Person* is thus the agent and ideal term of this process: a real subject totalizing a real world.

But *personnage* denotes an imaginary subject totalizing an unreal world. (See I, 962, and II, 1222ff.) The various roles Flaubert assumes throughout his life—for example, *le Garçon*, a caricature of himself as a middle-class boor—not only are forms of self-derealization, but also constitute attempts to derealize the world—the world as image of itself. These *personnages*, in addition to being hedges against the real, function as traps leading others to join in their own derealization by "playing the game." Sartre signals the basic difference between *person* and *personnage* when he implies that one *lives* the former but merely *interprets* the latter. (I, 737)[37]

K. *Reciprocity*. Our next point of contrast is overtly valuational. Sartre writes that in order to know who adapts best to "reality" one must employ a value system; in other words, that "reality," at least in the context of social adaptation, is a value-laden word.[38] And what is Sartre's highest psychosocial value? Since his play *The Devil and the Good Lord* and the *Critique*, it has been *reciprocity*—the kind of interpersonal relationship in which mutual interiority is enhanced and mutual object-being minimized, though not entirely overcome.[39] Its antithesis is seriality, a purely exterior relationship such as for Sartre that exhibited by laughter and the comic. As he argued in the *Critique*, this desired mutuality is impossible in an exploitative society. Psychosocial relations in such a context, we may conclude, are *unreal* in this valuative sense. Indeed, this explains why Sartre in *L'Idiot* can claim that there are no "real bonds" among the atomized individuals of bourgeois society and can add that the bourgeois individual is an "imaginary being."[40]

---

37. In Flaubert's case the distinction is blurred by his choice of the vocation of artist, according to Sartre; see I, 736-737 and 762ff. "He is without the means of effecting what I call an accessory reflection [one that constitutes an empirical ego and psychic temporality; see BN, pp. 159-170; Fr., pp. 206-218]" (I, 771). When he tries to reflect, "he is already in the hands of others—that is to say, originally, his parents. Consequently, his *real* ego seems to him partially alienated, i.e., an alter ego, somewhat lacunary—he is ignorant of what others think of him in so many respects—and rather flabby, wishful, unstable and dazed" (ibid.).
38. See III, 12. In this he reflects the opinion of his admirer and commentator R. D. Laing.
39. Apropos of laughter he writes: "The fundamental relation between men, masked, deviated, alienated, reified as much as you will—is reciprocity" (I, 816). And later he observes in a more political vein: "The true relationship between men is reciprocity which excludes commands properly speaking" (III, 48). Confirming one of our previous categories of contrast, Sartre emphasizes that "one *desituates* himself by breaking or concealing the relationship of reciprocity" (III, 12 n.). Nonobjectifying, or "free," reciprocity is the apex of human relations analyzed in the *Critique*. See my "The Alienating and the Mediating Third in the Social Philosophy of Jean-Paul Sartre," in *Heirs and Ancestors: Studies in Philosophy and the History of Philosophy* (Washington, D.C.: Catholic University Press, 1973) 6:3-38.
40. See II, 1232-33.

L. *History and Ideology.* The valuational use of *real/unreal* suggests our final area of contrast: Sartre conceives of history and ideology as the real and unreal respectively. He has long accepted the basic theses of historical materialism and awarded explanatory priority to economic base over ideological superstructure.[41] In this respect *reality*, as in the phrases "real cause" or "true agent," refers to the genuine subject of history, that is, to that class and those groups and institutions that are historically efficacious. What counts as real in this sense will differ from historical age to age.

With tacit appeal to this usage, Sartre notes that the abortive "revolt" by Flaubert's high-school classmates shocked them into realizing that they were "the *patients of history.*" (II, 1371) Here, too, the Prussians incarnate that historical causality which Sartre's Flaubert identifies with the real (see section E, above), for history is the real as diachronically totalizing praxis.

Sartre depicts the antithesis when he writes:

> There is no society founded on the division of labor and exploitation which does not have an objective but false idea of itself, in particular when the idea is produced at the level of the leading classes as their self-justification and as the edifying mystification which the exploited classes must be made to swallow. This unreal but rather rigorously constructed totality is called an *ideology.* (III, 36)

It is here that we should locate Sartre's remarks about the "bourgeois real" to which Flaubert responds with imaginary destructiveness. (III, 663)[42] Besides the standard features of the self-image of the age—for example, the manners and mores of the ruling class (and that bourgeois humanism which we can expect Sartre to excoriate)—it is the specific cloak of unreality with which French society had wrapped itself—the "imperial mirage" of the Second Empire (III, 548)—that earns the censure of both author and critic. So ideology, a collective form of Sartrian bad faith, joins those other unreals which human freedom makes possible and from which, Sartre continues to believe, that same freedom can in large part deliver us.

These, then, are the dozen uses of the antithesis "real/unreal" that we have garnered from *L'Idiot.* Initially epistemic and psychological, they

---

41. He warns against the "economism," however, that a failure to recognize the role of individual praxis entails; see *Search for a Method,* p. 132. Recently he has distinguished "ethical systems," phenomena of the superstructure, from "living morality" (*la moralité vivante*), which is as basic as productive activity itself; see *On a raison,* pp. 118ff., 45.

42. Sartre is quick to note that the self-defeating behavior exhibited by the neurotic artists of Flaubert's generation, though a denunciation of the real, was an *imaginary* one; that it required as a condition "a modest but real integration" into the bourgeois real, e.g., Flaubert's comfortable living as a *rentier,* which it could then neglect or deny for the sake of art. Such indifference to economic reality is more difficult, he adds wryly, if you must work every day. (See III, 176.)

shade into the ontological with the category "*L'Échec* and the Magical."
The subsequent distinctions (sections E–J) are chiefly ontological, though
Sartrian ontology is never far removed from phenomenological anthropology. Drawing the contrast in terms of laughter, the other, and *personnage*
and *person* (sections I and J) extends the distinction to social psychology in
which the value "reciprocity" reigns supreme (section K). The four final
types of opposition (I–L) employ increasingly the discourse of the *Critique*,
culminating in a Marxist theory of history describable likewise in the language of real/unreal. The centrality of this distinction, therefore, not only
in *L'Idiot*, which we hope to have established, but throughout Sartre's philosophy, can be assumed as at least a reasonable hypothesis. It is beyond the
task at hand to establish any more in this regard.

Limiting ourselves to *L'Idiot*, can we discover any unity among these diverse uses other than the progression just noted?[43] It would seem that we
can. Whether we use the expression "family resemblance" or speak of the
analogous predication of the distinction real/unreal, one use emerges from
our typology as the "head" of the family, that is, as the *core* analogue,
which the other uses approximate. The core analogue of the real/unreal
throughout *L'Idiot* seems to be the "practical/imaginary."

The antithesis in each of our categories of contrast is a form of the imaginary in that peculiarly Sartrian sense that we summarized in section I, A.
Its distinguishing feature is the rendering "present-absent" of an object or
event by means of an *analogue*, which lends the image its stability while be-
traying its parasitical state as regards the real. Indeed, the analogue is the
source of the basic *ambiguity* that haunts the image as not simply "unreal"
but as "*de*-realization," that is, as really related to the real by an internal
negation. (One cannot glide, *vol à voil*, in a vacuum.) Although the imagination can thus be "at the service of *praxis* and consequently of the real" (II,
1327), this is a subordinate function. In its pure form the image is flight
from the real; and as "oneiric commitment,"—for example Flaubert's
"choice" of the unreal—it constitutes devaluation of the real: an ethicoaes-
thetic transvaluation that Sartre has observed in the works of Baudelaire
and Genet, as well.

The positive term in each category, on the other hand, is not primarily
the epistemological concept of perception, but emerges rather as that of the
practical. In some contrasts this is obvious; in others it requires elucidation.
In a remark displaying the practical orientation of the categories of truth,
knowledge, and possibility, for example, Sartre explains: "Evidence is a
moment in a praxis. . . . It is revealed as requiring transformation within a
practical field, but also as itself defining the conditions and limits of this
transformation. Evidence is the real showing itself to be the regulation of

---

43. This progression is ours, not Sartre's. Most of these distinctions occur repeatedly
throughout the three volumes.

possibles." (II, 1813n.) We have pointed out the vectorial nature of Sartre's reading of Husserlian intentionality and of Heideggerian being-"into"-the-world. In this regard, Sartre has always traded on the ambiguity of the French term *sens* ("meaning/direction"). And ekstatic temporality is practical as well, denoting the conditions for and limitations of concrete choice. There is a primarily practical character to even the most apparently theoretical categories in terms of which the real/unreal distinction is drawn. Indeed, Sartre enunciates a maxim in his understanding of the real/unreal when he asserts: "It is a general fact . . . that when we are unable to respond to the exigencies of the world by an action, [the world] suddenly loses its reality." (I, 666) Hence, it is not the perceptual as such, but rather the practical, including praxis, project, class interest, and reciprocity, and also time as the tram of concrete possibility and the other as limit to my *sens*-giving actions — it is the practical in this appropriately broad sense that stands out as the model of the real for Sartre.

And lest we be accused of contrasting the incomparable, let us recall that *imaginary* is the contrary of the practical to the extent that it obtains *apart from* the present world with its concrete possibilities, forming rather a "world" of its own.[44] It is the imaginary as the nonpractical, indeed, as the *anti*practical, that constitutes the other pole of Sartre's basic antithesis in *L'Idiot*.

The drawing of this fundamental distinction is the culmination of our typology and the main objective of our inquiry. In the two remaining sections we shall observe briefly how Sartre's Flaubert and Sartre himself face the *tension* that this core analogy engenders, the former as imaginary man and the latter as demoralizer.

III. Sartre's Flaubert as *L'Homme imaginaire*

Perhaps the main conclusion about Flaubert to be drawn from *L'Idiot* regarding our topic is the *ambivalence* of his attitude toward the real/unreal. The unreal is both an escape and a weapon for him. It must be sufficiently other than the real (truth, utility) to provide a genuine alternative, yet real enough to be taken seriously. Thus, two distinct and competing literary schools, the Symbolists and the Naturalists, can equally claim his parentage. The former prizes the imaginary because it is neither true nor false; the latter is concerned precisely with the truthfulness of fiction. (II, 1571)[45] Sartre underscores "that curious relation between imagination and truth, affirmed a hundred times since [Flaubert's] youth, that truth reveals itself

---

44. Already in BN, prior to his discovery of praxis but with its predecessor "project" clearly in mind, Sartre writes: "reality is presented to us neither as thing nor as instrument but as instrumental-thing" (BN, p. 320; Fr., p. 384). For his most recent affirmation of the practical and ethical nature of "reality," see *On a raison*, pp. 78–79.

45. Sartre's *ex professo* treatment of this problem is found in *What Is Literature?*, trans. Bernard Frechtman (New York: Philosophical Library, 1949).

only to imaginary beings as the meaning (*sens*) of their derealization." (III, 543) The meaning of Flaubert's self-derealization, consummated at Pont-l'Évêque, is that he is forever barred from the essence of man (praxis) but that this very *échec* is the necessary condition for great art. In a typically Sartrian ploy, "loser wins."

Yet Flaubert's attitude simply reflects the ambiguity of the imaginary itself, especially as understood by Sartre. A hybrid of the real (the analogue) and the other-than-real, the image can serve either as instrument in the service of the real or as end in itself, keeping the real "out of play." The tension we have witnessed stems from this dual capacity of the image to either foster praxis or foil it. Flaubert's "choice" of the imaginary merely heightens this tension to a neurotic extreme, aided not a little by family and contemporary society. In retrospect after Sedan, Flaubert avows that the image is a composite of being and nothingness, with too much of the latter to be causally efficacious but too much of the former not to modify the reality of the imaginer. (III, 519)

It follows that the basic antithesis, real/unreal, is itself ambiguous. In none of the categories treated above is the real an absolute. At best, it is a "relative-absolute," like the phenomena in *Being and Nothingness*. (BN, p. xlvi; Fr., p. 12) To this extent Austin is correct: we do articulate our understanding of the real by playing it off against the unreal. But, to turn an Austinism against its author, it is the real nonetheless that "wears the trousers"; for it has positive meaning, for example, the "practical," and it is both conceptually and ontologically primary, that is the imaginary is always the derealization of some reality. Moreover, it triumphs in the end. Flaubert's dismay at the powerlessness of the imaginary after the Prussian victory is echoed by a similar conclusion in Sartre's own autobiography.[46] The very act of self-derealization serves to realize the artist; flight from the real is abdication in favor of the real; holding the real at bay as if the real would reciprocate is a futile and self-defeating gesture. In fact, for Sartre's Flaubert as for the Bonapartists, "oneiric commitment" is an exercise in massive *bad faith* — the chief moral lesson of *L'Idiot*. Specifically, it is that type of bad faith that Sartre has termed *conduite d'échec*, namely, "behavior with two objectives, the more superficial being to achieve a definite goal and the deeper being to fail to achieve it." (III, 173) For Sartre's Flaubert, *l'homme imaginaire* from inception to term is *l'homme-échec*.

IV. Sartre (of *L'Idiot*) as *Démoralisateur*

The ease with which Flaubert slips into Sartrian categories leads one to suspect that the subject of this extended study is equally Sartre himself. Parallels between the two abound. With regard to the real/unreal let us consider two.

---

46. "For a long time, I took my pen for a sword; now I know we are powerless" (W, p. 212; Fr., p. 159). For a similar realization ascribed to Flaubert, see III, 593 and 650.

Sartre shares Flaubert's ambivalence toward art. By insisting that what he calls "poetry" and music cannot be "committed," he relegates them to the sphere of "pure art," a stand not unlike Flaubert's regarding *l'art pour l'art*.[47] On the other hand, he displays a naturalist bent when he describes the artist as one who must lie to tell the truth.[48] Indeed, his Flaubert study, which he has characterized as "a novel which is true" (*un roman vrai*),[49] can be read as a work of art in the latter sense. The "lie" comprises hypotheses about Flaubert's infancy, inner states, and the like, as well as that imaginative reconstruction, the "novel" itself, which Sartre has erected from these fragments — *ex pede Hercules*. The "truth," as we observed at the outset, is what we can know about a man nowadays. It is the truth of Sartrian anthropology *in concreto*. As such, it is no mere theoretical analysis, but exhibits an evaluative and a practical dimension in accord with his understanding of the *real* as we have interpreted it in this essay. So the writing of *L'Idiot*, far from constituting the aesthetic "flight from reality" some have taken it to be, can itself be read as a *political act*, a matter of consciousness-raising, revealing the implicit hatred of man that grounds both *l'art pour l'art* and the bourgeois humanism that feeds, and feeds upon, it — standard themes of the politicized Sartre.

Finally, both authors share a high regard for what Sartre calls the "demoralizing" power of the unreal-imaginary. As he explains:

> To demoralize is to ruin an existence by maneuvering it with phantasms . . . but for the operation to be perfect, *trompe-l'oeil* and trick objects are not enough: the victim must be aware of their nonbeing, if not at the outset, as soon as possible. For it is at that moment of consciousness that he will discover the being of nonbeing [appearances] and the nonbeing of being [finitude], each by means of the other, and he will find to his surprise that all this was *nothing* and that this nothing has corroded his life inexplicably. (II, 1309)

This was Flaubert's project, if we may believe Sartre, from his schoolboy attempts at scandalizing to the "demoralizing derealization" in his projected

---

47. In addition to *What Is Literature?* see his essay "*L'Artiste et sa conscience*," reprinted in *Situations, IV* (Paris: Gallimard, 1964), pp. 17–37. In recent years, however, he seems to have shifted his position; see, for example, his remarks on "critical poetry" in *Situations, IX* (Paris: Gallimard, 1972), p. 31, and his discussion of commitment in the plastic arts in the essay "*Coexistences*," ibid., pp. 316–325. The concept of art as a "critical mirror" held before the face of bourgeois society, Sartre's current view, renders such art "demoralizing" for the class whose bad faith it reveals; see III, 106.

48. Thus, in *What Is Literature?* he insists that it is necessary "as always in art, to lie in order to be true" (p. 158, n. 12).

49. The expression as it first appeared, "a true novel," is ambiguous; see "Itinerary of a Thought," *Between Existentialism and Marxism*, trans. John Mathews (New York: William Morrow and Co., 1976), p. 49. Later retranslated into French as *un roman vrai*, ("a novel that is true"), the phrase lost its ambiguity — to some extent; see *Situations, IX*, p. 123. Still the questions remain: In what sense is it a novel? and What does it mean for a novel to be true?

final novel, *Sous Napoléon III*. (III, 656) But it is surely Sartre's as well —
from Roquentin's proposed novel, which would "make people ashamed of
their existence"[50] through the moral and aesthetic transvaluations of *Saint
Genet* to *L'Idiot de la famille*, itself interpretable as a work of demoralizing
derealization.

Let there be no misunderstanding. *L'Idiot* is primarily a concrete study
in Sartrian philosophical anthropology. As such it contains much that is
true and valuable for our understanding of the human condition, both
structurally and diachronically. It is not hyperbolic to see in these volumes
the apex of Sartrian rationalism, not the Cartesian deductivist but the Hegelian genetic variety.

But *L'Idiot* is also a work of imaginative literature, *un roman vrai*. It is
instructive to read it in this light. For example, it helps us appreciate how
Sartre at the height of his political activism could take the time to prepare
so demanding a study of a paradigmatically bourgeois artist. The imaginary
aspect clarifies the work's political (and, for Sartre, moral) significance: we
are being "maneuvered by phantasms," viz., imaginative reconstructions,
unconfirmable hypotheses, arresting examples, and creative interpretations, "to feel feelings traitorous to our class." (At a press conference for a
revival of *The Condemned of Altona* several years ago, Sartre remarked:
"What I want to do is give people a bad conscience.")[51] Literary Naturalism
understood as a critical mirror held up to the bourgeoisie is described by
Sartre as "an attempt at radical demoralization." (III, 106)

However, Sartre is not a nihilist; demoralization for him is not an end in
itself as it seems to have been for Flaubert. Rather, it functions like the first,
ironic move in Socratic dialectic, to be followed by the positive maieutic, in
Sartre's case the ethic of "disalienation" that must guide our lives this side of
a "socialism of abundance."[52] But Sartre remains pessimistic, an unquali-
fied demoralizer, to the extent that he seems to consider the bourgeoisie
completely unsalvageable. Having underlined the misanthropy, racism,
and general bad faith that masquerades as bourgeois humanism, he turns
to another class and a new generation, in which he hopes for a more promising audience.[53] But the irony persists; like Flaubert in the Second Empire,
Sartre's chief following continues to come from those whom he holds in low-
est esteem, middle-class intellectuals like himself.

---

50. Jean-Paul Sartre, *Nausea*, trans. Lloyd Alexander (New York: New Directions, 1964),
p. 178.

51. Quoted by Michel Contat and Michel Rybalka in their compilation *The Writings of
Jean-Paul Sartre*, vol. 1, *A Biographical Life*, trans. Richard C. McCleary (Evanston: Northwestern University Press, 1974), p. 468.

52. Though the theoretical basis for what we have termed Sartre's "ethic of 'disalienation'" is established in BN and especially in the *Critique*, its popular conception is perhaps
best formulated in *On a raison de se révolter*; see pp. 45, 76–79, 118–19, 341ff. For Sartre's
"socialism of abundance," see III, 189.

53. See Francis Jeanson, *Sartre dans sa vie* (Paris: Éditions du Seuil, 1974), p. 261.

Eugene F. Kaelin

7. *On* Meaning *in Sartre's Aesthetic Theory*

According to Sartre, *sens* is defined as the presence-in-absence of the object created by the imagination, found in all successful works of art, whether representative of natural objects or not. If there is such an object, the *sens* is the totality of the person, milieu, epoch, or human condition depicted by the work; and if not, the affective character of the presentation itself. Thus, even if by definition there is no signification in the nonfigurative "image," one would not be justified in claiming that such works lack meaning, since nonobjective works do present organizations of lines, colors, and forms possessing the all-important *sens*; or, should they fail to do so, they would simply be judged unsuccessful works.[1]

Although I do not disagree with the claim that a nonobjective work possesses a sense, I shall attempt in the following sections to show that this sense is perceptual and not imaginary; that even Sartre has claimed that no work of art signifies beyond itself any other thing in an extra-aesthetic context, except the original or fundamental project of its creator; and that Sartre himself has provided sufficient explanation of the affective consciousness to show how the expressiveness of nonobjective paintings and sculptures comes to be a property of our experiences of the objects in our worlds, even if they are interpreted as "meaning" nothing beyond themselves.

In order to achieve these ends, I shall have to trace the sources of Sartre's aesthetic theories to the phenomenological bases from which they were derived.

I.

The difficulty in discussing any facet of Sartre's aesthetic theory is apparent to anyone who has tried. Since Sartre has nowhere written a com-

---

1. In a recent reexamination of the role of images in Sartre's "aesthetic theory," Thomas R. Flynn rejects the claim, made against the theory, that the imagination has no role to play in the appreciation of nonfigurative, perceptual art: "To insist that much modern art simply *is* but doesn't mean anything, is to confuse *sens* with signification and to overlook the affective

plete, consistent theory of aesthetic experience, the discussant's first task is to construct a reasonable description of what would count for an aesthetic theory had Sartre written one. The sources are many and various.

The first of his philosophical works was a small, quasi-historical treatise on the imagination, published in 1936.[2] *Nausea* (1938),[3] his first novel, is a fictionalized account of the development of an artist's consciousness, ending with the protagonist's decision to change directions in life, and to seek whatever surcease being a creative writer may bring to the "meaninglessness" of that person's existence. Characters in other novels and plays are fascinated by the properties of art works: along with the paintings of *Nausea* that have fixed their subjects in a pose of bad faith, and the music that precipitates the hero's decision, one is reminded of the statue of *No Exit*,[4] which symbolizes for Garcin the essence he has become in death.

As if in explanation of this symbolism, the *Psychology of the Imagination*,[5] an essay in pure phenomenology, appeared in 1940. There, in Husserlian terminology, we find the eidetic description of "the mental image" and its implications for an explanation of aesthetic objects, together with "solutions" to a number of outstanding debates within aesthetics over the nature of aesthetic pleasure, the disinterestedness of the aesthetic attitude, the actor's paradox, and the ontological characterization of aesthetic objects as "unreal."[6]

And, in addition to the sources dedicated to the essential description of images, there are others, dedicated to the ontology of the person who imagines. From these we understand that in order to be able to imagine, a consciousness must be situated in a world and be motivated by that situation. The artist's freedom, a function of a consciousness of being a lack, is able to interpret the realities of the situation as possibilities for overcoming that lack in an act of self-transcendence. This self-transcendence is worked out by personal decision and the dialectic of the negative consciousness, which as consciousness can never simply be what it is. Thus, the conclusions of the earlier works necessitated further phenomenological justification: human freedom, most clearly exercised through the imagination, needed the clarification of a fundamental ontology, the inspiration of which is no longer purely Husserlian, but Heideggerian as well.

---

dimension of art; or else it bespeaks a certain aesthetic anarchism where everything (and thus nothing) is a work of art." "The Role of the Image in Sartre's Aesthetic," *The Journal of Aesthetics and Art Criticism* 33 (summer 1975): 437.

2. Sartre, *L'Imagination*, 3d ed. (Paris: Presses Universitaires de France, 1950). Original, 1936; translated by Forrest Williams as *Imagination* (Ann Arbor: University of Michigan Press, 1962).

3. *La Nausée* (Paris: NRF, 1938); translated by L. Alexander as *Nausea* (Norfolk, Conn.: New Directions, 1949).

4. *No Exit and Three Other Plays* (New York: Vintage Books, 1958).

5. *L'Imaginaire*, (Paris: Gallimard, 1948); translated by Bernard Frechtman as *The Psychology of the Imagination* (New York: Philosophical Library, 1948).

6. The Psychology of The Imagination, pp. 230–246.

What must the human reality be in order to be able to imagine? The technique for answering such a question will be the same as that sketched out in his brief *Theory of the Emotions*:[7] to study phenomena — things as they appear to consciousness — not for their own sakes, but for what they mean. Corresponding to every phenomenological reduction there is a possible eidetic reduction. For the perceptive consciousness, the meaning of a series of phenomenal appearances of an object is an essence, which may be intuited from a single example; and every consciousness, perceptive, intuitive, or imaginative, signifies beyond itself toward the totality of a human project.

So, just as one may look at phenomena to discover the essences they reveal, one may look at conscious human choices to discover what the chooser's fundamental human project may be. Whence the existential psychoanalysis that Sartre has practiced on Baudelaire (1947),[8] Genet (1952),[9] Tintoretto (1957),[10] and Flaubert (1971);[11] indeed, he was even prompted to practice the same technique on himself in *The Words* (1964),[12] the work instrumental to his being named Nobel laureate of literature in that year. Perhaps characteristically for this social rebel, he scandalized the literary world by refusing the award; that action, too, revealed something of his total human reality.

It seems clear from the repeated use he has made of the technique that Sartre thought the greatest discovery of his *Being and Nothingness* (1943)[13] was existential psychoanalysis. Since, as mentioned above, the poet and art critic, the novelist and dramatist, the painter, and the very incarnation of the "bourgeois" novelist were all amenable to existential analytic treatment, some authors have been led to look upon it as an important part of Sartre's aesthetic theory. But they are mistaken: instead of criticism, the method produces biography; and instead of aesthetics, psychology. And even Sartre's own description of his *L'Idiot de la famille* (the study of Flaubert) as

7. *Esquisse d'une théorie des émotions*, 2d ed. (Paris: Hermann, 1948); translated by Philip Mairet as *Sketch for a Theory of the Emotions* (London: Metheun, 1962) and by Bernard Frechtman as *The Emotions: Outline of A Theory* (New York: Citadel, 1971).

8. *Baudelaire* (Paris: Gallimard, 1947) translated by M. Turnell (Norfolk, Conn.: New Directions, 1967).

9. *Saint Genet: comédien et martyre*, 3d ed. (Paris: Gallimard, 1952); translated by B. Frechtman as *Saint Genet: Actor and Martyr* (New York: Mentor Books, 1964). The reaction of Genet to this analysis was a period of some seven years in which he was unable to write another word. The story is apocryphal, but betokens what might be expected from having one's "essence" determined.

10. "Le Séquestré de Venise," *Les temps modernes* 13 (1957): 761–800.

11. *L'Idiot de la famille: Gustave Flaubert de 1821à1857*, 3 vols., (Paris: Gallimard, 1971–72).

12. *Les Mots* (Paris: Gallimard, 1964); translated by B. Frechtman as *The Words* (New York: Braziller, 1964).

13. *L'Être et le néant* (Paris: Gallimard, 1943); translated by Hazel E. Barnes as *Being and Nothingness* (New York: Philosophical Library, 1956).

"un roman vrai" will not make of that work a true work of art.[14]

More useful, for the purposes of sketching out the implications of *Being and Nothingness* for an understanding of Sartre's "aesthetic theory," is his discovery of the "pre-reflective *cogito*," the self-awareness of any consciousness as it is aware of some other, transcendent object, whether that object be real or unreal. But this is a theme to which I must return.

Besides the longer works already mentioned above, Sartre has written hundreds of smaller critical articles, both for his own review, *Les Temps Modernes* (edited at first in collaboration with Merleau-Ponty), and for those of others, on topics of art, literature, and society. A number of these articles were collected into a single volume entitled *What Is Literature?* (1947),[15] taken from those already assembled in volume two of his *Situations* (1947-73).[16] Finally, "A Question of Method," an article written for a Polish review, has been republished as the initial chapter of his magnum social and political opus, *Critique of Dialectical Reason*.[17] In these works he is concerned with explaining the relations between his earlier existentialism and contemporary Marxism; the *Critique* itself is written in Hegelian logic, and contains in outline the theory of the state.

Since the theory of a literature of commitment was most fully expounded in the literary essays — making the call for a literature suited to the times — precisely the kind being produced by Sartre and the other "Mandarins of the Left," they caught the attention of Merleau-Ponty, who, in *The Adventures of the Dialectic*,[18] did some existential psychoanalysis of his own: Sartre's decision to renew his commitment to leftist causes in spite of the evidence of unmitigated social repression in Russia some thirty years after the Revolution only proved to Merleau-Ponty that Sartre had decided to "enclose himself in words,"[19] that is, to have "deliberately taken up a position in the realm of the imaginary."[20] Sartre, of course, admitted the charge by his subsequent autobiographical psychoanalysis entitled simply *Les Mots*: not just any words indeed, but those he had deliberately chosen to work out his fundamental project, as Roquentin, of *Nausea*, had already prefigured in 1938. But Merleau-Ponty's irony still hurt; for to take up a position in the

---

14. See Situations, IX (Paris: Gallimard, 1972), p. 123; translated by John Mathews, *Between Existentialism and Marxism* (New York: Pantheon, 1974), p. 49.

15. *What is Literature?*, trans. B. Frechtman (New York: Philosophical Library, 1949).

16. Sartre's critical essays are periodically edited and published in collected volumes as *Situations*, (Paris: Gallimard, 1947-73).

17. *Critique de la raison dialectique* (Paris: Gallimard, 1960); translated by Alan Sheridan-Smith, ed. Jonathan Rée, as *Critique of Dialectical Reason* (London: New Left Books, 1976). *Search For a Method* is published separately, translated by Hazel Barnes (New York: Vintage, 1963).

18. *Les Aventures de la dialectique* (Paris: Gallimard, 1955); translated by Joseph Bien as *Adventures of the Dialectique* (Evanston, Ill,: Northwestern University Press, 1973).

19. Merleau-Ponty, *Les Aventures*. p. 270; translation mine.

20. Ibid., p. 262; translation mine.

realm of the imaginary is to admit that one is dealing with the unreal, just as Sartre had criticized Flaubert for abstaining, as a bourgeois writer, from comment on the social unrest of the 1840s.

The personal barbs contained in these ploys and counterploys did not begin, however, with Merleau-Ponty's overt criticism of his former associate; they may have grown from their prior friendly decision to split the task of introducing Frenchmen to phenomenological philosophy: Sartre was to investigate the realm of the unreal in the phenomenology of the imagination, and Merleau-Ponty was to plumb the depths of the real in his own *Phenomenology of Perception*.[21] Each tended to view aesthetic experiences in terms of the one attitude at the expense of the other; where Sartre extolled the virtues of a free, derealizing imagination, Merleau-Ponty insisted that whatever is artistically imagined must be perceived and expressed in sensuous terms for all to see.

The difficulty was compounded by Sartre's insistence that perception and imagination were two irreducible structures of human consciousness. I have tried to show elsewhere that this contention is false,[22] that every imaginative act presupposes a perceptive one as the source of the concepts implicit in what Sartre calls the *savoir imageant* employed by an artist to project his images, unless the human mind may be said to be graced by its Creator with the innate ideas so dear to Descartes. But the method of phenomenology, as shown by Merleau-Ponty in *The Phenomenology of Perception*, does not permit the distinction between mind and body that Descartes had carried into his philosophy from his classical and medieval training, so another source of conceptual knowledge must be discoverable within a purely phenomenological analysis.

In the context of creative communication, which constitutes the field of aesthetic inquiry, the connection between perception and imagination is established by the "motivating situation" in which the artist, as human reality, must always find himself. Indeed, while engaged in the act of creating a work of art, the artist's consciousness seems to change intermittently from imagination to perception and from perception to imagination until the artist sees that his work is done. It was for this reason, it should be remembered, that John Dewey referred to artistic creation as a series of actions and reactions during which the artist alternatively does something and undergoes the effects of having done that very thing. The artist is said by Dewey to learn from his experience as he is led to comprehend the relations between the "doings" and the "undergoings."[23]

There is no point in repeating here what has already been done twice be-

---

21. *Phénoménologie de la perception* (Paris: Gallimard, 1945); translated by Colin Smith as *Phenomenology of Perception* (New York: Humanities Press, 1962).
22. See E. F. Kaelin, *An Existentialist Aesthetic* (Madison: University of Wisconsin Press, 1962) and *Art and Existence* (Lewisburg, Pa.: Bucknell University Press, 1970).
23. John Dewey, *Art as Experience* (New York: Minton, Balch and Co., 1934), p. 44.

fore. But Thomas R. Flynn has called into question my appraisal of Sartre's aesthetic theory as being limited to the mimetic arts.[24] He also finds some grounds for caviling with other interpreters of Sartre who have maintained that any theory distinguishing between the physical artifact and the so-called aesthetic object that makes its appearance when an appreciator attends to the properties of the physical artifact is open to the charge of "idealism," that is, of multiplying entities beyond necessity for an understanding of the creative process.[25] For if one attends to the properties of the physical medium in which the artist happens to be working, one ought to be able to see how that "aesthetic surface" is organized, even if some depth references may be overlooked in the interpretation of any signified meanings.

To make sense of all this, that is, to decide what interpretation can and ought to be made of Sartre's seemingly endless production of thoughts on matters aesthetic, and how it is to be judged—as sufficient or insufficient for a coherent aesthetic theory—perhaps the first move is to make clear what is expected of any such theory.

We should expect, for example, that some account be given of the entire process by which aesthetic objects are created and appreciated, that is, how an aesthetic object becomes a vehicle of communication between an artist and his audience; and within that account, there must be a description of aesthetic objects that does justice to all forms of aesthetic expression, from the most "realistic" to the most "abstract." Whether such accounts and descriptions are themselves realistic or idealistic should be of little consequence, since any theorist needs and is entitled to all the constructs at his disposal for an adequate account, in which the "adequacy" of this account is defined in reference both to the internal consistency of the theory and to its external, referential properties. No aesthetic theory need be bound to a particular metaphysics, and the virtue of phenomenological aesthetics is the avoidance of any claims of describing the nature of the "real" world.

II.

For an understanding of Sartre's phenomenological aesthetics, the *Psychology of the Imagination* is still the best place to begin, as indeed Flynn does begin, with Sartre's eidetic description of the essence of the image:

> The image is an act which intends an absent or non-existent object in its corporality by means of a physical or psychical content which is given not for its own sake but only as an "analogical representative" of the intended object.[26]

The class of things being so described constitutes an abstractive hierarchy

---

24. Flynn, "The Role of the Image," p. 437.
25. Ibid., p. 438.
26. Ibid., p. 432; the translation is Flynn's.

of the imaginative function: from the most physical images — a portrait or caricature — to printed signs, mimed imitations, drawings, faces in flames, spots on a blank wall, rocks in a human shape, and so on to hypnagogical images and, lastly, purely mental images, in which the analogue is freely created by the imagining consciousness out of kinesthetic and sensible structures of that particular consciousness. And in each case, the same consciousness is armed with conceptual meanings (the *savoir imageant*) that motivates its intention. But, for a clarification of this view, Sartre's background in Husserlian phenomenology must be considered.

For Husserl, an image is a particular consciously lived experience (an *Erlebnis*) found in reflection within the stream of a personal global consciousness. It is an event by which consciousness intends an object not contained in that consciousness. Thus, an image is not a content of consciousness that may be seen, although it is composed in part of a "content" by virtue of which it intends the transcendent object. Husserl called such a content a *hyle*, the matter of an image, which is given form by the intending consciousness.

Husserl's example was Albrecht Dürer's etching *Knight, Death, and the Devil.*[27] A perception of a print of the etching intends the lines, shapes, and forms of the drawing that represents the knight and two personifications, Death and the devil, along with the knight's faithful dog. As soon as awareness is given to the represented figures, consciousness changes from the perceptive mode (in which the "object" is the drawing as such) to the imaginative, wherein the figures are understood as representing their corresponding transcendent objects, which are thereby "given" in their concreteness, but only as absent. Thus, according to Sartre, the imaginative consciousness intends its objects as "not being there" (as nonexistent, or as existing elsewhere, or as merely absent, or as having no commitment to any existence at all); they are present only to the imagination, and this in their very absence.

Following Sartre's analysis of this process, the imagination "derealizes" the real world (in which objects of perception are related in time and space) and projects its "unreal" world of absolute significance, measured in effect by the total structure of the intentional object itself. The Husserlian influence is clear: that a particular image is as it is may be the result of an artist's conscious decision; Dürer's imagination was guided by the concepts applicable to the figures of his drawing and to the world view they help depict, but the exact manner of the depiction is the spontaneous result of Dürer's conscious noetic synthesis guiding his artistic hand.

---

27. *Ideen zu einer reinen Phaenomenologie und phaenomenologischen Philosophie*, in *Husserliana* (The Hague: Martinus Nijhoff, 1950-56) 3:269-270; bk. 1 translated by W. R. Boyce Gibson as *Ideas* (New York: Collier Books, 1962), pp. 286-287.

It should be clear from the foregoing that Dürer's initial creative act is one of intending *the drawing* that as yet does not exist, but which, once created, further intends the absent objects signified therein. When this same drawing is viewed by an appreciator, a second consciousness perceives the physical analogue (the line and forms), and *must* perceive them so that the aesthetic surface may motivate the imagination "to see in the mind's eye only" the world depicted in the image. And when this occurs, it may be said that the surface perception "deepens" to include the appreciation of the represented objects and whatever ideas they may suggest.

The artist, of course, is his first viewer, and may discover his ideas in the same way as his audience, by responding to the features of the created object —whether or not his creative activity is preceded by an original, "subjective" intention that corresponds to the intentionality of the work itself. Nothing precludes the possibility of having such an intention, since what can be seen can be imagined; but nothing necessitates the existence of a primal intention either, since the actual making of a drawing is one way of producing the image. It is for this reason that the so-called intentional fallacy is a fallacy: if the artist had no original purely mental image of the work to be created, it is a mistake to look for one; but it he did, and has succeeded in creating the physical analogue that presents the essence of that image, then the perceptive viewer need not inquire after the artist's original intention, since by hypothesis the essence appearing on the basis of the percept is the same as that of the original image. And how can an image be created by manipulating a physical medium? Just think of all those proofs by "construction" used in geometry: the essence of the theorem to be proved is made manifest as the proper figure is generated.

At this point Flynn objects: "The imagined object . . . is not some bloodless essence which we contemplate with detached curiosity."[28] And his objection has some point—the same stated by Heidegger, who asked the rhetorical question "Who could maintain that the meaning of a temple is the idea of a temple?"[29] But Heidegger distinguished between the inessential essence of things (a *quidditas*) and their *Wesen* (a nominalized verb).[30] The manner in which a thing comes to be and remains what it is—as a temple becomes the "House of God" in the human perception of the strife between "the Earth" and "the World," or the tension between the surface of the building as built and the depth significance in the use to which the building is put—at least offers a clue as to how surface experiences deepen

---

28. Flynn, "The Role of the Image." p. 434.

29. Martin Heidegger, *Holzwege* (Frankfurt am Main: Klostermann, 1950), p. 26. For a fuller discussion of this point, see my "Notes towards an Understanding of Heidegger's Aesthetics," in Lee and Mandelbaum, eds., *Phenomenology and Esistentialism* (Baltimore: Johns Hopkins, 1967), pp. 59-92.

30. Heidegger, *Holzwege*, p. 39.

in aesthetic perception. Sartre too has an idea of the deepening of the aesthetic consciousness, but to follow out that idea it will be helpful to retrace his interpretation of Husserlian phenomenology in some greater detail.

III.

Since Flynn has a different notion of Sartre's dependence upon Husserl, I shall begin with Flynn's account, and then proceed to explain why I cannot agree with him in every detail. Analyzing the "components" of the Sartrian imaginative consciousness, Flynn finds 1) the object of the imagining act, 2) its content, and 3) the imagining act itself. He diagrams the whole as

Mental Act (intending)   ⟶ via Content   ⟶ Object[31]

Although I think this diagram is a bit inexact, since the content is always found *within* the act and, in the case of aesthetic creations, the mental act need not precede the manipulation of a medium, it is on the whole informative. Yet, if I am allowed the pun, the image it conveys would be clearer if one diagramed the relations involved in the following manner:

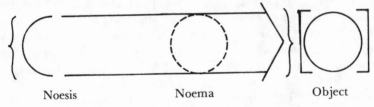

Noesis   Noema   Object

In this diagram, with the brackets of the phenomenological *epoche* placed where they occur, the *C* stands for the intending act, which carries over to a transcendent object, *O*. This intending is itself what Husserl referred to as a "noetic synthesis." It gives structure and hence meaning to the object, whether it be perceived or imagined. *All* consciousnesses are conscious of something. What is synthesized may be very complex, but in every case, in order to be found immanent within consciousness, this matter must be a meaning: a concept (for the *savoir imageant* of Sartre) or an essence, such as "thing," "extended thing," "colored thing," "part of a body," or "hand." I have used quotation marks on the names of these essences to indicate their intentionality: they are intuited from prior acts of perception; and the listing of the essences is presented above in the reverse order to that in which they are revealed in Descartes's analysis of a percept in the dream hypothesis of the first *Meditation*. It should not be forgotten that Descartes was

---

31. Flynn, "The Role of the Image," p. 433.

working under the hypothesis that whatever appeared to him in perception was nothing more than a dream image. Husserl, indeed, interprets the essences as definitive of various regional "ontologies," the interpretation of which must occur prior to any empirical investigation in a positive science.

Moreover, no consciousness exists apart from its body. Hence, some meanings of the hyletic nucleus of the noema (represented by the broken O in the diagram) may be kinesthetic—such as those that motivate the appearance of spots on blank walls—or sensory-affective—such as those that motivate the appearance of hypnagogical images. As such, they constitute the "psychic" elements of the noema. Where the conceptual structure of the noematic nucleus may be purely formal, as in the geometric proofs noted above, the kinesthetic and sensory-affective meanings give "flesh" to the images of art. And once the total image has been formed, the creator or his appreciator may react in an emotional way to the objects depicted in the image.

Such reactions are secondary intentions. Caught in the unreal world of its own creation, the consciousness of the artist engages in the logic of "magic." Finding the right word, or the right formal expression, is sufficient to make the unreal world appear; and in its appearance the deeper consciousness, which we loosely refer to as an "emotion," forms a new intention—precisely the emotive properties thus created in the depicted world: in the case of Dürer's etching, the feeling of loneliness, abandonment, and melancholic commitment of the knight's world. And for this total structure of the imagined universe, in the image present-in-its-absence, Sartre uses the appropriate term *presence*.

But the question arises whether in our perceptions of nonfigurative works of art this same presence is made to appear. For an answer to this question look once again at the diagram of the "bracketed" consciousness. Within the brackets we find only the noesis and the neoma; and since the transcendent object is bracketed outside the consciousness, the investigator cannot commit himself on the "reality" or "unreality" of that object: the natural attitude has been suspended once and for all. And should we remove the brackets and attend to our further experience, in the case of perception we shall find only a physical or psychical analogue (the physical and affective properties of a drawing) or nothing at all (in the purely mental image). So, what kind of presence makes its appearance when an art critic attends to the properties of a nonobjective work of art?

Before considering the answer to this question, please note the limitations of the method. The critic must already have had the experience (whether it be "thinly" perceptive or "thickly" imaginative); his judgment is reflective, and is limited to a description of the conditions under which the experience was had in the first place. In reflecting, he may now intend the noetic and noematic structures of the original consciousness. Therefore, what one describes in phenomenological criticism will be either a manner of synthesizing the "contents" of an experience (the noesis) or the various layers, or "strata" (to use Ingarden's term), of content within the noematic nucleus.

No reference to the "real" properties of objects, which themselves may be real or unreal (the knight and the devil in Dürer's etching), is possible for the critic, since the context of significance has been limited by the phenomenological reduction. And on this point, Sartre's substitution of the Kantian transcendental deduction for the Husserlian reduction on the assumption that they are "equivalent" procedures is a mistake. Kant's procedure is an inference — from the existence of some phenomenon to the necessary structures that would render an explanation of the phenomenon's possibility. Husserl's technique is an intuition of the structure of the phenomenon as the essential necessity for that phenomenon's occurrence. As such, it is a direct object of conscious awareness to the reflecting consciousness, that is, to the phenomenological analyst; it is not the phenomenon itself, but the meaning of the phenomenon, an essence given along with the phenomenon itself.

Whence the source of the ambiguities associated with the transportation of phenomenology into French. In French, the "meanings" of phenomenological analysis became in general *significations*, a generic term not limited to semantical reference. They are, indeed, any object of any conscious awareness qua meant; whether reflective or nonreflective, their being is purely intentional. What Sartre has done, and what Flynn has made abundantly clear, is to limit *signification* to its semantic usage and to employ the cognate *sens* to refer to the total organization of an image, whether it be figurative (composed of a semantical component) or nonfigurative (and lacking semantical "signification").

Thus, should we return to our original question — whether in nonfigurative art there is a *sens* revealing a nonexistent presence — there seem to be two ways of answering. One is that of Sartre and Flynn. As the latter explains,

> . . . Sartre distinguishes between representation, in the usual sense of that term, which the artist gives of a *realité-pilote* (properly derealized into an imaginary object), and "the presence which finally descends into the composition." Borrowing concepts from his image theory, he describes presence as "the thing itself, without detail, in a space without parts." And he suggests that abstract art, having freed itself from the figurative, concentrate on achieving "incarnate presence." But even though presence is revealed a little more each time we effect an imaginative synthesis, it is never fully realized: for presence, finally, "is nothing but the work itself considered as an organic whole (*organisme*)."[32]

---

32. Ibid., p. 436.

The passage is not without its difficulties, which its author readily admits, but the whole debate may be put on a single issue. What is this presence that is the thing itself making its appearance without detail in a space without parts? It is clear that such a space must be phenomenological and not natural, since all natural spaces are composed of homogeneous parts. It must occur, then, as a psychological tension; but that still leaves both the perceptive and the imaginative modes of consciousness. If imaginative, the tension is felt between the image serving as sign and what it signifies (its signification); and if perceptive, the tension is directly presented in the sense (*sens*) of the image or sign as "self-referring."[33]

The logic of "self-referring" entities has always been baffling. The least sense that may be made of the expression is that our *perception* of the spatial tensions of an organized sensuous surface does not refer to anything beyond itself. Nor, if Sartre is right, do the signifieds of an aesthetic depth. It is for this reason that he can truthfully say that in its totality no work of art signifies anything beyond itself.[34] A work of art may be constructed of meanings, but none, in its totality, has a meaning (signification). If the signifieds occurring within the aesthetic context are purely imaginative, and permit the appearance of the aesthetic object in its totality,[35] can the same be said for the *sens* of a nonobjective piece? Sartre's appeal to "the symphony" as that which makes its appearance[36] makes no sense, however, since in answer to the question What is the symphony?, one would have to respond with a description of the tensions felt in an experience of the music as heard.

The symphony is presented in the experience of the music, but the symphony is heard, not imagined.[37] The symphony, too, is an intentional object, but one that is constructed of perceived tensions. Call that a "presence" if you will or must, but do not confuse the modes of intentionality. Music that is not heard is nothing more than periodic waves of sound in the purely physical sense.

Nor will it do to refer to "presence" as the sense of organic unity within the work itself,[38] for organic unity is nothing more than a principle of organization of first-order sensuous percepts and hence, itself an object of our perception: it corresponds roughly with Husserl's "essence" of a perceived object and directly with Merleau-Ponty's notion of a primitive, meaning-given *sens*.[39] The idea that in perception the human consciousness is passive

33. Ibid.
34. As per Flynn, ibid.
35. Ibid.
36. Cf. ibid., p. 433.
37. I.e., the essence we refer to as "the symphony" makes its appearance in its various performances and by means of them. For a discussion of the ontology involved in this claim, see C. I. Lewis, *Analysis of Knowledge and Evaluation* (LaSalle, Ill.: Open Court, 1946), p. 478.
38. As per Flynn, "The Role of the Image," p. 437.
39. See his "Le doute de Cézanne," in *Sens et non-sens* (Paris: Éditions Nagel, 1948), pp.

before the impressions of sense is as inadmissible as that according to which the imagination is said to be so active that it creates its objects or presences without the prior possession of sedimented meaning structures gained through the activity of active perceptions in the past.[40] Perception, too, is intentional, conscious activity in the strict Husserlian sense; and consciousness gives meaning to the world in first perceiving objects as they really are.

Flynn's further suggestion that "presence" is a third alternative between the "hallowed pair" of representation and expression in the popular conception therefore rings hollow.[41] To say that not all art is representative is to say that some works of art express what they do without making a depth reference. And this accords with the popular conception of the difference between "realistic" and "nonfigurative," or "abstract," art. But whether it is figurative and realistic or nonfigurative and totally abstract, all art is expressive; and if there is "presence" in both styles of art, then it must occur in two different manners, which now need to be described.

IV.

In this section, I shall attempt my own eidetic description of the conditions under which aesthetic objects make their appearance.[42] Instead of using "sense" to translate the French *sens*, as used by Sartre to refer to the presence of an aesthetic object, I shall use it to translate the same word as used by Merleau-Ponty to refer to a structured perceptual noema. In terms of aesthetic theory, all such noemata are organized sensuous surfaces.

I begin with a noncontroversial claim: without a prior experience of the artist's work, which may be called a "physical analogue" only in cases of representational art, there is nothing to be analyzed or described. As Dewey puts it, all aesthetic judgment presupposes our having had the experience to be analyzed. But whereas Dewey looks for that one pervasive quality that makes *an* experience of an organism's contact with its environment, I shall state that the context of aesthetic significance (a term to be defined later) is

---

15-49; translated by H. L. Dreyfus and P. A. Dreyfus as *Sense and Non-sense* (Evanston: Northwestern University Press, 1964), pp. 9-25.

40. It is not absurd to suppose, as Descartes did in the exposition of the dream hypothesis of the first Meditation, that an imagination could be so all-powerful; for he reasons only that *if* such a power existed the objects it produced would have to be visible; hence, to be colored, and extended.

41. Flynn, "The Role of the Image," p. 437. I know of no aesthetician who supposes that "expression" and "representation" are alternatives, since some expressions contain mimetic elements. Perhaps Flynn has Croce in mind, for whom expression (intuition) is opposed to "sensations," "associations," and "representations," in the strict epistemological sense of these terms. But then Croce could not be called "a popular" mind; his language is highly technical. See Benedetto Croce, *Aesthetic*, trans. Douglas Ainslie (London: Vision Press, 1953; original edition, London: Macmillan & Co., 1909).

42. This section is a revision of the three postulates found in my "Method and Methodology in Literary Criticism," *Art and Existence*, pp. 100-104; see also my "Aesthetic Education: A Role for Aesthetics Proper," *Journal of Aesthetics Education* 2 (April 1968): 51-66.

established by an exercise of the phenomenological reduction. Within the brackets of the reduction there is found, in reflection, only noetic intendings and their corresponding noematic strata. Whence, postulate one: *All aesthetic expressions are context-bound.*

But that context is composed of stratified conscious noematic structures and their synthesizing noeses. At the simplest level, the object of these intendings is perceptual. In absolute music, nonobjective painting, and all other nonfigurative arts, the primitive counters of the context are sensuous. "Counters" are anything that may be discriminated within the context. Thus, if a colored patch is a counter, so is the relation between two colored patches. Depending upon the values of those colors and their juxtaposition within context, the relation between the patches sets up a space tension that is felt by the perceiving organism. On the whole, the warms will tend to come forward and the cools to recede in the perceptual field.

Husserl was right, and Sartre did well to note, that feelings may be a phenomenon of the natural world, that is, an intersubjective property of objects in human experience, such as the "horror" of the Japanese mask and the "anguish" of the yellow in Tintoretto's Venetian sky. Lines, explicitly or only implicitly drawn, engage the kinesthetic responses of the subject, and "movement" is predicated by the design.

In addition to the sensuous properties of the "object," given in noematic reduction, there is always the corresponding noetic synthesis. The discovery of Sartre's *Being and Nothingness,* and his principal contribution to contemporary phenomenology, is the description of these noetic syntheses as pre-reflectively self-aware. While the consciousness attends to the perceived relationships between colored patches, and these are not so organized as to represent any further objects, the consciousness is "thetically" or "positionally" aware of the colors and their relations, and at the same time non-thetically or non-positionally aware of itself as intending those objects. Such a non-positional awareness is a feeling perceived in the apprehension of the object, and cannot be had without such an apprehension. The expressivity of this "surface" object is a quality of the object, but is felt in our cognition of that object, and may be felt by anyone who perceives the same object structured as it is. The experience is purely perceptual; and the cognitive-affective awareness of the object, within its own internal structures, constitutes a sense. It is indeed the meaning created by the artist in manipulating the counters of his medium.

But some contexts are so organized as to include layers of depth: lines and forms allow figures to appear; and when they do, the imagination is called into play. The lines and forms present the figures, which represent and therefore are said to signify the objects associated by resemblance or some other form of analogy with the figures. And, in a further layer of depth, such figured objects, in their relationships, may be said to represent an idea, a world view, an ideology, or what have you.

Again, the virtue of Sartre's theory of the image is that it explains the way in which purely depth counters express an affective content. By a secondary intention the consciousness may lose itself in the "unreal" world depicted within the image. "Depth" feelings are called out by the manner in which the depiction is made. Lines of stress are felt as one attends to the manner of depiction. Look again at Dürer's etching. The loneliness of the drawing is in the depiction of the knight having left his castle on the hill or else bypassing the castle of another in pursuit of his mission. Although accompanied by his faithful dog, he is beset by the threat of death and the temptations of the devil. In this way, through the emotive-cognitive grasp of the depicted universe, depth expressiveness is experienced by the viewer.

Surface expressiveness on the one hand, and depth expressiveness on the other. Which predominates? That all depends upon the context. If there is no depth reference, the entire expressivity of the context is explained by the perception of the value of the perceptual counters. But where there is depth representation, the surface values merely contribute to the total expressiveness of the piece. And quite obviously if there are depth counters, their presence alone does not determine the total expressiveness of the piece. The value of the perceptual counters, as signifiers, cannot be abstracted from but must be put into relation to the values of the signifieds of the sign in order for there to be a complete determination of the context. Whence, postulate two: *An aesthetic context is composed of counters, either surface alone or both surface and depth, and their relationships.*

Perhaps the best expression of the relationship between surface and depth of aesthetic contexts has been made by contemporary structuralists: a work of art is a functional relationship between a signifier and its correlated field of signifieds. That, too, is a tension felt in the consciousness aware of the relationship between the signifiers and the signifieds. Whence, postulate three: *The significance of an aesthetic context* (occurring within the brackets of a phenomenological reduction of an artwork) *is the felt expressiveness of all the counters of that context as they fund, or come to closure, within an experience of that context.*

And there follows from the three postulates stipulated above a fourth: *No single counter, or set of counters, is absolutely significant;* that is, all counters of the context have only that significance which accrues to them by virtue of a relationship to some other counter or counters. This last postulate is, once again, a contribution of Merleau-Ponty, whose aesthetic theory was inspired by both Husserl and de Saussure, the founder of modern French linguistics. Since Sartre's aesthetic theory violates this postulate — emphasizing depth at the expense of the value of the surface counters — the theory of images upon which it is based is insufficient for a complete aesthetic theory. Images, when they occur, are only a part of the total aesthetic context.

V.

If nonobjective works of art are totally explicable by our perception of organized sensuous surfaces, expressing a "vague" feeling[43] that is equivalent to a consciousness's pre-reflective awareness of its own states in the act of perception, there seems to be no need of the concept of "presence" for nonobjective works. An aesthetic surface is always a necessary condition of perceptual art, and is sometimes sufficient; and where it is not sufficient, the missing structures are supplied by the imaginative consciousness. Consequently, there can be no complete theory of aethetic experiences that does not take into account both surface and depth structures of human consciousness.

And if a physical artifact may be interpreted as a sign, expressive in its own right of surface feeling, or of both that feeling and a depth signification, with its attendant depth feeling,[44] then there must be some third concept used to name the relationship between signifier and signified. Since Sartre uses *presence* to refer to both the significance of the signifier and the significance of the signified, he cannot use that term for those complex arts in which the expressiveness is controlled by both surface and depth, as in the figurative arts. I prefer the term "total expressiveness," which may be used for both surface and depth expressions, since the manner in which that total expressiveness is achieved is consistently described in the postulates of section IV without respect to the differences between figurative and nonfigurative arts.

For a complete theory of the aesthetic object, as phenomenologically reduced, one must make an appeal to *both* the phenomenology of perception *and* to the phenomenology of the imagination; and, in addition to these, to some version of linguistic structuralism. It is for this reason that I refer to my own theory as a "phenomenological structuralism." Within it, only three aesthetic categories are necessary: surface (the signifier), depth (the signified), and total expressiveness (the significance of the sign).

In retrospect, I am grateful to Flynn for having provided the occasion to review my commitments, and I can express my gratitude only by admitting the fact that my original assessment of Sartre's theory of aesthetic objects was, indeed, wrong. Although it is true that Sartre's theory of images is not applicable to nonobjective works of art, if we take into consideration the total expressiveness of aesthetic objects, as we must, it is likewise true that the theory does not give a complete explanation even of figurative works. The concept of *presence* is suggestive, but only of one significant part of the

---

43. This expression is D. H. Parker's; see his *The Principles of Aesthetics*, 2d ed. (New York: F. S. Crofts & Co., 1946), pp. 48–50.

44. Cf. ibid., pp. 50–53.

mechanics involved in the experience of aesthetic contexts as they are isolated in phenomenological reduction.

It should likewise be clear from the foregoing why existential psychoanalysis of an artist has no part to play in the description or evaluation of aesthetic objects. Sartre's interest in existential psychoanalysis led him to treat aesthetic objects as significant beyond themselves — as symptomatic of the artist's fundamental project. This certainly is a meaningful inquiry, but it is not an aesthetic one.

In Husserlian terms, the analyst has a choice: either to pursue the ontology of aesthetic objects, in which case we seek to determine how art works are made and appreciated (constituted for and by consciousness), or to pursue the ontology of personal existence, in which case the task is to show how an individual artist has determined his own existence by a set of personal choices. Unfortunately, as an artist interested in his own commitment to imaginative creation, Sartre was led to an investigation of his works to discover an image of his self-development as the ultimate sense of his creative acts.

In this way, I think, Sartre was misled by one of his own creations — the character of Roquentin, who projected the life of an artist as his salvation from the nausea of brute existence. The image of such a salvation was presented to him by the "essence" of a piece of music. Sartre should have known that music may be essentially determined (in the relationship between its sensuous counters), but that a human personality, on this side of its own death, can never fulfill the conditions of an imaged essence. That is what he had shown so forcefully in *Being and Nothingness*.

Old images never die; they merely fade away, as consciousness changes its intentions from the unreal world of the imagination to the real world of our perceptions. From there we need only place the brackets of the phenomenological reduction and proceed as above, either as critical aestheticians or as existential psychoanalysts, but not both in the same way, or at the same time. Indeed, if Sartre did find the sense of his own creative project in *The Words* — and in the signs as the functional relationship between signifiers and signifieds — he found it between surface and depth expressions where the tension occurs in all representational arts. If we are to understand how works of art enter our lives, both the imagination and perception must be given their due.

Garth Jackson Gillan

8. A Question of Method: History and Critical Experience

In subjecting Sartre's conception of historiography to scrutiny, the concept of *problematic* as developed by phenomenology and structuralism will provide us with an avenue of approach. As elaborated by Husserlian phenomenology and post-Saussurean structuralism, the concept of *problematic* focuses upon the manner in which theoretical questions are posed. Theory is as much the search for an object and the specification in discourse of a domain of objectivity as it is the expression of statements about that object and domain. The manner in which the question concerning the object is phrased creates the domain of objectivity to which it refers. Sartre's thought falls naturally into that characterization, for from *Nausea* through *The Roads to Freedom* to the *Critique of Dialectical Reason* his thought has been a search *for* history. And not in an idle sense, for from the start the concept of the being of consciousness as freedom, the project, in *Being and Nothingness* meant that nothing would do, but that the actions of men and, consequently, history must have a political urgency animating them. The question is one of man's fate. And everything hangs in the balance.

From its side, Husserlian phenomenology emphasized the necessity of outlining the complex of concepts that in their interrelationships specify a particular objectivity and, in that way, concentrated on the programmatic nature of philosophical method and discourse. Although deeply involved with its content, the phenomenological method retained the appearance of a formal discourse. It was to be a way of introducing the world into philosophical discourse; it did so by suspending the thesis of the natural world, so that the natural world and the layers of objectivity founded upon it could shine forth, appear, as phenomena. This, however, was a program; philosophy remained an introduction to the world; it could never pretend to equate itself with the world. As such an introduction to the world, it was up to philosophy to provide the initial concepts that would allow the world to be seen and spoken: to present the world as a program for thought.

Since de Saussure's *Course in General Linguistics*, structuralism has emphasized the concept of system as the concept that makes it possible to tie down the concrete analysis of phonological systems or kinship relations. Linguistic or anthropological data become relevant only when they become the indices of relations. The significance of facts lies in their interrelationships; their meaning lies at the level of the network of those relations, in their specific coherence. The task of theoretical reflection is, then, to elaborate from the oppositions found in the sensible given the sytematic interconnections that elaborate it into a system. The object of theory is promoted to the level of meaning at the moment when it takes on the characteristics of a network, of a text, of a paradigm, or of a discourse.

What both of those conceptions emphasize is that the specific coherence of a thought is to be found on the axis of synchrony. Thought is suspended in the daze of the question. Before it can move on along the axis of diachrony or exposition, it must bring that question to the point: In what way does the problem at stake become a problem? Hence, the concept of *problematic*: the network of interrelated concepts — the web of discourse — that introduces thought to a new domain of objectivity.

The above considerations make it possible to pose or to formulate as the essential problem the *question* of history. The first task in the construction of history is the manner in which the question of history is asked. The *problematic* of historical theory is that complex of concepts which locate it within the world as an object of discourse and provide an introduction to its theoretical explanation. The question of history is, in that way, the problem of historiography: *how* is one to write history? Sartre accentuates this aspect of the matter in the very title of his major work on history and historical method, *Critique of Dialectical Reason*.[1] The term *critique* is used, above all, in the sense of the search for the real outlines of the question of history. The form which that search takes is by reason of necessity one of criticism of the *status questionis*. What is the state of the question?, as a question, requires that the fog of dogmatism be pierced by the bright rays of a political passion for the meaning of history. Through critique, history becomes a question, carrying with it all the insecurity and the submerged anguish of a humanity constantly threatened by economic scarcity, the inertia of things, and the counter-humanity of others.

In order to sharpen our focus upon the elements entering into the structure of the question of history for Sartre, it is necessary to introduce two preliminary matters: the terrain of history — the question of historiography — and the subject of history — the question of politics. Both of these questions are interwoven and are what give historical and political theory within the Marxist stream of the Western revolutionary tradition its particular cast and conflicts. The first stage in our analysis can be reached through a con-

---

1. Jean-Paul Sartre, *Critique of Dialectical Reason*, trans, Alan Sheridan-Smith, ed. Jonathan Rée (London: New Left Books, 1976). Henceforth cited in the text as CDR with original French ("Fr."): *Critique de la raison dialectique* (Paris: Gallimard, 1960).

sideration of the opposition between the theory of history, or historiography, and the philosophy of history in *The German Ideology*.[2] The second stage can be achieved by examining the role of the proletarian movement as the subject of history in Lukács's *History and Class Consciousness*.[3]

The German Ideology of Marx and Engels is a transitional work, not only in the mere chronological sense of the term, but also because it marks out a new theoretical terrain for social and political criticism. It establishes a break, or *coupure*, to use the phrase that Althusser has introduced, between the philosophy of history and the theory of history. In introducing "the mode of production" as a guiding concept for history, Marx was introducing a new way of "writing" history.[4] The concepts involved, then, in setting the writing of history on a materialist foundation are methodological concepts that have relevance only in the organization of historical events. But they themselves do not provide a meaning for concrete, diachronic history. "They can only serve," in the words of *The German Ideology*, "to facilitate the arrangement of historical material, to indicate the sequence of its separate strata. But they by no means afford a recipe or schema, as does philosophy, for neatly trimming the epochs of history."[5]

The terrain for the theory of history is established for Marx in a space created by the interrelationships of historical events. Although not a formal theory in the strict sense in which those terms are understood today, historical theory is concerned with the form that events possess as they occur in material reality. The opposition between the theory and the philosophy of history, consequently, focuses upon the issue of historical methodology. The philosophy of history provides a categorization of historical facts, prior to a confrontation with their form. It is an interpretation of the sequence of historical events and not a comprehension arising from the organization of historical events into a text, into an exposition. Once that point is established, it becomes clear that the opposition between historical theory and the philosophy of history is between a methodology for the exposition, or "writing," of history and a schema emphasizing the arrangement of historical periods along a line. As a consequence of that opposition, "when reality is depicted, philosophy as an independent branch of activity loses its medium of existence."[6] The idealist nature of philosophy, which consists in the fact that it creates a schema for historical facts prior to exposition, results in its absolute condemnation. There is no Marxist philosophy of history; there is only a Marxist historical methodology.

---

2. Karl Marx and Frederick Engels, *The German Ideology* (New York: International Publishers, 1965).
3. George Lukács, *History and Class Consciousness*, trans. Rodney Livingstone (Cambridge, Mass: MIT Press, 1970).
4. Marx and Engels, *German Ideology*, p. 7.
5. Ibid., p. 15.
6. Ibid.

The problem, however, is not quite that clear-cut. The philosophy of history conceives of historical facts as ranged along a line leading from the past into the present. And its interpretation focuses upon the stages into which that line can be graduated. From that linear conception come the concepts of progress, inevitable development and evolution, concepts to which, at one time or another, the Marxist tradition has been extremely hostile, particularly as seen in Luxembourg and Lenin. Because it is involved with the form of facts and hence with different levels of history — economic, political, religious, social, cultural, artistic — and with their foundation in the modes of social production, historical theory would, on the contrary, seem to be located on the axis of synchrony. It would seem to be concerned with historical forms of human production at various levels to which time — the essential factor in historical explanation — would be an extrinsic factor. From that point of view, the materialist conception of historical methodology would not in fact match the real nature of the material of history, events whose character is to be the marks of transition, repetition, or revolutionary change. Hence, the ever-recurrent temptation to see Marxism as a pure science in an empiricist or positivist sense. But, on the other hand, once the axis of synchrony is dissolved for the benefit of diachrony, historical theory lapses inevitably into a variant of the philosophy of history. It, once again, becomes a chronicle of epochs and a teleology guided by subjective ideals.

But, rather than being the sign of a failure, the conflict of synchrony and diachrony in historical method exposes an underside to history, the question of historical subjectivity. Historical theory as the theory of the social production of human life leads in Marx's view to the discovery of the real movement of history and to the subjectivity that is at work in that development. It is not a subjectivity that bears that development, for the idea of carrying along certain anticipated forms of historical development to their completion belies an implicit idealism, a subjectivity that explains history rather than being explained by it. The theory of history, on the contrary, discovers a material subjectivity, one that erupts from the description of the capitalist mode of production, a subjectivity that is defined as the *practice* of a form of historical production. Form this vantage point, historical subjectivity is not the bearer of history but the practice of history, an intersubjectivity *at work* in the social production of life. Its unity is not that of an epistemological subject that is assured by the unity of its internal life. Rather, it is a unity across dispersion: a subjectivity existing between individual subjects. Whether that conception still retains the characteristics of subjectivity remains in question, for the difficulties involved in specifying class consciousness and in establishing a politics based upon the existence of potential or actual proletarian class consciousness points to an unresolved problem: whether the "subjectivity" of history can be created or thought of

as arising from or between—the "inter" of intersubjectivity—individual
subjects.

In *History and Class Consciousness* Lukács places the emergence of proletarian consciousness in the modern era at the center of the development
of historical theory.[7] The dialectical, unreified understanding of history
and society is reached in the principle of totality. Historical processes at
work in society can be understood, not on the basis of their isolated singu-
larity, but on the basis of their social totality—the totality of social relations
—in which they occur. It is at that moment that they are seen not as brute,
irreducible facts, but as relationships, or as facts mediated by one another
within society. However, that theoretical viewpoint is dependent upon the
emergence within bourgeois society of a consciousness that is its negation
and transcendence.

The possibility of a dialectical understanding of history and society demands that a singular perspective can be taken upon history that is at once
the opening up of the room necessary in order to see the functioning of
social processes in their totality, and its own validation. The proletariat fulfills that function, for it is at once a rupture with and a negation of bourgeois society and the consciousness of being that negative moment.[8] It is
consciously a revolutionary class. The specific consciousness of the working
class is not limited to the reified forms of consciousness typical of bourgeois
society, in which social relations are masked in the commodity fetish. As a
rupture with bourgeois society, the proletariat is the only perspective upon
history and society that can occur outside of the social exchange that sees
every social relation as a commodity. Bourgeois consciousness contains its
own theoretical limitations. It cannot really understand; it can only "fetish-
ize" social relations. Hence, as Lukács states, the principle of totality is the
revolutionary principle in theory.[9]

The unity of historical theory and its material—the events and social
movements of history—are achieved along the same lines for Lukács. The
rubric under which that unification is effected is the unity of theory and
practice: the unity of historical theory and proletarian politics. That unity
rests upon the dialectical idea that the proletariat as a social consciousness
is both the subject and object of history. To that point Lukács writes, "Only
when a historical situation has arisen in which a class must understand society if it is to assert itself; only when the fact that a class understands itself means that it understands society as a whole and when, in consequence,
the class becomes both the subject and the object of knowledge; in short,
only when these conditions are all satisfied will the unity of theory and prac-

---

7. "What is Orthodox Marxism?", Lukács, *History and Class Consciousness*, pp. 1-26.
8. Ibid., p. 20.
9. "Reification and the Consciousness of the Proletariat," Lukács, *History and Class Consciousness*, pp. 83-222.

tice, the precondition of the revolutionary function of the theory, become possible."[10]

In the "Preface to the New Edition" (1967) Lukács expresses some serious doubts about the primary role *History and Class Consciousness* originally gave to historical subjectivity in the exposition of historical rationality. The first reservation Lukács states about his original views is that nature was seen solely within the immanence of society; nature was a social category and not something exterior. His second reservation is that the central role played by the mediation of labor in social production, the exchange between society and nature, is missing. The consequence of the first two theoretical distortions leads to a third: the overvaluation of knowledge as a practice.[11] While Lukács's self-critique on this occasion and on others is almost universally downplayed in the literature that has grown up around his works, in this instance it points to a fundamental weakness in the position that accords to proletarian subjectivity as class consciousness the primary role in historical theory. Can the concepts or the historical method arising from the dialectics of subjectivity effect the material exposition of historical events and movements? Lukács, without rewriting *History and Class Consciousness*, indicates that the answer must be in the negative. The dialectical rationality of history has to be recovered on a new terrain. In the *Critique*, Sartre has willingly accepted the task.

The *Critique of Dialectical Reason* does not attempt to pose the problem of the dialectical rationality of history in the same terms and to solve it by effecting a new synthesis. The *Critique* attempts, rather, to recover the dialectic in historical method and place in on a new footing, or on a new terrain. As a consequence, the *Critique* has all the power and pulse of a work rediscovering the concrete dimensions and developing the requirements of historical methodology toward the formation of a new approach to historical comprehension. Its rigor and irreducibility lie in the fact that Sartre will not shun one of the most embarrassing issues in modern historiography: the study of the way in which the general, anonymous structures and movements of history are sustained by the daily life of men. Not *man*, but *men*; and the shift in terms here points to the need to expose the rationality of collective praxis in the praxis of individual consciousness.

The *Critique* as we have it is the first of two projected volumes; the second, which may never appear, is an exposition of the history of the contemporary era. The first volume is itself composed of two somewhat distinct works that, Sartre warns us, are uneven. The first part, "Search for a Method," describes the overture to history in terms of the existential project as it is concretely lived within specific material conditions. And it retains the tone of existentialism, for, in Sartre's intentions, it is the incorporation

---

10. Ibid., p. 3.
11. Ibid., p. xvi.

of the existentialist program into what Sartre terms the unsurpassable philosophy of our time, Marxism. The second part of the *Critique*, the *Critique* properly so called, opens on to the horizon of history from within the experience of praxis as it is a totalization of natural and social conditions. The problem and its terms remain the same, but the orientation of the second part is more clearly a response to the possibility of a materialist conception of history. Its terrain is the critique of the critical experience of historical structures.

The first volume of the *Critique of Dialectical Reason* is, then, clearly situated within the historiographical question: in Sartre's terms, the a priori determination of the limits of dialectical reason and its validation as the form of historical movement within a totalization of historical truth. (CDR, p. 823; Fr., pp. 10-11) The historical question for Sartre is thus strung out along the axes of both synchrony and diachrony. The suggestion that the limits of dialectical reason can be determined a priori points to a synchronic moment. And, in turn, the idea of history and historical truth as a totalizing process, and not a totality, indicates that the limits of dialectical reason are to be found within the boundaries of the actual course of history, that is, along the axis of diachrony.

The manner in which Sartre develops the question of historical rationality in the *Critique* constitutes a break with the philosophy of *Being and Nothingness*, particularly in the shift from action as choice to action as praxis. The latter concept fulfills its role in focusing upon the way in which the dialectical comprehension of transindividual history arises from a description of the experience that praxis has of itself. Yet, even though existentialism is reduced to an "ideology" within Marxism,[12] Sartre's concern is still anthropology. The *Critique* is concerned with the foundation of a philosophical anthropology. (SM, pp. xxxiv-xxxv; Fr., 10) Ethics, however, has given way to history; the meaning of the human adventure can be discovered only by reflection upon man's materiality. The *Critique* is, in spite of its focus upon praxis, in accord with the phenomenological starting point of *Being and Nothingness*: the sense of being or the meaning of history can be revealed only through human behavior.

That phenomenological or existentialist starting point secures the concrete characteristics of reflection and prevents it from losing its way in the entanglements of an abstract and universal dialectic. (SM, p. 91, n. 3; Fr., p. 63, n. 2) Everything depends upon this first step. For, if the transindividual character of history is reduced to a play of abstract concepts and universal descriptions, as has taken place in what Sartre terms transcendental materialism (CDR, p. 27; Fr., p. 124), then the very historical character of

---

12. Jean-Paul Sartre, *Search For a Method*, trans. Hazel E. Barnes (New York: Vin Fage, 1963), p. 8; henceforth cited in the text as SM. French page reference is to *Critique de la raison dialectique*, p. 18.

history—historicity—is lost. Access to the uniqueness and generality of historical movements can be gained only by reflecting upon an experience which, in order to be self-conscious, must be a dialectical comprehension of itself and its world. That experience is the critical experience of praxis.

The recovery of the dialectic from the hands of dogmatism serves to discover a critical dialectic founded upon the experience of an observer situated within the dialectic. To that point Sartre writes, "the dialectic reveals itself only to an observer situated in interiority, that is to say, to an investigator who lives his investigation both as a possible contribution to the ideology of the entire epoch and as the particular *praxis* of an individual defined by his historical and personal career within the wider history which conditions it." (CDR, p. 38; Fr., p. 133) The recovery of the dialectic installs the concept of the project at the center of historical comprehension. If the dialectic is to be a real portrayal of the movement of history and not a logical method to subsume historical particulars under universals, then it must encompass the self-comprehension of action, of the way in which human action is temporalized by the past and the future. That is, at once to restore to praxis both its positivity and its negativity: "The most rudimentary behavior must be determined both in relation to the real and present factors which condition it and in relation to a certain object, still to come, which it is trying to bring into being. This is what we call the project." (SM, p. 91; Fr., pp. 63-64) What the dialectical comprehension of history captures, then, is the "original temporalization" in which an action is a temporal movement. In possessing a future, action, or praxis, opens up a field of possibilities; its meaning is its possibility. The transindividual, or collective, nature of history appears at this point, for the field of possibilities is not a *zone of indetermination*, but a *strongly structured region* in which every individual possibility is at the same time a social possibility.

In choosing an action, the individual inserts himself into history, that is, into the field of past and present conditions and of future possibilities that are sustained by the material existence of human objects, the practico-inert. The individual is from that point on an objective being; in choosing he has objectified himself. The counter-movement to that objectification is internalization. The field of social conditions and possibilities are taken up and surpassed toward their future by becoming part and parcel of the temporality of the project; they become its conditions and possibilities lived from within. In this sense, the project, or praxis, is itself the dialectic, for it unites within itself the play and counterplay of subjectivity and objectivity, not in a unilateral determination of one by the other, but in a reciprocity, in a movement of objectification and internalization taking place within action. The recovery of the dialectic within history is, from that vantage point, the recovery, as with Lukács, of subjectivity within the objectivity of social conditions. History is the movement of a subjectivity within the collective dimensions of history. It is no longer a subject, but praxis.

The substitution of praxis for the concept of the subject in the comprehension of history is a crucial step made possible by the introduction of the idea of totalization. The "original temporalization" of human action means that social conditions, social possibilities, and the social complex do not appear as a totality, as they did for Lukács, but as a process of totalization: "The only conceivable temporality is that of totalization as individual process." (CDR, p. 53; Fr., p. 143) Subjectivity does not give birth to the meaning of history. Nor is the meaning of history borne on the shoulders of subjectivity toward its realization. History is a meaning in the course of being made on the basis of past conditions in the process of being transformed by the work of the future: totalization. It is, from the vantage point supplied by the dialectical comprehension of praxis, always history in the making. (CDR, p. 47; Fr., p. 139) The task of historical understanding is to comprehend that meaning as it comes to be within the actions of individuals, confronting one another in a world of scarcity. As historical agents, men define themselves in terms of one another and against one another, for their reciprocity is discovered through need and through the lack of food, clothing, and shelter. (CDR, pp. 125-134; Fr., pp. 205-215) They are in conflict; the synthesis of their actions, thus, never forms a totality, a whole in which equilibrium is the rule, but rather an unstable collective overcoming of past and present conditions.

The concept of action, or praxis, can sustain the meaning of history in the *Critique*, because it provides a terrain in which the transition from individual action to collective action can be made within the material conditions constituted by the practico-inert. Within the project, objectification and internalization both mean that the concrete temporality of the project — what its past, present, and future really are — comes into being only by means of the insertion of the individual into the objective conditions of history and by means of the social conditions taken up and transcended in the choice of the future. The meaning exposed within praxis is thus dialectical. That raises the perspective of collective action, or praxis, within the structure of the individual project. And yet, the dialectical structure of praxis, its reciprocity and interchange with others and nature, means that its sense is particular to itself. The individual subject is not the paradigm for the disclosure of the subjectivity of history; nor is totality the term in which social conditions, modes of production, ideology, and culture can be understood. The work of praxis sustains at the same time both poles of what was Lukács's dilemma.

The comprehension of history occurs within the course of the experience of totalization by means of a progressive-regressive reflection based upon the experience of a praxis caught up in that process of totalization. The incorporation of human objects and others into a process of totalization can be understood by understanding past conditions, the regressive moment, in terms of the future possibilities that arise upon them, the progressive moment, through the action of praxis. Hence, historical comprehension is at once an understanding of historical movement from within history and an understanding that grasps that movement as an objective movement at work within the transformation of nature into objects of use and into the conditions of collective action, totalization. (CDR, p. 49; Fr., p. 141) The characterization of critical experience as within history and yet capable of assuming a perspective on history paves the way for the dialectical intelligibility of history. The unity of theory and practice — which, as we have seen with Lukács, is also the unity of subject and object — for Sartre arises from the unique place that the critical experience of praxis occupies within historical methodology. It is "the fundamental identity between an individual life and human history (or, from the methodological point of view, of the 'reciprocity of their perspectives')." (CDR, p. 70; Fr., p. 156)

That reciprocity of historical perspectives is the founding moment of the methodology of the *Critique*, for it defines the very nature of critical experience. Its impact depends upon the epistemological rigor of the view that "the epistemological starting point must always be consciousness as apodictic certainty [of] self and as consciousness of such and such an object." (CDR, p. 51; Fr., p. 142) The same rigor can be felt in the very notion of critique that is to establish criteria in which the false can be separated from the true, or, more important for Sartre, "to define the limits of totalizing activities so as to restore to them their validity." (CDR, p. 50; Fr., p. 141)

The understanding (*intellection*) of the totalizing forces at work within society rests upon the comprehension (*compréhension*) of each individual praxis as totalizing. (CDR, p. 45-46; Fr., 138-139)[13] "Therefore, if there is to be any such thing as totalization," Sartre writes, "the intelligibility of constituted dialectical reason (the intelligibility of common actions and of *praxis*-process) must be based on constituent dialectical reason (the abstract and individual *praxis* of man at work)." (CDR, p. 67; Fr., p. 154) The limitations to be given to totalizing forces — the critical recovery of the dialectic from the abstract and universal dialectic of transcendental Marxism — arise from the understanding (*intellection*) of totalizing forces at work in society on the basis of the methodological concepts derived from the comprehension (*compréhension*) of individual praxis, from its transparence to itself as a totalizing of objects and others within its project. (CDR, p. 60; Fr., p. 149)

The self-comprehension of individual praxis is, thus, the methodological base upon which the sense of history that arises from collective praxis can be understood. Individual praxis is not the transformation of nature and the assumption of the work of others that creates the meaning of history; that is the role of collective praxis. Rather, individual praxis provides the

---

13. See also CDR, pp. 74-76 (Fr., pp. 160-161) for the distinction between *intellection* and *comprehension*.

point of departure for the elaboration of the a priori methodology of history; it supplies history with the tools of comprehension. The problematic of the question of the intelligibility of history—the historiographical question—is contained in the concepts that arise from the structural components of the self-comprehension of individual praxis: project, totalization, the practico-inert, and the group. The problematic of a materialist theory of history is provided by the transparence of individual praxis to itself. The founding rationality of history is that of the constituting dialectic, the dialectic of individual praxis. This contrasts with the substitution of praxis for the concept of subjectivity at the level of the *exposition* of the diachronic movement of history for which the *Critique* is an introduction. In that respect, individual praxis is a methodological paradigm, but not a paradigm for the *exposition*, or writing, of history. The meaning of history in its exposition lies, for Sartre, at the level of collective praxis. The axes of synchrony and diachrony are once again at right angles to each other. They intersect, but they form neither a vertical nor horizontal synthesis.

Sartre recognizes the problem, for at the end of the *Critique* he has posed it in somewhat similar terms. "Thus," he writes in summing up the achievements of the *Critique*," on the one hand, we have remained on the level of synchronic totalization and we have not portrayed the diachronic depth of practical temporalization; on the other hand, the regressive moment has ended upon a question: that signifies that it must be completed by a synthetic progression which will attempt to raise itself to the double synchronic and diachronic movement by which history totalizes itself without respite." (CDR, p. 817–818; Fr., p. 755) That second, progressive, diachronic part of the *Critique* will, perhaps, always remain an uncompleted task. The reason for that suspension of the exposition of diachronic history indirectly pinpoints the nature of the problem of history in its entirety: it would, in Sartre's mind, require a vast collective effort.[14] The exposition of history lies at another level than that of the *Critique*'s methodological paradigm. The transparence of praxis to itself may be instrumental in gaining a foothold upon the terrain of history: as an experience it shows us where to look and what to see; it specifies, in that exact sense, the objectivity of history and its internal structure. However, the transparence of praxis to itself does not allow us to occupy that terrain.

The contestation of the primacy of subjectivity in the formation of historical theory posed by Lévi-Strauss's *Savage Mind* and the writings of Michel Foucault and the *Les Annales* group in the name of the exposition of history has, then, a counterpart in Sartre's thought. The roles played in the formation of historical theory by ideas such as the mode of production

---

14. Michel Contat and Michel Rybalka, *The Writings of Jean-Paul Sartre*, vol. 1, *A Biographical Life*, trans. Richard C. McCleary (Evanston: Northwestern University Press, 1974), pp. 373, 546.

(Marx), discursive practice (Foucault) and the long duration (Braudel) bring forth aspects of diachronic history that are exterior to subjectivity. They refer to an exchange between subjectivity and what is irreducible to it; what subjectivity works with without ever assimulating: a realm of exteriority. The exposition of history works at the level of nonintuitive facts, discursive facts, which only become facts once they are assembled together into a text.

In the *Critique of the Gotha Programme*, Marx noted that "labour is *not the source* of all wealth. *Nature* is just as much the source of use values (and it is surely of such that material wealth consists!) as labour, which itself is only the manifestation of a force of nature, human labour power."[15] Focusing upon the mode of production in the explanation of history does not, then, confine history within the creations of human activity, or labor. Labor is, itself, a natural force; its meaning is not exhausted in its subjectivity. It is a praxis in as much as it is a natural force and exterior to itself. Exteriority is installed within the concept of action itself, for the concept of praxis occupies a ground common to itself and nature, not a ground confined to the relation of self to self. History at the level of praxis, then, is the repetition of an overture to what is exterior to itself, both within itself and in its objects, nature. The question asked of history cannot be answered, consequently, by citing a cause or discovering an origin in the past for subsequent events. In this respect, the exteriority of nature in Marx's thought has a direct relationship to the exteriority of language in Foucault's. The relationship exists not in specific answers given to the question of history, but in the structure of the question itself: in the way and on what terrain history is interrogated about its meaning.

The exteriority of language to consciousness is the acquisition of structural linguistics and structural anthropology: language is first of all a system independent of expression. In Michel Foucault's *The Archeology of Knowledge* this exteriority is assumed in the concept of discourse.[16] Discourse, for Foucault, is a system of signs whose unity rests not upon the self-expression of subjectivity, but upon the practice of discourse in discursive formations. Discursive *practice* defines a field of statements that arises through the specification of its object, through enunciative modalities — concepts and strategies — and takes the shape of a discursive formation. The latter is not a unified field of discourse with an internal essence, unifying theme, or singular type of expression, but a "system of dispersion."[17] It arises across different levels and planes. The subject of discourse, then, rather than defining the way in which discourse is used — is defined by it. The subject is accorded a position within a discursive formation; he is given

---

15. Karl Marx and Frederick Engels, *Selected Writings* (New York: International Publishers, 1969), p. 319.
16. Michel Foucault, *The Archeology of Knowledge* (New York: Random House, 1972).
17. Ibid., p. 37.

a *site* from which he speaks.[18] "Thus conceived," Foucault writes, "discourse is not the majestically unfolding manifestation of a thinking, knowing, speaking subject, but, on the contrary, a totality, in which a network of distinct sites is deployed."[19]

What is at work here in this transformation of the historical subject is the corresponding transformation, in the sources of historical exposition, of the document into a monument.[20] Linking up with the *Annales* critique of the dependence of historical method upon documents, Foucault sees the crucial turning point in historical method in the contestation of the privilege of the document as the witness to historical events and as the testimony of consciousness to its own historical intentions and content. The document is, rather, an item to be disassembled into its elements, planes, levels, unities, and relations. Historical method — the posing of the question of history in exposition — revolves around this transformation. "History is undoubtedly constructed with written documents. When there are any. But it can be constructed, it must be constructed, without written documents, if there are none. . . . In one word, with all that which exists for man, depends on man, serves man, expresses man, signifies the presence, the activity, the preferences and the ways of being man."[21] There is an anthropological remnant in those words of Lucien Febvre that Foucault would most likely criticize, but they express very well Febvre's intention to submerge the primacy of political and diplomatic history with its dependence upon written documents into a wider historical *problematic*: a posing of the question of history in terms of facts dispersed among different levels and planes of human activity. The document owes its sway over historical method to its preconceived unity and plenitude of meaning. But once transformed into a question, a subject cannot speak in historical events from the plenitude of its preestablished unity. Subjectivity remains to be specified; rather than being the *place of* history, it has a *place in* history.

Beginning with the *Annales* group, with Febvre and Bloch, and then with Braudel and his colleagues, history is no longer conceived as linear, as the history of events (*l'histoire événementielle*), the time, *par excellence*, of political history. The long duration (*la longue durée*) opposes the dominance of linearity in historical method. The long duration is the time of a "history whose passage is almost imperceptible, that of man in his relationship to the environment, a history in which all change is slow, a history of constant repetition, ever recurring cycles."[22] The conception of the history of the long duration is not the only history. There is the history of the con-

---

18. Ibid., p. 51.
19. Ibid., p. 55.
20. Ibid., p. 6.
21. Lucien Febvre, *Combats pour l' histoire* (Paris: , 1953, p. 428.
22. Fernand Braudel, *The Mediterranean and the Mediterranean World in the Age of Phillip II*, vol. 1, trans. Sian Reynolds (New York: Harper & Row, 1972), p. 20.

juncture and of the event. In Braudel's words, "history is the sum of all possible histories."[23] But history can avoid the error of "historizing" history—
that is, of dissipating the work of time in history—only if the question of
history is *posed* across the multiple levels of historical exposition.

The amplification of historical methodology in the *Annales* conception
of historical time brings with it the posing of the question of history in terms
of that which is exterior to subjectivity: the relationship of man to nature,
to his environment, to the slow work of time. The exposition of that history
is a writing whose style and structure—whose method—rest upon another
historical problematic than that which can be provided by historical subjectivity. It poses the question of a history whose sense is derived from what
is outside of man, exterior to him and incapable of internalization, as much
as it is derived from the exchange of men *with* it.

The conception of the exposition of history in the *Critique of Dialectical
Reason* brought us to the threshold of this other history. Rigorously focused
upon the crucial importance of the concept of praxis in historical method,
it exposes, along with Marx, the horizon of a dispersed subjectivity at work
in and, at the same time, worked upon by history. But the question remains
whether Sartre's posing of the question—his way of defining what concepts
must come into play in the exposition of history—makes it possible to cross
that threshold. The substitution of praxis for subjectivity is irreducible to
Sartre's starting point: the transparence of praxis to itself. Braudel's conception of the long duration and Foucault's theory of discursive formations
do not dispel the dilemma. Although they do show that the philosophy of
consciousness is a failure as a basis for the formulation of the problematic of
history, they do not make any clearer what the *Critique* has shown to be
crucial: the exchange of exteriority and consciousness in praxis. Perhaps
the solution is not only a new way of writing history, but a new way of creating it.

---

23. Fernand Braudel, *Écrits sur l' histoire* (Paris: Flammarion, 1969), p. 55.

PART THREE

Comparisons and Contrasts

Frederick A. Elliston

9. Sartre and Husserl on Interpersonal Relationships

The relationship between Sartre's existentialism and Husserl's phenomenology has been tempestuous at best, at least according to the critics. Does
Sartre employ the familiar techniques of transcendental reduction and
eidetic variation? Is he right to reject the egological conception of consciousness that emerges in Husserl's later writings? In his radical reinterpretation of the key concept intentionality as *néant*, has he abandoned classical phenomenology?

Though these are undoubtedly major questions that must be answered
for an adequate appraisal of Sartre's place in twentieth-century philosophy,
I shall not take them up directly here. Rather, I shall try to shed some light
on the agreements and disagreements between Sartre and Husserl by comparing what they have to say about interpersonal relationships.

This theme is of critical importance for Husserl, because he defines
objectivity — whether in the case of mathematical truths, logical theorems,
scientific propositions, or the world of everyday life — as the correlate of intersubjectivity. Failure to solve what analytic philosophers have termed "the
problem of other minds" marks the collapse of his entire philosophical enterprise into solipsism. For Sartre, on the other hand, it marks the rounding
out of his philosophy — not just that existence is social but that without others a dimension of my being is missing, the lived coincidence of myself as
object. Husserl's phenomenology of empathy lays the foundations for his
transcendental philosophy much as Sartre's phenomenology of the look
completes his kind of existential analytic and lays the basis for his later
Marxist social philosophy.

In an earlier paper I sought to defend Husserl's account of intersubjectivity in his Fifth Cartesian Meditation against "internal" critics who attack
it from within his phenomenological framework — taking for granted basic
tenets of his philosophy as well as his formulation of the problem.[1] This
paper will also serve to extend my defense by examining the more radical

---

1. Frederick A. Elliston, "Husserl's Phenomenology of Empathy," in *Husserl: Expositions*

challenge of Sartre, an "external" critic who calls these tenets into question and rejects Husserl's formulation of the problem.

In part one I shall summarize briefly Husserl's account and my earlier defense of it. In part two I shall turn to a comparison of Sartre's alternative account with Husserl's — stressing some similarities ignored by both Sartre and his interpreters. Then in part three I shall examine Sartre's objections to Husserl's account and assess his own success in overcoming these. Finally I shall conclude with a short reflection on Sartre's positive accomplishments.

I. Husserl's Phenomenology of Empathy

For Husserl the problem of intersubjectivity is a hermeneutical one: How do I come to interpret something within the purview of my experience as an other self, or alter ego? His task is to locate a type of experience called "empathy" (*Einfühlung*) — namely any experience I have of another person — and to analyze it into its constituents. This "intentional analysis" — so called because it is breaking down a mode of intentional consciousness into its constituents — has two dimensions: the noematic dimension in which the sense alter ego is analyzed into its four components; and the noetic dimension in which pairing (*Paarung*) is uncovered as the mental process whereby this sense is constituted.

The first step in intentional analysis is descriptive: to report the content of the everyday and commonplace experience of empathy by immersing oneself in it. According to Husserl, this procedure yields the following results:

> In changeable harmonious multiplicities of experience I experience others as actually existing and on the one hand as world objects — not as mere physical things belonging to Nature (though indeed in one respect as that too). They are in effect experienced also as always governing psychically in their respective natural organisms. . . . On the other hand I experience them at the same time as subjects for this world, as experiencing it, this same world that I experience, and in so doing, they experience me too, even as I experience the world and others in it. (CM, p. 123)[2]

Others are ordinarily experienced as *actually* existing *physical* things that *control* their bodies and *experience* a world I share. These four features form the explanandum.

---

and Appraisals, ed. F. A. Elliston and P. McCormick (Notre Dame: University of Notre Dame Press, 1977), pp. 213–231.

2. All reference to the standard edition of Husserl's *Cartesianische Meditationen* Husserliana, Vol. 1 (The Hague: Nijhoff, 1950) is abbreviated CM. Translations from this text are my own. I shall use the abbreviation BN to refer to *Being and Nothingness*, translated by Hazel E. Barnes (New York: Philosophical Library, 1956).

To locate the conditions for the possibility of such an experience, Husserl resolves to carry out a new kind of *epoche*: "We disregard all constitutive achievements [*Leistungen*] of intentionality which relate either directly or indirectly to another subjectivity." (CM, p. 124) By stripping the world of all sense [*Sinn*] that refers directly to others—as in the ascription of pain to another body—or indirectly to them—as in interpreting something as a book with its shared social significance—Husserl hopes to abstract to a basic level of experience that founds knowledge of others and all higher forms of social interaction. This new reduction, which marks a transition from description to explanation, strips the world of all "spiritual predicates" and of all objectivity, since by "objective" Husserl understands what is "there for everyone." (CM, p. 124)

Husserl calls the stratum of experience that remains the sphere of ownness [*Eigenheitsphäre*]. On the noematic side it includes a field of kinesthetic sensations that are intentionally related to one body in particular as their noetic correlate, the animate organism [*Leib*] that is my body. This peculiar relation that singles out my body from this domain is illustrated by the radical visual and auditory transformation that takes place in the world when I close the eyes of my body or stop my ears. No such global change occurs when I perform a similar action on any other body.

Yet within this sphere there are bodies that look and act similarly to mine. These resemblances in bodily appearances and movements motivate an apperceptive transfer of sense [*Sinn*] based on imagination and taking the form of a counterfactual conditional: What would I feel and what would I see if I were "there," in the place of the body that resembles mine in these two ways?

Since my body is an actually existing physical entity with its kinesthetic field "in which I rule and govern immediately" (CM., p. 128), apperceptive transfer confers a similar sense on the body of the other, a sense that has the four constituents of alter ego analyzed earlier. The ensuing conjunction of these two bodies is a form of association termed "pairing," which has two defining characteristics:

> First that the instituting original is continuously present as something alive. . . . and second . . . that what is appresented . . . can never actually become present. (CM, p. 142)

Husserl hereby avoids recourse to forms of rationality such as an argument from analogy: just as I need not compare this pen with past objects it resembles to apprehend it analogously as like (or unlike) them, so too I need not compare the other explicitly with myself as I would be in his situation to apprehend his pain as like (and unlike) the pain I might then feel.

The two main objections to Husserl's account are that the requisite similarities are lacking and that the reduction lacks the linguistic means necessary for its execution. But the first, as I have argued elsewhere, overlooks the counterfactual character of pairing that ties the other not to myself as I am but to the self I would be if I were there. And the second confuses the philosopher who uses language with the *Leib* rendered mute by the new *epoche*: that these two selves are identified along a methodological continuum entails no inconsistency, any more than my reporting my birth date is inconsistent with the acknowledgment that the child referred to (cf. *Leib*) could not then talk, though I (cf. philosopher), who am the *same* as this child, can. Moreover, the schema of apperceptive transfer in pairing, based on indirect similarities in appearances and behavior, provides a useful model for social scientists to analyze prejudicial attitudes of individuals towards others and the mythological ascription of human features to inanimate objects.

Yet Husserl's account does fail to meet the transcendental realists' demand to prove the existence of others as entities in their own right rather than merely as a sense constituted through pairing within my actual and possible consciousness. Husserl rejects this demand as "nonsensical" (*widersinnig*). (CM, p. 122) According to the transcendental phenomenological principle of meaningfulness, "every sense which any entity has and can have for me . . . is [a] sense which is clarified and revealed for me *in* and *in terms of* my intentional life, in terms of its constitutive synthesis, and in systems of harmonious verification." (CM, p. 123) This transcendental principle violates the realists' hypothesis of others as noumenal entities existing in and of themselves, rendering transcendental realism a logically incoherent position. Conceding this incoherence, the problem of intersubjectivity requires the intentional analysis of empathy Husserl provides.

II. Sartre and Husserl on the Other

Sartre's celebrated phenomenology of the look combines insights from Husserl, Hegel, and Heidegger. Yet he seems to reject as much as he borrows from Husserl. This impression, instigated by Sartre and perpetuated by his critics, obscures some shared features of their two accounts that unite them as phenomenologists.[3]

First, each rejects any claim that the relation between self and other is an inferential or rational relation. In so doing they stand in opposition to many philosophers within the Anglo-American tradition, who explain knowledge of other minds by reason of an argument by analogy: by noting similarities between the appearance and behavior of others and myself, I

---

3. For two recent studies of this theme, see Marjorie Grene's *Sartre* (New York: Franklin Watts, 1973), pp. 139–180, and Arthur Danto's *Jean-Paul Sartre* (New York: Viking Press, 1975), pp. 107–146. Two earlier studies of Sartre's philosophy also emphasize this theme: Mary Warnock's *The Philosophy of Sartre* (London: Hutchinson & Co., 1965), pp. 63–87, and Wilfred Desan's *The Tragic Finale* (New York: Harper & Row, 1960), pp. 61–73.

infer (either inductively or deductively) truths about their mental life.[4] Husserl undercuts this rational reconstruction of social life by introducing the notion of assimilative apprehension. Though generally Husserl's philosophy is an effort to reclaim the rigor of science as one form of rationality, here he eschews rationality as logic by denying that it is fundamental: my awareness of others is not based on the explicit formulation of arguments in my head or specific inferences executed as identifiable mental processes locatable within my stream of consciousness. Appeal to this logical form of rationality belies the content of ordinary experience and introduces an unbridgeable gap between philosophical analysis and everyday life.

> There is to be a sort of comparative apperception but by no means therefore an inference by analogy. Apperception is not an inference, not a thinking act. (CM, p. 141)

Within the unity of one act or process, I take an expression as a look of love, just as I take this implement as a pair of scissors. And just as I need not draw an explicit comparison between these scissors and the ones I saw yesterday, I need not infer the emotion the other feels on the basis of similarities and differences to what I might feel in his place. Arguments do not and need not play any role at this level of experience: rather, at one stroke I apprehend the mental qualities of another self.

Sartre, too, rejects any appeal to comparisons and inferences.

> Shame is by nature *recognition*. I recognize that I am as the Other sees me. There is however no question of a comparison between what I am for myself and what I am for the Other. . . . (BN, p. 222)

And later:

> . . . the meaning of "the Other" can not come . . . from a reasoning by analogy effected on the occasion of the experience; on the contrary, it is in the light of the concept of the Other that the experience is interpreted. (BN, p. 234)

Of course, what they juxtapose to any argument from analogy is quite different: Husserl speaks of "pairing" as the basis for any such inferences; Sartre appeals to emotions as an alternative form of experience. Husserl is trying to locate a stratum of experience more fundamental than reasoning. Sartre is seeking a noncognitive mode outside rather than underneath the domain of reasoning. They are in agreement, however, on what they oppose.

---

4. See, for example, Bertrand Russell's *Human Knowledge: Its Scope and Limits* (New York: Simon and Schuster, 1948), pp. 482–86, and A. J. Ayer's "One's Knowledge of Other Minds" in his *Philosophical Essays* (London: Macmillan & Co., 1954), pp. 191–214.

Second, each maintains that the relation between self and others is not external but rather *internal* and *reciprocal*. In his description of pairing, Husserl speaks of an "intentional overreaching, of a living reciprocal mutual awakening, a reciprocal converging or self-coinciding." (CM, p. 142) Through this process, the self and others are united in both their similarities and differences: I grasp the other as both like and unlike myself. This reciprocity of meaning makes self-understanding and knowledge of others emergent features of one process.[5] Sartre is equally insistent on this point. He criticizes the realist for not establishing "an immediate reciprocal action of thinking substances upon each other." (BN, p. 223) But the term *action* signals Sartre's departure from Husserl: within the dialectic of the look, I objectify the other when I stare him down — stealing his world by asserting my power over it and reducing him to an object within the field of my concerns. Sartre's reciprocity is not solely a function of meaning, interpretation, or identity, as in Husserl, but refers additionally to the constant possibility of a reversal, whereby the other can divest me of my everyday world and reduce me to something at his disposal.

Third, for neither Sartre nor Husserl is the other a noumenal entity. Though each works within a Kantian perspective that seeks to delineate the conditions for the possibility of social life, neither categorizes others as things in themselves beyond the phenomenal world.

Sartre is quite explicit: "When I aim at the Other in my daily experience, it is by no means a noumenal reality that I am aiming at." (BN, p. 225) In accord with the phenomenalism he espouses at the outset of *Being and Nothingness*, Sartre insists that "the Other is a phenomenon which refers to other phenomena." (BN, p. 225)

Husserl's reasoning is couched in terms of a critique of transcendental realism adumbrated briefly at the outset of the Fifth Cartesian Meditation. He terms the postulate of others as noumena "nonsense" (*Widersinn*, CM, p. 121): since meaning is constituted within consciousness, a noumenal entity beyond this realm is meaningless. Moreover, to postulate such an entity when no proof for its existence is or can be given is to violate the radical spirit of phenomenology, that takes nothing for granted but justifies all assumptions.

Fourth and more positively, Sartre and Husserl agree that the other is a subject intended through various modes of experience, whose otherness must be preserved against its collapse into a mirror image of myself. But they interpret this subjectivity differently. For Sartre, the subjectivity of the other is experienced in terms of my own objectivity: when the other enters my field of action, my world becomes a world at his disposal; and when he

---

5. Because Husserl does not argue from self-knowledge to knowledge of others, he is not vulnerable to the attack of Anglo-American critics on private languages and private knowledge. For a more general discussion of privacy, see Robert Solomon's "Husserl's Private Language," *Southwestern Journal of Philosophy* 5 (Fall 1974): 203-228.

looks at me I am reduced to an object under his dominion. In short, for Sartre subjectivity is defined in terms of bodily actions and the consequent exclusivity of control and controlled. Husserl's account, by contrast, is not marked by this denial of mutual subjectivity, nor of mutual objectivity, either. Indeed, he insists on the simultaneous conjunction of subject and object: the *Leib* is both a subject that experiences the world through its body and an object of its own experiences within this same world; similarly, the other is both an intentional object of my experiences and a subject directing its own experiences of the world (and of me as an entity within that world). Husserl's *Leib*, or animate organism, both touches and is touched, both sees and can be seen, both hears and can be heard. Consequently, Husserl's account is not vitiated by the dualism that prevents Sartre from acknowledging any subject-subject relation.

This fundamental difference is partly due to their different orientations: Husserl's focus on experience as interpretation allows one thing to be simultaneously both the subject and the object of experience, and allows two people to *experience* the same thing in the same way—that is, with the same interpretation (*Sinn*); but Sartre's emphasis on action generates conflicts when two people try to *possess* the same thing or to cooperate in mutual endeavors. Knowledge can be shared in a way that possessions cannot. But more basic than this shift from epistemological to pragmatic affairs is Sartre's reconceptualization of intentionality as a nothingness (*néant*);[6] by transforming consciousness into the pure process of nihilating Sartre introduces an irreconcilable opposition between the self that nihilates and the self that is nihilated. This schism between subjectivity as the process of nihilating and objectivity as that which is nihilated makes conflict an irreducible dimension of all human interaction: the Hegelian dialectic of master and slave has been arrested, with no possibility of a subsequent synthesis of two equal and harmonious subjects.[7] Consequently, any harmonious form of social life is condemned to eventual disruption and collapse.

Sartre's emphasis on nihilating generates an account of otherness radically different from Husserl's: for Sartre the other opposes me as something totally unlike me; for Husserl, by contrast, pairing involves similarities as well as the differences Sartre celebrates.[8] For Sartre there can be no features shared by self and other, because the other has no positive traits to share. As a pure negating, his look is simply and solely the process of objectifying me.

Husserl's account of intersubjectivity delineates this otherness not just in

6. This reconceptualization is explicitly and dramatically presented in his early enthusiastic endorsement of Husserl. See "Une Idée fondamentale de la phénoménologie de Husserl," *Nouvelle revue française*, 1939, p. 129-32. A translation by Joseph P. Fell appeared in *Journal of the British Society for Phenomenology* 1 (1970): 4-5.

7. G. W. F. Hegel, *The Phenomenology of Mind* (New York: Humanities Press, 1966), pp. 228-240. See as well A. Kojeve's celebrated and influential commentary *Introduction to the Reading of Hegel*, tr. J. H. Nichol, Jr. (New York: Basic Books, 1969), pp. 41-70.

8. See CM, section 51.

terms of differences in specific traits but in terms of two additional features: the immediacy of control and the directness of self-awareness. My body is something "in which I rule and govern immediately" (CM, p. 128): I lift my arm without performing any intervening action of the sort necessary in order to lift yours; this power I exercise over my own body is unlike any I exercise over any other body. Conjoined with this power is a distinctive form of awareness:[9] when I close my eyes the world undergoes a visual transformation totally unlike the change that occurs when I close the eyes of any other living thing; and when I stop my ears the world loses an audible dimension that survives virtually any other change in the world. In short, my body is related to a field of kinesthetic sensations in a way that distinguishes it from every other body in the world — including that of the other.[10] And finally, I have direct access to my own mental life, whereas the thoughts and feelings of others are presented indirectly — appresented, along with their gestures, expressions, and other behavior.[11] If I could directly grasp another's lived experiences, he and I would not be two selves: "he would be a mere moment of my own nature and hence he myself and I myself would be as one." (CM, p. 139)

III. Sartre's Critique of Husserl

Despite several substantive points of agreement in the details of their accounts, Sartre is very critical of basic tenets of Husserl's entire philosophy as exhibited by his phenomenology of intersubjectivity. He charges Husserl with inconsistency in his use of *intuition* and with failure to account for my *certainty* about the existence of others.

Taking intuition as a direct or immediate apprehension, Sartre asks rhetorically:

> But within Husserl's philosophy, at least, how can one have a full intuition of an absence? The other is the object of empty intentions, the other on principle refuses himself to us and flees. (BN, pp. 234–235)

As already noted, Husserl insists that the mental life of others is not and cannot be directly available to me, otherwise otherness would disappear: "nothing of what belongs to his very nature becomes originally given." (CM,

---

9. See CM, p 128.
10. This distinction is marked terminologically by calling my body apprehended from my point of view *Leib* instead of *Körper*. See CM, sections 44–46.
11. For a discussion of appresentation as applied to intersubjectivity, see section 50 of CM. As Alfred Schutz points out, the term has a venerable history. See "The Problem of Transcendental Intersubjectivity in Husserl" in Schutz's *Collected Papers* (The Hague: Nijhoff, 1970) 3: 61–67, and "Symbol, Reality and Society" in the first volume of his *Collected Papers* (The Hague, Nijhoff, 1962), pp. 294–305.

p. 139) But is Husserl committed to identifying intuition with direct apprehension? He uses the first concept generally to characterize the moment that marks the fulfillment of a process—either the process of imaginative variation that culminates in an intuition of essences, or the process of making evident (*Evidenz*) that yields an intuition of what truly exists.[12] In section fifty-two of *Cartesian Meditations*, Husserl makes implicit use of intuition as part of the process of verifying truths about others:

> The experienced animate organism of another continuously proves itself really to be an animate organism only in its changing but always harmonious behavior in such a way that the latter has its physical side and indicates the psychic by way of appresentation that must now emerge by way of a fulfillment in original experience. (CM, p. 144)

The fact that the thoughts and feelings of others are never grasped like my own does not preclude an "intuitive" knowledge of others; this restriction only makes such knowledge a function of the harmonious fulfillment of expectations about the physical appearances and bodily behavior of others.[13] Husserl concedes that the evidence thereby secured is neither adequate nor apodictic.[14] The horizon of my future experiences of others cannot be exhausted: there are an infinite number of things I could do to verify my beliefs about others but only a finite time in which to do them. And nonfulfillment of any set of expectations cannot be ruled out in advance—hence, error is always possible and apodictic certainty cannot be achieved. This lack of adequacy and apodicticity leads Sartre to a second objection: Husserl has failed to account for my certainty about the existence of others. This deficiency is symptomatic for Sartre of a more general deficiency of Husserl's entire philosophy—his epistemological idealism: because Husserl takes knowledge as the measure of Being and because my knowledge of others is only probable, the Being of others is only conjectural.

Does Husserl subscribe to this general philosophical position? If so, does it vitiate his account of others in particular? Does Sartre's alternative account successfully avoid this objection?

Several texts could be cited to confirm Sartre's interpretation of Husserl:

---

12. Husserl's own statement of essential intuition is adumbrated in sections 3 and 4 of *Ideas* and elaborated more fully in sections 86 to 93 of *Experience and Judgment*. His position has been widely attacked. For a recent defense see J. Patočka, "The Husserlian Doctrine of Eidetic Intuition and Its Recent Critics," in *Husserl: Expositions and Appraisals*, ed. F. Elliston and P. McCormick (Notre Dame: University of Notre Dame Press, 1977), pp. 150–159. For a discussion of intuition and evidence, see Henry Pietersma's contribution to this same collection, "The Evident and the True," pp. 38–53.

13. See section 52 of CM.

14. Not all texts distinguish these two terms. See section 6 of CM, where *inadequacy* is identified with unfulfilled components accompanying an experience and *apodicticity* is identified with the indubitability attributed to the first principles of science.

the Third Cartesian Meditation is entitled "Truth and Actuality," indicating that what is actual is correlated with what can be shown to be true through a process of making evident; and the fourth division of *Ideas* has the Hegelian heading "Reason and Reality." The validity of Sartre's objection to Husserl turns on the discrepancy he claims between the certainty we feel about the existence of others and the mere probability of the best knowledge attainable of them. But is this initial claim to certainty itself legitimate?

Sartre concedes that the existence of any particular other *as object* is not certain. Here he agrees with Husserl that the best knowledge "can be only probable." (BN, p. 276) According to Sartre, it is the existence of the other as subject that is beyond all possible doubt: in my shameful apprehension of myself under the others' gaze, the other is experienced as an indubitable dimension of my very own consciousness — as certain as my own self-conscious existence. Such emotional experiences exhibit a dimension of interpersonal relations that — according to Sartre — Husserl's account does not and cannot accommodate: the unshakable confidence I have in the existence of the other as subject.

As a first defense of Husserl it is worth emphasizing what a strange creature Sartre's other as subject is. One moment he is on the creaking stairs, the next moment he is at the rattling window, and at no moment was he at any of the intervening places: he comes to me from "beyond the world" as a presence "without distance." (BN, p. 270) Indeed, to refer to the other as "he" is misleading, for the other has no gender. Because the other's ties to any particular object in my world are radically "contingent," (BN, p. 277) I may discover nothing whatsoever when I turn to oppose the other's stare: I was looked at, when no one was looking! Anonymous, elusive, and sexless, the other is a totally undifferentiated presence without locus.

And what of the certainty Sartre claims for this presence? Sartre's examples are affective not cognitive, so the certainty has no epistemic value. Perhaps I misidentified my feeling as shame instead of embarrassment. If I can be mistaken about the emotions through which the other is disclosed, can I not be mistaken about the other? Sartre's certainly cannot be the infallibility of a claim to know, for my emotional life is not immune to error. The semblance of an unshakable belief about the existence of the other is maintained by two restrictions never defended: first, by confining the experience to the pre-reflective level, where it has not yet been subject to critical reflection; and second, by confining the experience to emotions such as shame or pride, thereby excluding rational appeals to evidence in support of truth claims about them. The apparent indubitability is not the product of a trial by fire whereby the other's existence proves itself immune to reasonable doubt, but rather it follows from the failure to subject such experiences to rational scrutiny. Consequently, Sartre has not proved that the existence of others is impervious to reasonable doubt, and so cannot fairly fault Husserl for failure to do so either.

IV. Concluding Reflections

What has Sartre accomplished, then, through his phenomenology of shame and pride? He has not supplanted Husserl's account of intersubjectivity, but rather supplemented it. He has expanded the domain of phenomenological inquiry beyond the epistemological confines that delineated Husserl's main preoccupations into the noncognitive realm of our emotional life. But to justify this departure from orthodox Husserlian phenomenology, Sartre erroneously believed he had to disprove Husserl's epistemological claims. If he had assessed his own originality in terms of expansion rather than confrontation, his genuine contribution to phenomenology might have been appreciated more, and one of the needless and fruitless battles between phenomenology and existentialism might have been avoided.

Michel Haar

10. *Sartre and Heidegger**

. . . a meaning can come only from subjectivity[1] —Jean-Paul Sartre

In the heyday of postwar existentialism, the names Sartre and Heidegger were often linked, evoking two aspects of a single doctrine. Today, more than thirty years later, it seems clear that no kinship ever bound the two philosophers, but that, on the contrary, they are radically opposed in every respect. Indeed, one may notice that to each of his principal theses Sartre attaches a vigorous and methodical refutation of the corresponding Heideggerian doctrine. In *Being and Time* Heidegger calls into question the very essence of man through the notion of *Dasein* and being-in-the-world, and he undertakes a "destruction" of metaphysics in order to recover the forgotten meaning of being. In the face of this audacity, Sartre appears conciliatory and *conservative*: he seeks to safeguard the great principles of Cartesian and Hegelian metaphysics. The *cogito* appears to him to be "the sole secure point of departure" (BN, p. 244; Fr., p. 300),[2] and Hegelian negativity scaled down to the dimensions of individual consciousness offers him the key to the mind.[3] It is also in order to save the essence of traditional subjectivity that he places himself in opposition to Heidegger, when interpreting the phenomena of nothingness and anxiety: he reduces them to "inner" dimensions. In the same way, because he respects the logic of the subject-object duality, he strongly rejects the positive meaning Heidegger gives to the other as well as to the relationship with death. He tries in general to preserve the fundamental structures of metaphysics: the presence of consciousness to itself is an act of self-foundation and the origin of all meaning; being in totality gets its coherence and justification through the absolute responsibility of human liberty. Always reacting defensively against Heideg-

---

*Translated by Elizabeth Kinlock
    1. Jean-Paul Sartre, *Being and Nothingness*, trans. Hazel E. Barnes (New York: Philosophical Library, 1956), p. 539; hereafter incorporated in the text as BN. Original French: *L'Être et le néant* (Paris: Gallimard, 1943), p. 623 hereafter cited as Fr.
    2. The word "secure" is lacking in the translation.
    3. "Hegel rather than Heidegger is right when he states that Mind is the negative" (BN, pp. 18–19; Fr., p. 54).

ger, Sartre goes so far as to reproach him for a method too offhand, will-ingly revolutionary, and speaks of "his abrupt, rather barbaric fashion of cutting Gordian knots rather than trying to untie them." (BN, p. 244; Fr., p. 300) It seems that Heidegger has served Sartre not as a source of inspira-tion but as a foil.

How, then, were the two able to be assimilated and confused under a sin-gle heading? Doubtless it was Sartre who had the illusion of an intuition common to Heidegger and the existentialists: the primacy of existence over essence. When Heidegger writes, *"The 'essence' of Dasein lies in its exis-tence,"*[4] In *Existentialism is a Humanism*, Sartre transposes the sentence in-to "existence precedes essence." For Heidegger, such an interpretation re-duces this characterization of *Dasein* to a simple reversal that is maintained *inside* the structures of traditional metaphysics and which consequently just reiterates them. For him there is not "the slightest point in common" be-tween these two sentences. In particular, Sartre has not understood that if the word *essence* is written in italics, this is meant to indicate that there is no question of a *what*, but only of a *how*. Sartre has never responded to Hei-degger's criticism in his *Letter on Humanism* (1946) that Sartre's claim perpetuates the metaphysics of subjectivity. The numerous references to Heidegger in *Being and Nothingness* disappear entirely from Sartre's later work. How may this silence be interpreted if not as the sign of an insoluble quandary? Indeed, the *Critique of Dialectical Reason* contains one reveal-ing note: "The case of Heidegger is too complex for me to discuss here."[5] Actually, what Sartre judges as "too complex" is to confront the problem of metaphysics and to call into question human subjectivity as the source and foundation of all meaning.

I. Consciousness versus Dasein

[Heidegger . . . has completely avoided any appeal to con-sciousness in his description of Dasein. —Sartre (BN, p. 85; Fr., p. 128)]

From the outset of *Being and Nothingness*, Sartre resolutely sets himself apart from Heidegger: he rejects as contradictory the notion of *Dasein* and avoids prolonged questioning of the meaning of being, thus remaining within the framework of a philosophy of consciousness. "The pursuit of Be-ing," undertaken in the introduction, is in point of fact promptly suspended, at least temporarily; but no new ontological proposition is added later to

---

4. Martin Heidegger, *Being and Time*, trans. John Macquarrie and Edward Robinson (New York: Harper & Row, 1962), p. 67; hereafter referred to as BT.
5. Jean-Paul Sartre, *Search for a Method*, trans. Hazel E. Barnes (New York: Knopf, Vintage Books, 1963), p. 15 n. Original French: *Critique de la raison dialectique* (Paris: Gal-limard, 1960), p. 21 n.

those propositions made in the opening pages. In these pages we learn that "the concept of Being has this peculiarity of being divided into two regions without communication." (BN, p. lxiii; Fr., p. 31) Being in general cannot form a whole. For on the one hand we have being as *in-itself*, which is defined as a perfect identity to itself: it is full, solid, opaque; "it is what it is." (BN, p. lxvi; Fr., p. 34) Being in itself is so "heavy," so "glued to itself," that it can be neither active nor passive, neither self-affirmative nor self-denying. Not only things, objects, but in general every being that is not conscious, every being in the world partakes of the in-itself. On the other hand, consciousness and the *for-itself* is called "nihilation" and active nothingness. In fact, consciousness emerges as the negation of the in-itself, as "a decompression of being," a hole, an emptiness, a lack in the in-itself that it will never be possible to fill. Contrary to the in-itself, the for-itself is pure transparency; it is present to itself, but without ever being able to identify with itself. Always being other than it is, because of its negating activity, the for-itself is haunted by an unattainable ideal: to coincide with itself in the same mode as the in-itself. But it is condemned to freedom, to the impossibility of having a stable identity. With regard to the for-itself, the in-itself provokes fascination and a threat: it fascinates as that fullness which consciousness alone lacks; it threatens as death, which arrests the continual movement of negation by which the for-itself escapes the in-itself. The Sartrian metaphysical climate is a climate of struggle and despair inasmuch as the in-itself is alway the victor. All existence is doomed to failure, because every free subject returns to the state of the inert object, first under the effect of the other's stare and finally in death.

Sartre subjects Heidegger's *Dasein* to this ontological pattern and asks, in a very Cartesian way, on which side it is to be situated. Is it part of the in-itself, or of the for-itself? *Dasein*, which we are, says Heidegger, comprehends being as well as its own possibilities. Its being is not simply given, it has to be. It is defined by care. It is not defined by consciousness. Thus, says Sartre, it is bound to "lapse into a thinglike, blind in-itself." (BN, p. 73; Fr., p. 115)

But why, according to Sartre, does Heidegger take *Dasein* as a starting point, and not consciousness? It is with the best of intentions: to avoid falling into the error Husserl commits by interpreting all the relations between consciousness and the world ultimately on the basis of a relationship of knowledge. Husserl did so because he sought, as Kant did, a pure and universal transcendental ego. The for-itself has at least one thing in common with the *Dasein*: it is "always mine," always individual. On this specific point, Sartre at first sides with Heidegger in opposing Husserl. He follows the Heideggerian analysis in *Being and Time*, which shows that knowledge is a derived or secondary attitude that presupposes a preoccupation that has already revealed a world of things ready-to-hand. Theoretical knowledge is a reduction of that original concern to a disinterested look, which considers things as neutral, simply present-at-hand. It is impossible to analyze a transcendental subject apart from its concrete relationship to the world, to decompose the unity of being-in-the-world-alongside-things, whence the deliberate bias that leads to the notion of *Dasein*: "Heidegger is so persuaded that the 'I think' of Husserl is a trap for larks, fascinating and ensnaring, that he has completely avoided any appeal to consciousness in his description of *Dasein*. His goal is to show it immediately as care, that is, as escaping itself in the projecting of self toward the possibilities which it is." (BN, p. 85; Fr., p, 128) This projecting of possibilities, which Heidegger calls understanding (*Verstehen*), forms part of the very being of *Dasein*. Here Sartrian criticism intervenes: "Understanding has meaning only if it is consciousness of understanding. My possibility can exist as *my* possibility only if it is my consciousness which escapes itself toward my possibility. Otherwise the whole system of being and its possibilities will fall into the Unconscious — that is, into the in-itself. Behold we are thrown back again toward the *cogito*. We must make this our point of departure." (BN, p. 85; Fr., p. 128) Sartre's reasoning is founded once again upon the sole alternative between the for-itself and the in-itself. It excludes the possibility of a "third kind of Being,"[6] as Merleau-Ponty says. Understanding must be conscious or unconscious, it cannot fall between the two, for there are only two modes of being. Let us note that Sartre, while believing himself to be a nonrationalist, submits to the logical principles of rationalism, those of contradiction and of the excluded middle. By refusing an understanding not linked to consciousness, he is reaffirming the preeminence of knowledge.

In fact, if the "I think" is the trap of knowledge, how can Sartre at once maintain the *cogito* and avoid falling into this trap? He believes he succeeds through the notion of the unreflecting, or *pre-reflective, cogito*. Indeed, he distinguishes immediate, spontaneous consciousness, which does not posit itself, and reflective, or self-positing, consciousness. Reflection is the attempt, destined to fail, at recovering retrospectively the spontaneous negativity of consciousness and of giving it a being in-itself. Descartes's error is to identify consciousness, reflection, and knowledge. The pre-reflective *cogito* is paradoxical in this sense, in that it does not reveal itself directly but only in retrospect. In itself it is elusive. In fact, immediate, or pre-reflective, consciousness is to such a degree *ekstatic*, lost in and confused with the sighting of its object, that it is nothing for itself. It has no content as such. It is always absorbed in what it perceives, imagines, or feels. It is pure transcendence, pure escape from itself. The activity of transcendence and of original nihilation *does not know* and *does not know itself*. And yet there is *already consciousness*. Proof of this is easy to provide. In all unreflecting activity, I may at any moment "become conscious" and express what was there

---

6. Maurice Merleau-Ponty, *Le Visible et l'invisible* (Paris: Gallimard, 1964), p. 104. Translation mine.

implicitly. For example, says Sartre, when I count the cigarettes in this package, I do not know myself to be in the act of counting. But if someone asks me what I am doing, I can answer without hesitation, "I am counting my cigarettes." This is what Sartre expresses in saying that all consciousness of an object contains a non-positing consciousness (of) oneself; the "of" is in parentheses in order to emphasize the absence of all reflection. But does not this *implicit* positing by the self mean that openness to the world is conditioned by openness to oneself?

Within the prereflective *cogito*, Sartre claims to have reconciled at once his Cartesianism of principle, Husserl's discovery of the preobjective (that which precedes judgment), and the Heideggerian notion of *being-in-the-world*. Nothing could be more illusory. Indeed, the prereflective is actually a "presubjective" that in no way presupposes any area of being in which the future "ego," future "others," and the "world" would still be indistinct and intermingled. The pre-reflective, on the contrary, presupposes consciousness as the preliminary positing of the subject. Just as in Hegel mind (*Geist*), with all its knowledge, is implicitly present from the very beginning in immediacy itself, so consciousness in a way precedes itself. The Sartrian prereflective constitutes, as Merleau-Ponty says in *The Visible and the Invisible*, "a reflection preceding reflection."[7] As pure transparency, pure escape from itself and from the in-itself, spontaneous consciousness is freed in advance of any possibility of density, opacity, primitive involvement, or indistinctness of the ego with respect to the world. It may certainly decline towards the in-itself and be alienated or "glued," but its essence is to be detached. As a metaphysical principle, consciousness could never be *compromised* by complicity with the world; from it comes openness to the world that it dominates and masters, and this *excludes* any situation of truly primal and irrecoverable *passivity*.

Here it is necessary to make a careful distinction between Sartrian *facticity* and that passivity which determines Heidegger's *Dasein* to have structures forever anterior to the spontaneity of its projects. Indeed, Sartre's *facticity* means merely that consciousness does not choose the given that it must nullify, that the original bond between the for-itself and the in-itself is contingent. In other words, I do not decide that I have a particular body, specific ethnic and social affiliations, a detailed past, but I have free access to the meaning of this facticity. Up to the instant of my death, I can change the significance of all my past acts by a single act. For Heidegger, on the contrary, there are dimensions of *Dasein* that definitely escape all mastery. Thus, the possibility of getting lost in the *they* (*das Man*) is not only more fundamental than the possibility of being-oneself, but it is a permanent possibility of *Dasein*. No one is free either to do without the meanings given by the *they*, or to avoid inauthenticity entirely. On the other hand, Sartre

---

7. Ibid.

affirms that "it is in complete freedom and by an original choice that I realize my being-with in the anonymous form of the 'They.' " (BN, p. 246; Fr.,
p. 302) For him bad faith is the work of an isolated consciousness that
through its solitude is already saved from dispersion into the *they*. For Heidegger, *falling* (*Verfallen*) into the *they* is preliminary to the constituting of
the self: to begin with, I am not given to "myself" in the sense of my own
self, but in terms of the "they-self" (*Man-selbst*). It is phenomenologically
unjustified to think that consciousness is originally self-determined even before reflection, that its autonomy and its immanence are such that its
moods and emotions are produced by itself, indeed that consciousness affects itself with joy or sadness with a definite aim, most often out of bad
faith, in order to avoid direct confrontation with reality. By contrast, *Dasein* always finds itself in some mood or other that reveals its thrownness, its
already being situated in the world. "We are never free of moods," says Heidegger, nor are we ever free to master a mood in whatever way we like.
Moods are prior to cognition or will, prior to and ontologically deeper than
consciousness. "Indeed from the *ontological point of view* we must as a general principle leave the primary discovery of the world to 'bare mood.' "[8]
Dasein cannot lay hold of itself and be assured of itself as an absolute
source. Certainly Sartre shows that reflection is incapable of recapturing
the movement of nonreflective consciousness and cannot seize it as a fixed
self, but this failure merely bears witness to the preeminence, the power,
and the irreducibility of consciousness.

II. Two Opposing Interpretations of Nothingness and Anxiety

. . . *anxiety is the reflective apprehension of freedom by itself.* (BN, p. 39; Fr., p. 77) — Sartre

. . . *Being in-the-world itself is that in the face of which anxiety is anxious.* — Heidegger[9]

As a general rule, Sartre takes inspiration from Heidegger only in so far
as the preeminence of consciousness is not shaken. This appears clearly
from his analyses of nothingness and anxiety. For Sartre in fact adopts at
first the Heideggerian idea that negation as an act of judgment or purely
intellectual operation of logic is a derivative phenomenon that presupposes
the existence of an actual nothingness anterior to logic. "Without a doubt
Heidegger is right in insisting on the fact that negation derives its foundation from nothingness." (BN, p. 18; Fr., p. 54) When I say, after having
looked for him in vain, "Pierre is not in this café," I am stating a relation of
real negation produced by my disappointed expectation. Such a negation is
of a different nature from "judgments I can make subsequently for my

---

8. BT, p. 177.
9. Ibid., p. 232.

amusement, such as 'Wellington is not in this café'; 'Paul Valéry is no longer here,'" (BN, p. 10; Fr., p. 45) which are merely abstract negations. But I can play with abstract negations only on the basis of a possible, real, lived negation. Negative judgments are ultimately possible only because I can meet something like a "real non-being."

But where does that non-being come from? Here Sartre sets himself apart from Heidegger. Non-being is brought into the world by man. Nothingness is not somewhere in the world or beyond the world; rather, it constitutes the inner structure of consciousness. As such it is not a given fact. It is rather an act of consciousness, not simply nothingness but nihilation. Like Hegelian negativity, nihilation is an indefinite process of negation from which the positive necessarily results. But Sartre sets himself apart from Hegel, and especially from Heidegger, considering that for him negation comes solely from the subject: being, the in-itself, remains absolutely immune to negation. On one side we find pure negativity, on the other pure positivity, incorruptible and full. Being is; non-being is not.

Therefore, when Sartre grants to Heidegger that anxiety is "the apprehension of nothingness," (BN, p. 29; Fr., p. 66) their disagreement on the concept of nothingness gives a totally divergent meaning to their definition. "The apprehension of nothingness" becomes for Sartre the apprehension of consciousness "as such," that is, in its nihilating activity *taken in itself* without tending toward any exterior object. Now, inasmuch as spontaneous consciousness is inseparable from the consciousness *of something*, anxiety becomes a property of reflective consciousness taking as its object the very activity of spontaneous consciousness. Anxiety is consciousness reflecting upon its sheer uprooting from the in-itself, upon its sheer upsurging, which nothing outside itself can determine, limit, or require. But why does this reflection cause anxiety? Because consciousness discovers that nothing, no authority or power in the world, no safeguard of any law, be it physical, moral, or social, no previously made decision, can protect it from its own power to deny and to deny itself. Nothing separates it from the nothing that it is. I am anxiety-stricken to be what I am not, what I have to be. Thus, I have decided this or that, to go to see a friend, to write a book: I discover that the continuity of this project is not guaranteed by anything unless it be by an act of consciousness, constantly to be renewed, which reconfirms it and pulls it at every moment out of inertia, laziness, or forgetfulness, into which all projects would lapse if left to themselves. As I reflect upon this emergence of my consciousness, which has no support and which supports itself upon its own nothingness, I am stricken with anxiety for my freedom: "anxiety is then the reflective apprehension of freedom itself." (BN, p. 39; Fr., p. 77)

By contrast, Heidegger situates nothingness and anxiety outside the sphere of inner life, reflectiveness, and subjectivity. Nothingness is described as an event that arises unexpectedly in the world; it is "a withdrawal of being in its totality."[10] Sartre has recognized this "objective" dimension, noting that "Heidegger . . . makes of nothingness a sort of intentional correlate of transcendence." (BN, p. 19; Fr., p. 55) By applying this Husserlian vocabulary to Heidegger, Sartre tries to suggest that he commits the error of hypostatizing nothingness, of projecting the phantasmal double of transcendental subjectivity: an error of logic that amounts "simply to a denial of the predicate to a subject." (Translation modified: BN, p. 19; Fr., p. 55) Or else he is displaying "bad faith" in his description of *Dasein*, by cloaking implicit negations in positive terms. "*Dasein* is 'outside of itself, in the world'; it is 'a being of distances.' . . . All this amounts to saying that *Dasein* 'is not' in itself, that it 'is not' in immediate proximity to itself, and that it 'surpasses' the world inasmuch as it posits itself as *not being in itself* and as *not being the world*." (BN, p. 18; Fr., p. 54) This Heideggerian claim, however, is neither error nor bad faith, for *Dasein* does not posit itself as an internal negation; it does not posit itself as not being the world. On the contrary, *world* is defined in *Being and Time* as that "wherein" *Dasein* understands being.[11] Being-in-the-world is the very unity and identity of *Dasein*, and cannot be split into two independent parts, such as "consciousness" and "world." Two inverse movements appear: in Sartre the world falls on the side of the in-itself; in Heidegger the world, without being subjectified, constitutes a dimension of *Dasein*, since the latter is not a subject but rather the openness of the world. Far from being the seizing of consciousness "as such," Heideggerian anxiety is the seizing of the world "as such." What awakens anxiety in *Dasein* is absolutely not any intraworldly being but the worldhood of the world as such. Properly speaking, this worldhood is not any *thing*, but is at most a horizon; specifically, it is not what Sartre calls "an extra-worldly nothingness." (Translation modified: BN, p. 19; Fr., p. 55) The horizon of the world is not anything in the world, and it is not outside of the world, either!

Sartre is so firmly persuaded of the solidity of the in-itself and of the fragility of man that he fails to imagine that nothingness might appear not from the human side but *from the side of things*. What, according to Heidegger, does anxiety reveal? It reveals not an absence of things, but an absence of the meaning of things. This "nothing" that floats between *Dasein* and things is not "subjective," for *Dasein* could not be stricken, by itself, with anxiety. "The utter insignificance which makes itself known as the 'nothing and nowhere' does not signify that the world is absent, but tells us that entities within-the-world are of so little importance in themselves, that on the basis of this insignificance of what is within-the-world, the world in its worldhood is all that still obtrudes itself."[12] When the finality of tools or

---

10. Martin Heidegger, *Was ist Metaphysik?*, (Frankfurt" Klostermann, 1955), p. 33; hereafter referred to as WM. Translation mine.

11. BT, p. 119, paragraph 18.

12. Ibid., p. 231.

the system of reference from one instrument to another collapses, what is revealed is not absolute nothingness or emptiness, but the possible structure of a world. What shocks Sartre's Cartesianism is that the world, or the in-itself, might be able to lose its consistency and take on a coloring, so to speak, of unreality and of nothingness. "In anxiety," say Heidegger, "Nothingness presents itself together with Being in totality."[13] If one admits (as Sartre does) that nothingness *is*, it can be no more than a modification of being; it cannot be elsewhere, outside of being! Anxiety is merely more clear-sighted, more sensitive to the fact that nothingness is always a dimension of being. "Nothingness does not form the concept antithetical to Being, but from the start, the essence of Being itself involves Nothingness."[14] Sartre diverges most when he bypasses nothingness as well as anxiety and moves toward concepts, by making anxiety a question of *reflection*. Now for Heidegger these phenomena are situated at a prejudgmental, preconceptual level, which he seeks to safeguard at all costs: "that the world as world is disclosed first and foremost by anxiety . . . this does not signify that in anxiety the worldhood of the world is conceptualized."[15] Moreover, he emphasizes this point in *What Is Metaphysics?*: "Anxiety is not the act of conceiving Nothingness."[16] For Sartre, the concept of nothingness is consciousness, and the concept of anxiety can be formulated with complete precision: it is freedom.

III. The Sartrian Refusal of the Other and of Death

Being-for-others is a radical refusal of the Other. —Sartre (BN, pp. 224-225; Fr., pp. 309-310)

. . . there is no place for death in being which is for-itself. —Sartre (BN, p. 540; Fr., p. 624)

Confronting the fragile ray of consciousness, others and death are the two great forces — allied, moreover — that seek to reduce the spontaneity of the for-itself to the inertia of the in-itself.

The Sartrian theory of being-for-others is once again developed with a refutation of the corresponding Heideggerian theory of "being-with" others as its point of departure. Here too, Sartre reproaches Heidegger for not making consciousness and negation intervene in the definition of my relationship to the other. By its mere look, the other denies me as the subject that I am for myself, despoils me and posits me as an *object*. What is the look? It is not the fleshly eye, but the ideal abstraction of the consciousness

---

13. WM, p. 33: "das Nichts begegnet in der Angst in eins mit dem Seienden im Ganzen."
14. WM, p. 35.
15. BT, p. 232.
16. WM, p. 33: "Die Angst ist kein Erfassen des Nichts."

of the other. In being looked at "it is never the eyes which look at us; it is the *Other-as-subject*." (BN, p. 277; Fr., p. 336)

His second objection is that Heidegger does not understand that intersubjective relationships are based not on coexistence but on struggle. "The essence of the relations between consciousnesses is not the *Mitsein*; it is conflict." (BN, p. 429; Fr., p. 502) In his own name Sartre takes up the Hegelian dialectics of the master and the slave, except that slavery becomes our permanent and insurmountable condition. "I am a slave to the degree that my being is dependent at the center on a freedom which is not mine and which is the very condition of my being." (BN, p. 267; Fr., p. 326) This radical dependence is due to the fact that it is the other from whom I take my objective being—my *nature*, my *body*, and all my outwardness. I am a slave because I need the other to constitute me as a body in a world of which I am not the center. But I am at the same time master, because I am able to turn the other's aggression against him and make of him in his turn an object. Thus, there is a perpetual reversing of roles, but there can never be any equal or reciprocal recognition. For consciousness seeks only to be recognized as master or subject but can never succeed, for to dominate and objectify the other is part of its activity as a subject. "I am at the very root of my being the project of assimilating and making an object of the Other." (BN, p. 363; Fr., p. 430) The master could not be satisfied unless he were recognized not by a slave but by another master, another subject. But he is never to meet one unless he himself becomes a slave, and so on in an endless play of exchanged roles.

Thus the doctrine of *Being-with* (*Mit-sein*) appears to Sartre as at once insipid and alienating. For beyond coexistence he perceives the notion of collaboration effacing any individual encounter, not to mention any individuality, for the sake of a "we" that is destined to a common labor. "The empirical image which may best symbolize Heidegger's intuition is not that of conflict but rather of cooperation. . . . Heidegger's Being-with is not the clear and distinct position of an individual confronting another individual. . . . It is the mute existence in common of one member of a crew with his fellows. . . ." (Translation modified: BN, pp. 246–247; Fr., p. 303) There is alienation inasmuch as there is a vague recognition of the other as being the same as oneself, because he is bound to the same project of instrumental exploitation of the world. Heidegger lacks the sense of encounter: for him "our relation is not a *frontal* opposition, but rather an oblique interdependence." (BN, p. 246; Fr., p. 302) Individuals do not encounter each other directly; they merely meet through common interests or projects. For Sartre it is obligatory that one be subjected to the violence of the other's stare, be reduced to the state of an object; in return one has to do the other this violence in order for an intersubjective relationship to be established.

However, Sartre distorts the Heideggerian analysis of coexistence by schematizing it: far from an "ontological solidarity" with others, Heidegger insists on a tension between the possibility of being-oneself (authenticity) and the possibility—always realized beforehand—of being subjected to the domination of others, to their interchangeable possibilities, that is, to the petty ways of thinking and behaving of the *They*. There is no conflict between me and the other, but between my adopting the first and fundamental possibility to be *They* and the possibility to be myself, for whom a resolute struggle is required. For Sartre, the conflict is between me and *an Other*, who gives me a possibility of bad faith, which consists of interiorizing the objective being that he makes of me. I can either submit to or refuse the objectification he imposes upon me, the way he defines me from without. But being-oneself is neither nonexistent nor problematic. On the contrary, for Heidegger I am not myself originally, but the others. For him the relation to others is given as preobjective and presubjective, while Sartre thinks that it is given in utter objectivity and founded not only on a *reflection* but also on *knowledge*: "it is necessary that there should be *some knowledge* (*quelque savoir*) of what the Other is . . . I am with . . . But with *whom?*" (BN, p. 428; Fr., p. 500) In Heidegger, by contrast, an understanding—and not a knowledge—of the other appears already on the preobjective level: "because *Dasein*'s Being is Being-with, its understanding already implies the understanding of others. This understanding, like any understanding, is not an acquaintance derived from knowledge about them. . . ."[17] The understanding of the other appears at a level at which there is not yet either ego or alter ego: "When Others are encountered, it is not the case that one's own subject is proximally present-at-hand. . . ."[18] In this respect, the Sartrian position appears both more optimistic and more desperate: it is more optimistic because there is no alienation prior to the appearance of the for-itself; yet it is more desperate because the encounter with other is compared to an ontological catastrophe—"my original fall." (BN, p. 263; FR., p. 321)

The other causes the passion and agony of the for-itself. The meeting of the other exposes the for-itself to the torture of feeling its being, as sovereign subject, center and organizer of the world, turned again into an object whose definition is unpredictable. Let us notice here that the other is reduced to its look. The body of the other does not count, says Sartre, not even its eyes. The look is the ideal abstraction of the subject. It is everywhere present, even when I am alone: "Wherever I am, they are perpetually looking at me. . . ." (BN, p. 282; Fr., p. 342) Because it is unforseeable, elusive, unable to be situated, the look is *the* threat. In front of the other "I am in danger," (BN, p. 268; Fr., p. 326) in ontological danger, for the other can inflict upon me any qualification he pleases. Exposed defenselessly to his "watchful" look, I am not only petrified—"the petrifaction into in-itself is the profound meaning of the Medusa myth" (translation modi-

---

17. BT, p. 161.
18. Ibid., p. 155.

fied: BN, p. 430; Fr., p. 502) — but also wounded, bleeding. The metaphor of bleeding expresses the idea that my vital substance, my freedom, flows out of me from the wound made by the other's eyes, which are reorganizing the world without me. "He is that object in the world which determines an internal flow of the universe, an internal hemorrhage." (BN, p. 257; Fr., p. 315) This "flow of blood" means that "I flow outside myself," (BN, p. 261; Fr., p. 319) that is to say, that I am dispossessed unto my very death. If the other wounds me mortally, it is because in fact he puts beyond my reach and outside my range of vision those possibilities that define me to myself. "The Other is the hidden death of my possibilities insofar as I live that death as hidden in the midst of the world." (BN, p. 264; Fr., p. 323) Others are linked to my death, especially insofar as death is the final victory of the others' point of view over my own. Indeed, once dead, I am defenseless against objectification by the other.

This violent exacerbation of the conflict from a Heideggerian standpoint is the result both of Sartre's reduction of the other to a pure object and his interpretation of the other out of the mode of instrumentality, what Heidegger calls "readiness-to-hand." If the other is a tool that is not at my disposal and whose functioning escapes my world and my control, it comes as no surprise that the other becomes an arm turned against me. Sartre would seem to forget that, in Heidegger's view, my possibilities are always at first[19] those of the others: it is necessarily among possibilities not my own in the beginning that I choose those which I will appropriate. If the other were this total exteriority, how could I even understand the possibilities he offers to me? For there are perhaps no possibilities that could from the outset define me in isolation.

However, it is with respect to the interpretation of death that Sartre is most vigorously and most viscerally opposed to Heidegger, and to such a degree that he seems to run short of arguments very rapidly. Whereas in *Dasein* the fact of confronting and anticipating the possibility of one's death makes death the source of all authenticity and individualization itself, Sartre declares flatly that death is "absurd." (BN, p. 533; Fr., p. 617) When he sums up the Heideggerian position, he seems to understand well that being-unto-death means for *Dasein* "an anticipation and a project of its own death as the possibility of no longer realizing presence in the world." (BN, p. 533; Fr., p. 616) This possibility as what is most entirely its own, that which no one can assume in its place, permits *Dasein* to be free of the *They* and to discover itself in its individual uniqueness. Sartre rejects these two points: that death may enter into a project, and that it may be a possibility truly different from others. "Death," says Sartre, "cannot be awaited. . . . To *expect* death is not to *wait for* death. We can 'wait for' only a determined event." (BN, p. 535; Fr., p. 619) But this criticism does not bear up,

---

19. Or, in Heidegger's words: "proximally and for the most part" (zunächst und zumeist). Bt, pp. 37, 76.

for if death is a *project*, that is to say a pro-jecting of an extreme possibility from which the horizon of all my possibles is sketched, it could not be an event that *Dasein* awaits, in the passive sense of the word. Death could not then be situated in a more or less far-off future, since it is a possibility sighted *now*. Death is no longer a stark, exterior fact, but a permanent ontological structure. *Dasein* has to recover from the obnubilation of what *They* say about death: that death comes at the end of everything and that it is the "others" who die. Nor can one say, either, as Sartre does, that death is man's mortality, for it is *my* death. His second objection, notably that what Heidegger expresses is trite, and that one could as easily say that no one else can *love* in my place, shows clearly that Sartre considers death as a particular event situated at the end of life and not as a present possibility. On the one hand one can certainly affirm that another can love in my stead, for that it be I or another who loves is a contingency. But no one can die in my place; this is a possibility that is necessarily mine. For Heidegger being-unto-death is in fact only a certain aspect of anxiety that confronts me with being-in-the-world as such and for which I alone am answerable. Being-unto-death is also the experience of nothingness as the revelation of *my* ultimate possibility: "*Dasein* finds itself *face to face* with the 'nothing' of the possible impossibility of its existence."[20] This bond between death and my actual possibility, this confrontation with the essentially possible, disappears in Sartre. If "there is no place for death in the being which is for-itself," (BN, p. 491; Fr., p. 631) it is because the for-itself in its total reflection on itself attempts to tear itself from contingency and to establish itself in transparence. Thus it rejects chance, limitation, the irrational, and the absurd on the part of the in-itself. Death is reduced to its pure facticity: it is pure de facto destruction from *without*, from the in-itself. For Sartre the relationship to death is not present throughout all of existence; it appears only in anxiety! But Sartrian anxiety is that of the "anything is possible" variety; it is the dizziness of the all-powerful consciousness that excludes limitation, finitude — other names for death — from the possible.

IV. The Heideggerian Evaluation of Existentialism

Metaphysics shuts itself off from the simple and essential given, that man unfolds his essence only insofar as he is addressed by Being.[21]

Man is not the master of being [seiende]. *Man is the shepherd of Being* [Sein].[22]
                                                                        —Heidegger

The evaluation of Sartre's philosophy that is sketched rather than elaborated in Heidegger's *Letter on Humanism* is no more that a particular case

---

20. Ibid., p. 310.
21. Martin Heidegger, *Platons Lehre von der Wahrheit, Mit einem Brief über "Humanismus,"* (Bern: Francke, 1947), p. 72; hereafter referred to as BuH. Translations mine.
22. Ibid., p. 72.

of his general criticism of metaphysics, of the modern metaphysics of sub-jectivity that deduces all reality from a worldless human subject. Sartre takes up again and repeats naively, involuntarily but necessarily, the prin-cipal axioms of post-Cartesian philosophy: the transparent and self-sufficient presence of the subject to itself; the evidence of that presence (the *cogito*) which is the ultimate foundation for being and knowledge; the self-affection by which the subject is assured of its self-certitude; the dualism of the ego and the nonego; and finally a humanism truly absolute inasmuch as the human subject is the sole source of all meaning. Sartre actually inter-prets time, the possible, and being itself as productions of subjectivity: all that is draws its being from man. "I am the being by whom 'there is' (*es gibt*) Being." (BN, p. 248; Fr., p. 305) Doubtless we touch here upon the point at which the two philosophers are diametrically opposed. To the Sartrian for-mulation "precisely we are on a plane where there are only men," Heideg-ger responds by a sharp inversion of the original French: "Precisely we are on a plane where there is principally Being."[23] For Heidegger man is not an origin, but an answer to and correspondence with "the sending" (*Geschick*) of being. The project is not a pure upsurging of subjectivity outside the pas-sive in-itself, but a pro-ject (*Ent-wurf*) that responds to the primordial being-thrown.

According to Heidegger, the reason for Sartrian naiveté lies in the ab-sense of any criticism of the language of metaphysics. Sartre does not see the layers of meaning that traditional words and expressions such as "hu-man reality" convey. He does not see why the term *Dasein* is preferred to the term *man*, which is so difficult to detach from the notion of a composite of body and soul and which always refers to this duality rather than to the unity of being-in-the-world. Like Husserl, Sartre believes naively that one can go directly "to the things themselves" without interposing any screen of words. His fidelity to Husserlian intuitionism is constant and manifests itself par-ticularly in the importance given to the look. If existentialism, like Husserl's phenomenology, remains imprisoned in metaphysics, it is because of the lack of attention paid to words and to their traditional weight. Thus, when Sartre formulates the principle of existentialism, "existence precedes es-sence," "he is taking *existentia* and *essentia* in the sense of Metaphysics, which has reiterated since Plato that *essentia* precedes *existentia*. But his reversal of a metaphysical proposition remains a metaphysical proposition. As such this proposition persists with Metaphysics in forgetting the truth of Being."[24] Accomplishing one of the last possibilities still open to Metaphys-ics in its death throes, Sartre reverses the propositions traditionally domi-nant. He is the anti-Leibnizian. Thus, he develops the implications of this sentence in *Nausea*: "the essential is contingency." For Leibniz the essential was necessary. To "nothing is without reason" or the rationality of being, he

23. Ibid., pp. 79–80.
24. Ibid., p. 72.

opposes its characteristic absurdity, unjustifiability: "Being is without reason, without cause and without necessity." (BN, p. 619; Fr., p. 713)

The for-itself engenders itself not by being thrown into being but by tearing itself from the in-itself through the power inherent in it. It is founded by itself and affects itself in a totally transparent presence to itself. The very idea of foundation presupposes a duality of which the in-itself is incapable. Only the for-itself, says Sartre, is self-creative; "it is the cause of its own way of being." (BN, p. iv; Fr., p. 22) But one must distinguish the idea of foundation from the idea of necessity. A being that would be both a cause of itself and a necessity would be God, but this being is the ideal and impossible synthesis of the in-itself and the for-itself. It is necessary to maintain at once the principle of the contingency of existence. "Consciousness is its own foundation, but it remains contingent that there may be consciousness rather than an infinity of pure and simple in-itself." (BN, p. 82; Fr., p. 125) With the idea of a contingent foundation, Sartre maintains the prior metaphysics, merely inverted. In the same way, the distinction between a superior being that has the power of founding and an inferior being that is founded remains purely metaphysical: the traditional relation is simply turned inside out. The in-itself is inferior by an excess of positivity and substance, while what constitutes the superiority of the for-itself is its insubstantial, its elusive character, its "liberty." The for-itself is in fact a "contingent necessity": it is necessary as the *basis of the self*, as the "origin of negation," contingent through the bond that unites it with that which it denies and which it has not itself posited, by the fact that it surges up here rather than there in the immensity of the in-itself.

The theme of *self-affection*, a consequence of *self-founding*, is one that recurs most insistently in *Being and Nothingness*. "Man presents himself . . . as a being who causes Nothingness to arise in the world *inasmuch as he affects* himself with non-being to this end." (Translation modified, *italics mine*: BN, p. 24; Fr., p. 60) Man, or rather consciousness, is "*its own Nothingness.*" (BN, p. 23; Fr., p. 59) It is a being that "affects itself" perpetually with a breaking into being. In every way man makes himself what he is because he is nothing originally. Even feelings and moods, and especially feelings, do not express a dependency within a situation or a passivity like that of the Heideggerian *Stimmung*, which seizes *Dasein*. Rather, moods are freely produced by an act of self-affection on the part of consciousness. "Is it not consciousness which affects itself with sadness as a magical recourse against a situation too urgent?" (BN, p. 61; Fr., p. 101) The "magic" is that of the consciousness that makes something out of nothing. All sentiments and emotions have a dimension of bad faith and are destined to fail inasmuch as they are an attempt by consciousness to affect itself with an in-itself. I would like to be sad the way a stone is a stone, in order to be delivered once and for all from the anxiety of having perpetually to decide my being. But "if I make myself sad, it is because I *am not* sad—the being of

sadness escapes me by and in the very act by which I affect myself with it."
(BN, p. 61; Fr., p. 101) Vainly consciousness seeks to identify with a reassuring in-itself; it can affect itself only with nothingness. We can only play,
as the café waiter does, at taking this role or that one in turn. But in our
very abjectness we remain free, because "consciousness *affects itself* with
bad faith." (BN, p. 49; Fr., p. 87) In contrast with Heideggerian inauthenticity, which is a structure of passivity into which *Dasein* is thrown, bad
faith is yet another testimony to the self-producing activity of consciousness. The prereflective *cogito* is, in reality, nothing more than the discovery
of self-affection, self-determination: the primitive act of consciousness is an
act of self-negation that isolates it forever in its own immanence, not "in the
world" but outside it.

As in all of metaphysics, the for-itself as the being of beings is marked
with the trait of *presence:* "the law of Being of the for-itself, as the ontological foundation of consciousness, is to be itself in the form of the presence to
itself." (BN, p. 77; Fr., p. 119) Certainly, presence to the self implies *the
contrary* of what one usually means by this: coinciding with the self. Paradoxically, the in-itself alone can be itself, but its presence cannot reveal itself "to itself," for it is complete identity enclosed in itself. To be present to
the self implies *not* being altogether oneself; it implies distance and separation. But strictly speaking, *nothing* separates the subject from itself. The
for-itself is not separated from itself by anything but its *own power to deny
itself.* "This empty distance" (BN, p. 77; Fr., p. 120) that defines it is not
the duality of two in-itself's, but a flight out of the in-itself and out of the
identity to itself.

In his analysis of the relation between time and being, Sartre, like all of
the metaphysicians since Plato, gives priority to the dimension of the *present.* In its first stage the Sartrian analysis seems to join Heidegger's position,
which shows that the original *ekstasis* of temporality is the future. Indeed,
since the past constitutes a return to the in-itself and since the present is the
very movement of nihilation in view to realizing a never-realizable self, the
meaning of the for-itself should derive from the project of being the self.
The future is just this project which uproots the for-itself from any closed
presence of the in-itself kind. Consequently, the future would seem to condition the relation of the self to itself. Indeed, "the future," says Sartre,
"constitutes the meaning of my present for-itself." (BN, p. 128; Fr., p. 173)
But this constitution turns out to be an illusion; I shall never be in the present that filled gap that I have the project to be. The project of the for-itself
toward the future is the result of the unfulfillable desire to be in-itself.
Thus, the future, linked to the in-itself, is an inauthentic dimension: it represents "the ontological mirage of the Self." (BN, p. 137; Fr., p. 182) It is
not the source but simply a frame, a pre-outline "within which the for-itself
will make itself be as a flight making itself present to Being in the direction
of another future." (BN, p. 128; Fr., p. 173) The only authentic future is

the present, because it is the condition for the possibility of temporality itself. Of course, the for-itself is at once present, past, and future, but the
unity of the three dimensions is made by the present. It is for this reason
that "it is best to put the accent on the present ekstasis and not on the future
ekstasis as Heidegger does." (BN, p. 142; Fr., p. 188) In order to bind the
dimensions of time together, negation has to be very active: thus, the present "is the mould of indispensable non-being for the total synthetic form of
temporality." (BN, p. 142; Fr., p. 188) One may note in passing that temporality is conceived, in a very Platonic way, as a fall, a loss, a dispersion for
which there must always be compensation. The only difference from Plato
is that lack does not correspond to any real plenitude.

As Heidegger asks, why is authenticity on the side of the future rather
than the present? Because the future is not the *objective* project Sartre
would make of it, but a preobjective understanding by which *Dasein* grasps
its possibilities as "ahead of itself." This "ahead" is not a before me that I
can overtake and which is situated in the temporal flow. In short, the
meaning of the possible does not disappear in *Dasein*, even if some possibilities are realized. Man, says Heidegger in the *Letter on Humanism*, is open
to the dimension of the possible; he does not create it, nor can he master it
entirely. The possible cannot be identified with the sum of the projects of
human subjectivity; it refers to a temporality that is not possessed, but
which possesses man. If Sartre favors the present dimension, it is because he
sees in it the reign of activity and mastery. "Making present" — as the operation of reducing things and *Dasein* to substantiality, to the "present-at-
hand" (*Vorhandenheit*) — constitutes for Heidegger the very source of "falling" (*Verfallen*). If metaphysics gives preference to presence, it does so
because metaphysics seems most to permit the appropriation or domination
that makes possible in its turn technological mastery of the world.

Taking its basis in itself, affecting itself and possessing itself in its presence to itself, the for-itself is, not surprisingly, called the "absolute." Of
course it is a "non-substantial absolute," but nevertheless, "it can be considered as the absolute." (BN, p. lvi; Fr., p. 23) Like Descartes, Sartre thinks
he has found the *fundamentum absolutum inconcussum veritatis*. The subject is absolute in the sense that nothing is possible without it; nothing happens in the world without it. "Absolute" signifies also totalization: "The for-
itself makes being in-itself exist as a totality," (BN, p. 90; Fr., p. 133)
although without a totality made of the in-itself-for-itself. The totality of
the in-itself is opposed to the totality of the for-itself; but the first exists
solely through the second. So it is that "the appearance of the for-itself is the
absolute event which comes to being." (BN, p. 619; Fr., p. 713) Sartre fulfills the wish of all ontology, which is to discover the unconditional source.

Metaphysics is, however, indissolubly onto-theological. Could there be a
Sartrian theology? In its place he offers a discourse on the impossibility —
which does not mean the absurdity — of a God: an a-theology. Sartre is

doubtless one of the rare philosophers who have attempted to demonstrate the *nonexistence* of God. God, the *ens causa sui* of theology, is a being that does not have its foundation in nihilation, but that, like the in-itself, is at once total identity with itself (being), and total freedom (nothingness). If such a synthesis is contradictory because one of the principles would necessarily absorb the other in an eventual fusion, what is noteworthy is that God keeps a meaning even in a-theology. God is man's vain wish to achieve being-in-itself, to be as dense as a rock and as free as a thought. "Human reality is the pure effort to become God, without there being any substratum for that effort. . . ." (BN, p. 576; Fr. p. 653) The very meaning of man is failure: he is without ground, standing in emptiness. God is the symbol of universal failure. Not only does man fail — "the for-itself in its being is failure" (BN, p. 89; Fr., p. 132) — but the whole of reality fails: "the real is an abortive effort to attain to the dignity of the self-cause. Everything happens as if the World, Man, and Man-in-the-World succeeded only in realizing a missing God." (BN, p. 623; Fr., p. 717) Disharmony, whether preordained or not, suggests "an ideal synthesis," which is called God. "Ideal" means "false" here. The bankruptcy of the ideal in general along with that of God is declared. It would seem that Sartre should thus be led to that nihilism which is the result, according to Nietzsche, of a disappointed belief in an absolute ideal inscribed at the root of things. If, as Sartre says in the last sentence of *Being and Nothingness* before the conclusion, "man is a useless passion," is not this a real pessimism, a profound nihilism that says, "nothing has any meaning"?

But Sartre seems to reject any nihilistic attitude in order to affirm a humanistic and moralizing activism. On the one hand, it is a question not merely of humanizing things, but of appropriating them to oneself. All the relations between man and the world are described as relations between master and slave, relations of domination and assimilation: "art, science, play are activities of appropriation." (BN, p. 585; Fr., p. 675) On the other hand, Sartre affirms that the freedom of the individual, even in his solitude, makes him entirely responsible for all others. This humanism, from a Heideggerian viewpoint, serves only to mask a radical nihilism: man wants desperately to master nature and, in a way, to carry on his shoulders the fate of the whole species. For Heidegger this is nihilism, because if nothing exists except through man, nothing exists finally except man; and also because others and the entire world draw their existence and their meaning from this nothingness, which constitutes individual subjectivity. While Sartre declares that man is "responsible for everything," this responsibility is not in fact a moral one, but ontological: it is because he is the source of existence and of essence. His responsibility is "overwhelming," since he is not only the one who makes himself as well as the other be, but "the one by whom it happens *there is* a world." (BN, p. 553; Fr., p. 639) We are enclosed in a nihilistic circle, where man meets nothing but himself, where everything including earthquakes, says Sartre, partakes of human responsibility. There are no "natural" disasters, indeed, except insofar as they bear upon human works! "There is no non-human situation." (BN, p. 554; Fr., p. 639)

Thus, in spite of its surface atheism, we see the reappearance in an assertive way of the most traditional of theological motifs. Man as the being of beings, as causing himself to be, is in point of fact a *causa sui*: he cannot, therefore, complain of his suffering and the evil that exists in the world; for evil, like everything else, depends on him. There is a reiteration of the old theme of *theodicy*. How can one fail to see a parallel between Sartre's expression "It is therefore senseless to think of complaining since nothing foreign has decided what we feel, what we live, or what we are" (BN, p. 554; Fr., p. 639) and that of Descartes in the Fourth Meditation: "I have no subject for complaint that God has not given me a more capacious intelligence. . ."[25] Since for Sartre man is his own God, in fact if not by right, he must be totally justified through and by himself.

There is a great distance between this anthropo-theology and Heidegger's prudent expectancy: the thought of being can be neither atheist nor theist, because neither man nor God is any longer thought of as the absolute founder of the world. It is only after the destruction of metaphysics that a new dimension of the sacred and of divinity may perhaps become apparent. Such an interrogation is once again opposed to Sartrian dogmatism.

Can we say that in his later work Sartre has come closer to Heidegger? Certainly not directly, for he has ignored the criticisms Heidegger has addressed to him. But in the *Critique of Dialectical Reason* Sartre has in fact considerably modified the extreme dualism that was his earlier point of departure, doubtless in order to respond to Merleau-Ponty's objections. The later Sartre finds himself objectively less distant from Heidegger inasmuch as he develops, rather unexpectedly, a theory of *passivity*. Man is *passive* in the first place through his submission to need: all of his activity tends first to satisfy organic and economic needs in an environment governed by "scarcity." Of course, freedom is the principal spring of action, but it is no longer defined as an absolute upsurging, revealing and overtaking its own facticity. From another angle, Sartre shows that certain structures of passivity impose themselves as a necessary condition prior to any project: for example, historical context or membership in a social class. Thus, he says, exploitation reveals to the working class its "passive unity." In such remarks we witness the reversal of his original theory of freedom. It is no longer the

---

25. René Descartes, "Meditations," in *The Philosophical Works of Descartes*, vol. 1, Trans. E. S. Haldane and G. R. T. Ross (Cambridge: University Press, 1911), pp. 133–199. See esp. Meditation Four.

negation of the in-itself by the for-itself that is the primordial event, but, on the contrary, that the project is first denied: "the organizing project in *everyone* begins by being denied by that which it surpasses and denies."[26]

Nevertheless, Sartrian passivity partakes of a contingent historical alienation that can, and must, be surmounted through revolutionary struggle. As in Marx, the dialectic implies in an optimistic way that man may recover his full and total freedom. The possibility for man to *give himself* liberty is simply postponed, but already it belongs in itself to the essence of man. Man is the being who makes himself be. There lies the secret of the opposition to Heidegger, for whom liberty is *given* to us and thereby cannot flow from a purely human source. "Man does not 'possess' liberty as property, but on the contrary, liberty possesses man,"[27] writes Heidegger in *Of the Essence of Truth.* That man is possessed by freedom does not mean that "man is condemned to be free," as Sartre says: that he cannot avoid being free. Nor does it amount to a certain fatalism by which man would recognize himself as being played upon by forces more powerful than he. It means that man does not decide the relation between being and himself, which, as openness to the world, is the primal freedom. Man does not make himself be. There lies the radical and insurmountable passivity: "That which, in the project, has the power to *throw* is not man, but Being itself, which destines man to ek-sistence. . . ."[28] Man is not the *ultima ratio*. He does not create his own destiny. There is no action, thought, or writing, except as the accomplishment or the receiving of a manifestation of being that has *always already* taken place, in an irrecoverable anteriority. Sartrian man refuses to have a destiny, that middle ground between opacity and transparence.

---

26. Jean-Paul Sartre, *Critique of Dialectical Reason*, trans. Alan Sheridan-Smith (London: New Left Books, 1976), p. 310; Fr., p. 352 (translation modified).

27. Martin Heidegger, *Vom Wesen der Wahrheit* (Frankfurt: Klostermann, 1954), p. 16. Translation mine.

28. BuH, p. 84.

Ingbert Knecht

11. Seriality: A Ground for Social Alienation?*

Sartre employs the terms *series* and *collective* to speak of the role played by the complex of relations between men and things in his theory of alienation. From the perspective of Marx's thought, the collective or series is an attempt to further develop and generalize the dialectic[1] as presented in the section of *Capital* (volume one) on "fetishism of commodities."[2] Sartre claims that Marx did not fully develop the function of dialectic in the phenomenon of fetishism. Since, in Sartre's eyes, this development has still not taken place, he considers a full expansion of a dialectical rationality for fetishism a desirable aim of Marxist philosophy. This aim must now be examined in terms of his theory of series.[3]

I. Alienation and Fetishism in Marx

A presentation of fetishism in Marx must take its point of departure from division of labor as a reality. Marx understands division of labor as the first historical basis of alienation emerging in society as a product of labor. Division of labor is held responsible for the transformation of the product of labor into an "objective power" that "outgrows our control and ruins our expectations." Division of labor should entail this "alienation," but only under definite social conditions, namely, when the product of labor is appropri-

---

*Translated from the German by James Bernauer and Hugh J. Silverman

1. Klaus Hartmann, *Die Marxsche Theorie: Eine philosophische Untersuchung zu den Hauptschriften* (Berlin: de Gruyter, 1970), pp. 299ff.

2. Karl Marx, *Capital*, vol. 1, ch. 1, section 4. Translated by Samuel Moore and Edward Aveling (New York: International Publishers, 1967), pp. 71-83.

3. Jean-Paul Sartre, *Critique de la raison dialectique* (Paris: Gallimard, 1960), pp. 55 ff. The English translation of the introductory section to the *Critique* has been published as *Search for a Method*, trans. Hazel E. Barnes (New York: Knopf, Vintage Books, 1963), pp. 77ff.; hereafter incorporated in the text as SM. The remaining parts of the *Critique* have been published as *Critique of Dialectical Reason*, trans. Alan Sheridan-Smith, ed. Jonathan Rée (London: New Left Books, 1976); hereafter incorporated in the text as CDR. The French original in all cases is cited as Fr.

ated as private property. In this case, the contradiction between the individual's interest and that of the totality accompanies the division of labor.[4] Marx sees this combination as the origin of competition. The separation of labor and property is accompanied by a conflict of interests.[5] Division of labor, private property — the worth of which is created by labor — and competition: all are regarded as characteristic of a social state that exists as a multiplicity of isolated individual worlds. According to Marx, in such a society each person follows only his own individual interest. Individuals deal with one another as "autonomous producers of commodities." The only "authority" that they recognize is that alleged compulsion "which the pressure of their reciprocal interests exercises upon them."[6] In this connection, Marx also speaks of the "atomistic behavior of men in their process of production."[7]

The atomistic character of men's combined efforts is the basic structure of the phenomenon of fetishism. Although fetishism is developed in detail only in terms of illustrating the constitution of value in the exchange of commodities, it takes on a significance in Marxist theory that goes beyond the scope of its original use. The fetishism of commodities can be regarded as the fundamental pattern for thinking all forms of the alienating effect that emerges as the product of human activity.

The analysis of the fetishism of commodities must begin from the value character that attaches to the commodity.[8] Marx bases the determination of the value of the commodity upon the simple fact that the commodity produced by men's labor is, in its basic significance, a useful object. The transformation of the product of labor, which is provided with a use value, into commodity is accounted for by the fact that the producer does not make use of it, but rather exchanges it in return for other products. The "exchange value" (*Tauschwert*) furnishes the norm for the exchange. This exchange value is determined as the "quantitative relation" according to which products provided with a use value are exchanged.[9]

While labor, which only produces use values, continues to remain in that area of the unmediated life of the individual (an area that can be controlled), the production of commodities makes the producer dependent upon society. For Marx, the product as commodity emerges from individual private labor and becomes a social object. Marx thus justifies the social determination of the product of labor by showing that it stands in a correlation with the "system of social division of labor." It fulfills a "definite social

---

4. Karl Marx and Frederick Engels, *The German Ideology*, pts. 1 and 2 (New York: International Publishers, 1947), pp. 21–24.

5. Ibid., pp. 65–66.

6. Marx, *Capital* 1: 356.

7. Ibid., p. 92.

8. Cf. Klaus Hartmann, *Die Marxsche Theorie*, pp. 299ff.

9. Marx, *Capital* 1: 356.

need" in the context of the society producing commodities through division of labor.[10]

The exchange of commodities is the origin of the phenomenon of the fetishism of commodities. For Marx, a fetishism occurs because the individual producer does not control the process of establishing commodity value. Rather, it arises "independent of the will, foreknowledge, and action of those who do the exchanging."[11] According to Marx, the possibility of such a process is rooted in the competitive situation, which excludes agreement among individual producers. The absence of organization and control make individual activities appear "accidental" (als "Zufall"). In that regard Marx wants to say that the effect of the individual's activity evades the influence of the individual and finds its "truth" in the outcome of many individual activities. The individual sees himself placed under the "law" of exchange processes that are determined by competition.[12]

As Marx portrays it, the process of generating value represents, on the one hand, a movement of which the commodity seems to render itself independent as an object of value in relation to its producer. Therefore, Marx indicates that, for individuals, their "own social movement" has the form of a "movement of things," which they do not control but which controls them.[13] On the other hand, this explanation of the generation of value does not ignore the constitutive role of human activity. Rather, transformation of the individual into a component within the context of things is decisive in providing evidence of alienation. Marx emphasizes that the social characteristics of the product come to it through the exchange and activity of individuals. However, to the extent that the product becomes a social thing, it detaches itself from the individual and becomes something alien for him. This shows itself when the relation among individuals, who also produce and exchange, reduce themselves to value relations among commodities. These relations with others prove to be relations among things that cannot be influenced by the individual. Here Marx wants to speak of alienation. For him, the "alienation of the individual from himself and from others" is indicated in the "generality" of the thing relations.[14] The activity of the individual producer, which is objectified in the value of the commodity, comes to confront him in the form of a social power that is independent of him.[15]

Subjugation to the laws of exchange of commodities is the point from which Marx's theory of alienation logically takes its departure. The phe-

---

10. Ibid., p. 73.
11. Ibid., p. 75.
12. Marx, *Capital*, 3: 828.
13. Marx, *Capital* 1: 75.
14. Karl Marx, *Grundrisse: Foundations of the Critique of Political Economy*, trans. Martin Nicolaus (Baltimore: Penguin, 1973), p. 162.
15. Ibid., pp. 196–197.

nomenon of fetishism is not restricted to the exchange of commodities. In the analysis of Marx's theory of capitalism, it shows itself to be far more: it is the basic structure of that alienation that is met with over and over again on all levels of the capitalistic mode of production. What is special about fetishism, and of that alienation lodged within it, is that they do not necessarily imply the existence of laborers and, therefore, of the class division of society. The commodity type must not only be considered as a phenomenon independent of capitalism insofar as historically it existed before capitalism, but it also can be described in its logical genesis, within the theory of capitalism, as a type independent of typical capitalist structures.[16] The commodity type has, as it were, a "pre-capitalist" character.[17]

Howeover, the value of the commodity depends upon the initial phases of the capitalist process, insofar as it is the formation of surplus value. Furthermore, the fetishism of commodities is presented as a typical structure of all capitalism. Marx justifies his position by ascribing an atomistic structure both to all human multitudes involved in the process of capitalism and to their activities. Fetishism, which is traced back to the social atomization of the producer of commodities, obtains, therefore, the character of a universal phenomenon.

The formation of commodity value does not presuppose class division. This becomes a consideration only with the appearance of surplus value. In Marx, surplus value entails division into 1) private owners, to whom the product of labor belongs, and 2) laborers who receive wages for their work and are not the owners of the product. The one thing that workers are able to sell is their labor. They do sell it because they must live. And so, to the market, labor appears as a commodity.[18] In the labor market, workers meet one another as competitors. The "isolation of workers through competition" subjugates them to the condition of selling labor as a commodity, just as it subjugated the private producers of a product of labor to the laws of the commodity market.[19] The fetishism of commodities is thus also a moment in the development of the labor market. These features of the market are due to competition among the workers, which holds wages at a level determined by those necessities of life required for an individual to return to work and by the development of needs corresponding to social situations.[20]

The isolation of workers through competition results in their subjugation to the laws of the market. Furthermore, the powerlessness of workers

16. Karl Marx, Fragment des Urtextes von "Zur Kritik des politischen Ökonomie" (1858) and Grundrisse der "Kritik der politischen Ökonomie" (Berlin: Dietz, 1953), p. 907.

17. Helmut Klages, Technischer Humanismus (Stuttgart: F. Enke, 1964), pp. 62ff.

18. Marx, Capital 1: 167.

19. Karl Marx and Frederick Engels, The Communist Manifesto, trans. Samuel Moore (New York: Washington Square Press, 1964), p. 78.

20. Karl Marx, Wages, Price and Profit (Peking: Foreign Language Press, 1970), pp. 71-73.

against the capitalist's activities is rooted in another form of competition, which draws them into the use of capital.

The activities of the capitalists, however, are not regarded as concerted measures of a united capitalist class. Marx reasons that the capital that is involved in a branch of the economy is divided among many capitalists, who are in competition with one another. Each of them is concerned with eliminating the other producers by improving the instruments of production. In this competitive battle, the owners of greater capital succeed against those who produce less.[21] For Marx, this struggle to enlarge capital is not an individual tendency of particular capitalists. Rather, it demonstrates the subjugation of the individual capitalist to the compulsion of the system: whoever does not improve his instruments of production and does not enlarge his capital will be ruined by the others.[22] Without following Marx by entering into the particulars of economically grounding the historical development of capital, it becomes clear that both workers and capitalists are together subjugated to the laws of capital. The same fundamental structure continues to reveal itself: workers compete in the labor market and capitalists compete by struggling with one another for their existence. Competition and the divisions bound up with it (the absence of organization and the synchronization of the economic process as a whole, the partitioning of property) are to be regarded as the condition establishing alienation in the structure of capitalist society. Thus, abolition of alienation seems to be possible only if the atomization of capitalist society is overcome through a process of unification.[23]

Sartre ties the phenomenon of fetishism that Marx was describing to his own theory of the series. He thinks that he has found here the rationality of social relations that accounts for social alienation. As we shall see in the later course of our investigation, seriality constitutes a fundamental condition for social alienation.

Sartre plainly agrees with Marx on the importance of fetishism as a social structure for the theory of alienation. Certainly, however, the theory functions on a different level in the thought of Sartre from that of Marx. With Marx, the phenomenon of fetishism appears in the context of the theory of a historically-concrete object, the capitalism of bourgeois society. Even alienation in this case has a concrete, historical form. It reveals itself in the contradictions of capitalism. Sartre's formulation of the question is different. In his thought, alienation is situated in the context of a social philosophy that takes a transcendental-philosophical orientation.[24] At stake is the demonstration of principles through which understanding can

21. Marx, *Capital* 1: 626.
22. Ibid., p. 592.
23. Marx and Engels, *German Ideology*, pp. 69–70.
24. Cf. Klaus Hartmann, *Sartres Sozialphilosophie: eine Untersuchung zur "Critique de la raison dialectique"* (Berlin: de Gruyter, 1966).

discover its justification in the domain of the social. These principles should be grasped by ascertaining their principle-concepts, and by demonstrating their range and meaning.[25] Discussion of alienation must be seen against the background of this formulation of the question. Sartre begins with the logical structures of Marx's theory of alienation in his determination of the concept of alienation. The determination of the concept is supposed to result in drawing out the full theoretical consequences of what was restricted to a historical-concrete object in Marx's theory.

Even in Marx the dialectic of alienation does not necessarily follow the historical development of its object. It is a dialectic of meaning that has its own logical character. While the moment of fetishism occupies us in the movement of this dialectic, the dialectic is restricted in its meaning to the economy of bourgeois society. This is one of the reasons why Sartre wants to treat once again Marx's theme of fetishism. He would like to expand the range of application of those structures contained in fetishism to other social phenomena. Sartre thinks that the rationality of fetishism can be made fruitful for a theory of alienation that transcends the context of bourgeois society's economy. At the same time, he can unite it with a sure reference to Marx himself. As we have already seen, the fetishism of commodities appears as a precapitalist structure that certainly fits into the theory of capitalism.[26]

II. Massification as Social Background of Seriality

Sartre's discussion of seriality proceeds from the fact that many individuals find themselves in a system of practico-inert relations. He joins the viewpoints of objectification and depersonalization with that of "massification" by the practico-inert. (CDR, p. 257; Fr., p. 308) Massification signifies that the individual stands in relationships in which he, as a person, is unessential. Sartre is thinking here of the fact that a great number of concrete complexes, such as factories, streets, shops, and train stations, exist without reference to individuality. The exigencies, directions for application, and meanings bound up with these have a diffuse character directed toward an indefinite plurality. Here the individual is, in Sartre's interpretation, "anyone." He appears as the "whoever," nameless in the midst of a multitude of men. The generality that is determined by matter and then ascribed to the individual is decisive here for Sartre.[27]

Massification not only means the reduction of the individual to the

---

25. Ingbert Knecht, *Theorie der Entfremdung bei Sartre und Marx* (Meisenheim: Anton Hain, 1975), pp. 1, 22ff.

26. Klages, *Technischer Humanismus*, pp. 62ff.

27. Jean-Paul Sartre, *L'Être et le néant* (Paris: Gallimard, 1943), pp. 500ff. English translation by Hazel E. Barnes as *Being and Nothingness* (New York: Philosophical Library, 1956), pp. 427ff.; henceforth incorporated in the text as BN. Cf. also CDR, pp. 257ff.; Fr., 309ff.

generality of practico-inert givens, but it also includes the "isolation" of individuals from one another. The intensity of isolation is understood as a measure of the massification of the society's entire complex. (CDR, pp. 257ff; Fr., pp. 309ff.)

As the moment that determines the structure of the plurality in the domain of the practico-inert, isolation is the comprehensive expression for a large number of factors of disintegration and disharmony. It expresses the impossibility of establishing a consensus among the members of a multitude when shaped by a scarcity of organization and control, by disagreement on the basis of interests, by competition, by an absence of communication among individuals, by a scarcity of information about the whole, and by a deficient synchronization of activities. Here the factors that exclude a conscious and organized mutuality predominate. Isolation is also to be understood as a socially mediated structure. It is rooted in the fact that a plurality mediates a practico-inert domain that prefigures its own division. Sartre asserts that the plurality mediating the practico-inert must accommodate to pre-given conditions and, therefore, the inner organization of the plurality is influenced by the practico-inert. In this case, isolation seems to be brought back to external conditions.

For Sartre, the phenomenon of isolation allows for pure demonstration in specific areas of public life, such as public means of commerce, means of mass communication, the market. These areas are viewed as evidence that isolation as a characteristic of human collectivities corresponds to the peculiarity of practico-inert actuality. He asserts that the practico-inert is so constituted that men emerge as isolated. In the first instance, the automobile driver, the reader, the listener, the competitor are implicated in no other relationships with one another than those of observing certain rules of utilization and dealing with a prefabricated practico-inert domain. The plurality of people involved in commerce, of readers, and so forth, presents in its wholeness no practical communities that have united for the accomplishment of definite tasks and for the pursuit of specific goals. Rather, they are collectivities of isolated men whose external unity is the practico-inert object.

III. The Concept of Seriality

Sartre develops *seriality* from the reciprocal mediation of a plurality and the practico-inert. His description of the rationality of this type of mediation proceeds from the presupposition that isolation is a characteristic of these pluralities.

We can pursue the relationship of the plurality and the practico-inert in the first instance with those examples that Sartre has introduced: waiting at a bus stop and using the underground, respectively. Sartre describes the following situation: a plurality of isolated men find themselves within a common practical field; among their activities there exists no synchronization; they pursue no common goal. Each of those waiting at the bus stop or using the underground finds his possibilities prescribed in the same manner. The timetables and the information at the station are valid for the individual as well as for everyone else. The steps that lead the underground's users up to the street, the traffic island that protects those waiting at the bus stop from the traffic that is flowing by, the behavior that must be employed (giving signs, getting in, canceling the travel ticket, entering through the front door, exiting through the back door, and so forth) have no relationship to the personal character of the individual. Borrowing from Heidegger, Sartre says that the individual is "anyone" who uses the underground, who waits at the bus stop.[28] Certainly, each individual distinguishes himself from his neighbors by the details of his life, by his family, by the objectives that he pursues, by his past. However, with respect to the proximate objectives of waiting for the bus, of using the underground, the individual is simply "anyone." In his individuality, he is unessential. Everyone could stand in his place. The individual appears as interchangeable with any of his neighbors. (CDR, pp. 255ff.; Fr., pp. 308ff.; and BN, pp. 423ff.; Fr., pp. 495ff.)

Collectivities of the type treated first present themselves as though they were exclusively structured by the field of objects. Sartre would like to make it clear that the structure, which seems imposed upon the plurality from the outside, can really only establish itself through the cooperation of the plurality. Accordingly, seriality is not to be understood as a reflection of an external structure in a collectivity. Rather, it is traced back to how a grouping conducts itself toward a domain of objects.

We want to continue with our example of how the structure of seriality is created. Sartre advances from the position that the collectivity of people waiting for the bus sees itself over against a complex of exigencies and things. He imputes the following givens. The bus travels at definite times established in the timetable. In order to be taken in the bus, one must draw a number from an automatic machine that determines the order of those waiting. Depending upon how many places are available in the bus, the number entitles one to enter it, although it may be necessary to stay outside and wait longer. A travel ticket is canceled upon entering. When one wants to leave, he must give a signal. There is a specific door set aside to be used as an exit, just as there is another for an entrance. Everything is rigidly ordered. One must insert oneself into the given order or else choose another means of transportation.

In the plurality there is clearly a structure that is mediated through the

---

28. Martin Heidegger, *Being and Time*, trans. John Macquarrie and Edward Robinson (New York: Harper & Row, 1962), section 27.

common object. A series has been established among the individuals by the numbers. The possibilities of the individual are determined by his place in the series. Whether one can be taken in the bus is dependent upon how many free places are available. On the other hand, the place of the individual is still not determined just by objects. His place in the series is dependent upon other individuals, who also wait. It is dependent upon the fact that someone has come before and another after him. (CDR, pp. 258-262; Fr., pp. 310-313)

What matters for Sartre in the previous example can be indicated by two points. First of all, he would like to show that the practico-inert indeed presents a pre-given order for the relations within the plurality, but this order must be effected by individuals themselves. It should also be made clear that, on the basis of a presupposition of isolation, there is a mediation of the practical field by a plurality as a whole. Sartre maintains that the individual, as long as he appears in collectivities, occupies definite possibilities from which others are excluded. In this way a diversity of relations of reciprocal dependence arises within a plurality of isolated individuals. These relations produce the integration of isolated individuals into a common mediation of the practical field. On the other hand, this common mediation occurs only on the foundation of the practico-inert object. The evident givens of the local bus organization determine the structure of relations within the series of waiting people. The "totality" of all the determinations shape the possibilities of the individual. This totality is fixed by the pre-given external organization and by the mediation of the plurality. (CDR, pp. 263ff.; Fr., pp. 314ff.) Here the practico-inert appears as the dominating realm. The formation of relations among particular individuals appears, therefore, not as the production of a synchronizing praxis but rather as the actualization of a predetermined reality by social atoms. (CDR, pp. 268-269; Fr., p. 318)

The structural conditions of alienation can already be recognized. Sartre would like to elucidate the rationality of the process that leads to the formation of a system of relations that are both rigid and not controlled by individuals, a system to which they are subjugated. The alienation is derived from the individual's participation in constituting the system and at the same time his inability to determine which possibilities are open to him within that system. Here alienation first arises in a provisional way. Nevertheless, the structures of the appearances of alienation already point to those we have come to know in our sketch of fetishism in Marx's thought. There too, alienation consisted in a system of relations that had become autonomous over against those very individuals who had participated in creating it. The difference between Sartre's and Marx's intentions is already clear. Sartre is not concerned with the description of concrete phenomena such as the constitution of price and the process of capital. Rather, he prefers to explain in greater generality the schema of determination by which many isolated individuals find themselves subjugated to a social system. Alienation ought to be presented as a structure.[29]

IV. Seriality and Powerlessness

The collection of people who are waiting for a bus is a simple example of a series. There exist "direct relations" among the members of this series, namely, all members are present in it. Interaction among these particular individuals could take place immediately. One could start up a conversation with his neighbor just by chance. Sartre now shows that the dependence of the individual upon others is intensified by factors that increase the degree of isolation among members of the plurality. Such factors include, for example, the reduction or enlargement of numbers. In the collective of people who are waiting, an individual who would like to have a place on the next bus could request of those ahead of him a position further up in the series. Such an attempt to abolish isolation can be condemned to failure in larger groups and in the absence of others. Sartre sees in this case the source of the phenomenon of serial powerlessness. (CDR, pp. 269ff.; Fr., pp. 319ff.)

The presupposition for powerlessness is a more acute isolation. In our example of people who are waiting, some elementary givens that characterize large masses of people who live together—in a large city, for instance—were taken as factors that are relevant for isolation. In this case, the isolation consists in the fact that people do not know one another and therefore, following custom, do not speak to one another. Perhaps one isolates himself from the others by reading the newspaper he has just bought or by thinking of his job or by continuing to think of his family, which he has just left. As we have already said, the factual isolation that exists among the members of a collective could be easily abolished. In other situations, the isolation among the members of a plurality that is joined by a practico-inert object operates more seriously insofar as it seems impossible, in any case under the given conditions, to reach agreement. Sartre also imputes other meanings of isolation to this case. Isolation consists now in factors such as the dispersion of the members of a series over a geographical area, the diversity of their intentions and interests, their definite opposition through competition or enmity, their variety of world views. Isolation is no longer the indifferent and more or less accidental coexistence of social atoms.

Sartre wants to clarify why, in cases of absence or opposition, one's insertion into a serially structured system of relations can signify coercion. While it was possible, in our previous example, to conceive of withdrawing from the system, thought is now subjugated to an inescapable system. In our context, the coercion should not be rooted in men or in the authority exercised

---

29. Knecht, *Theorie*, pp. 259–265.

upon them. Rather, its source is due to the impossibility of the plurality itself controlling the practical field. Therefore, the coercion is indirect and
consists in the powerlessness experienced in view of the system.

Sartre's description of the phenomenon of powerlessness does not depend upon the concrete meaning of definite forms of isolation. His only
presupposition is that the spatial isolation of the individual from the other
members of the series cannot be abolished under the given circumstances
and that a certain opposition exists in the series. The relation of the individual to the others is otherwise left open. The other is thought of as a contingent other who appears to the rest of the members of the series in a sort of
"counter-orientation." The decisive factor is that, under the conditions of
the series, the contingency of the other makes him inscrutable to everyone
else. The practical field becomes insecure — particularly when the determination of possibilities given by the practico-inert object is less rigid and,
thus, the latitude of the individual is greater. For the individual, then, others appear in their contingency as completely ungraspable. To a certain extent, contingency strengthens the gravity of isolation.

Sartre elucidates the moment of powerlessness by the example of a radio
broadcast whose political message is heard by a great number of listeners.
The specific content in the example is not essential for our context. It serves
as an illustration of seriality as a structure. The audience is interpreted as a
series of isolated individuals structured by the practico-inert object, that is,
the radio. The reception at home breaks the audience into particular individuals or small groups. Other factors are added to the spatial isolation and
intensify it. The contingency of the other subjectivities is indicated by the
relationship of the individual members of the series to the broadcast. Sartre
distinguishes the listeners who are in agreement with the broadcast from
those who are in opposition to it; these are further distinguished from those
who are undecided, those who are waiting, those who are already half persuaded, those who are without an opinion, those who are easily influenced,
those who are opportunists, and so forth. Considered from the standpoint
of the particular listener, the others are capable of taking up these various
positions in response to the broadcast. Under the conditions of isolation a
sphere of insecurity emerges for the individual. He does not know how the
others will react. Will they let themselves be persuaded? Will they be unsure?

Sartre interprets the possible reactions of the other listeners from the
perspective of seriality. The possible reactions of the others determine the
conduct of the particular individual. According to the example, the individual may be determined by the probability that the view articulated in
the broadcast will influence other listeners and that the actual processes of
political life will also be affected. To a certain extent, the particular individual listens to the whole broadcast from the perspective of the other. Perhaps he obtains only a prereflective awareness of his sense of powerlessness

before the practico-inert object and the plurality of others. He senses that the future activities of others will be influenced by this broadcast and that they will shape his own fate. Perhaps the formation of opinion owing to the influence of the broadcast will affect an important political event, for example, an election. This process withdraws, however, from the control of the individual. What will happen is decisively dependent upon others. Powerlessness manifests itself in that the future is not shaped by the goal of the individual. Rather, it appears as a dimension of alienation. (CDR, pp. 270–276; Fr., pp. 320–325)

Alienation appears in the form of a rotating deprivation of power among the members of the series. The social significance of powerlessness as a moment of seriality cannot, however, be viewed as only the powerlessness of an individual confronting the whole. Sartre would like to indicate that, in addition, the powerlessness of the individual members of the series results in the powerlessness of the series itself. Hence, the serial structure of a plurality also always implies the possibility of domination.

V. Recurrence as a Pattern of Alienating Repercussion

Up until now the series has appeared as fundamentally a static collection of separate individuals. Sartre now takes into consideration additional moments in the structure of seriality. As an illustration, he employs basically nonstatic series in which individuals affect one another by their actions within a common practical field. Furthermore, he no longer considers the members of the series as particular individuals. Pairs joined by reciprocal relations now emerge as members of the series. The pairs themselves are, to be sure, separated from other pairs. As members of the pair relation, particular individuals do not necessarily appear at all times. Even groups can be incorporated into a pair relation. A pair relation can also consist of a relation between one group and another or between a particular individual and a group. (CDR, pp. 280–281; Fr., p. 328)

The market, public belief, social class are introduced as examples of collectivities with serially structured associations of pairs. Sartre maintains that there is always a reciprocal relation in totalities of this type: the relation of buyer to seller, seller to his customers, and competing sellers to one another. Also there is the relation between the person who publicly voices a current belief and the person who follows it. Then, there is the relation among colleagues at work and that between the particular worker and his union. For Sartre, the significance of seriality for the characterization of social givens is adequately determined when its applicability to the type of associations that have been introduced can be shown. This is especially important for him in the light of his effort to generalize Marx's description of the phenomenon of fetishism. Sartre would like to show that, under definite conditions in which men face the result of their activities, they realize their position of powerlessness—even when positive reciprocal relations exist among them.

We will follow the structure of complex series through the example of price formation as determined by competition within a market. Here isolation exists on the side of competing sellers. The isolation of the buyers consists in their entering into the market as particular individuals. Because of the absence of an agreement among them (for example, not to buy commodities that exceed a certain price limit), they become social atoms.

Sartre points out that price formation is the outcome of the activities of the seller-buyer totality and that this outcome is generated upon the foundations of relations existing among individuals within the market. Supply and demand are not to be understood as categories of political economy, which serve to explain the process of price formation. Rather, they are concrete actions of individual men. A seller offers his commodities at a definite price, while the buyer announces that he is prepared to pay this or that price.

The market is conceived of as an ideal unity of communication. All stand in a relation with one another and, therefore, every variation in supply and demand spreads to the whole and operates upon the price. On the one hand, the rise in supply at a lower price immediately forces the other sellers to reduce their price. On the other hand, an increase in demand compels the buyers to pay a higher price if they wish to obtain the commodity. In this case, for Sartre, the activity of others, owing to a lack of agreement, determines the activity of every single individual. The engaged individual looks toward the plurality of others. The market necessitates acquiescence in the collectivity if one's interests are to be safeguarded. The market appears as a unity within which the individual's activity accommodates to the activity of others. (CDR, pp. 281-286; Fr., 329-332)

The interpretation that Sartre gives to the process of price formation should indicate that the individual perceives the market as a totality that always has reference to the activity of others. Therefore, the price, while based upon a buying transaction, does not appear as a purely private agreement between buyer and seller. Rather, it emerges within the totality of the market, a totality that seems to "flee" from the individual toward the others. Sartre maintains that within the series of pairs (buyers and sellers) there exists a rotating relationship that has actual reference to others and that determines the specific reciprocity within the collectivity of others. With respect to price, the individual finds himself in a position of powerlessness. As Sartre expresses it, the individual sees "his direct action deprived of its real meaning insofar as the Other governs it, and in his turn hastens to influence the Other, over there, without any real relation to his intention." The price prevails through a circular induction, which is sustained by all the members of the series without being an object of agreement. This imposition of price holds for the individual, because it governs his neighbor, and it holds for his neighbor, because it governs that person's neighbor, and so forth. (CDR, pp. 286-289; Fr., pp. 332-335)

The process of price formation demonstrates to Sartre a structure that is characteristic of serial activity in a plurality. On the one hand, the price seems to be the communal result of everyone's activities. On the other hand, it cannot be said that the price originates from the agreement of individuals. The price appears to us, rather, as a result that, to a certain extent, takes place behind the backs of the individuals; nevertheless, one could not speak of an interweaving of powers that is to be located outside the plurality. Rather, the price points back to activities of individuals, but under conditions of isolation and lack of organization.

Sartre employs this model of a plurality's serial activity for a characterization of alienation. He would like to show that alienation emerges from the opposition between individual activity and the totalization of multiple praxis. Sartre wants to show that alienation results from the activity of a plurality under conditions of seriality. Alienation consists in the totalization of multiple praxis dominating the actions of particular individuals. Again, we return to the position that a plurality's common action to realize a common project is not the basis of a totalization. As in the example of price resulting from totalization, totalization occurs by separate and discordant actions of particular individuals. For Sartre, alienation manifests itself in the form of a hiatus. Indeed, totalization demands the activity of isolated individuals. Nevertheless, it does not determine the result.

Sartre does not hold one system, created in whatever way, responsible for alienation. Rather, dependence upon the performance of others in a ready-made practico-inert field appears as the moment of alienation. This dependence is bound up with the situation that is characterized by the powerlessness of particular individuals in the face of the plurality of others. However, the powerlessness of the oppressed is not in question here. Instead, powerlessness is founded upon the nonconcurrence of particular individuals in their activities. For Sartre, this returns to the force exercised upon each person by the activities of many individuals. (SM, pp. 78-79; Fr., p. 56)

That which presents itself as compulsion, when objectively seen, seems to be an accommodation to the activities of others from a subjective perspective. The accommodation effects the totalization, which can be regarded simultaneously as a result and as a cause of serial powerlessness. It is the cause of powerlessness because, through it, the atomized plurality of others appears over against the individual as an alienating association. It is the result of powerlessness insofar as it is grounded in the activities of particular individuals who find themselves in a position of powerlessness when faced with the plurality of others. Since I cannot prevent the other from conducting his affairs in a certain manner, I hasten to insert myself into his affairs. Yet my possible behavior has already influenced that of the other. In the conduct of others, the behavior of each individual comes to the same point and influences him. According to Sartre, this is a question of "lateral totalization," which is typical of the series. This totalization does not issue in a direct agreement of individuals. The impossibility of arriving at an agreement with others is fundamental. (CDR, p. 289; Fr., 335) Alienation consists precisely in this. It shows that the individual, in his state of powerlessness when confronting the conduct of others, can accomplish only those goals that are accommodated to the goals of others. Alienation expresses itself when each individual conducts himself as "Other than himself." (CDR, p. 308; Fr., p. 350) Such a situation can be shown by an entrepreneur's introducing new machines under the pressure of competition, by the reactions of a listener to a radio broadcast, by the individual's accepting and repeating a public belief that can be neither verified nor falsified, by accommodation to the process of price formation in the market, by the behavior of individuals at a time of inflation (each seeks immediately to exchange his money for commodities, because he foresees that others will react in the same way). In the serial activity of a multitude, the individual appears determined by a future development that he cannot grasp. He can keep the connection only while he accommodates himself. (CDR, p. 289; Fr., p. 335)

Sartre has designated the totalization of the series and the constitutive lateral totalizations of individuals as *recurrence*. (CDR, p. 275; Fr., p. 324) The concept of recurrence designates the process of serial mediation. Recurrence constitutes for Sartre the fundamental structure of alienation in the context of which it is possible to understand all concrete forms of alienation. In this sense, he identifies it as *primitive alienation*. Here "primitive" does not refer to historical temporality. "Alienation by recurrence" does not describe the form of alienation that historically precedes the other forms of alienation. Rather, it occupies the position of a structural moment in the constitution of meaning for all appearances of social alienation: if the activities of a plurali y are characterized by recurrence, alienation is present.

The structural foundation of alienation accounts for Sartre's efforts to define alienation as beyond the opposition between capitalism and socialism. Sartre refuses the judgment that alienation exists only in capitalism and that it has lost its basis for existence in socialist countries.[30] This tendency, which has paralyzed the analysis of alienation, becomes evident when one is distinguishing between alienation resulting from recurrence and its "historically" identified forms, such as exploitation in capitalism. This exploitation is interpreted as the historical-concrete form of the structural alienation explained by recurrence. (CDR, p. 164; Fr., 234) The distinction provides an important foundation for evaluating Sartre's concept of alienation in its relationship to that of Marx. Whereas for Sartre the capitalist form of exploitation can be made to disappear — namely, by over-

---

30. Ibid., pp. 53ff.

throwing the social relations—alienation by recurrence is a state of affairs that can appear in any conceivable society, so long as the conditions of the series are given. (CDR, pp. 306–307; Fr., p. 349) The concrete appearance of alienation is dependent upon the conditions that the particular society furnishes. When we consider that the Sartrian theory of seriality describes the same structure of alienation as does fetishism in Marx, it strikes one at once that when Sartre draws examples from economics for illustration, he does not argue in terms of the economic in the same sense as Marx does.[31] Marx explains the price of commodities by the economic argument that socially necessary working hours provide a measure of the commodity's value.[32] We have already treated the Sartrian conception of price formation, which runs contrary to Marx's view. Sartre offers no role to economic arguments of this type. He attempts to clarify alienation, when it arises in the process of price formation, as occurring within the framework of the generally posited dialectic of practico-inert and social plurality. The process of price formation presents an elaboration of the anthropological structure of seriality with an economic content. The economic content serves to illustrate a structure. Isolation, powerlessness, recurrence, alterity are moments of a structure that is certainly suitable to the economic sphere but whose range is more comprehensive. Here alienation seems to be more generally grounded than in Marx.

The generalizing, after which the Sartrian theory of alienation strives, enlarges the sphere of realities to which the concept of alienation can be applied. This does not only mean that the concept of alienation is detached from its close association with the economic sphere. The generalizing also prevents the restricting of alienation to the critique of capitalism. Alienation is linked much more to the conditions that absolutely relate to the anthropological characterization of sociality.

Like Marx, Sartre departs from an atomized plurality. The mutuality on this point is, to be sure, only a formal one. In actuality, two different levels of reality are at the root of the theory. Sartre's anthropology bases itself upon the plurality of irreducible subjectivities. If particular individuals act, in Marx's theory of fetishism, it is, on the contrary, a matter of existentially diminished essences. They appear as personifications of categorical economic determinants. In this sense, Marx even indicates that he wants to understand persons only as the "personifications of economic categories."[33] They are apprehended "not as individuals."[34] In line with this, Marx speaks in another place of the "economic character-masks of persons" as being only the "personifications of economic relations."[35]

---

31. Hartmann, *Die Marxsche Theorie*, p. 325.
32. Marx, *Capital* 1: 38–40.
33. Ibid., p. 10.
34. Ibid., p. 162.
35. Ibid., p. 85.

Certainly a tendency to let the plurality of individuals recede behind economic categories is present in Marx's theory. Even if atomism is presupposed for all levels of the theory of capital, it does not mean that Marx is thinking of pluralities of irreducible, individual existences. Atomization states the condition for the process of capital to represent an autonomous movement over against a plurality of social atoms. Competition and the private character of the appropriation of values created by labor should make it clear that the result of the many individual activities cannot be determined by particular individuals.

In this perspective atomization can be considered as the "ground" for the possibility of an objective dialectic of capital. The atomized plurality of individuals appears here as subjugated to a movement that follows the dialectical rationality of capital. Exchange, price, money, surplus value, accumulation, and so forth are all determinations that can be defined only in relation to a social plurality, but even here, individuals are thought of only as personifications of economic meanings. Capital appears as an autonomous stage. It possesses its own necessity. It itself, not the praxis of individuals, is the beginning and the end of movement, in Marx's sense of dialectic.[36]

The objective dialectic of capital, which emerges as an independent stage over against the social plurality, forces the subjective moment into the background. Klaus Hartmann characterizes this form of dialectic as a "logic of essence" (*Wesenslogik*). He considers that the "treatment of society in terms of a logic of essence," as designated by the opposition between capital and labor, is a mistake in Marx's theory. He objects that a critical theory of the social — which remains on the level of a categorically comprehended essence of the social — can present a critique only as a "categorical development of the negativity of essence." And so the spontaneity and contingency of the individual remain neglected.[37]

Included within this tendency of Marx's theory is the comprehension of alienation as a moment in the essence of the capitalist system. Correspondingly, the necessity of its surpassing is presented as the contradiction that is immanent to the dialectical rationality of capital. The plural praxis pressing for modification of an alienated society reduces to the role of executing a dialectical-logical necessity. By asserting a dialectic of essence, Marx seems to have already decided about the development of society and the nature of alienation.[38]

Sartrian social theory presents a very different face. It is true that alienation reveals itself in his analysis of the exigencies of the practico-inert as a moment of a "system." However, alienation also has the character of an adaptation. In this, he expresses his conception that alienation must be actualized by freedom.[39] Sartre emphasizes this conception on the level of the

---

36. Marx, *Grundrisse*, pp. 106–107.
37. Hartmann, *Die Marxsche Theorie*, pp. 181ff.
38. Knecht, *Theorie*, pp. 12ff.
39. Ibid., p. 130.

series by maintaining that alienation is made comprehensible by a definite form of plural praxis, seriality. This assessment is indeed identical with that of Marx: like Marx, Sartre roots his view of alienation in social atomization. Certainly, there is an important difference. In Sartre's thought, *atomization*, insofar as it constitutes the foundation of alienation, does not simply evoke a movement of the system in which the alienated plurality is a moment, which it is for Marx. For Sartre, the social plurality, insofar as it is alienated, is not reducible to a moment of the system. Rather, social plurality is an irreducible stage of the social dialectic that is conceived along the lines of a reciprocal mediation between the plurality and the practico-inert. Here alienation is the result of activity by a serially structured plurality, as its "accomplishment."

At the same time, the plurality is not thought of as a super-subject. Sartre is oriented more in terms of the social being-in-the-world of particular individuals, who are placed under definite conditions — the coexistence of a plurality of individuals separated from one another in a social field full of exigencies. Thus, alienation is characterized by structural moments of relations that bind a particular individual to the plurality of others and to the givens of the practico-inert. And so, alterity, powerlessness, and recurrence are moments of alienation that are shaped by the orientation of individuals. In Sartre's thought, alienation seems exclusively characterized by anthropologically conceived structural moments. The concrete social areas to which reference is made in the development of these moments (the means of transportation, the instruments of mass communication, the market) have a paradigmatic character. For the sake of demonstration, these areas should fill out these structural states of affairs with historical-social contents. The demonstration of the structure itself does not obtain its orientation from a sociological or economic subject, but from the dialectical-anthropological relationship of the reciprocal mediation of the plurality and the practico-inert field.

Sartre is not satisfied by an organizational structure in the more precise demonstration of alienation on the practico-inert level. For him, the relationship between seriality and alienation is only incompletely described when the characterization of alienation is not finally related to individual praxis. The manner of doing this consists in showing, to the extent of the alienation, the falsification of individual purposes entailed by serial mediation. Alienation is characterized as a *counter-finality (contre-finalité)*.

VI. Alienation as a *Counter-finality*

In his description of alienation as a counter-finality, Sartre starts from the position that the actions of members of a series objectify themselves in terms of results. These objectifications of actions account for the experience of modifications that were not contained in the purposes of the actions. The modification of purposes is interpreted as alienation. Let us cite some examples. Sartre introduces the example of periodically recurring floods in the vicinity of China's great rivers, as a result of the continual clearing operations by Chinese farmers. The floods are the unintended result of activities directed toward winning back the land. The floods are traced back to the inner laws of the material realm: clearing the forest leads to an increase in the sedimentation of soil and raises the level of the river above that of the plain. Clearly, the realm of objectified action provides a context for the alienating modification. This is shown in another of Sartre's examples, that of the pollution of the air by exhaust gasses from an industrial plant. The gasses cause harm not only to human health but also, by corrosion, to the buildings and industrial plant. They are interpreted as a result that was not intended and which, to some extent, arises as a repercussion from the work being done on the particular industrial material. (CDR, pp. 193–195; Fr., pp. 258ff.) The material appears as a judgment directed against the society's praxis. It incorporates the plurality of activities objectified in it and binds them to its inherent lawfulness. As in the previous examples, the result can be the opposite of what was intended by human activity. Therefore, Sartre speaks of the counter-finality of the material that is worked upon.[40]

Characterizing the objectification as alienation cannot be limited to the material result of the objectification. It must include the structure of plural praxis that produces the alienated result. Sartre interprets the process of objectification by means of seriality. The floods arrived as a negative effect of human activity only because everyone was continually engaged in clearing the forest (for generations) without a fixed plan and in ignorance of possible consequences. The effort directed at recovering the land is deprived of its meaning, because a flood presents a new catastrophe each time. (CDR, pp. 175–176; Fr., p. 243) Dangers to health and harm to plants and buildings emerged only because all or almost all of the entrepreneurs of a particular epoch allowed the air pollution to take place. The alienating counter-finality of the material realm seems to be a result of human conduct. The material realm is only a vehicle. Its action is set into motion by men. Because, as Sartre presupposes, the powerlessness of a serially structured plurality frustrates the transformation of the situation, men seem to be an object of what is done, of something that has taken place because of the activity of all. The praxis of the plurality generates results that no longer correspond to its original intentions. For Sartre, the counter-finality of the material worked upon finally goes back to an opposition generated by praxis itself.

Sartre presents seriality as the social structure that can make objectification intelligible as a factor of alienation on the social level. The recurrent process of the series' disharmonious activities furnishes the model for dem-

---

40. Hartmann, *Sartres Sozialphilosophie*, p. 98.

onstrating the alienation of objectification. Alienation, therefore, affects not only the act of objectification but also its result. Alienation consists in powerlessness bringing the individual member of the series to accommodate his activity within the series. As we have seen, for that very reason his activity seems to be already alienated in its origin. The alienation is constituted by the individual's putting his goals aside into a realm of possibilities that external relations and the activities of the series of others permit him. Insofar as every member of the series finds himself in this situation of powerlessness, and the series allows him to seize possibilities that recur within the series, it seems that the series itself is what is fundamentally active. And this is Sartre's interpretation: the series becomes autonomous over against each of its members and it develops its own finality. Alienation consists in this. (SM, pp. 163-164; Fr., p. 102)

The explanation of alienation in Sartre's thought is based upon a fundamental criterion in which the counter-finality of the practico-inert is entailed in objectification. Accordingly, alienation is present when the projected aims of praxis are robbed of their authentic meaning by the reality that is allotted to them in the act of or in the result of objectification. And so he writes: "But the permanent possibility that an end might be transformed into an illusion characterizes the social field and the modes of alienation; it does not remove from the end its irreducible structure. Still better: the notions of alienation and mystification have meaning only to the precise degree that they steal away the ends and disqualify them." (SM, p. 158; Fr., p. 99) By pointing to this, Sartre characterizes the falsification of the aims of individual activities as alienation. Indeed, the counter-finality of the practico-inert cannot be understood as the alienation of aims for the series. The aims of the series could be included only if some sort of agreement and harmony existed in the series. The series, however, is characterized precisely in terms of the isolation and disharmony of the projected aims of its members. Alienation as falsification of aims is related, therefore, to the projected aims of particular individuals. (CDR, pp. 806-808; Fr., pp. 745ff.)

Sartre is not new in proposing that alienation consists in man's creating a reality in his product that does not correspond to the intention of his activity. This aspect of alienation is also found in Marx, who emphasizes that to the alienated and exploited worker, his labor seems "as an activity turned against him, as independent of him, as not belonging to him."[41] Sartre's novelty does not consist in his definition of the meaning of alienation, but rather in the type of explanation he offers. In Marx's thought, the phenomenon of alienation always appears in connection with the capitalist economy and the history of the division of labor. Sartre consciously advances

---

41. Karl Marx, *The Economic and Philosophic Manuscripts of 1844*, trans. Martin Milligan (New York: International Publishers, 1964), pp. 111-112.

beyond this context to the anthropological-structural state of affairs, with the intention of generalizing Marx's concept of alienation.

For Sartre the criterion of alienation is clearly not — as it is for Marx — a deterioration in the concept of the essence of true mutuality. The moment of strangeness is in the failure of aims and results to correspond to one another. Just as in the case of the criterion, the foundation of the alienation is also immanent to the plurality itself. Alienation should not be interpreted as a moment that comes from the outside. An inner structure is made responsible for it: social atomization and seriality of praxis return to it. Here the tendency of Sartrian thought shows itself: to define alienation extensively within a phenomenology of the social. This is not to say that the meaning of alienation is determined in an exclusively phenomenological manner and that it is introduced to the social realm without reference to an external standard of value. Certainly, the normative, in which definite social states of affairs appear as alienated, is here reduced to a minimum. Unlike Marx, Sartre does not refer to the notions of species-being or universally-developed labor. Sartre's conception of alienation is more extensive than that of Marx. The idea of emancipation is not linked to the realm of labor to such a decisive degree as in Marx. The conception that the falsification of individuals' projected aims is the criterion for alienation implies the accordance of project and realization as a positive contrast of an absent alienation. The Sartrian conception of alienation is clearly oriented toward a standard of freedom that accounts for a situation whose organization does not hinder it from realizing what it has proposed for itself.

Mikel Dufrenne

12. *Sartre and Merleau-Ponty**

Within Parisian intellectual circles, Sartre is no longer fashionable. Our present situation does not yet provide the distance needed to measure his work and to assign him a place in the history of ideas. On the other hand, posthumous judgments and laurels of a meager immortality make little difference, particularly to Sartre. But let us make no mistake: whatever the ebbs and flows of fashion may be, Sartre is profoundly present for our present age. We are all Sartrians — perhaps because, on the whole, Sartre is not Sartre. But he would certainly like to be the elusive power of reflection that is faithful only to a thoroughly generous inspiration. For this reason, outside academia and professional circles Sartre is *the* philosopher, the incarnation of militant philosophy — just as Picasso embodies painting.

Apparently, however, opposition to Sartre thrives among specialists. What is the counterposition? On the one hand, it is the philosophy of the concept, authorized by scientific, semiological, and structuralist knowledge. On the other hand, it is the philosophy of nonphilosophy — sometimes in terms of traces, sometimes in terms of flux. Nevertheless, has not Sartre contributed to knowledge and to analytic reason just as much as he has contributed to dialectical reason? And if we hold that knowledge is the ally of power, that science becomes ideology and that philosophy must have at least some force, must we not still look for the first manifestation of this force in Sartre? For him, philosophy ceases to be the authoritarian and totalitarian discourse of the master. It exists only by way of a subjectivity that "bursts forth towards the world" (following Sartre's interpretation of Husserlian intentionality).[1] Philosophy is carried out by the practice of a philosopher who writes plays, attempts a political reassessment, supports the Russell tribunal, creates a journal, and acts with militancy on many terrains.

---

*Translated from the French by Hugh J. Silverman and Frederick A. Elliston
1. See Jean-Paul Sartre, "Intentionality: A Fundamental Idea of Husserl's Phenomenology," trans. Joseph P. Fell, *Journal of The British Society for Phenomenology* Vol. 1, no. 2 (May 1970), pp. 4–5.

Despite this philosophical burgeoning, Sartre cannot claim a monopoly on philosophy. As for his contemporaries within the French context, another philosopher—Maurice Merleau-Ponty—can be set off against Sartre. They were once very close: classmates at the École Normale, comrades in battle at *Les Temps Modernes*, a solid friendship that later dissolved between them. We know of the emotion with which Sartre recalled their friendship on the occasion of Merleau-Ponty's premature death. And yet they diverged. Without crossing swords overtly they unequivocally maintained their dignity. Must we therefore, in turn, put one in opposition to the other—perhaps even to the extent of taking sides?

We cannot ignore the reasons that separated them. Their reasons were serious, yet they acted without excessive seriousness. Both were profoundly ethical—that is, political. What caused the break was Merleau-Ponty's attitude toward the Communist Party in *The Adventures of the Dialectic* (1955). This position was no longer the reticence of *Humanism and Terror* but an outright refusal. This is very significant. For French intellectuals, the Communist Party did not cease to be a problem, and did not cease to create problems. Witness the sometimes theatrical movement of adherence and resignation and even, most recently, the turns that *Tel Quel* has taken. The problem is above all that of allegiance to the party in Moscow. Today this subordination is undoubtedly less strong. It is even more intolerable now that the Soviet state has betrayed the Revolution and its only ambition is to be a partner—the equal—of the United States. Yet in France, the Communist Party continues to be the party of the proletariat. For a long time it was impossible—at least until 1968—to undertake any action in the streets, to work in spite of, or even outside the party. Can we disengage ourselves from all the workers whom the party unites and who are the living force of the proletariat? Can we be content to say that these workers are mystified and neutralized? Thus, we adopt a good conscience—at little cost to ourselves. Must we sacrifice the solidarity and efficacy that is too easy for the privileged to reject in favor of purity? It makes little difference today whether purity flies the colors of the impure, the perverse, and the schizoid. Purity always runs the risk of being a pretext for someone's resignation. Sartre never resigned from his position as a beautiful revolutionary soul, and as one who passively awaits a miracle.

Neither Sartre nor Merleau-Ponty ever believed that they could situate themselves outside history and become disinterested toward the present. They were both committed—initially side by side at *Les Temps Modernes*. Yet even then they were committed in terms of their different styles. When Merleau-Ponty in *The Adventures of the Dialectic* distanced himself from his friend, he left Sartre with a moral project of the Kantian sort. Simone de Beauvoir became indignant, as if it were shameful to be a Kantian. And yet Merleau-Ponty was not wrong. Even if Sartre's commitment does not have the rationality of a formal imperative (which, for Kant, is supposed to be

forged into empirical choices), it acquired the character of an absolute decision. Nourished within bourgeois culture, Sartre chose to put himself un-
reservedly at the service of the oppressed. His was an original and, we might
add, unreflective or nontheoretical choice, because it remained prior to all
deliberative reflection on history. The *Critique of Dialectical Reason* was
not published, and not even written, until 1960 — whereas the break with
Merleau-Ponty occurred in 1955. This choice induced Sartre to join in
common cause with the Communist Party, at least on precise and limited
subjects. Whatever the case, he certainly knew that the Party is the instrument of Russian imperialism, that the Revolution in the Soviet Union had
been stifled by the bureaucracy and the police, and that the proletariat was
in no way a dictatorship that could prepare for the abolition of the state.
But he also knew that the Party in France is, objectively speaking, the sole
force capable of rallying the proletariat, because the proletariat recognizes
itself in the Party. Sartre refused, therefore, radically to cut himself off
from the Party. Merleau-Ponty made a different choice. Indeed, he chose
not to choose. He did not offend history by throwing himself into it.
Rather, he maintained his distance, just because he considered himself already thrown. This passive commitment within history preserved him from
an active commitment. The unreflected that surrounded him — the complexity and opacity of historical situations — brought him to a reflection
that compelled him to "decipher the probable" without compromising itself
with radical options. Their situation parallels the relationship between
Hume and Kant.

Thus, what separates Sartre from Merleau-Ponty is a tactical problem.
But their divergence expresses the difference between two beings-in-the-
world, one who is more abrupt, more willful, more concerned with disengag-
ing himself from his context; the other who is more reserved, more subtle,
more prudent. This inevitable difference reverberates in their philosophies.
But does it extend to the point of placing them in opposition? I would like
to show that little by little Sartre's thought, especially when he wrote the
Critique, cautions above all that his philosophy does not conflict with that
of Merleau-Ponty.

In 1955 Merleau-Ponty became hardened to what he could not accept in
Sartre, even to the point of caricature: the passion for freedom, the idea of
a radical upheaval of the for-itself outside the shadows of the in-itself, and
what he calls "the folly of the *cogito*." And certainly Sartre forcefully affirms the irreducibility of the subject. Yet consciousness is not always purely
personal. Since it is self-consciousness, nothing issues forth from it. But the
dualism to which this initial affirmation seems to lead is not the last word.
Acts of consciousness are not pure acts; choices are not sovereign decisions.
And indeed, as Francis Jeanson has indicated, Sartre describes images of
the bastard in his novels and plays: "Roquentin, Orestes, Mathieu . . .
three failures in freedom." Freedom fails to interrogate itself, to take itself

as an end. It is found only when it is engaged in an action in which it forgets itself. In effect, the for-itself always has an obligatory relation to the in-itself. At the end of *Being and Nothingness*, beyond the dualism that a "phenomenological ontology" suggests, Sartre asks a "metaphysical" question in order to determine whether this relation can be articulated within a totality. It is perhaps true that this totality must always remain "both indicated and impossible," that we can no longer be Spinozists. To think this totality would be to think God, and furthermore to think myself as God. For in me the for-itself is first advanced to the in-itself without alienating itself. And I am a bastard more easily than God is.

This totality is no less lived because it is unthinkable. It is not mastered within a dialectic but lived in ambiguity. The philosophy of *Being and Nothingness* could also have been called a philosophy of ambiguity, as De Waelhens and others have described Merleau-Ponty's work.

First there is the fact—the metaphysical fact, if you like—of birth. The for-itself bursts forth abruptly. It acts in accordance with a celebrated formula: "carried by the in-itself, the for-itself is born." Yet the umbilical cord will never be cut. Consciousness will not cease to live this relation to the object that defines its intentionality. It is a power of "bursting forth toward the world," and it is only that. The relation of the self to the self that accompanies this burst does not constitute the subject as an object. Let us stress the "burgeoning" rather than the aim (*visée*). This substitution of terms is the measure of the distance between Sartre and Husserl. Sartre would not be tempted by the idealism whereby the aims (*visées*) of consciousness are constitutive acts and in which consciousness is accorded a properly transcendental status. Quite the contrary, there is the charter of a fundamental realism that would bear all of its fruit within the confrontation with Marxism: "Existentialism and Marxism aim at the same object; but Marxism has reabsorbed man into the idea, and Existentialism seeks him everywhere *where he is*—at his work, at his home and in the streets."[2] Being-in-the-world is presence to the world. The critique of representation that is intoxicated by contemporary thought finds its source here: the world is not my representation; it is what I am present to and there is no "I" except at the heart of this presence. Merleau-Ponty had already described the dissolution of the pact that perception effects between man and the world. He had taught us that there is no more an interior man than an external world. In doing so, was he not following Sartre's teachings? We must admit that presence to the world is not neutral. Being-in-the-world is not only openness on to the world, it is also compromised by it to the extent that its presence is mediated by the body. The relation of the for-itself to the in-itself, in that it

---

2. Jean-Paul Sartre, *Critique de la raison dialectique* (Paris: Gallimard, 1960), p. 28. English translation of this introductory essay is entitled *Search for a Method*, translated by Hazel E. Barnes (New York: Knopf, Vintage Books, 1963), p. 28; henceforth cited in the text as SM.

is obligatory and unthinkable, is therefore the relation of freedom to facticity. Sartre has not forgotten this, for it is through the body as body that I am in the world. It is possible that certain formulas from *Being and Nothingness* appear to refine the body by making it into a sign rather than a reality; for example, Sartre describes the body as "the contingent form that holds the necessity of my contingency."[3] But Sartre also knows that this contingent form is man's destiny. It is not only the matter in him that gives him balast but also the form that informs him and thereby determines and limits him. That I am my body signifies that I am not what I want; and life that animates me perseveres in me without me. No matter what the impact of the psychic on the somatic, I cannot measure its effects nor master the effects of the inverse relation. For me to be living signifies that the relation of the for-itself to the in-itself cannot be categorized. But there is still more: being-in-the-world is not just compromised; it is also betrayed. And here Sartre's thought ultimately goes in the same direction as that of Merleau-Ponty.

After being-alive, another dimension of being-in-the-world must be considered: being-in-society. If Merleau-Ponty in *The Structure of Behavior* was more explicit than Sartre on the theme of life, Sartre in the *Critique of Dialectical Reason* is more explicit than Merleau-Ponty on the theme of society, for the *Critique*, published in 1960, is a response to objections that Merleau-Ponty had raised in 1955. Merleau-Ponty contested Sartre's earlier account of the primary opacity of social life, within which consciousness is incarnate. Sartre held that history has a meaning but it is neither clear nor distinct, and no dialectic can master it. However, such a dogmatic philosophy of history is a trap. From this, Merleau-Ponty took up the challenge—but his was no less categorical than Sartre's. Moreover, we might even ask whether his conclusion was justified. If history carries us and moves us like life, can we disengage ourselves from it in order to interrogate it from without? To be within the world or to be within history is always at the same time to be both inside and outside. But then the philosopher, sanctioned by history, appeals to its wisdom and recommends a reformist attitude. This is still a choice, as with Sartre, of a revolutionary attitude, neither more nor less justifiable by a philosophy of history. What distances Merleau-Ponty from Sartre is precisely this existential choice, more so than any doctrinal partisanship.

But in fact, Sartre has attempted to justify his choice, or in any case to clarify it. He has striven to think history, or at least to "establish the basis for a prolegomenon to any future anthropology."[4] In other words, to do

---

3. Sartre, *L'Être et le néant* (Paris: Gallimard, 1943), p. 371. English translation by Hazel E. Barnes: *Being and Nothingness* (New York: Philosophical Library, 1956), p. 309.
4. Sartre, *Critique de la raison dialectique*, p. 153. English translation by Alan Sheridan-Smith; edited by Jonathan Rée (London: New Left Books, 1976), p. 66; henceforth cited in the text as CDR.

what Merleau-Ponty should have done would be to do for social life what he had done with natural life. Merleau-Ponty showed that the natural world, which is our own environment and which he calls the transcendental field, is entirely opaque to us. Perception is the emergence of a lived meaning for the body in its presence; a world is expressed across appearances; and the arts bear witness to this world by taking up a movement of blossoming. Now why does the social dimension of the world not reveal itself in perception, too? To inhabit the world (to repeat Hölderlin's expression) is always to co-inhabit, to grasp the already articulated presence of others at least as a watermark on the things themselves. The social is abandoned to feeling, and extends to aesthetic experience. Meanwhile, Sartre does not explore the meaning of history according to a "phenomenology of perception," and thus he does not explore it as an extension of Merleau-Ponty.

Sartre speaks of intelligibility more than sense. The *Critique* is, in a Kantian way, the search for the conditions of intelligibility within the social. Sartre understands this intelligibility as comprehension,[5] following the traditional opposition between comprehension and explanation. This allows him to refuse the intelligibility of the natural sciences as elaborated by analytic reason. In *Being and Nothingness* the principle of intelligibility always resides in the immediate transparency within the relation of the self to itself, which defines the for-itself as consciousness (of) self and whereby understanding is primarily self-understanding — that is, consciousness of the self. But the great novelty of the *Critique* consists in substituting praxis for consciousness. Because the relation of the for-itself to the for-itself — if not of self to self — is necessarily mediated by matter, Sartre appeals at the same time to dialectic: "The *praxis* of men is the sole intelligible reality." (CDR, p. 717; Fr., p. 674) Why? Because praxis is still consciousness. And could we not also say that all consciousness is praxis, that every relation to the world — even passive relations such as emotion — is still in some respect active? Sartre does not develop this point. What he underlines in praxis is rather his relation to matter as "worked matter." And what interests him is that it can communicate its intelligibility to the whole sociohistorical field. How can it do that? By totalizing.

"Totalization" is the key word here. At the end of *Being and Nothingness* totality already appeared as a metaphysical problem, but in that case it made no difference whether it was confronted or neglected. Its meaning, however, has changed: as far as the for-itself is concerned, emphasis has shifted from consciousness to praxis, and the in-itself is henceforth the matter on which praxis affixes its seal; "matter as a passive totality is revealed by an organic being seeking its being." (CDR, p. 81; Fr., p. 167) First, the totality does not exist by itself. We do not encounter it, we do not undergo it — except as a provisional product of a totalizing act. In nature there is no

---

5. *Compréhension* can also be translated as "understanding" or *Verstehen*.

totality. Outside of the act that brings the object together (outside of perception, we might say) or outside of the act that unifies a practical field (in other words, outside of work), there is only multiplicity and exteriority. All meaning and everything social, to the extent to which the totality makes sense, remains suspended in a subjectivity, but hereafter of a practical sort. Furthermore, intersubjectivity, the confrontation of consciousness, and the look of the third are no longer thematizations of the social: "The relation of reciprocity and the relation to the third party are not in themselves social." (CDR, p. 255; Fr., p. 308) This relation of the practical organism acting on the environment occurs in a context that is affirmed by materialism. In this respect, a whole theory of individual totalizing praxis serves as a prelude to a theory of the social. To totalize is to confer unity on the practical field by a project. From this it follows that totalization implies matter. And here already the dialectic that inaugurates history — and which in truth is antidialectical, as Sartre would say — will play a role such that we can call it, with Adorno, a negative dialectic: not a surpassing but a return. This misfortune of praxis is indicated in several ways. First, man makes himself inert in order to act. This, we dare to say, is not very convincing, for one can choose to make oneself inert without alienating the individual. We could even extend the analysis to show how means too often pervert the ends or become themselves the ends such that man sees himself as stealing meaning from his own enterprise. The history of the Russian Revolution provides a rather probing example of this shift. Here we have rejoined the Sartrian theory: the totality turns itself back against the totalization while totalizing man finds himself totalized by the matter he has totalized. He submits to the history he has made. But this submission demands that we also take the other into consideration. And indeed the other is always already there: individual praxis is never solitary. The individual's unhappiness arises because the first relation between men is always one of opposition. No longer is it owing, as in *Being and Nothingness*, to the look of the other objectifying me and stealing my world from me, in other words, to each consciousness pursuing the other's death. Rather, it is owing to each praxis entering into competition with the other — because "the practical field is originally conditioned by scarcity." (CDR, p. 331; Fr., p. 269) Matter is always at the heart of human relations, and in this case each person is excessive in relation to the other. Scarcity is the fundamental fact — the necessity of our contingency, just as the body in *Being and Nothingness* was that which orients all history.

Scarcity is assuredly an evil. But all evil cannot be attributed to scarcity. Evil comes from the success of totalization in the totality. For what becomes individual praxis also becomes common practice instituted in the group: "the unity of exteriority" is opposed and often substituted for "the unity of interiority." "Any social field is constituted to a large extent by structured ensembles of groupings that are always both praxis and practico-inert, even though either one of these characteristics may constantly tend to cancel itself out." (CDR, p. 254; Fr., p. 307) Passing through a series of admirable analyses, Sartre describes two phases of the social. The first is the place of a possible liberation when the group is truly totalizing. It is linked by a common enterprise and does not bind itself as does the heated group of rioters at the moment of a revolutionary action. The second is the place of alienation when the group cools down, institutionalizes, and hardens itself, when objectivity becomes inertia — the fall into materiality.

Is all this so far from Merleau-Ponty? By moving in a direction counter to that of Merleau-Ponty, does Sartre open up the possibility of a science or philosophy of history? No, but he does indicate the possibility of an experience rather than a concept. The intelligibility that he first proposes is not what is demanded by knowledge. To understand is not to explain. To understand is to resume, to reincorporate, to participate. On the other hand, should history be studied theoretically? In the *Critique* presented as only the first volume of a larger projected study, Sartre says nothing about history as a totalizing act of becoming. In the process of formalization, he notes only the abstract elements of social reality. He joins them according to a logical genesis that remains explicitly indifferent to chronology. This formalization is at the heart of the real whose intelligibility he guarantees but does not situate historically. Certainly, totalization can have some relationship to time. It is also the unity lived by the subject of temporal *ekstases*.

But what is the relation between this unity and the flow of a transindividual act of becoming? What sort of grounding is available to a becoming whose subjectivity is intelligible? But must we trap Sartre in his own questions? Whether he holds to his promises or not, we must not expect that he will provide a theory of history similar, for example, to Althusser's — namely, a structuralist theory that explains instead of understands and which relegates the subject to an all-encompassing ideology, which renounces its right to think how the structure is operated or lived. Sartre can be only partially structuralist. The structure must be thought, but we cannot think it like a thing — simply in terms of exteriority. The structure is the object of a negative dialectic that is at the same time "the inert object of calculation when seen as an ossification without taking account of totalization or an effective power activated by the praxis of each and every person." (CDR, p. 500; Fr., p. 503) Anthropology cannot place the human in parentheses. He who is attached to the lived must take into account what Van Gogh called the terrible human passions. We no longer write treatises on the passions; rather, we make a strong case for desire. By mystifying it with elements of eros and thanatos, or at least by depersonalizing it, one might still write a libidinal history devoid of a subject. But such a study is nevertheless about historical subjects, which in the last analysis are individuals — not necessarily the great men or names inhabited by a will to power, but anonymous people lost in the masses. In them, we show the relationship between the libido and their work.

Sartre, in his own way, does refer to the passions. Instead of desire, he speaks of violence. When in conflict, he says, men continually try to remove themselves from it. However, violence does not derive its full meaning from its use in a historical totalization. How can we understand torture without also appealing to sadism? Must we suppress "the incredible ferocity of the English proprietors in the nineteenth century," even though it is "quite deliberate"? (CDR, pp. 742-743; Fr., p. 694) If the theory does not account for that aspect of violence, it will construct only abstract models and in turn will undergo the same failures as bureaucracies. On the practical plane, bureaucracies juggle statistics or strategies without considering the incredible courage of the Vietnamese. By accounting for the human, the theory also encounters the inhuman. What was nonhuman in inert matter becomes antihuman through the mediation of historical agents. A theoretician — when his name is Sartre — cannot remain indifferent to this presence of evil. His theory finds a more stringent link with its practice than epistemologists derive from Marxism, which is animated by indignation and anger — the avatars of generosity. Lucidity loses nothing there. Something from history is revealed in sentiments that actively engage man in history and his historical moment, just as something from the world is revealed to perception where a body proves itself in the flesh of the sensory.

Sartre and Merleau-Ponty are not so different in their opening up of the transcendental field. However, we would say that Sartre indicates a greater debt to dialectic as the spring of history and the instruments of its intelligibility. Yet what is primarily intelligible is the praxis that, like consciousness, is a relation of the self to itself. If we say that the totalization that it accomplishes is dialectical, it is on the basis of a rather uncertain meaning of *dialectic*. What is properly dialectical is a return or circularity: man is mediated by things to the same extent that things are mediated by men. True dialectic is this antidialectic that steals from man the meaning and fruit of his enterprises. Antidialectic is this fall of totalization into the totality that confers on the group the objectivity of inertness. For "the group in fact does not exist anywhere except *everywhere*, that is to say, it belongs to each individual *praxis* as an interiorized unity of multiplicity. . . . If we abandon every mystical or magical interpretation, then it is clear that this ubiquity not only signifies that no new reality has been incarnated in each individual, but on the contrary that it is a question of a practical determination of everyone by everyone, by all and by oneself within the perspective of a common praxis." (CDR, p. 507; Fr., p. 506) When the group cools down, becomes fixed, and is immobilized in a structure — in short, when it becomes institutionalized — it escapes praxis to some extent and takes on the consistency of the inert. Sartre effectively illuminates this status of the practico-inert or the subjective-objective as the bastard reality of society, and, why not say, of ambiguity? It is precisely ambiguity that Sartre is describing, and dialectic helps him to systematize it. But he does so without producing a complete system, that is, without proclaiming a path that is simultaneously chronological in dealing with the experiences of consciousness and logical in dealing with the becoming of the concept—in other words, the truth of consciousness. In short, Sartre succeeds without opposing a dogmatic epistemology to Merleau-Ponty's phenomenology.

While Merleau-Ponty wrote—and rewrote—a *Phenomenology of Perception*, Sartre wrote a *Critique of Dialectical Reason*. In the end, the problems they confront are not the same: Merleau-Ponty's world is above all the natural world; Sartre's world is the social world. Even if their approaches, despite all appearances, do not diverge radically, their emphases are different. Must we say that this difference is insignificant? No, philosophy is not a competitive game between doctrines, a trial case upon which fashion provisionally passes its verdict. It is not a question of determining who is right and who is wrong, as if some sovereign court could decide—God's judgment or that of history. Yet this difference can govern choices. We must not choose as if we were choosing between two consumer goods. Rather, this difference is at the very least a matter of orienting our sympathies.

PART FOUR

An Interview with Sartre

Leo Fretz

An Interview With Jean-Paul Sartre*

Introduction

On November 25, 1976, I arrived at the home of Jean-Paul Sartre, as agreed, at about twelve o'clock in the afternoon. As the door opens, I stand facing a small man, clearly still recovering from a stiff grippe, who resembles Sartre. With a few civilities I am led into the study and placed in a large armchair. Then Sartre takes his place directly opposite me on a small stool: the same piece of furniture from which he spoke for about three hours in *Sartre par lui-même*, the film by Michel Contat and Alexandre Astruc, which I had gone to see the previous evening in Montparnasse. Suddenly he says that there is no question of an epistemological break in his thought, thereby pitching into a passage in my introductory letter. I turn on my tape recorder and hope that everything will go well. We part after a conversation of one and a half hours. I have seldom seen a greater contradiction between intellectual power and physical frailty.

The conversation was the result of a written request concerning an exchange of ideas about the interpretation of Sartre's philosophical work. With nineteen neatly written questions I traveled to the man whom Gombrowicz called the Eiffel Tower of French culture. However, right from the beginning of the conversation it was clear that there could be no systematic reading of my questions. Strangely at ease, I felt the fear of French quickly vanish and I defended my theses as strongly as I could. The original goal of the discussion — to inform me about a number of technical problems — was exceeded by Sartre's conciliatoriness. The conversation contains a number of assertions that might be of interest to a large public — philosophers and nonphilosophers. Therefore, it is published here in translated and somewhat abridged form. This translation does not aspire to suppleness. Rather, I have opted for as literal a copy as possible. As an introduction to the text I present the most important conclusions of my research, as well as

---

*Translated from the Dutch by George Berger

a brief indication of the structure and contents of the discussion. The text is provided with a few footnotes, which may contribute to a better understanding of it.

My interest in Sartre's philosophy originally centered upon the question of the extent to which one can speak of an epistemological break between the two main works, *Being and Nothingness* and the *Critique of Dialectical Reason*. In the CDR Sartre undertakes the at first risky attempt at a synthesis of an existentialist and a Marxist view of man. One can correctly wonder if it is at all possible to unite an anthropology wherein the uniqueness and self-determination of each separate person is central with a philosophical conception wherein the emphasis is placed on the social and economic conditions that to a large extent determine each individual life. It became increasingly clear that the question of a break could be answered only if the concepts of individuality employed by Sartre were subjected to an accurate analysis. It was decided to reconstruct carefully the development of the concept of the individual in Sartre's entire philosophical oeuvre. The investigation led to a number of conclusions: those most relevant to the conversation are reproduced here in the form of theses.

1. The concept of an individual and impersonal *pseudo-cogito*, developed in *The Transcendence of the Ego*, exhibits a striking resemblance to the concept of the *historical man* that is developed in the CDR in the expositions of the so-called regressive analysis.

2. The concept of the *pre-reflective cogito* in BN deviates from the characterization of the prereflective consciousness that is given in TE. In the prereflective consciousness, as it is characterized in the first main work, levels of consciousness, which in the earlier essay were still strictly separated, are inseparably coupled.

3. The transcendental consciousness in BN is consequently not only an individual but also a *personal* consciousness, which implies a total change in Sartre's epistemological position with respect to TE.

4. If one can indeed speak of an epistemological break in Sartre's philosophical development, then this break should be localized at a very early stage, to wit, between TE and BN.

5. However, it is unjustified to speak of a break if one surveys Sartre's overall philosophical development. There is, rather, a continuity within his thought. Positions are sometimes quite drastically modified, but the total development displays a dialectical structure, whereby contradictions between separate works are finally removed. In this manner the concept of the historical man from the CDR can be considered as a matured, materialistic version of the early pseudo-cogito concept from TE.

6. As a consequence of the connection mentioned above under 2., the transcendental consciousness of BN displays a pathogenic structure. To be sure, Sartre has posed the question of the transcendental precondition of pathological behavior (neurotic behavior, bad-faith behavior) very clearly and has answered it in an impressive fashion. But the explanation for the pathogenic character of this transcendental structure is not supplied by him.

7. The attempt, undertaken in BN, to solve the problem of solipsism must be considered a failure. The reason for this is not only the pathogenic structure of the transcendental consciousness, but also its "narcissistic" character. The for-itself indeed implies the for-others, but consciousness alienates itself not only by *constituting itself* as an interiorized other, as a "superego," but at the same time by *constituting the other* as an alienated self.

8. The transcendental consciousness in BN should therefore be characterized as solipsistic, in the full sense of the word. To be sure, it acknowledges the in-itself as a necessary condition for its "existence," but at the same time it creates (constitutes) its own *mode* of existence as an alienated self. By doing so it renders its relations with the in-itself problematic by confinement in a premature neurotic subjectivity. Moreover, it loses contact with the other by depriving him of his own identity.

9. It is true that Sartre's theory of the "for-others" can be considered as a *theoretical* foundation for Freud's *empirical* theory of a (pathological) *Mitsein*. But a theoretical foundation for the inter-individuality on the natural level of a consciousness *in* the world, together with others, is totally absent in BN.

10. In the CDR the problem of solipsism, considered both from a more liberalistic and a more Marxist standpoint, is deepened in a productive manner. Sartre's solution of this problem gives a new impetus to the dialogue between supporters of liberalistic and Marxist conceptions of man. The dualism between for-itself and in-itself is transcended, since the interpersonal relations mediate between both forms of materiality, while inversely the interpersonal relations are founded in the individual dialectical experience.

11. The regressive analysis, as it is developed in the CDR, offers a fruitful starting point for a new ethic. With the help of the concept of the historical man, the concept of an impersonal individual, tensions between philosophical anthropology and ethics — and thereby tensions betwen the so-called individual and social ethics — can be removed.

The central question in part one of the interview is the extent to which the structure of consciousness in BN (1943) deviates from that in TE (1936). It is striking that Sartre refuses to recognize more than two levels of consciousness — a pre-reflective and a reflective level — whereas *three* degrees of consciousness are distinguished in the earlier essay, the *first two* of which are pre-reflective and the *third* reflective. My questions are primarily intended to clarify the remarkable phenomenon that the pseudo-cogito from TE — the transcendental consciousness of the first degree — plays no role at all in BN. The pseudo-cogito is characterized in TE not merely as individual, but at the same time as *impersonal*, whereas the pre-reflective transcendental consciousness in BN exhibits a *personal* structure. My question, whether the two pre-reflective levels of consciousness are inseparably coupled in BN, is answered in the affirmative; this coupling is explained by the fact that consciousness always — thus also on the pre-reflective level — carries a certain measure of reflectivity in itself. Sartre is apparently alluding here to the thesis, already put forward in section three of the introduction to BN, that every consciousness is a form of self-consciousness. On the other hand, however, the pseudo-cogito in TE was also characterized as a consciousness of itself. Therefore, in my opinion, it is legitimate to ask why this pre-reflective reflection—if this paradoxical term is permitted—in BN seems possible only by the confluence of the two pre-reflective levels, which were still strictly distinguished in TE. An answer to this question is naturally of the greatest importance for the tenability of thesis three. The question re-mains undecided and the discussion ends a little abruptly when Sartre, a bit irritated, speaks about "those degrees of yours," as if I were the person who had introduced the three-degree distinction. In any case, it is surprising that in a later phase of the conversation — part two — Sartre seems willing to accept the term *third-degree consciousness* for reflection on the unifying activity of what he himself calls second-degree consciousness. In my opinion it is hereby still implicitly admitted that a "true" first-degree consciousness, wherein there is as yet no question of an adulterating synthesizing activity of consciousness, can independently occur. (For a more complete understand-ing of this problematic I refer to part one of TE and to section three men-tioned above from the introduction to BN.) Although in my opinion no conclusive explanation is given for the disappearance of the pseudo-cogito in BN, I consider this first round of great importance, not least because of the discussion concerning the time consciousness in Husserl. See also theses 2. and 4.

In part two the discussion becomes acute. By assuming the thesis that the pre-reflective consciousness as positional consciousness of an object is al-ways a non-positional consciousness of itself as well (as defended in both TE and section three of the Introduction to BN), the question arises if this "it-self" must be conceived as personal or as impersonal. Or, in terms of the discussion in part one: Is this non-positional consciousness a consciousness of the first or of the second degree? Sartre's answer is a consistent extension of the standpoint that he adopted earlier. In this connection the question is raised in passing concerning the extent to which one may speak of a break in Sartre's theory of the emotions. But the central problem is whether the "self" exhibits a *personal* structure and if this "self" is not constituted as a *thing* by a more or less objectifying attitude of consciousness. These two problems stand in the closest connection with each other. In my questions one can discern the thesis that the consciousness as a *witness consciousness* —a term that is already introduced in part one—"looks" at itself as if it were another and alienates itself from itself in this objectifying, which finds its residue in a superegolike person structure of pre-reflective consciousness. In my opinion, Sartre's position on these matters is clearly put forward in the discussion about Freud. See also theses 6., 7., and 9.

In part three Sartre claims that the problem of solipsism is not satisfacto-rily solved in BN, but that it *is* solved in the CDR (1960). He agrees that the epistemological exposition of the regressive analysis in CDR can be considered the basis for a new ethic. He announces that he will formulate the first principles of this ethic in a new book, *Pouvoir et Liberté* ("power and freedom"). He confirms the suggestion that a greater relation exists between TE and CDR than between the two main works. Moreover, he remarks that he is trying, in his most recent phase, to regain a connection with the philosophical intuitions that he set down in *Nausea* (1938). See also theses 1., 5., 8., 10., and 11.

In part four Sartre's materialism comes up for discussion, as a result of renewed questioning concerning the pathogenic character of transcendental consciousness and the theory of the emotion in BN. Sartre sketches his conception of the materiality of consciousness in a long answer. The significance of interpersonal relations in the dialectical intercourse between for-itself and in-itself is illustrated by our conversational situation. The debate is closed with an autobiographical sketch of the connection between Sartre's life and work, and with Sartre's cautious agreement with the vision I presented of his development. See also theses 1. and 5.

Part I:

S. — I think that there is more continuity in thought. I do not believe that there is a break. There are naturally changes in one's thinking; one can deviate; one can go from the one extreme to the other; but the idea of a break, an idea from Althusser, seems to me to be mistaken. For example, I do not think that there is a break between the early writings of Marx and *Capital*. Naturally there are changes, but a change is not yet a break[1].

F. — But is there also no epistemological break? Break, that is a weighty word. I agree with you there, but perhaps there is an epistemological break, since I think that the concept of individuality in BN is a totally different concept than that in CDR[2].

S. — Certainly, certainly, but that is perhaps because BN is a general point of view, a fundamental point of view. And CDR is a point of view that on the contrary is social and concrete. The one is abstract, studies general truths, and the other is not so concerned with that and places itself upon the plane of the concrete.

---

1. For the concept "break" (coupure) see L. Althusser, e.g. Pour Marx, Paris 1965, pp. 23ff.

2. For the different meanings of the concept "epistemological break" (coupure épistémologique) see, e.g. Sami Naïr and Michael Lowy: *Lucien Goldmann*, Paris 1973. See therein the interview with Goldmann by Brigitte Devismes concerning the "emploi actuel du concept de 'coupure épistémologique' ", pp. 135ff. The meaning of the term "epistemological break" in our discussion becomes clear in what follows.

F. — Can one say that there is an epistemological break between TE and BN? There are great differences between the individuality-concepts in the two works, in the sense that transcendental consciousness in TE is characterized by you as individual but at the same time as impersonal, while in BN the pre-reflective consciousness is provided with a personal structure.

S. — Yes, absolutely.

F. — In both TE and BN you try to avoid idealism. In the Introduction to BN the in-itself remains a necessary condition for consciousness as a *fact*[3]. But when you propound the thesis that the existence of consciousness implies the essence of consciousness and that for that reason consciousness is the cause of its own *mode* of existence, does this not mean that you defend an epistemological idealism?

S. — Oh no, since consciousness is consciousness *of* something. And that leads me at the very start to reject all forms of epistemological idealism. Consciousness never stands apart. It is never just itself. One would never be able to consider a consciousness that is not consciousness of something. Consciousness of an object — whatever form that object might have — thus never remains in itself. It is a relation to being.

F. — Does the in-itself always remain a necessary condition for consciousness in that sense?

S. — Yes, ultimately. There should be an ontology — which we cannot create — wherein one can see how the in-itself has produced the for-itself; produced it in a certain manner which is not a causal manner. I say that often. But we do not have the means for this, and we will never know it.

F. — But when you say: the existence of consciousness implies its essence; is that to say that the two levels of consciousness which you still distinguish in TE become inseparably connected? In §3 of the Introduction to BN for example, you speak of a witness-consciousness[4]. And if I have understood it well, that is a consciousness of the second degree, which posits the nothingness of consciousness.

S. — Yes, that is reflexivity. Consciousness of the second degree is reflexivity. There is no other consciousness of the second degree. It is the only consciousness that as object — that would be a wrong word, but after all one can say it quickly — that has a consciousness as object. The consciousness that I have of you is never just consciousness of a consciousness. It is a consciousness of a being that is animated with a consciousness, that possesses a consciousness, that is a consciousness and at the same time a body. Consciousness of a *consciousness* however, only exists in the form of reflexivity.

F. — Indeed, but why do you characterize that consciousness as pre-reflective? You speak about a pre-reflective cogito.

---

3. Some words in the text are italicized, when this is considered necessary for a better comprehension.
4. "Conscience-témoin".

S. — Yes. Each consciousness, consciousness "of itself" in a certain sense, is, as an introspection of itself, of pre-reflective order. Consequently the being of consciousness — if one can speak of it — the existence of consciousness is indeed always a relation to itself. It is the for-itself — it is for this reason that I call it this — which thus already presupposes a pre-reflectivity. But the reflectivity comes later, as a new consciousness, that is consciousness of the pre-reflective consciousness. It is thus a strengthening of the reflection which one calls the real reflection. Since that reflection lies already in the very nature of consciousness.

F. — But what is the difference between the pseudo-cogito in TE and the pre-reflective cogito in BN? If I have understood it well, the pseudo-cogito is a cogito of the first degree. Well then, in BN you never use the term "pseudo". I believe that this is because BN is concerned with a pure cogito, whereas the pseudo-cogito is a form of materiality. Why doesn't that pseudo-cogito come back in BN?

S. — Because a cogito is never a pseudo-cogito. The non-reflected[5] consciousness comprises — as we have just said — a reflective structure, which however is no pseudo-cogito. It is a cogito that is as yet poorly developed, and which presupposes real reflection in order to become really developed; that is to say, a certain consciousness *on* a consciousness, which however is not "pseudo". "Pseudo" means unauthentic. It is not unauthentic, it is, let us say, an element that must be developed.

F. — And the pseudo-cogito in TE, is that of material order? You speak not only of a unification of consciousness by *objects*, but also about an internal unification. I can easily conceive of that unification of the pseudo-cogito by the objects of the world, but I have difficulty with that internal unification through the "internal time-consciousness" of Husserl. It is obvious that this "time-consciousness" can unify consciousness of the second degree, but I do not believe that it can bring about the consciousness of the first degree[6].

S. — Yes, I allude there to the "time-consciousness" of Husserl. There is no doubt about that. And I have spoken about a connection between the moments of consciousness, which is a pre-reflective connection. But I think that in fact the real connection, the cognitive and epistemological, just as much as the ontological

---

5. "Conscience irréfléchie" is consistently translated as "non-reflected consciousness". Sartre sometimes also uses the expression "conscience non-réfléchie". Both expressions are more or less synonymous with each other and with the expression "conscience préréflexive".

6. In TE Sartre appeals to Husserl's "innere Zeitbewusstsein" for the unification of both first-degree consciousness (the pseudo-cogito) and second-degree consciousness (see Husserl's *Die Phänomenologie des inneren Zeitbewusstseins*). But the sharp distinction between the two levels of consciousness in the early essay makes this appeal incomprehensible in the case of the pseudo-cogito. On this level there is still no question of any sort of subject-forming, but exclusively of an impersonal "transcendental field", which is unified by the consciousness-transcendent objects towards which consciousness is intentionally directed. In other words: it seems that an internal and external unification are mutually exclusive. The plural "con-sciences" is, with one exception (cf. note 15) always translated with "moments of consciousness", since the English "consciousnesses" is not only ugly, but is also misleading: this can also be a term for the consciousness of *diverse* people.

connection between the moments of consciousness, the moments by which consciousness is always consciousness of something, . . . only reflection can supply
this [connection]. But it still holds that temporally we are not dealing with successive moments without mutual connection on the pre-reflective level. I cannot
say that I see you and that I should only be conscious on the reflective level of
having seen you. There exists a pre-reflective connection of the moments of consciousness without real synthesis. Simply, just like that. Moments of consciousness that succeed each other and that hook on to each other in their succession
show that they have existed and continuously determine the form of the consciousness that follows. For example: I perceive you and I am conscious of perceiving you, but I am conscious of perceiving you as the one whom I have already
perceived a moment ago and whom I will perceive in the following moment. It
cannot be doubted that you do not appear without this connection. The moments of consciousness wherein I am conscious of you do not appear without
connection with the consciousness that I have had earlier or later shall have. But
you are not going to appear and then disappear.

F. — But who causes this unification? I or you? There is the problem.

S. — Oh, both. You in the sense that your are indeed a being that remains facing me
and that thereby gives rise to the fact that I am constantly conscious of you; but
at the same time also myself in the sense that I constantly connect my momen-
tary consciousness with the consciousness that precedes it.

F. — But are you not then on the second level?

S. — No, we are talking about the pre-reflexive consciousness. This is approximately
what Husserl has said. But he lingered here all too briefly. He stopped at precisely that level where he should have spoken of the reflective synthesis. But
time-consciousness is still a sort of connection between successive moments of
consciousness, as opposed to objects which themselves continue to exist. But
consciousness, time-consciousness, can only be achieved on the reflective phase.
I mean: after this one comprehends the three time-dimensions of the object,
starting from a consciousness that is already conscious of the temporal development of reflected consciousness, and that is a reflective consciousness.

F. — In §3 of the Introduction to BN you give an initial characterization of the pre-
reflective cogito. In that paragraph you defend the thesis that non-positional
consciousness (of) itself[7] is a sufficient and necessary condition for a positional
consciousness of an object. If I have understood it correctly, you maintain that
consciousness must be conscious (of) itself in a non-positional manner in order
to make possible a positional consciousness.

S. — That's right.

F. — To speak in Kantian terms: According to you a transcendental and non-
positional consciousness is a condition for all experience.

S. — That's right.

---

7. "(of) itself" with parentheses indicates, following Sartre, that we are dealing with a
non-thematic (non-positional) self-consciousness.

F. — But that consciousness which is a necessary and sufficient condition, is that a consciousness of the first or of the second degree?

S. — But I have told you, I conceive of those degrees of yours as pre-reflective of rather as non-reflective consciousness *and* reflective consciousness. I see no other degrees of consciousness.

Part II:

F. — In that §3 also the following problem occurs. You write: "The immediate consciousness which I have of perceiving does not permit me either to judge or to will or to be ashamed. It does not know my perception, does not *posit* it". It seems to me that this assertion is perfectly applicable to the pre-reflective cogito of TE and of BN. But the problem is that you give three examples of a pre-reflective cogito: a perception such as seeing, one which I simply call semi-perception (counting cigarettes) and an act of consciousness like pleasure, which according to your interpretation is of the same order as seeing and counting. That I don't understand. I cannot understand how a perception such as seeing can be of the same order as, for example, having pleasure. I mean: when I perceive you, I am also non-positionally conscious (of) myself, but it need not be the case that that perception is, for example, pleasure or anguish.

S. — It is perceived in the same manner. It is conscious in the same manner. I cannot distinguish the origin of anguish from what the perception of the world for example will be, the consciousness of the world. One is only dealing with a quality of the consciousness of the world.

F. — I understand that. But in your EM you describe the anguish that always expresses itself bodily, whereas in BN you describe an anguish of a higher level, such as for example the flight away from oneself in bad faith. Is that another anguish?

S. — Another, that is saying too much. They are connected with one another. There is, for example, a reflective anguish which is connected with the anguish of object-consciousness, of non-reflected consciousness. Anguish and flight from anguish are one and the same for me. It has nothing to do with two separate attitudes, with a passive feeling that is supposed to be anguish, and the flight, which is supposed to be active. No, there is a feeling that flees from itself, which is flight *and* anguish. I do not make those distinctions; I find them academic. Anguish has the flight from itself in itself. But that resides in the center of anguish itself.

F. — Have you been inspired by Kierkegaard in your analysis of anguish?

S. — The problem at least came to me via Kierkegaard, although I do not approach it in the same manner as he does. But one cannot maintain that there is any question, with respect to anguish, of a solution or an attitude à la Kierkegaard. Simply and solely of a global, total influence upon a total world of thought. *That* stood out clearly, when I read Kierkegaard. When I was reading *The Concept of Dread* I said to myself: there is a *problem* of anguish. And I worked on it, I thought about it from my own point of view.

F. — But isn't your "self"-concept in *one* form or another a concept of christian origin, but secularized? I believe that your "self" in BN is a "self" that is constituted as a thing.

S. — Not as a thing, but almost. It is just like a thing. It lies *before* consciousness. It does not at all lie behind it, as does the "ego" of Husserl for example. I think that a "selfhood"[8] of consciousness exists, which is not identical with the self, which is a relation to the self, a sort of "in-itself"-being, which brings it about that consciousness can recognize itself, can turn towards the past, etc. But the self — in the proper sense of the word — that lies outside. Those are the connections of the moments of consciousness outside, insofar as these lie in the objects.

F. — I posed this question about the self to you, because the key to your solution of the solipsism-problem in BN is to be found in the epistemological expositions in part I and III. Although on the one hand you maintain that each individual for-itself is confronted with its unique self as a presence-absence[9], you also say that the for-itself implies the for-others. One wouldn't dream of interpreting that for-others as a being-for-God, as Kierkegaard. . . .

S. — By no means.

F. — . . . because God has disappeared in your thought. Nor can one interpret the for-others as a *Mitsein* à la Heidegger. For you — if I have understood it well — the for-others is a becoming objectified by the gaze of the others.

S. — That's correct.

F. — But is this being seen by the gaze of the other not of the same order as the *Mitsein* of Freud? Not the *Mitsein* of Heidegger, but the *Mitsein* of Freud? I'll explain myself further: In your analysis of bad faith you come up with a thesis which at first sight is paradoxical, namely that behavior in good faith is also a specimen of bad faith. You explain that thesis by a concrete example: Not only the homosexual who confesses his homosexuality because his friend demands it, but also the homosexual who does it because he demands it from himself; even he, according to your interpretation, is in good faith and as such in bad faith.

S. — Correct.

F. — You adduce as an argument that the homosexual in the latter case is looking at himself. But if he is looking at himself, as you say, is his self not then constituted by an interiorized other, and can one not say, that this self is already a super-ego which is constituted by the other?

S. — Yes, that might be so in certain cases. But in fact the viewing of oneself by oneself, that is, the reflective consciousness which views the series of non-reflected moments of consciousness, in general merely supplies syntheses that are too simple; with parts that are ejected and crowded out, with continuities that are sharper or less sharp than in non-reflected consciousness. In brief, it provides primarily an object that is poorly constituted, that strives too much towards

---

8. "ipséité".
9. "présence-absence".

unity, that is too synthetic. It does not supply the truth of the non-reflected consciousness. A truth, which doesn't exist, because there is no divine consciousness which supplies the veritable synthesis, a truth which is nothing else as the unreflected consciousness itself. However the synthesis that is brought about by the reflective consciousness always contains the defect of being a *consciousness*, a synthesis by consciousness which is bent on achieving a total unity. Whereas the true unity of the non-reflected consciousness is in reality given in the non-reflected consciousness. But this unity is not itself explicit; it does not present itself as such, but we live it in the non-reflecting and in the unity, so that the reflective unity is a unity of the second degree and a unity which as such falsifies the true unity. Do you see what I mean?

F. — I'm beginning to understand it. Is it a true consciousness on the level of third degree consciousness?

S. — If you wish. But then third degree must be understood as a consciousness that reflects upon the reflection.

F. — I have asked you this question because you have said nothing about the concept of transference in Freud's work, although it is a most essential concept in his thought.

S. — Absolutely. But I just wanted to indicate the starting point for a critique. I have given a more sound critique in the *New Left Review*[10]. But I judged that the transference concept could only be properly understood as a concept of philosophical order through an attempt at making all of Freud's thought philosophical; for I did not consider Freud a philosopher. I was of the opinion that the concepts which he forged were forged empirically; and that if one wants to give them a philosophical value, one must try to rethink them one by one and to preserve them in a philosophical form which is not Freud's.

F. — I agree with you that many philosophers have committed an error by interpreting Freud as a philosopher.

S. — Most certainly.

F. — But when you criticize the "id"-concept in BN, do you not criticize Freud as a philosopher? Is this an ontological critique or not?

S. — Yes, but not as a philosopher. I criticize him insofar as he remains on the empirical plane. That is to say *I* assume standpoints with respect to an object that appears to contradict what I say, but which is only an object in consciousness. I mean: Freud has said nothing at all of philosophical importance when he, for example, talks about consciousness. He developed his theories and he took his own logic and gave them again a definite purport; but that is not philosophy. And if one wishes to render an account of a freudian philosophy one would have to create it in a certain sense, to create it with the same doctrines, with the same collections[11], but nevertheless to create it.

---

10. Sartre is apparently referring here to an interview that is included in *Situations IX* (pp. 99–134).
11. "ensembles".

F. — I did not know that you did not want to interpret Freud as a philosopher.

S. — Oh no, I do not want that. I do not think that he is one.

F. — Not at all?

S. — No, not at all.

F. — In your critique of Freud in BN you say: Freud unjustly introduced the *Mitsein* into subjectivity. Well now, I think, once again, that this for-others is implied by the for-itself and vice versa, that this is a *Mitsein*. Is it a *Mitsein* or not? Or is it another *Mitsein?*

S. — If you at any cost want to employ the term *Mitsein*, then let us say that it is another *Mitsein*, completely other. That of Freud, precisely by lacking a principle, remains on a plane that is not demonstrated, not defined. There are beings that live together. *There* is the fact given by Freud, but which each of us is also able to give, insofar as he is not a philosopher. But he has no theory of that *Mitsein*. Freud has not said why those beings who lived together knew each other with reciprocal relations.

F. — Yes, naturally. Freud has no theory of *Mitsein*. Could one say that your theory of the *for-others* is a foundation for the *Mitsein* of Freud?

S. — If one wants to. It is a foundation for every *Mitsein*.

Part III:

F. — I ask you these questions about Freud, because I am largely occupied with what you have to say about the problems of solipsism and interindividuality. In TE you say: there is no problem of solipsism at all, since there is no subject. In BN you say: yes, there is indeed a problem, since one must explain how the (one) transcendental field[12] is connected with the other. And you give a solution to that problem by showing that the for-itself implies the for-others.

S. — That is precisely right.

F. — But you have given no solution for the problem of interindividuality on the level of the pseudo-cogito. Have you given that solution for the problem of interindividuality on the first level in the CDR?

S. — Undoubtedly, if you wish. I would agree with you. I am of the opinion that what I said about solipsism in BN is an abstract and general point of view; it is much more complicated. And the solution seems to me indeed to come in the CDR.

F. — Aren't you satisfied with your solution in BN?

S. — Now, that is abstract, it is not wrong, it is abstract. In fact it is more complicated. One has to look at things on an historical plane.

F. — Do you think that one could interpret the figure of Fosca in the novel of Simone

---

12. I think that the word "field" expresses the *impersonal* character of the pseudo-cogito.

de Beauvoir *"Tous les hommes sont mortels"* as a literary concretization of your concept of the impersonal individual, as you developed it in the CDR under the title "regressive analysis"?

S. — Yes, if you want. But that was not done on purpose. It is a thought which we have in common, but in different forms.

F. — Naturally. But could one interpret that figure in this fashion?

S. — Certainly. It is in effect about the impersonal individual, the individual as it is made, that is to say, is created as a large multitude of concepts which are given to him from without.

F. — Can one say that regressive analysis, as you developed it in CDR, is a foundation for every future ethic? One can indeed find a relation with other people in that analysis.

S. — Yes, certainly.

F. — But what would that ethic on the basis of the CDR look like?

S. — Well, I am writing a book with a friend[13] about power and freedom, and in that book I will provide the first principles of morals. We are doing it in dialogue form, because I can no longer write, so that it is a dialogue just like ours, whereby each says what he has to say and the other answers. And I will try to show that morals and politics can only make sense from the moment when the concept of power and the reality of power are truly removed. A society without power starts to become an ethical society, because a new form of freedom is established, which is the freedom of reciprocal relations of persons in the form of a we. Democracy does not mean free individuals, that is the relation on all levels, with respect to everything, of all individuals, who are mutually free in the form of a we. That is what I am doing at this moment, but we have just begun.

F. — In the film of Contat and Astruc you also spoke about two morals. One moral up until — let us say 1948. And thereafter a new moral, which you are still developing. What is in your opinion the difference between those two morals?

S. — The first moral was abstract, it depended ultimately on the pre-reflective and the reflective cogito. And it only took account of the external circumstances in the rather vague and badly described manner of BN. From the moment that I transformed the point of view of BN and the cogito and made something empirical from the cogito, the moral became something different. It had to be sought elsewhere, in a relation of the cogito with the external world, wherein the external world and the cogito had an equal value. I am seeking that. That is to say: I am trying to show how a cogito, which is immersed in the world and is not anterior to it, but which is on the same plane as this lamp or this chair; how that cogito is related with, for example, the social circumstances which modify its thoughts, . . . and that it is the relation of the social, of the world in all its forms *with* the cogito, which must constitute a moral.

---

13. Sartre is referring here to Pierre Victor.

F. — Could one say that that new moral, wherein the individual — as you say — is immersed in the world, is already to be found in TE[14]?

S. — Yes, already there.

F. — Can one say as well that a stronger connection exists between TE and CDR than between TE and BN?

S. — Yes, that is right.

F. — Is that right?

S. — That is correct, i.e. speaking more generally *Power and Freedom* returns to concepts which lie before BN, as for example contingency in N, more generally as everything that I said in N. And I am trying to recover it, because it seems to me that it is the starting point of my thought. And I am trying to close the circle, to link up my first thoughts with my latest, by giving up some of my ideas from BN and CDR.

Part IV:

F.   Consciousness as you described it in BN is pathogenic in one way or another. Not pathological, but pathogenic in this sense, that with the help of that transcendental consciousness one can give an explanation of, for example, bad faith consciousness and neurotic behavior. I believe that one can give no explanation for that behavior with the aid of the cogito in TE. In the film you say about TE: I have been influenced by Husserl, but I cannot take something over without also resisting it. That is the position of an intellectual. But it is not natural behavior. It is not the behavior of a consciousness that gives way to the world.

S. — No, it is not a non-reflected consciousness, it is a reflexive attitude which comes precisely from the attempt to unify the non-reflected consciousness. From this moment on the problems pose themselves on the plane of unity. A theory, a theory of Freud, a theory of Kierkegaard, can neither be confirmed nor denied by the non-reflected consciousness. It can only register explanations, possibilities for understanding itself with reference of anything whatever, even of theories which do not keep to the general lines of consciousness; but it can accept a Freudian interpretation, while in its most essential depth it is completely opposed to the fundamental principle of psychoanalysis. Where a distinction is really made between what one accepts and what one doesn't accept is in the reflective consciousness. That is to say, this consciousness unifies the non-reflected moments of consciousness in the way I just described, and then finds the contradictions, finds what flatters the non-reflected consciousness even if it is a freudian interpretation, what on the contrary displeases it, in an interpretation which makes use of an unconscious for example. It is up to reflective consciousness to bring about the synthesis, that is to say, to see the contradictions and to try to

---

14. "plongé". This term is already used in TE to indicate the profound relation of consciousness with the world.

establish a connection between what one accepts in psychoanalysis and what one rejects on the plane. . . . , the non-reflective plane in the same psychoanalysis of the unconscious. It must find a synthesis, it must find a possibility.

F. — Can one say, with reference to your theory of emotion as you have developed it in EM and as you have developed it in BN, that you sketched in EM the emotions of a first level and in BN those of a higher level? Is that correct, considering that the emotions. . . . Anxiety for example which you described in BN, no longer manifests itself in the body.

S. — That is correct. But despite all this it is related to a bodily disposition that lets itself get afraid or angry. There is nothing that is not also bodily. As you know I am a materialist, although I cannot exactly account for consciousness in a materialistic *theory*. But it is still a material problem for me.

F. — In CDR you speak of two forms of materiality, the materiality of consciousness and the materiality of the in-itself.

S. — That is so.

F. — Can you characterize those two forms of materiality, which enter into a synthesis in dialectical experience, in somewhat more detail? You not only characterize the "practico-inert" as material, but also the "practical organism". But these are two forms of materiality, also for you.

S. — Yes.

F. — But if you say that you are a materialist, which form of materiality are you thinking about, if you speak about the "practical organism", and which form if you speak about the "practico-inert"?

S. — The "practico-inert" is simple. That is materiality as one conceives of it in some given materialistic theory, but taken up again by consciousnesses[15] and presenting itself simultaneously as materiality endowed with meaning and simultaneously on a higher level as materiality which has meaning: a meaning which will be materially given here and now and which is nothing else than the precipitate of the meaning which consciousness has of itself, but which does not have the same form. Let us take a book for example, a book which I have in the bookcase, it doesn't matter which one. I grab it. I read it. I'm dealing with materiality. That object exists. But there are signs which determine a meaning. That meaning is in the collection of pages, with the printed signs, and these constitute a certain meaning. That meaning is an object, it is given. It is there, I grasp it, just as I grasp the meaning by means of an object that serves to provide light, a lamp for example; and in the same way I grasp that meaning [i.e. of the book] from the outside. But that meaning itself is nothing but the precipitate of what corresponds with the meaning which is grasped by the consciousness, the consciousness of him who has written and who grasped a meaning which is no longer the same meaning as that which one grasps if one reads the book. That

---

15. "consciences". In my opinion Sartre does refer here to the consciousness of different people (see footnote 6).

(original) meaning was broader, psychological. It can endure changes which the author did not take into account in the book, because this was not his affair. There is therefore the meaning of the consciousness which creates this meaning when it sees objects, in order to unite certain objects with one another, to arrange them, to make from them something unified, something developed, something adapted. That is the consciousness that creates this meaning, which gives this meaning and simultaneously discovers it. But those two things belong together. And then once this meaning has been given to the object, when it has been transformed into print, it undergoes a complete modification, it becomes the material meaning of the object itself, i.e. a meaning like that which I am now (while reading the book) taking account of and which I find in the object. I do not discover it and I do not invent it as on the level of the creative consciousness, but I grasp the meaning in the object from without.

F. — Well, if I have understood it well, consciousness for you is no longer a hole in being, but you find consciousness in the in-itself itself.

S. — In the social in-itself in any case. And sometimes also in the natural in-itself. Yes, I find it everywhere. To put it differently: there is no in-itself that could get away from the for-itself, nor a for-itself that should not be provided with the in-itself. Those two are distinct, but one constantly finds the relation of the one to the other; and in particular the meanings of the in-itself, which are infinite in number, are discovered by consciousness. They are meanings for man.

F. — With respect to the role of human relations between the two forms of materiality, could one say that the relations of consciousness with the in-itself is mediated by the other?

S. — Yes, constantly. That is so.

F. — In your CDR you talk about the role of the "third"[16]. I am not sure that I have properly understood that concept of the third.

S. — That is an arbitrary person in a group. Who is an outsider with respect to the reciprocity between two people. If there is a group of three persons, then there are two who stand in a relation of reciprocity . . . and the third, who is the relating element in this notion of reciprocity, and who consequently is indispensible because the notion of reciprocity is incomplete by itself.

F. — But who, for example, is that third in the relation between you and me at this moment?

S. — There is none. But if you write a book there will be one, the public, the public wherein you situate yourself as a possibility of saying what you think and making it comprehensible. And I direct myself to that same public, in so far it is more or less acquainted with my ideas.

F. — Thus that third can also exist as a possibility and not only as concrete reality?

---

16. "le tiers".

S. — No, but as a possibility with a more or less real meaning. For example, that public is possible and real at the same time: they are the philosphers who read books about one or other. That public is therefore simultaneously composed of possible and real elements. There are elements who might be witnesses who will acquire it [the book] and others who will certainly acquire it, and again others who will not acquire it. It is thus not only something possible, it is also something real. It is something that, as something possible, is something real. Do you understand what I wish to say?

F. — I am beginning to understand. And those thirds they are not yet persons? That are impersonal individuals such as. . . .

S. — Impersonal or personal, that depends. If there is a large meeting, a demonstration in the street, the "third" is a real person.

F. — Yes, a real person. But if I avail myself of the concept of person, I am also referring to the concept of the person in BN. That is another person.

S. — Yes, certainly.

F. — Well, what then is the difference between the person-concept in BN and in CDR? You have not worked out the person-concept in CDR.

S. — No, that should have come in the second volume. Well now, in BN the person is really a synthesis of the various notions which I clarified, more or less discovered, or in any case rediscovered, and the result of this is something perfectly abstract. No mortal can compare himself with a person from BN. That is a critical-theoretical work. But my aim in CDR — but this required two volumes and I never wrote the second — was the concrete individual, i.e. what remains, what is true in BN plus the truth about the person; i.e. his real life, the fact that he finds himself in a definite social situation with definite opinions, etc. *There* is the great difference. But one cannot say that BN supplies the principles and that CDR supplies their application. For the principles of BN are not always true according to my current conception. And some of them remain true. But roughly you can say that it is as follows: One can consider BN as a general and abstract vision of how I see and understand things, and then view CDR as the contingent and rich grasp of the person in the world, which was merely the case in abstracto in BN. And naturally, when I analyze an impression from BN the bad faith for example, then that impression is right, but one should also give an explanation of that bad faith, for example of a couple at a table in a café, where everyone is flirting; that bad faith should be explained, not simply as I have done in abstracto, but as a fact of the twentieth century; since men and women have not always associated that way. This association has known many other divergent forms, which have developed in the course of history and which have changed in the course of history; the description would not be successful for a Roman or Gallic-Roman couple. And yet its main point still stands. Thus one should always realize that the people in BN lack a foundation. They are surely real, but they lack a foundation.

F. — Can one feel sympathy for such a person? For example, do you see Flaubert in your study as a person?[17]

S. — Yes.

F. — But you feel no sympathy for him?

S. — No sympathy.

F. — You just feel empathy?

S. — Empathy, exactly, since there are too many actions, principles, and thoughts in Flaubert which conflict with mine. Consequently I can feel no sympathy for him. When I read certain formulations in his letters I react with repugnance — now, repugnance, that is too strong — but in any case with antipathy, even though I recognize that the man is worth the effort of being studied as a person.

F. — I believe that one gains much with that person-concept and with that empathy-concept, but that one also loses something. Can one still love given that concept?

S. — Yes, if the person who appears, whom you bring to mind, whom you see before you, is loveable. That means a lot: to be loveable. The old nineteenth-century theory claims that you love a person for psychological and personal reasons, who is neither loveable nor non-loveable, [but] who is the loved person. But according to me that is not correct. Persons are loveable or they are not loveable, and it is to that extent that one can love them or not love them.

F. — Is there still a place for the analysis of human relations as you described them in BN?

S. — Yes, surely. That becomes more possible.

F. — In BN there is as yet no place for what you have called empathy. There is only room for subject-object relations.

S. — That is right.

F. — And now, have you changed your opinions?

S. — Oh yes, certainly.

F. — Can that also be explained historically? I mean: in the 40's you thought differently about human relations than today. You are now — if I may say so — more friendly towards people.

S. — Yes.

F. — How do you explain that?

S. — Oh, I explain that by the context. Do not forget that I wrote BN during the occupation. We were occupied here. I did some work in the resistance like everyone else, and BN was also a book against the Germans. It has an anti-German aspect and there is most certainly some violence in it and more generally some antipathy, which undoubtedly can be explained in this way.

---

17. I am naturally referring to the Flaubert-study *l'Idiot de la Famille*.

F. — Were your analyses of intersubjectivity strongly influenced by the war?

S. — Without any doubt. Personally I see my life as the life of an anarchistic individualist until '39 . . . and in '39 a certain sort of communication with the people whom I loved during the war and thereafter in captivity; then from '40, under the monstrous conditions that characterized the occupation, the societal comes into my field of vision; I see how people associate with each other and I see that as something that must be changed by the disappearance of the occupation forces; and thus since '45 I began to take part in politics and to think about the social, which terminated, as you know, with the CDR.

F. — That is new for me. You have never, I believe, stated so clearly that the analyses of interpersonal relations were so strongly influenced by the war.

S. — Oh, but very clearly. That is true. I do not know if I have said it. I must have said it somewhere; I don't know any more. In any case my life certainly consists of three parts. An anarchistic individualistic part, a transition period, wherein one may speak of a development, of a coming into contact with the societal in many ways, — the war taught me the societal, as did the prison camp, and thereafter the return home and the struggle of the French against the Germans, the resistance and the liberation — , and from that moment there is a new attitude, that of the individual in the society, of the person in society.

F. — I would like to defend the following thesis: In CDR you return to a standpoint which was developed very early in TE.

S. — Yes, yes, but it is somewhat later. It is N. For me N was my first printed book — now first, well yes, there were articles — but N is the first printed book, and that is important to me, it is the only [book] of which I really consider myself the author. And as for the others, there are certainly influences, you have to dose, but N is the book wherein I set down my first intuitions. And I am returning to it in *Power and Freedom*. That will be the same sort of work.

F. — Do you think I am on the right track?

S. — Yes, I think so. . . , I think so. . . . That depends upon where you place the most emphasis: on a general movement or on a particular work. According to me the general movement is the proper standpoint.

F. — And when will *Power and Freedom* appear?

S. — In three years.

F. — Then we must have patience.

S. — (laughing) Yes!

Selected Bibliography
The Philosophy of Sartre in English

The following bibliography lists writings by and on Jean-Paul Sartre in English. They are divided into five sections: (1) Sartre's Life and Writings, (2) General Studies on the Philosophy of Sartre, (3) Existential Phenomenological Themes, (4) Philosophical Problems, and (5) Historical and Comparative Studies. A more complete set of entries including materials in other languages can be found in the bibliographies by Michel Contat and Michel Rybalka, *The Writings of Jean-Paul Sartre,* trans. Richard C. McCleary (Evanston: Northwestern University Press, 1974), Vol. 1: A Bibliographical Life (primary source); and by Robert Wilcocks, *Jean-Paul Sartre: A Bibliography of International Criticism* (Edmonton, Alberta: The University of Alberta Press, 1977) and François and Claire Lapointe, *Jean-Paul Sartre and his Critics: An International Bibliography* (1938-1975) (Bowling Green, Ohio: Philosophy Documentation Center, 1975) (secondary sources).

I. *SARTRE'S LIFE AND WRITINGS*

A. Chronological Listing of Writings and Events in Sartre's Life

(Sartre's writings in English translation including the date of original publication situated in the context of some major events in Sartre's life)

1905: Jean-Paul-Charles-Aymard Sartre born in Paris on June 21.

1906: Death of his father Jean-Baptiste Sartre on September 17. Moves with his mother to the home of his grandparents in Meudon (near Paris).

1911: His grandfather Charles Schweitzer moves with his wife, daughter (Anne-Marie Sartre), and Jean-Paul to Paris, where he founds a modern language institute.

1912-13: Reads *Madame Bovary*; rewrites the fables of La Fontaine in alexandrines, writes "novels": "For a Butterfly" and "The Banana Man."

1916: His mother remarries to a naval engineer, Mr. Mancy while "Poulou" remains with his grandparents and attends the Lycée Henri IV in Paris.

1917: Moves with his mother and step-father to La Rochelle.

1920: Returns to the Lycée Henri IV.

1922: Completes his *baccalauréat* exams; and begins a two year program of study at the Lycée Louis-le-Grand in preparation for the Ecole Normale Supérieure competitive entrance exam.

1923: "The Angel of Morbidity." In M. Contat and M. Rybalka, *The Writings of Jean-Paul Sartre, Vol. II: Selected Prose.* Translated by Richard C. Mc-Cleary. Evanston: Northwestern University Press, 1974, pp. 3-8. [Henceforth cited as *WS II*].

"Jesus the Owl, Small-Town Teacher." In *WS II*, pp. 9-21.

1924:   Passes the entrance exam to the Ecole Normale Supérieure and begins taking courses mainly in philosophy and psychology.

1926:   Writes a thesis on the imagination under the direction of H. Delacroix.

1927:   Writes "A Defeat," a novel inspired by the loves of Nietzsche and Cosima Wagner, "Er, the Armenian," and participates with Paul Nizan (whom he first met in 1916) in the translation of Karl Jaspers' *General Psychopathology.*

"The Theory of the State in Modern French Thought." In *WS II*, pp. 22-36.

1928:   Fails the written exam for the *agrégation* in philosophy.

1929:   Begins his friendship with Simone de Beauvoir. He passes the *agrégation* exam in first place, Simone de Beauvoir in second place.

1930:   Begins his eighteen months of military service at Saint-Cyr.

1931:   Appointed professor of philosophy at a Lycée in Le Havre.

"The Legend of Truth." In *WS II*, pp. 37-52.

"Motion Picture Art." In *WS II*, pp. 53-59.

1932-33:   Vacation trips to Spanish Morocco, Spain, England, and Italy.

1933-34:   Obtains a grant to the French Institute in Berlin, studying Husserl and Heidegger.

1934-39:   Teaches philosophy in *lycées* at Le Havre, Laon, and then Paris.

1936:   *The Transcendence of the Ego.* Translated, annotáted, and with an introduction by Forrest Williams and Robert Kirkpatrick. New York: Farrar, Straus, and Giroux, 1957.

Imagination: A Psychological Critique. Translated with an introduction by Forrest Williams. Ann Arbor: University of Michigan Press, 1962.

1937:   "The Wall." In *The Wall and Other Stories.* Translated by Lloyd Alexander. New York: New Directions, 1948, pp. 1-17. [Henceforth cited as *Wall*]. First published under the title *Intimacy.*

1938:   Finishes a 400-page work in psychology, entitled "The Psyche." Only a segment of this work is published as *The Emotions* (1939).

Nausea, or *The Diary of Antoine Roquentin.* Translated by Lloyd Alexander. New York: New Directions, 1949. Translated by Robert Baldick. Middlesex, England: Penguin Books, 1965.

"The Room." In *Wall*, pp. 18-40.

"William Faulkner's *Sartoris.*" In *Literary and Philosophical Essays.* Translated by Annette Michelson. New York: Collier Books, 1967, pp. 18-83. [Henceforth cited as *LP*].

"Intimacy." In *Wall*, pp. 55-83.

"John Dos Passos and *1919.*" In *LP*, pp. 94-103.

"Foods." In *WS II*, pp. 60-63.

1939:   Mobilized at outbreak of World War II.

The Wall and Other Stories is published and includes the previously unpublished stories "Erostratus" (pp. 41-54) and "The Childhood of a Leader" (pp. 84-144).

"Intentionality: A Fundamental Idea of Husserl's Phenomenology." Translated by Joseph P. Fell. *Journal of the British Society for Phenomenology,* vol. 1, no. 2, May 1970, pp. 4-5.

The Emotions: Outline of a Theory. Translated by Bernard Frechtman. New York: Philosophical Library, 1948. Also translated by Philip Mairet as *Sketch for a Theory of the Emotions.* London: Methuen, 1962. "François Mauriac and Freedom." In *LP,* pp. 7-25.

"On *The Sound and the Fury*: Time in the Work of Faulkner." In *LP,* pp. 84-93.

"Official Portraits" and "Faces." Translated by Anne P. Jones. In *Essays in Phenomenology.* Edited by Maurice Natanson. The Hague: Nijhoff, 1969, pp. 157-163. Also in *WS II,* pp. 64-71.

1940: Taken prisoner at Padoux, in Lorraine, on June 21 and sent to the *gardes mobiles* barracks in Nancy, where he remains for about two months. Then transferred to Stalag XII at Trèves, where he gives a course on Heidegger to a group of imprisoned priests and where he writes and stages his Christmas play *Bariona, or the Son of Thunder.*

Psychology of the Imagination. Translated by Bernard Frechtman. New York: Philosophical Library, 1948.

"Jean Giraudoux and the Philosophy of Aristotle." In *LP,* pp. 45-59.

1941: Liberated at the end of March by passing himself off as a civilian. Founds (with Merleau-Ponty) the intellectual's Resistance group, "Socialism and Liberty," but breaks with them seven months later.

Teaches at the Lycée Pasteur, then at the Lycée Condorcet until 1944.

"Herman Melville's *Moby Dick.*" In *WS II,* pp. 137-140.

1942: Meets Albert Camus in Paris.

"Sick at Heart." In *WS II,* pp. 141-151.

1943: *Being and Nothingness: An Essay in Phenomenological Ontology.* Translated by Hazel E. Barnes. New York: Philosophical Library, 1956.

The Flies. Translated by Stuart Gilbert. In *No Exit and Three Other Plays.* New York: Vintage, 1949, pp. 49-127. [Henceforth cited as *NE*].

"Camus' The Outsider." In *LP,* pp. 26-44.

"'Aminadab,' or the Fantastic Considered as a Language." In *LP,* pp. 60-77.

"Drieu la Rochelle, or Self-Hatred." In *WS II,* pp. 152-154.

1944: The editorial board of *Les Temps modernes* is established, including Sartre, S. de Beauvoir, R. Aron, M. Leiris, M. Merleau-Ponty, A. Ollivier, and J. Paulhan.

Writes for Camus' resistance newspaper *Combat.*

"Departure and Return." In *LP,* pp. 133-179.

No Exit. Translated by Stuart Gilbert. In *NE,* pp. 1-47.

"A More Precise Characterization of Existentialism." In *WS II,* pp. 155-160.

"On Dramatic Style." In *Sartre on Theatre.* Edited by Michel Contat and Michel Rybalka. Translated by Frank Jellinek. New York: Pantheon, 1976, pp. 6-29. [Henceforth cited as *ST*].

"Dullin and Spain." In *ST,* pp. 30-32.

"Paris Alive: The Republic of Silence." Translated by Lincoln Kirstein. *Atlantic Monthly,* vol. 174, December 1944, pp. 39-40.

1945: Visits the United States from January to May as special correspondent for *Combat* and *Le Figaro.* First number of *Les Temps modernes* appears in October. Returns to the United States for lectures at American universities in December.

"Introduction to *Les Temps modernes.*" Translated by Françoise Ehrmann. In *Paths to the Present.* Edited by Eugene Weber. New York: Dodd Mead and Co., 1960, pp. 432-441.

The Age of Reason. Translated by Eric Sutton. New York: Knopf, 1947.

The Reprieve. Translated by Eric Sutton. New York: Knopf, 1947.

"American Cities." In *LP,* pp. 114-125.

"Cartesian Freedom." In *LP,* pp. 180-197.

"The Liberation of Paris: The Apocalyptic Week." In *WS II,* pp. 161-164.

"New Writing in France." *Vogue,* May 1945, pp. 84-86.

1946:   Lectures in Switzerland and Italy.

Existentialism. Translated by Bernard Frechtman. New York: Philosophical Library, 1947.

The Victors. Translated by Lionel Abel. In *Three Plays.* New York: Knopf, 1949.

The Respectful Prostitute. Translated by Lionel Abel. In *NE,* pp. 252-281.

Anti-Semite and Jew. Translated by George J. Becker. New York: Schocken, 1948.

"The Mobiles of Calder." Translated by Wade Baskin. *Essays in Aesthetics.* New York: Philosophical Library, 1963, pp. 78-81. [Henceforth cited as *EA.*]

"New York, The Colonial City." In *LP,* pp. 126-132.

"American Novelists in French Eyes," *Atlantic Monthly,* vol. 178, no. 2, 1946, pp. 114-118.

"Forgers of Myths." In *ST,* pp. 33-43.

"Materialism and Revolution." In *LP,* pp. 198-256.

"We Write for Our Own Time." Translated by Sylvia Glass. In *Creative Vision.* Edited by Haskell Block and Herman Salinger. New York: Grove Press, 1960, pp. 187-194. [Henceforth cited as *Creative Vision*].

1947:   *Baudelaire.* Translated by Martin Turnell. New York: New Directions, 1950.

The Chips are Down [screenplay]. Translated by Louise Varese. New York: Lear, 1948.

"N-Dimensional Sculpture." In *WS II,* pp. 165-171.

"We Write for Our Own Time." In *WS II,* pp. 172-178.

"The Historical Process." In *WS II,* pp. 179-181.

"Nick's Bar, New York City." In *WS II,* pp. 182-184.

"The Responsibility of the Writer." In *Creative Vision,* pp. 165-185.

"For a Theatre of Situations." In *WS II,* pp. 185-186.

"Black Presence." In *WS II,* pp. 187-189.

What is Literature? Translated by Bernard Frechtman. New York: Philosophical Library, 1949.

1948:   *Dirty Hands.* Translated by Lionel Abel. In *NE,* pp. 129-248.

In the Mesh. Translated by Mervyn Savill. London: Andrew Dakers, 1954.

"The Quest for the Absolute." In *EA,* pp. 82-92.

"Nathalie Sarraute." In *Situations.* Translated by Maria Jolas. New York: Braziller, 1965, pp. 136-141.

"Consciousness of Self and Knowledge of Self!" Translated by Mary Ellen Lawrence and Nathaniel M. Lawrence. In *Readings in Existential Phenomenology.* Edited by Nathaniel M. Lawrence and D.J. O'Connor. Englewood Cliffs, New Jersey: Prentice-Hall, 1967, pp. 113-142.

"The Encounter, or Oedipus and the Sphinx." In *WS II,* pp. 190-191.

"We Must Have Peace in Order to Remake the World." In *WS II,* pp. 192-195.

1949: Visits Latin America, including Cuba.
Troubled Sleep. Translated by Gerard Hopkins. New York: Knopf, 1951.
"Foreword." In Jean Genet, *The Thief's Journal.* New York: Grove Press, 1964, pp. 7-8.

1950: Along with Merleau-Ponty, objects to the existence of Soviet concentration camps.
Travels to the Sahara and Black Africa.
"On Being a Writer." In *WS II*, pp. 196-201.
"The Artist and his Conscience." In *Situations.* Translated by Benita Eisler. New York: Braziller, 1964, pp. 142-155. [Henceforth cited as *S.*]
"Life Begins Tomorrow!" A film by Nicole Vedres in which Sartre appears. In *WS II*, pp. 202-206.

1951: Travels with S. de Beauvoir to Norway, Iceland, Scotland.
The Devil and the Good Lord. In *The Devil and the Good Lord and Two Other Plays.* Translated by Sylvia Leeson and George Leeson. New York: Knopf, 1960. pp. 1-149. [Henceforth cited as *DGL*].
"The Living Gide." In *S*, pp. 50-53.

1952: Breaks with Camus over *The Rebel.*
Participates in the People's Peace Congress in Vienna.
Lectures in Freiburg-im-Breisgau and visits Heidegger.
Saint Genet, Actor and Martyr. Translated by Bernard Frechtman. New York: Braziller, 1963.
The Communists and Peace. Translated by Martha H. Fletcher. New York: Braziller, 1968.
"Reply to Albert Camus." In *S*, pp. 54-78.

1953: From 1953 on (with the exception of 1960), spends his summers in Rome.
Publishes (with others) *L'Affaire Henri Martin,* defending the sailor arrested for opposition to the Indo-Chinese war.
"Reply to Claude Lefort." Translated by Philip Berk. In *The Communists and Peace.*
"Mad Beasts." In *WS II*, pp. 207-211.

1954: Participates in the World Peace Council in Berlin.
Visits USSR.
Later travels with S. de Beauvoir to Germany, Austria, Czechoslovakia, and Italy.
Kean. In *DGL*, pp. 151-279.
"The Paintings of Giacometti." In *S*, pp. 124-135.
"Julius Fucik." In *WS II*, pp. 212-216.

1955: Participates in the Congress of the Peace Movement in Helsinki, where he meets Lukács.
Spends two months in China with S. de Beauvoir and returns via Moscow.
Nekrassov. In *DGL*, pp. 281-438.
"An Unpublished Act from Nekrassov." In *WS II*, pp. 217-224.

1956: Sartre meets Arlette El Kaim, whom he adopts in 1965.
Visits Italy, Yugoslavia, and Greece.
Condemns the Soviet intervention in Hungary.

1957: Travels to Poland for the Polish premiere of *The Flies.*
The Ghost of Stalin. Translated by Martha E. Fletcher. New York: Braziller, 1968.
"Brecht and the Classical Dramatists." In *WS II*, pp. 225-228.
Search for a Method. Translated by Hazel E. Barnes. New York: Knopf, 1963.

"The Prisoner of Venice," In *S*, pp. 9-49.

1958: Participates in anti-Gaullist demonstrations concerning human rights in Algeria.

"A Victory." Introduction to Henri Alleg's *The Question*. Translated by John Calder. New York: Braziller, 1958.

"Of Rats and Men." In *S*, pp. 227-256.

"Theater and Cinema." In *ST*, pp. 59-63.

1959: Brief stay in Ireland for the movie *Freud* with John Huston.

The Condemned of Altona. Translated by Sylvia Leeson and George Leeson. New York: Knopf, Vintage, 1961.

1960: Travels to Cuba with S. de Beauvoir and meets Fidel Castro, Che Guevara. Received in Belgrade along with S. de Beauvoir by Tito.

Visits Brazil with S. de Beauvoir.

Critique of Dialectical Reason. Translated by Alan Sheridan-Smith. Edited by Jonathan Ree. London: New Left Books, 1976.

"Paul Nizan." In *S*, pp. 82-123.

"Sartre on Cuba!" Translated anonymously. New York: Ballantine, 1961, pp. 146-160.

"Albert Camus." In *S*, pp. 79-81.

"*Soledad*, by Colette Audrey." In *WS II*, pp. 236-238.

"Epic Theater and Dramatic Theater." In *ST*, pp. 76-120.

1961: "Preface." In Frantz Fanon, *The Wretched of the Earth*. Translated by Constance Farrington. New York: Grove, 1965.

"The Unprivileged Painter: Lapoujade." In *EA*, pp. 60-77.

"Merleau-Ponty." In *S*, pp. 156-226.

1962: Received by Kruschchev in USSR; also visits Poland.

"Science and Dialectic." Translated by Frederick L. Bender and Thomas E. Wren. In *Man and World*, vol. 9, no. 1, February 1976, pp. 60-74.

Bariona, or the Son of Thunder. In *WS II*, pp. 72-136. [Written in 1940].

1963: Returns to Moscow and makes contacts for an International Writers' Community.

Discusses the novel at a European Writers' Community congress in Leningrad.

Later visits Prague with S. de Beauvoir at the invitation of the Writers' Union; discusses the idea of decadence.

The Words. Translated by Bernard Frechtman. New York: Braziller; 1964.

"The Movies have Given Us Their First Tragedy, *Les Abysses*." In *WS II*, pp. 239-240.

1964: Visit to USSR; stay in Rome.

Awarded the Nobel Prize for Literature, but refuses it.

"Foreword." In R.D. Laing and D.G. Cooper, *Reason and Violence: A Decade of Sartre's Philosophy*, 1950-1960. New York: Vintage, 1971.

"Determinism and Freedom." In *WS II*, pp. 241-252.

"Kierkegaard: The Singular Universal." Translated by Peter Goldberger. In *Kierkegaard: A Collection of Critical Essays*. Edited by Josiah Thompson. New York: Doubleday Anchor, 1972, pp. 230-265. Also in *Between Existentialism and Marxism*. Translated by John Mathews. New York: Pantheon, 1974. [Henceforth this latter cited as *BT*].

1965: Petition to adopt Arlette El Kaim is granted.

Refuses to go to the U.S. for a series of lectures at Cornell University.

Trip to USSR.
The Trojan Women. Adaptation of a play by Euripides. Translated by Ronald Duncan. New York: Knopf, 1967.
"Why *The Trojan Women?*" In *ST*, pp. 309–315.

1966:   Travels to USSR, Greece, Japan, and W. Germany.
Participates in the "Russell Tribunal" investigating American war crimes in Vietnam. Preliminary meeting in London.
"A Plea for Intellectuals." In *BT*, pp. 228–285.
"Tintoretto: *St. George and the Dragon.*" In *BT*, pp. 179–196.
"Mallarmé: The Poetry of Suicide." In *BT*, pp. 170–178.

1967:   Conversation with Nasser in Egypt and visits refugee camps.
Travels to and lectures in Israel; conversation with Eshkol.
Serves as executive president of the Russell Tribunal in Stockholm; also in Roskilde, near Copenhagen.
Later in the year visits Spain.
"Myth and Reality in Theater." In *ST*, pp. 135–157.
On Genocide. Translated anonymously. With a summary of the evidence and judgments of the International War Crimes Tribunal by Arlette El Kaim-Sartre. Boston: Beacon, 1968. Also in *BT*, pp. 67–83 under the title "Vietnam: Imperialism and Genocide."

1968:   Trip to Yugoslavia.
Favors the May-June student movement against police repression and enters into debates with students at the Sorbonne.
Publicly condemns Russian invasion of Czechoslovakia.
"*In the Mesh.*" In *ST*, pp. 316–319.

1969:   Death of Mme. Mancy, Sartre's mother.
Condemns American atrocities at My Lai and Songmy in Vietnam.
"The Man with a Tape-Recorder." In *BT*, pp. 199–205.
"France: Masses, Spontaneity, Party." In *BT*, pp. 118–137.

1970:   Becomes editor of the Maoist-oriented *La Cause du peuple.*
Visits Norway and the Scandinavian countries.
Becomes editor of the newspaper *Tout!*
"Czechoslovakia: The Socialism that Came in from the Cold." In *BT*, pp. 84–117.
"A Friend of the People." In *BT*, pp. 286–298.

1971:   Publication of *J'accuse*, a journal for which Sartre writes regularly.
J'accuse and *La Cause du peuple* merge (in May).
Becomes editor of *Revolution!*
Publishes the first two volumes of *L'Idiot de la famille: Gustave Flaubert de 1821 à 1857*, which total over two thousand pages.
"The Actor." In *ST*, pp. 158–170. [From *L'Idiot, Vol. 1*].
"The Comic Actor." In *ST*, pp. 171–179. [From *L'Idiot, Vol. 1*].
"The Burgos Trial." In *Life/Situations: Essays Written and Spoken.* Translated by Paul Auster and Lydia Davis. New York: Pantheon, 1977. [Henceforth cited as *L/S.*]

1972:   Publishes the third volume of *L'Idiot de la famille.*
"The Maoists in France." In *L/S*, pp. 162–171.
"Justice and the State." In *L/S*, pp. 172–197.

1973:   Serious health difficulties and failing eyesight. Curtails his political activities.
Sartre on Theater. Edited by Michel Contat and Michel Rybalka. Translated by Frank Jellinek. New York: Random House, Pantheon Books, 1976.
"Elections: A Trap for Fools." In *L/S*, pp. 198–210.

"Sartre on Amnesty," *The New York Review of Books,* April 19, 1973, p. 45.

Politics and Literature. Translated by J.A. Underwood and John Calder. London: Calder & Boyars, 1973.

1974: Publishes discussions with Philippe Gavi and Pierre Victor, entitled *On a Raison de se révolter.*

Becomes editor of the collection *"La France Sauvage,"* published at first by Gallimard, then by the Presses d'Aujourd'hui.

Between Existentialism and Marxism. Translated by John Mathews. New York: Pantheon, 1974. [Selections from *Situations VIII* (1972) and *IX* (1972).]

The Writings of Jean-Paul Sartre, Vols. I-II. Edited by Michel Contat and Michel Rybalka. Translated by Richard C. McCleary. Evanston: Northwestern University Press, 1974.

1975: Travels to Greece.

Various appeals on behalf of Basque nationalists.

Life/Situations. Translated by Paul Auster and Lydia Davis. New York: Pantheon, 1977. [A translation of *Situations X* (1975)].

1976: Appeals with others in favor of liberating Soviet political prisoners.

Receives honorary doctoral degree from the University of Jerusalem.

"Socialism in One Country," (a fragment from the continuation of the *Critique of Dialectical Reason*), *New Left Books,* no. 100, November 1976-January 1977, pp. 143-163.

1977: Publishes a description in *Libération* of how his collaboration with Pierre Victor on a work to be called "Power and Freedom" began in 1975.

Sartre by Himself. Translated by Richard Seaver. Screenplay of the film by Alexandre Astruc and Michel Contat. New York: Urizen, 1978.

1978: Grants an extended interview with Michel Sicard on writing and publishing for a special number of *Obliques,* no. 18-19 including over thirty-five articles on or by Sartre with an update of the Contat-Rybalka primary bibliography. Articles by Sartre include a 1952 or so essay on Mallarmé's commitment and a substantial extract from his 1947 notebook on Ethics. Publication of the first collection of photographs of Sartre, gathered by Liliane Sendyk-Siegel with a commentary by S. de Beauvoir.

1979: First major conference in France on Sartre's work takes place during the summer at Cerisy-la-Salle, lasting ten days, under the direction of Geneviéve Idt and Michel Rybalka, with the participation of over fifty Sartre collaborators, scholars, and critics.

1980: Dies of a lung edema in Paris on April 15.

B. Chronological Listing of Interviews with Sartre

(Interviews with Sartre available in English and marked by the year of first publication. Does not include interviews reported only in summary form in Contat and Rybalka, The Writings of Jean-Paul Sartre, *Vol. 1)*

1946: "Existentialist." Anonymous. For *New Yorker,* March 16, 1946, pp. 24-25.

1947: "Existentialism: A New Philosophy—Or Is It Only A Word?" With Vincent Brome. For *Picture Post* (London), vol. 36, no. 5, August 2, 1947, pp. 4, 31.

1948: "Revolutionary Democrats." With Mary Burnet. For *New York Herald Tribune* (Paris), June 2, 1948.

1949: "Sartre Enters a 'New Phase!" With Joseph A Barry. For *New York Times*

Magazine, January 30, 1949. Also in Joseph A. Barry, *Left Bank Right Bank: Paris and Parisians.* New York: Norton, 1951, pp. 99–109.

"Author! Author?" With Roderick MacArthur. For *Theater Arts,* vol. 33, March 1949, pp. 11–13. [Concerns the New York adaptation and production of the *Red Gloves* (*Les Mains Sales*) in 1949].

1951:   "On *The Devil and the Good Lord.*" With Jean Duché. For *Le Figaro littéraire,* June 30, 1951. Translation in *ST,* pp. 232–237.

"There Is No Difference Between the Devil and the Lord — Personally, I Choose Man." With Marcel Peju. For *Samedi-Soir,* June 2–8, 1951. Translation in *ST,* pp. 226–231.

1953:   "About *Kean.*" With Renée Saurel. For *Les Lettres françaises,* November 12, 1953. Translation in *ST,* pp. 242–246.

1955:   ". . . Said Jean-Paul Sartre." With Henri Magnan. For *Le Monde,* June 1, 1955. Translation by Rima Drell Reck in *Yale French Studies,* no. 16, Winter 1955–56, pp. 3–7.

"By Denouncing the Methods of the Anti-Communist Press in My New Play, I Wish to Make a Writer's Contribution to the Fight for Peace." With Guy Leclerc. For *L'Humanité,* June 8, 1955. Translation in *ST,* pp. 248–250.

"The Play Aims at Institutions, Not Individuals." With J.F. Rolland. For *L'Humanité-Dimanche,* June 19, 1955. Translation in *ST,* pp. 250–252.

"Jean-Paul Sartre on the Theater." With Bernard Dort. For *Théâtre populaire,* September–October 1955, pp. 1–9. Translation in *ST,* pp. 44–54.

"Sartre Views the New China." With K.S. Karol. For *New Statesman and Nation,* December 3, 1955, pp. 737–739.

1956:   "After Budapest." For *L'Express,* November 9, 1956. Anonymous translation in *Evergreen Review,* vol. 1, no. 1, 1957, pp. 5–23. [Sartre's criticism of Soviet suppression of Hungarian intellectuals].

1957:   "Jean-Paul Sartre on His Autobiography." With Oliver Todd. For *The Listener* (London), June 6, 1957, pp. 915–16. [English translation of a BBC interview].

1959:   "Francis Jeanson Interviews Sartre." With Francis Jeanson. For *Verités pour. . . ,* June 2, 1959. In *WS II,* pp. 229–235.

"The Author, The Play, and the Audience." With F. Giroud, R. Kanters, F. Erval, and C. Lanzmann. For *L'Express,* [Originally appeared in English in *Evergreen Review,* vol. 4, no. 1, January–February 1960, pp. 143–152.

1960:   "The Purposes of Writing." With Madeleine Chapsal. For Madeleine Chapsal, *Les Ecrivains en personne.* Paris: Julliard, 1960, pp. 203–233. Translated by John Mathews. In *BT,* pp. 9–32.

"On *The Condemned of Altona.*" With Bernard Dort. For *Théâtre populaire,* January 4, 1960. Translation in *ST,* pp. 253–267.

"About *The Condemned of Altona.*" With Alain Koehler. For *Présence du théâtre,* March–April 1960. Translation in *ST,* pp. 271–285.

"All of Us Are Victims of Luther." For *Der Spiegel,* May 11, 1960. Translation in *ST,* pp. 285–306.

"Sartre on Violence." With K.S. Karol. For *Verité-Liberté,* no. 3, July–August 1960. Translation of excerpts in *New Statesman and Nation,* June 25, 1960.

1961:   "An Interview with Jean-Paul Sartre." With Oreste F. Pucciani. For *Tulane Drama Review,* vol. 5, no. 3, March 1961, pp. 12–18.

"Interview with Kenneth Tynan (1961)." For *The Observer* (London), June 18 and 25, 1961. In *ST,* pp. 121–134.

1962: "An Interview with Jean-Paul Sartre." With Ryo Tanaka. For *Sekai Magazine* (in Japanese), March 1962. Translation in *Orient/West* (Today's Japan), vol. 7, no. 5, May 1962, pp. 63-69.

"Two Hours with Jean-Paul Sartre." With L. Gendlin and S. Razgonov. For *La Culture et la Vie* (French language monthly in Moscow), no. 19, September 1962. Translation in *Culture and Life* (Moscow), no. 9, September 1962.

"Encounter with Jean-Paul Sartre." With Laszlo Robert. For *The New Hungarian Quarterly* (Budapest), vol. 3, no. 8, October-December 1962, pp. 246-248.

1964: "Conversation with Paolo Caruso about *Dirty Hands.*" With Paolo Caruso. In *ST,* pp. 210-225.

"A Long, Bitter, Sweet Madness." With Jacqueline Piatier. For *Le Monde,* April 18, 1964. Translation by Anthony Hartley, *Encounter,* vol. 22, June 1964, pp. 61-63 and under the title "Jean-Paul Sartre Speaks," *Vogue* no. 145, January 1965, pp. 94-95, 159.

"Sartre on the Nobel Prize." For *Le Monde,* October 24, 1964. Translation by Richard Howard in *New York Review of Books,* vol. 3, December 17, 1964, pp. 5-6.

1965: "The Condition of the Novel." For the Conference of European Writers at Leningrad, Summer 1963. Translation in *New Left Review,* no. 29, January-February 1965, pp. 19-40.

"Why I Will Not Go to the United States." For *Le Nouvel Observateur,* April 1, 1965. Excerpts translated by Lionel Abel in *The Nation,* April 19, 1965, pp. 407-411.

"Playboy Interview: Jean-Paul Sartre. A Candid Conversation With the Charismatic Fountainhead of Existentialism and the Rejector of the Nobel Prize." With Madeleine Gobeil. For *Playboy,* vol. 12, no. 5, May 1965, pp. 69-76. [Reprinted in *Playboy Interviews.* Chicago: Playboy Press, 1967, pp. 162-179.]

"Sartre Talks of Beauvoir." With Madeleine Gobeil. Translated by Bernard Frechtman for *Vogue* (American edition), no. 146, July 1965, pp. 72-73.

"The Writer and his Language." With Pierre Verstraeten. For *Revue d'esthétique,* July-December 1965. In *Politics and Literature.* Translated by J.A. Underwood and John Calder. London: Calder and Boyars, 1973. [Henceforth cited as *PL*].

"An Interview with Sartre." With Ali El Samman. For *Al Ahram* (Cairo), December 25, 1965. Translated (from the Arabic) by Amnon Kapeliuk in *New Outlook* (Tel Aviv), vol. 9, no. 2, February 1966, pp. 58-62.

1966: "Sartre on Israel and Other Matters." With Simha Flapan. For *Al Hamishmar* (Journal of the Israeli MAPAM), 1966. Translated in *New Outlook,* vol. 9, no. 4, May 1966, pp. 8-11.

"Imperialist Morality." For *Le Nouvel Observateur,* November 30-December 6, 1966. Translated in *New Left Review,* no. 41, January-February 1967, pp. 3-10.

"Replies to Structuralism." For *L'Arc,* no. 30, 1966. Translation by Robert D'Amico in *Telos,* no. 9, Fall 1971, pp. 110-116.

1967: "A Structure of Language." With Jean-Pierre Berckmans. For *Le Point,* no. 8, February 1967. Translation in *PL,* pp. 69-75.

"Sartre to De Gaulle." For *Le Nouvel Observateur,* April 26-May 3, 1967. Translation in *Against the Crime of Silence.* Edited by John Duffett. New York and London: Bertrand Russell Peace Foundation, 1968; Flanders, N.J.: O'Hare Books, 1968, pp. 29-36.

"A Theoretician in Brazil." With Jean-Claude Garot. For *Le Point*, no. 10, July 1967. Translation in *PL*, pp. 7-12.

1968: "Revolution and the Intellectual." With Jean-Claude Garot. For *Le Point*, no. 13, January 1968. Translation in *PL*, pp. 13-35.

"Communists are Afraid of Revolution: Two Interviews." With Gustav Stern, Georg Wolff, and Dieter Wild. For *Der Spiegel* (Hamburg), July 15, 1968. Translation by Elaine P. Halperin in *Midway*, vol. 10, no. 1, Summer 1969, pp. 41-52.

1969: "France: Masses, Spontaneity, Party." With the editors of the Italian journal *Il Manifesto*, August 1969. Translation in *BT*, pp. 118-137.

"Sartre Looks at the Middle East Again." With Arturo Schwartz. For *Quaderni del Medio Oriente* (Milan), vol. 1, nos. 3-4, January 1969, pp. 2-11. Translation in *Midstream*, vol. 15, no. 7, August-September 1969, pp. 37-38.

"Itinerary of a Thought." With Perry Anderson, Ronald Fraser, and Quintin Hoare. For *New Left Review*, no. 58, November-December 1969, pp. 43-66. Also in *BT*, pp. 33-64.

1970: "A Friend of the People." For *L'Idiot International*, October 1970. Translation in *BT*, pp. 286-298.

"Sartre on Mexico." For *The Spokesman*, no.6, October 1970, pp. 35-38.

1971: "On *The Idiot of the Family.*" With Michel Contat and Michel Rybalka for *Le Monde*, May 14, 1971. Translation by Paul Auster and Lydia Davis in *L/S*.

"Sartre Discusses Quebec." For *Guardian* (New York), May 19, 1971.

"Iron in His Soul." With John Gerassi. For *Manchester Guardian*, September 4, 1971. Also in *New York Times Magazine* under the title "Sartre Accuses the Intellectuals of Bad Faith," October 17, 1971.

1972: "What Is Jean-Paul Sartre Thinking Lately?" With Pierre Benichou. For *Esquire*, vol. 78, no. 6, December 1972, pp. 2, 4, 208, 280-286.

1973: "On Maoism: An Interview with Jean-Paul Sartre." With Michel-Antoine Burnier. For *Actuel* (Paris), no. 28, February 1973, pp. 73-77. Translation by Robert D'Amico in *Telos*, no. 16, Summer 1973, pp. 92-101.

1974: "A Conversation with Jean-Paul Sartre." For *Ramparts*, vol. 12, no. 7, February 1974, pp. 34-39.

1975: "Interview with Sartre." With Pierre Vicary for the Australian Broadcasting Commission's Radio 2 early in 1975. In Max Charlesworth, *The Existentialists and Jean-Paul Sartre*. London: George Prior, 1976.

"Self-Portrait at Seventy." With Michel Contat. For *Le Nouvel Observateur*, June 23, June 30, and July 7, 1975. Translation in *L/S*, pp. 3-92.

"Simone de Beauvoir Interviews Sartre." For *L'Arc*, no. 61, 1975. Translation in *L/S*, pp. 93-108.

1977: "Sartre and Women." With Catherine Chaine. For *Le Nouvel Observateur*, January 31-February 6, 7-13, 1977. Translation in *Playboy*, December 1977, pp. 103-104, 116-118, 124, 239.

"Sartre at 72: Still Hopeful." With Anne B. Zulli. For *The Washington Post*, February 13, 1977.

"Interview with Sartre." With Leo Fretz. For *De Gids* (in Dutch), nos. 4-5, 1977, pp. 338-355. Translation by George K. Berger. In *Jean-Paul Sartre: Contemporary Approaches to His Philosophy*. Edited by Hugh J. Silverman and Frederick A. Elliston. Pittsburgh: Duquesne University Press, 1980.

C. Biographical Accounts

(The major biographical studies of Sartre's life and writings available in English listed alphabetically according to author)

Beauvoir, Simone de. *Memoirs of a Dutiful Daughter*. Translated by James Kirkup. Cleveland and New York: World Publishing Co., 1959. [Also in Harper Colophon edition].

Beauvoir, Simone de. *The Prime of Life*. Translated by Peter Green. Cleveland and New York: World Publishing Co., 1962. [Also in Harper Colophon edition].

Beauvoir, Simone de. *Force of Circumstance*. Translated by Richard Howard. New York: G.P. Putnams, 1964. [Also in Harper Colophon edition in two volumes].

Beauvoir, Simone de. *All Said and Done*. Translated by Patrick O'Brien. New York: G.P. Putnams, 1974.

Contat, Michel and Rybalka, Michel. *The Writings of Jean-Paul Sartre, Vol. I*. Translated by Richard C. McCleary. Evanston: Northwestern University Press, 1974.

Madsen, Axel. *Hearts and Minds: The Common Journey of Simone de Beauvoir and Jean-Paul Sartre*. New York: Morrow, 1977.

Thody, Philip. *Sartre: A Biographical Introduction*. New York: Scribners, 1972.

II. GENERAL STUDIES ON THE PHILOSOPHY OF SARTRE

(Books, chapters, and articles which address Sartre's philosophy in its entirety and which provide an introduction to major aspects of his thought).

Albérès, René-Marill. *Jean-Paul Sartre, Philosopher Without Faith*. Translated by Wade Baskin. New York: Philosophical Library, 1961.

Allen, E.L. *Existentialism from Within*. New York: The Macmillan Co., 1958.

Aronson, Ronald. *Jean-Paul Sartre*. New York, Schocken Books, 1980.

Barnes, Hazel E. *Humanistic Existentialism: The Literature of Possibility*. Lincoln: University of Nebraska Press, 1959.

_____. "Jean-Paul Sartre and the Outside World." *Chicago Review*, vol. 15, no. 1, Summer 1961, pp. 107-112.

_____. *Sartre*. New York: Lippincott, 1973.

Barrett, William. "Talent and Career of Jean-Paul Sartre." *Partisan Review*, vol. 13, no. 2, Spring 1946, pp. 237-246.

Behar, Jack. "Jean-Paul Sartre: The Great Awakening." *The Centennial Review*, vol. 14, no. 4, Fall 1967, pp. 549-564.

Bochenski, I.M. "Jean-Paul Sartre," In *Contemporary European Philosophy*. Berkeley: University of California Press, 1959, pp. 173-180.

Boas, George. "Sartre." In *Dominant Themes of Modern Philosopy*. New York: Ronald Press, 1957, pp. 646-652.

Busch, Thomas. "Sartre: From Phenomenology to Marxism." *Research in Phenomenology*, vol. 2, 1972, pp. 111-120.

Carson, Ronald A. *Sartre*. Guildford, Surrey: Lutterworth Press, and Valley Forge, Pa: Judson Press, 1974.

Caws, Peter. *Jean-Paul Sartre*. Arguments of the Philosophers series. London: Routledge and Kegan Paul, 1979.

Cranston, Maurice W. *Jean-Paul Sartre*. New York: Grove Press, 1962.

_____. *The Quintessence of Sartrism*. New York: Harper Torchbooks, 1971.

Cumming, Robert D. "Introduction" to his edition of *The Philosophy of Jean-Paul Sartre*. New York: Randam House, 1965, pp. 3-47.

Danto, Arthur C. *Jean-Paul Sartre*. New York: Viking, 1975.

Dempsey, Peter. *The Psychology of Sartre*. Westminster, Maryland: Newman Press, 1950.

Grene, Marjorie. *Sartre*. New York: New Viewpoints, 1973.

Kaelin, Eugene F. "Three Stages on Sartre's Way: An Essay in Contemporary French Philosophy." In *European Philosophy Today*. Edited by George L. Kline. Chicago: Quadrangle paperback original, 1965, pp. 89–111.

Kern, Edith, ed. *Sartre: A Collection of Critical Essays*. Englewood Cliffs, New Jersey: Prentice-Hall, 1962.

LaCapra, Dominick. *A Preface to Sartre*. Ithaca: Cornell University Press, 1978.

Lafarge, René. *Jean-Paul Sartre: His Philosophy*. Translated by Marina Smyth-Kok. Notre Dame, Indiana: University of Notre Dame Press, 1970.

Manser, A.R. *Sartre: A Philosophic Study*. London: Oxford University Press, 1966.

Masters, Brian. *A Student's Guide to Sartre*. London: Heinemann, 1970, Reprinted as *Sartre: A Study*. Totowa, New Jersey: Littlefield Adams, 1974.

McMahon, Joseph J. *Humans Being: The World of Jean-Paul Sartre*. Chicago: University of Chicago Press, 1971.

Mészáros, István. *The Work of Sartre, Volume I: Search for Freedom*. Hassocks, Sussex: Harvester Press, 1978.

_____. *The Work of Sartre, Volume 2: The Challenge of History*. Hassocks, Sussex: Harvester Press, forthcoming.

Mihalich, J. "Jean-Paul Sartre." In *Existentialist Thinkers and Thought*. Edited by Frederick F. Patka. New York: Philosophical Library, 1962, pp. 126–137.

Miller, James. *The History of Human Existence: From Marx to Merleau-Ponty*. Berkeley: University of California Press, 1979.

Molnar, Thomas. *Sartre: Ideologue of Our Time*, New York: Funk and Wagnalls, 1968.

Murdoch, Iris. *Sartre: Romantic Rationalist*. London and New Haven: Yale University Press, 1953.

Naess, Arne. "Sartre." In *Four Modern Philosophers*. Chicago: Phoenix Books, The University of Chicago Press, 1968, pp. 265–359.

Olafson, Frederick A. "Sartre," *The Encyclopedia of Philosophy, Volume 7*: New York: Collier Macmillan Co., 1967, pp. 287–293.

Peyre, Henri. *Jean-Paul Sartre*, Columbia Essays on Modern Writers, no. 31. New York: Columbia University Press, 1968.

Richter, Liselotte. *Jean-Paul Sartre*. Translated by Fred D. Wieck. New York: Frederick Ungar, 1970.

Salvan, Jacques L. *To Be Or Not To Be*. Detroit: Wayne State University Press, 1962.

Schilpp, Paul Arthur, ed. *The Philosophy of Jean-Paul Sartre*. The Library of Living Philosophers Series. LaSalle, Illinois: Open Court Publishing Company, forthcoming.

Sheridan, James F. *Sartre: The Radical Conversion*. Athens, Ohio: Ohio University Press, 1969.

Solomon, Robert. "Jean-Paul Sartre and French Existentialism." In *From Rationalism to Existentialism*. New York: Harper and Row, 1972, pp. 245–324.

Stern, Alfred. *Sartre, His Philosophy and Psychoanalysis*. New York: Liberal Arts Press, 1953. 2nd rev. ed. New York-Los Angeles: Delacorte Publishers 1967.

Streller, Justus J. *Jean-Paul Sartre: To Freedom Condemned*. Translated by Wade Baskin. New York: Philosophical Library, 1960.

Thody, Philip. *Jean-Paul Sartre: A Literary and Political Study*. New York: Macmillan, 1961.

Warnock, Mary. *The Philosophy of Sartre*. New York: Hillary House, 1965; London: Hutchinson and Company, 1965.
_____. "Jean-Paul Sartre (1) and (2)." In *Existentialism*. Oxford: Oxford University Press, 1970, pp. 92-130.
_____, ed. *Sartre: A Collection of Critical Essays*. Garden City, New York: Doubleday, 1971.
Zuidema, Sytse Ulbe. *Jean-Paul Sartre*. Translated by Dirk Jellema. Philadelphia: Presbyterian and Reformed Publishers, 1960.

III. *EXISTENTIAL PHENOMENOLOGICAL THEMES*

(Books and articles concerned primarily with the first phase of Sartre's philosophy, focusing on his early major work Being and Nothingness *and the writings that surround it. Some of the themes treated include freedom, anxiety, nausea, bad faith, concrete relations with others, the body, situation and psychoanalysis.)*

Abel, Lionel. "The Existence of Jews and Existentialism." *Politics*, vol. 6, no. 1, 1949, pp. 37-40.
Abrams, Fred. "Sartre, Unamuno and the 'Hole Theory'." *Romance Notes*, vol. 5, no. 1, Autumn 1963, pp. 6-12.
Alexander, Ian W. "Jean-Paul Sartre and Existentialist Philosophy." *The Cambridge Journal*, vol. 50, no. 12, September 1948, pp. 721-738.
_____. "The Phenomenological Philosophy in France. An analysis of its themes, significance and implications." In T.V. Benn et al., *Currents of Thought in French Literature: Essays in Memory of G.T. Clapton*. Oxford: Basil Blackwell, 1965, pp. 325-352.
Ames, Van Meter. "Fetichism in the Existentialism of Sartre." *Journal of Philosophy*, vol. 47, 1950, pp. 407-411.
_____. "Reply to Mr. Natanson." *Journal of Philosophy*, vol. 48, 1951, pp. 99-102.
Anderson, Thomas C. "Is a Sartrean Ethics Possible?" *Philosophy Today*, vol. 14, Summer 1970, pp. 116-140.
_____. "Neglected Sartrean Arguments for the Freedom of Consciousness." *Philosophy Today*, vol. 17, no. 1, Spring 1973, pp. 28-39.
_____. "The Rationalism of Absurdity." *Philosophy Today*, vol. 21, Fall 1977, pp. 263-272.
_____. *The Foundation and Structure of Sartrean Ethics*. Lincoln, Kansas: Regents Press of Kansas, 1979.
Aquila, Richard E. "Two Problems of Being and Non-Being in Sartre's *Being and Nothingness*." *Philosophy and Phenomenological Research*, vol. 38, December 1977, pp. 167-186.
Arras, John D. "A Critique of Sartrian Authenticity." *The Personalist*, vol. 57, Spring 1976, pp. 171-180.
Ayer, A.J. "Novelist-philosophers, V: Jean-Paul Sartre." *Horizon*, vol. 12, no. 67, July 1945, pp. 12-26.
_____. "Sartre's Analysis of Man's Relationship." *Horizon*, vol. 12, no. 68, August 1945, pp. 101-110.
_____. "Some Aspects of Existentialism." In *The Rationalist Annual for the Year 1948*. London: Watts & Co., 1948, pp. 5-13.
_____. "Reflections on Existentialism." *Modern Languages*, vol. 48, no. 1, March 1967, pp. 1-12.

Atwell, John E. "Existence Precedes Essence." *Man and World*, vol. 2, Nov. 1969, pp. 580-591.

Barger, Bill. "Sartre on Original Choice." *Philosophy Research Archives*, vol. 2, no. 1082, 1976.

Barnes, Hazel E. "Jean-Paul Sartre and the Haunted Self." *Western Humanities Review*, vol. 10, 1956, pp. 119-128.

_____. "Transcendence Toward What: Is the Universe Like Us." *Religious Humanism*, vol. 4, Winter 1970, pp. 11-14.

Barrett, William. *What is Existentialism?* New York: *Partisan Review*, 1947.

_____. "A Study in Existential Philosophy." In *Irrational Man*. New York: Doubleday & Co., 1958, pp. 237-267.

Bell, Linda. "Sartre, Dialectic and the Problem of Overcoming Bad Faith." *Man and World*, vol. 10, 1977, pp. 292-302.

Berger, Gaston. "Existentialism and Literature in Action." *The University of Buffalo Studies*, vol. 18, no. 4, 1948.

Bergoffen, Debra B. "Sartre's Transcendence of the Ego: A Methodological Reading." *Philosophy Today*, vol. 22, Fall 1978, pp. 244-251.

Binkley, Luther. "Humanistic Existentialism: Jean-Paul Sartre." In *Conflict of Ideals: Changing Values in Western Society*. New York: Van Nostrand, 1967.

Blackman, H.J. "Jean-Paul Sartre" In *Six Existentialist Thinkers*. London: Routledge and Kegan Paul, 1952, pp. 110-148.

Bliltgen, Sister M.J. "No Exit: the Sartrean Idea of Hell." *Renascence*, vol. 19, 1967, pp. 59-63.

Blondel, Maurice. "The Inconsistency of Jean-Paul Sartre's Logic." *The Thomist*, vol. 10, no. 4, Oct. 1947, pp. 393-397.

Bobbio, Roberto. *The Philosophy of Decadentism. A Study in Existentialism*. New York: The Macmillan Co., 1948.

Boorsch, Jean. "Sartre's View of Cartesian Liberty." *Yale French Studies*, vol. 1, no. 1, Spring-Summer 1948, pp. 90-96.

Borrajo, Mogin, O.P. "Moral Perspectives in the Existentialism of Sartre." *Phillipp. Sacra*, vol. 3, 1968, pp. 531-570.

Breisach, Ernst. *Introduction to Modern Existentialism*. New York: Grove Press, Inc., 1962, pp. 94-106.

Brown, M. Jr. "The Atheistic Existentialism of Jean-Paul Sartre." *Philosophic Review*, vol. 57, no. 2, 1948, pp. 158-166.

Bruening, Sheila M. "Authenticity, Love, and the Reality of Hell." *Dialogue* (PST), vol. 19, April 1977, pp. 40-51.

Bukala, C.R. "Sartrean Ethics: An Introduction." *The New Scholasticism*, vol. 41, Fall 1967, pp. 450-464.

_____. "Sartre's Phenomenology of the Mask." *Journal of the British Society for Phenomenology*, vol. 7, October 1976, pp. 198-203.

Busch, Thomas W. "Sartre and the Senses of Alienation." *Southern Journal of Philosophy*, vol. 15, Summer 1977, pp. 151-160.

Butts, R.E. "Does Intentionality Imply Being? A Paralogism in Sartre's Ontology." *Kantstudien*, vol. 52, 1960-61, pp. 426-432. (An abstract appears in the *Journal of Philosophy*, vol. 55, 1958, pp. 911-912.)

Campbell, Gerald T. "Sartre's Absolute Freedom." *Journal Théologique et Philosophique*, vol. 33, Fall 1977, pp. 61-91.

Canfield, John V. and Gustavson, Don F. "Self-deception." *Analysis*, vol. 23, no. 2, December 1962, pp. 32-36.

Catalano, Joseph. *A Commentary on Sartre's 'Being and Nothingness'*. New York: Harper and Row, 1974.

Cerf, Walter. "Existentialist Mannerism and Education." *Journal of Philosophy,* vol. 52, no. 5, March 17, 1955, pp. 141–152.

Champigny, Robert. "God in Sartrean Light." *Yale French Studies*, no. 12, 1953, pp. 81–88.

Coates. J.B. "Existentialist Ethics." *Fortnightly*, vol. 181, May 1954, pp. 338–344.

Cole, Preston J. "The Function of Choice in Human Existence." *The Journal of Religion*, vol. 45, no. 3, July 1965, pp. 196–210.

Collins, James. "The Existentialism of Jean-Paul Sartre." *Thought*, vol. 23, no. 88, March 1948, pp. 50–100.

_____. *The Existentialists: A Critical Study*. Chicago: Henry Regnery Co., 1952, pp. 39–79.

Collins, Margery and Pierce, Christine. "Holes and Slime: Sexism in Sartre's Psychoanalysis." *The Philosophical Forum*, vol. 5, nos. 1–2, Fall-Winter 1973–1974, pp. 112–127.

Cook, Gladys Calkins. "Jean-Paul Sartre's Doctrine of Human Freedom and Responsibility." *Bucknell Review*, vol. 1, no. 2, June 1949, pp. 12–21.

Copleston, Frederick C. "Existentialism." *Philosophy*, vol. 23, no. 84, January 1947, pp. 19–37.

_____. "Atheistic Existentialism." In *Contemporary Philosophy*. Westminster, Md.: Newman Press, 1956, pp. 175–200.

Crawford, David R. "Interpretations of Self-Alienation." *International Philosophical Quarterly*, vol. 16, December 1976, pp. 323–340.

Cruickshank, John. "Existentialism after Twelve Years — an Evaluation." *Dublin Review*, no. 231, 1957, pp. 52–65.

Delfgaauw, B.M.I. *What is Existentialism?* Baarn: Het Wereldvenster, 1969.

De Ruggiero, G. *Existentialism*. Edited and introduced by Rayner Heppenstall. Translated by M. Cocks. London, 1946.

Desan, Wilfrid. *The Tragic Finale: An Essay on the Philosophy of Sartre*. Cambridge: Harvard University Press, 1954. New York: Harper and Row, Torchbook edition, 1960.

De Soto, Anthony Essex. "The Challenge of Existentialism — A Critical Analysis." *Journal of Thought*, vol. 5, April 1970, pp. 72–79.

De Tollenaere, M. "Intersubjectivity in Jean-Paul Sartre." *International Philosophical Quarterly*, vol. 5, 1965, pp. 203–220.

Dinan, Stephen A. "Intentionality in the Introduction to *Being and Nothingness*." *Research in Phenomenology*, vol. 1, 1971, pp. 91–118.

_____. "Sartre: Contingent Being and the Non-Existence of God." *Philosophy Today*, vol. 22, Summer 1978, pp. 103–118.

Doeswage, A.P. "Existential Psychological Analysis." *Journal of Philosophy*, vol. 52, July 1955, pp. 412–415.

Earle, William. "Man as the Impossibility of God." In *Christianity and Existentialism*. Edited by William Earle, James M. Edie, and John Wild. Evanston: Northwestern University Press, 1963, pp. 82–112.

Edie, James M. "Sartre as Phenomenologist and as Existentialist Psychoanalyst." In *Phenomenology and Existentialism*. Edited by Edward N. Lee and Maurice Mandelbaum. Baltimore: The Johns Hopkins University Press, 1967, pp. 139–178.

Etkin, Henry. "Comment on Sartre from the Standpoint of Existential Psychotherapy." *Review of Existential Psychology and Psychiatry*, vol. 1, 1961, pp. 189–194.

Farrel, B.A. "The Logic of Existential Psychoanalysis." *New Society*, vol. 6, no. 160, October 1965, pp. 9–11.

Fingarette, Herbert. "Sartre and *Mauvaise Foi*." In *Self-Deception*. New York: Humanities Press, 1969, pp. 92–100.

Frank, Joseph. "God, Man and Jean-Paul Sartre." *Partisan Review*, vol. 19, March 1952, pp. 202–210.

Gibson, A. Boyce. "Existentialism: an Interim Report." *Meanjin*, vol. 7, no. 1, Autumn 1948, pp. 41–52.

Goldthorpe, Rhiannon. "The Presentation of Consciousness in Sartre's *La Nausée* and Its Theoretical Basis: Reflection and Facticity." *French Studies*, vol. 22, April 1968, pp. 114–132.

Greene, Norman N. *Jean-Paul Sartre: the Existentialist Ethic*. Ann Arbor: University of Michigan Press, 1960.

Greene, Theodor. "Anxiety and the Search for Meaning." *Texas Quarterly*, vol. 1, no. 3, Summer-Autumn 1958, pp. 172–191.

Greenlee, Douglas. "Sartre: Presuppositions of Freedom." *Philosophy Today*, vol. 12, Fall 1968, pp. 176–183.

Grene, Marjorie. "Authenticity: An Existential Virtue." *Ethics*, vol. 62, July 1962, pp. 266–274.

_____. "Sartre and the Other." *Proceedings of the American Philosophical Association*, vol. 45, 1971–72, pp. 22–41.

Grimsley, Ronald. "An Aspect of Sartre and the Unconscious." *Journal of Philosophy*, vol. 30, 1955, pp. 33–44.

_____. "Jean-Paul Sartre." In *Existentialist Thought*. Cardiff: University of Wales Press, 1960, pp. 99–148.

_____. " 'Dread' as a Philosophical Concept." *The Philosophical Quarterly*, vol. 6, no. 24, July 1956, pp. 245–255.

Guthrie, G.P. "Importance of Sartre's Phenomenology for Christian Theology." *Journal of Religion*, vol. 47, January 1967, pp. 10–26.

Hamilton, Kenneth. "Life in the House that Angst Built." *The Hibbert Journal*, vol. 57, no. 224, October 1958, pp. 46–55.

Hanly, C.M.T. "Phenomenology, Consciousness and Freedom." *Dialogue*, vol. 5, March 1966, pp. 323–345.

Hardré, Jacques. "The Existentialism of Jean-Paul Sartre." *Carolina Quarterly*, vol. 1, no. 2, March 1949, pp. 49–55.

_____. "Sartre's Existentialism and Humanism." *Studies in Philology*, vol. 49, July 1952, pp. 534–547.

Harper, Ralph. *Existentialism, a Theory of Man*. Cambridge: Harvard University Press, 1948.

Hart, Samuel L. "*L'Existentialisme est un humanisme*." *Philosophy and Phenomenological Research*, vol. 9, no. 4, June 1949, pp. 768–771.

Hartmann, Klaus, and Santoni, R.E. "Sartre's Ontology." *International Philosophical Quarterly*, vol. 8, 1968, pp. 303ff.

Heinemann, F.H. "What Is Alive and What Is Dead in Existentialism?" *Revue Internationale de Philosophie*, vol. 3, no. 9, July 15, 1949.

_____. "The Philosophy of Commitment." In *Existentialism And The Modern Predicament*. New York: Harper Torchbooks, 1958, pp. 109–133.

Hellerich, G. "What is Often Overlooked in Existentialist Situation-Ethics." *Journal of Thought*, vol. 5, January 1970, 46–54.

Hook, Sidney. "Review of the English Translation of *Anti-Semite and Jew*." *Partisan Review*, April 1949, pp. 463–482.

Hopkins, Jasper. "Theological Language and the Nature of Man in Jean-Paul Sartre's Philosophy." *Harvard Theological Review*, vol. 61, January 1968, pp. 27–38.

Hudson, Yeager, "Existentialism: A Salvation Doctrine for Modern Man." *Religious Humanism*, vol. II, Winter 1977, pp. 21–38.

Kahn, Ludwig W. "Freedom: An Existentialist and an Idealist View." *Publications of the Modern Language Association*, vol. 64, no. 1, March 1949, pp. 5-14.

Kecskemeti, Paul. "Existentialism: A New Trend in Philosophy." *Modern Review*, vol. 1, no. 1, March 1947, pp. 34-51. Reprinted in *New Directions*, vol. 10, 1948, pp. 290-318.

Kaufmann, Walter. "Existentialism and Death." *Chicago Review*, vol. 13, no. 2, Summer 1959, pp. 75-93.

King-Farlow, John. "Self-deceivers and Sartrian Seducers." *Analysis*, vol. 23, no. 6, June 1963, pp. 131-136.

Kingston, F. Temple. "Freedom and Being Free." *Anglican Theological Review*, vol. 38, no. 2, 1956, pp. 153-160.

_____. "An Introduction to Existentialist Thought." *The Dalhousie Review*, vol. 40, no. 2, Summer 1960, pp. 181-188.

_____. *French Existentialism: A Christian Critique*. Toronto: University of Toronto Press, 1961.

Knight, Everett W. "The Politics of Existentialism." *Twentieth Century*, vol. 65, August 1954, pp. 142-153.

Kolnai, Aurel. "Existence and Ethics, II." *The Aristotelian Society*, supplementary vol. 37, 1963, pp. 27-50.

Kuhn, Helmut. *Encounter with Nothingness, an Essay on Existentialism*. Chicago: Henry Regnery, 1949.

Larrabee, Harold A. "Existentialism Is Not Humanism." *The Humanist*, vol. 8, no. 1, 1948, pp. 7-11.

Luijpen, William A. "The Atheism of Sartre." In *Existential Phenomenology*. Pittsburgh: Duquesne University Press, 1960, pp. 370-384.

Mackay, David. "Sartre and the Problem of Madness." *Journal of the British Society for Phenomenology*, vol. 1, May 1970, pp. 80-82.

Macleod, Norman. "Existential Freedom in the Marxism of Sartre." *Dialogue*, vol. 7, June-July 1968, pp. 26-44.

Macniven, C.D. "Analytic and Existential Ethics." *Dialogue*, vol. 9, June 1970, pp. 1-19.

Macquarrie, John. *Existentialism*. Baltimore: Penguin Books, 1973.

Macrae, D.G. "Private and Public Morality in Sartre's Existentialism." In *Ideology and Society*. New York: Free Press, 1961, pp. 198-207.

Manser, A.R. "Sartre and *le néant*." *Philosophy*, vol. 36, 1961, pp. 177-187.

_____. "Existence and Ethics, I." *The Aristotelian Society*, supplementary vol. 37, 1963, pp. 11-26.

_____. "The Imagination." *The Durham University Journal*, vol. 58, no. 1, December 1965, pp. 14-22.

Mansfield, Lester. "Existentialism: A Philosophy of Hope and Despair." *Rice Institute Pamphlet*, vol. 41, no. 3, October 1954, pp. 1-25.

Marcel, Gabriel. "Being and Nothingness." In *Homo Viator*. New York: Harper and Row, 1962, pp. 166-184.

_____. *The Philosophy of Existence*. New York: Philosophical Library, 1949.

Marcuse, Herbert. "Existentialism: Remarks on Jean-Paul Sartre's *L'Etre et le Neant.*" *Philosophy and Phenomenological Research*, vol. 8, no. 3, March 1948, pp. 309-336. Reprinted with a Postscript in his *Studies In Critical Philosophy*. Boston: Beacon Press, 1972, pp. 157-190.

Mark, James. "Sartre and the Atheism Which Purifies." *Prism*, no. 65, September 1962, pp. 5-22.

Maritain, Jacques. "From Existential Existentialism to Academic Existentialism." *Sewanee Review*, vol. 66, no. 2, 1948, pp. 210-229.

Martin, Michael W. "Morality and Self-Deception: Paradox, Ambiguity, or Vagueness?" *Man and World*, vol. 12, 1979, pp. 47-60.
_____. "Sartre on Lying to Oneself." *Philosophy Research Archives*, vol. 4, no. 1252, 1978.
McGill, V.J. "Sartre's Doctrine of Freedom." *Revue Internationale de Philosophie*, 1949, pp. 329-342.
_____. "The Transcendence of the Ego." *The Journal of Philosophy*, vol. 55, 1958, pp. 966-968.
McInerney, Peter K. "Self-Determination and the Project." *The Journal of Philosophy*, vol. 76, no. 11, November 1979, pp. 663-677.
Merritt, Richard N. "God, Sartre and the New Theologian." *Journal of General Education*, vol. 17, 1945, pp. 125-134.
Meyerhoff, Milton. "Sartre on Man's Incompleteness: A Critique and Counterproposal." *International Philosophical Quarterly*, vol. 3, December 1963, pp. 600-609.
Meyerhoff, Hans. "The Return to the Concrete." *Chicago Review*, vol. 13, no. 2, Summer 1959, pp. 27-39.
Mihalich, Joseph C. "Some Aspects of Freedom in Sartre's Existentialism." In *Existentialism and Thomism*. Totowa, New Jersey: Littlefield Adams, 1969, p. 9-22.
Molina, Fernando. "Sartre (1) and (2)." In *Existentialism As Philosophy*, Englewood Cliffs, New Jersey: Prentice Hall, 1962, pp. 73-102.
Morris, Phyllis Sutton. "Sartre and the Existence of Other Minds." *Journal of the British Society for Phenomenology*, vol. 1, May 1970, pp. 17-22.
Morriston, Wesley. "Freedom Determinism and Chance in the Early Philosophy of Sartre." *The Personalist*, vol. 58, July 1977, pp. 236-248.
Natanson, Maurice. *A Critique of Jean-Paul Sartre's Ontology*. Lincoln, Nebraska: University of Nebraska Press, 1951; The Hague: Nijhoff, 1973.
_____. "Sartre's Fetishism: A Reply to Van Meter Ames." *Journal of Philosophy*, vol. 48, 1951, pp. 95-99.
_____. "Jean-Paul Sartre's Philosophy of Freedom." *Social Research*, vol. 19, September 1952, pp. 364-380.
Netzky, Ralph. "Playful Freedom: Sartre's Ontology Re-appraised." *Philosophy Today*, vol. 18, Summer 1974, pp. 125-136.
Newman, F. "Origins of Sartre's Existentialism." *Ethics*, vol. 76, no. 3, April 1966, pp. 178-191.
Olafson, Frederick A. "Existential Psychoanalysis." *Ethics*, vol. 64, no. 4, July 1954, pp. 311-321.
_____. *Principles and Persons: An Ethical Interpretation of Existentialism*. Baltimore: The Johns Hopkins University Press, 1967.
Olson, Robert G. "Three Theories of Motivation in the Philosophy of Jean-Paul Sartre." *Ethics*, vol. 66, no. 3, April 1956, pp. 176-186.
_____. "Sincerity and the Moral Life." *Ethics*. vol. 68, no. 4, July 1958, pp. 260-280.
_____. *An Introduction To Existentialism*. New York: Dover, 1962.
O'Mara, Joseph. "The Meaning and Value of Existentialism." *Studies* (Dublin), vol. 40, no. 157, March 1951, pp. ll-22.
Owens, Thomas. "Absolute Aloneness as Man's Existential Structure: A Study of Sartrean Ontology." *New Scholasticism*, vol. 40, 1966, pp. 341-360.
Peterson, Joel. "Problems in the Sartrean Paradigm of Life as a Project." *Philosophical Forum*, vol. 7, Winter 1975-76, pp. 188-202.
Pivčević, Edo. "Existentialism Based on a Phenomenology of Consciousness." In *Husserl and Phenomenology*. London: Hutchinson University Library, 1970, pp. 122-131.

Pilkington, A.E. "Sartre's Existentialist Ethic." *French Studies*, vol. 23, January 1969, pp. 38-48.
Plantinga, A. "An Existentialist's Ethics." *Review of Metaphysics*, vol. 12, December 1958, pp. 235-256.
Pleydell-Pearce, A.G. "Freedom, Emotion and Choice in the Philosphy of Sartre." *Journal of the British Society for Phenomenology*, vol. 1, May 1970, pp. 35-46.
_____. "Freedom, Necessity and Existential Choice." *Journal of the British Society for Phenomenology*, vol. 7, 1976, pp. 204-208.
Portman, S. "Existentialist Ethics and Being as a Value." *Dialogue* (PST), vol. 14, October 1971, pp. 11-15.
Potoacki, Charles. "Freedom à la Sartre." *Annual Report, Duns Scotus Philosophical Association*, vol. 29, 1965, pp. 128-159.
Rau, Catherine. "The Ethical Theory of Jean-Paul Sartre." *Journal of Philosophy*, vol. 46, 1949, pp. 536-545.
Rintelen, J. von. *Beyond Existentialism*. Translated by Hilda Graef. London: George Allen & Unwin Ltd., 1961.
Roberts, David E. "Sartre." In *Existentialism And Religious Belief*. New York: Oxford University Press, 1957, pp. 193-226.
Roubiczek, Paul. "Some Aspects of French and German Existentialism." In *Existentialism: For And Against*. New York: Cambridge University Press, 1966, pp. 117-138.
Sahu, Sreenivassa. "The Humanism of Jean-Paul Sartre." *Philosophical Quarterly* (Asian), vol. 28, 1955, pp. 185-190.
Sanborn, Patricia F. *Existentialism*. New York: Pegasus, 1968.
Santoni, Ronald E. "Sartre on 'Sincerity': 'Bad Faith' or Equivocation?" *The Personalist*, vol. 53, Spring 1972, pp. 150-160.
_____. "Bad Faith and 'Lying to Oneself'. " *Philosophy and Phenomenological Research*, vol. 38, March 1978, pp. 384-398.
Scanlon, John. "Desire, Need and Alienation in Sartre." In *Dialogues In Phenomenology*. Edited by Don Ihde and Richard M. Zaner. The Hague: Nijhoff, 1975, pp. 211-223.
Schacht, Richard. "Alienation in Sartre's Major Works." In *Alienation*. New York: Doubleday Anchor Books, 1970, pp. 226-239.
Schindler, Stefan. " 'Consciousness' in Satisfaction as the Pre-reflective Cogito." *Process Studies*, vol. 5, Fall 1975, pp. 187-190.
Schrader, George A. "Existential Psychoanalysis and Metaphysics." *Review of Metaphysics*, vol. 13, 1959, pp. 139-164.
Schrag, Calvin O. "The Structure of Moral Experience: A Phenomenological and Existential Analysis." *Ethics*, vol. 73, no. 4, July 1963, pp. 255-265.
Schutz, Alfred. "Sartre's Theory of the Alter Ego." *Philosophy and Phenomenological Research*, vol. 9, 1948, pp. 181-199. Reprinted in *Collected Papers*, Vol. 1. *The Problem of Social Reality*. Edited & introduced by Maurice Natanson. The Hague: Nijhoff, 1962.
Scott, Nathan A. Jr. "Jean-Paul Sartre—Advocate of Responsibility in Solitude." In *The Unquiet Vision: Mirrors of Man in Existentialism*. New York: The World Publishing Co., 1969, pp. 120-149.
Shalom, Albert, and Yolton, John. "Sartre's Ontology." *Dialogue*, vol. 6, December 1967, pp. 383-398.
Sheridan, James F. "On Ontology and Politics: A Polemic." *Dialogue*, vol. 7, December 1968, pp. 449-460.
Shouery, Imad T. "Reduction in Sartre's Ontology." *Southwestern Journal of Philosophy*, vol. 2, no. 1-2, Spring-Summer 1971, pp. 47-53.
Smith, Colin. "The Search for Significance. Transcendence. The Pursuit of Mean-

ing as a Necessary but 'Useless' Passion. Sartre." In *Contemporary French Philosophy. A Study in Norms and Values*. London: Methuen, 1964, pp. 27–47.

Smith, Quentin. "Sartre and the Matter of Mental Images." *Journal of the British Society for Phenomenology*, vol. 8, May 1977, pp. 69–78.

Smith, Vincent Edward. "Sartre's Refuge in Atheism." In *Idea-men of Today*. Milwaukee: Bruce Publishers, 1952, pp. 288–310.

Smitheram, Verner. "Sartre and Ricoeur on Freedom and Choice." *Philosophy Research Archives*, vol. 3, no. 1105, 1977.

Spiegelberg, Herbert. "The Phenomenology of Jean-Paul Sartre." In *The Phenomenological Movement: A Historical Introduction, Vol. 2*. The Hague: Nijhoff, 1960, pp. 445–515.

Stack, George J. "Sartre's Social Phenomenology." *Studium Generale*, vol. 22, October 1969, pp. 985–1015.

_____. "Jean-Paul Sartre: Consciousness and Concrete Freedom." *Philosophy Today*, vol. 19, Winter 1975, pp. 305–325.

Stern, Guenther. "Emotion and Reality." *Philosophy and Phenomenological Research*, 1950, pp. 553–562.

Strasser, Stephan. "The Origin of the Emotional World-View According to Jean-Paul Sartre." In *The Phenomenology of Feeling*. Pittsburgh, Pa.: Duquesne University Press, 1977, pp. 65–86.

Sultan, Ather. "Sartre's Theory of Freedom and Choice." *Pakistan Philosophical Journal*, vol. 9, April 1966, pp. 13–18.

Tembeck, R. "Dialectic and Time in *The Condemned of Altona*." *Modern Drama*, vol. 12, May 1969, pp. 10–17.

Theobald, David W. "The Imagination and What Philosophers Have to Say." *Diogenes*, no. 57, Spring 1967, pp. 47–63.

Thévenaz, Pierre. "The Phenomenology of Sartre." In *What Is Phenomenology?* Translated and edited by James M. Edie. Chicago: Quadrangle Books, 1962, pp. 67–82.

Thody, Philip. "Sartre's Autobiography: Existential Psychoanalysis or Self-Denial?" *Southern Review* (Louisiana State University), vol. 5, pp. 1030–1044.

_____. "Existential Psychoanalysis." *Journal of the British Society for Phenomenology*, vol. 1, May 1970, pp. 83–92.

Thomson, J.S. "The Existential Philosophy." *Philosophy Today*, vol. 2, 1958, pp. 93–106.

Tollenaere, Mide. "Intersubjectivity in Jean-Paul Sartre," *International Philosophical Quarterly*, vol. 5, May 1965, pp. 203–220.

Topitsch, Ernst. "The Sociology of Existentialism." *Partisan Review*, vol. 21, no. 3, May–June 1954, pp. 289–304.

Tuedio, James A. "Sartre's Phenomenology of Lived-Immediacy." *Kinesis*, vol. 9, Spring 1979, pp. 72–87.

Tulloch, D.M. "Sartrean Existentialism." *Philosophical Quarterly*, vol. 2, no. 6, January 1952, pp. 31–52.

Ussher, Arland. "The Existentialism of Jean-Paul Sartre." *Dublin Magazine* (new series), vol. 21, no. 2, April–June 1946, pp. 32–35.

Ver Eecke, Wilfried. "The Look, the Body and the Other." In *Dialogues In Phenomenology*. Edited by Don Ihde and Richard M. Zaner. The Hague: Nijhoff, 1975, pp. 224–226.

Van de Pitte, M.M. "Sartre as Transcendental Realist." *Journal of the British Society for Phenomenology*, vol. 1, May 1970, pp. 22–26.

Vassilieff, Elizabeth. "Sartre on Imagination." *Meanjin*, vol. 10, no. 46, Spring 1951, pp. 267–286.

Vial, Fernand. "Existentialism and Humanism." *Thought*, vol. 23, no. 88, March 1948, pp. 17-20.

Wahl, Jean. "Freedom and Existence in Some Recent Philosophies." *Philosophy and Phenomenological Research*, vol. 8, no. 4, June 1948, pp. 539-556.

_____. *A Short History of Existentialism*. New York: Philosophical Library, 1949.

_____. *Philosophies of Existence*. Translated by F.M. Lory. London: Routledge and Kegan Paul, 1969, and N.Y. Schocken, 1969.

Walker, A.D.M. "Sartre, Santoni and Sincerity." *The Personalist*, vol. 58, January, 1977, pp. 88-92.

Warnock, Mary. "The Moral Philosophy of Sartre." *The Listener*, vol. 61, no. 1554, Jan. 8, 1959, pp. 64-65; and vol. 61, no. 1555, Jan. 15, 1959, pp. 105-106.

_____. *Ethics since 1900*. London: Oxford University Press, 1960, pp. 113-139.

_____. *Existentialist Ethics*. London: Macmillan and New York: St. Martin's Press, 1967.

_____. "The Concrete Imagination." *Journal of the British Society for Phenomenology*, vol. 1, May 1970, pp. 6-12.

IV. PHILOSOPHICAL PROBLEMS

(Materials which treat Sartre's discussions of traditional philosophical problems, stressing his views on art, literature, the self, history, metaphysics, religion, politics, and society. Unlike the preceding emphasis on his early work, these span the whole course of Sartre's thought, drawing comparisons on specific themes.)

Abel, Lionel. "The Retroactive I." *Partisan Review*, vol. 32, Spring 1965, pp. 255-261.

Adler, Franz. "The Social Thought of Jean-Paul Sartre." *American Journal of Sociology*, vol. 55, no. 3, November 1949, pp. 284-294.

Allen. E.I. "Justice and Self-Justification in Sartre." *Theology Today*, vol. 18, July 1961, pp. 150-158.

Ames, Van Meter. "Existentialism and the Arts." *Journal of Aesthetics and Art Criticism*, vol. 9, March 1956, pp. 252-256.

_____. "Back to the Wall." *Chicago Review*, vol. 13, no. 2, 1960, pp. 128-143.

Aronson, Ronald. *"L'Idiot de la famille*: The Ultimate Sartre?" *Telos*, no. 20, Summer 1974, pp. 90-107.

_____. "The Individualist Social Theory of Jean-Paul Sartre." In *Western Marxism: A Critical Reader*. Edited by New Left Review. London: New Left Review: Verso Editions, 1978, pp. 201-231.

Bach, Max and Bach, Huguette L. "The Moral Problem of Political Responsibility: Brecht, Frisch, Sartre." *Books Abroad*, vol. 37, Autumn 1963, pp. 378-384.

Bambrough, André. "Principia Metaphysica." *Philosophy*, vol. 39, no. 148, April 1964, pp. 97-109.

Bantel, Robyn A. "The Haunting Image of the Absolute in the Work of Sartre." *Research in Phenomenology*, vol. 9, 1979, pp.

Barnes, Hazel E. "Modes of Aesthetic Consciousness in Fiction." *Bucknell Review*, vol. 12, no. 1, March 1964, pp. 82-93.

Bauer, George H. *Sartre and the Artist*. Chicago: University of Chicago Press, 1969.

Bédé, Jean-Albert. "Sartre, Jean-Paul." *Columbia Dictionary of Modern European Literature*. New York: Columbia University Press, 1947, pp. 722-723.

Belli, Angela. "Jean-Paul Sartre: *Les Mouches*." In *Ancient Greek Myths and Mod-*

ern Drama. A Study in Continuity. New York: New York University Press and London: University of London Press, 1968, pp. 70-97.

Bentley, Eric. "Jean-Paul Sartre, Dramatist: The Thinker as Playwright." *Kenyon Review,* vol. 8, no. 1, Winter 1946, pp. 66-79. Reprinted in *The Playwright as Thinker.* New York: Reynal & Hitchcock, 1946, pp. 232-246.

Bergoffen, Debra B. "Jean-Paul Sartre's *Nausea*; Roquentin as Phenomenologist and Author." *The Personalist,* vol. 60, no. 1, January 1979, pp. 43-52.

Bondy, François. "Jean-Paul Sartre and Politics." *Journal of Contemporary History,* vol. 2, April 1967, pp. 25-48.

_____. "The Idiot or Sartre's Flaubert." *Encounter,* vol. 37, no. 6, December 1971, pp. 37-41.

Brée, Germaine and Guiton, Margaret. "Jean-Paul Sartre: The Search for Identity." In *The French Novel.* New York: Harcourt, Brace and World, 1962, pp. 203-217.

Brewster, Ben. "Presentation of Gorz on Sartre." *New Left Review,* no. 37, May-June 1966, pp. 29-52.

Brombert, Victor. "The Intellectual as Impossible Hero." In *The Intellectual Hero: Studies in the French Novel.* Philadelphia: Lippincott, 1961, pp. 181-203.

Bruening, Sheila M. "Sartre's Theory of Literature in 'The Wall'." *Dialogue* (PST), vol. 20, April 1978, pp. 49-56.

Burkle, Howard R. "Jean-Paul Sartre: Social Freedom in the *Critique de la raison dialectique.*" *Review of Metaphysics,* vol. 19, 1966, pp. 742-757.

Camus, Albert. "On Sartre's *Le Mur And Other Stories.*" In *Lyrical and Critical Essays.* New York: Random House, Vintage Books, 1970, pp. 203-206.

_____. "On Jean-Paul Sartre's *La Nausée.*" In *Lyrical And Critical Essays.* New York: Random House, Vintage Books, 1970, pp. 199-202.

Castoriadis, Cornelius. "Reply to Andre Gorz's 'Sartre and The Deaf'." *Telos,* no. 33, Fall 1977, pp. 108-109.

Champigny,Robert. *Stages on Sartre's Way: 1938-1952.* Bloomington: Indiana University Press, 1959.

_____. "Trying to Understand *L'Idiot.*" *Diacritics,* vol. 2, no. 2, Summer 1972, pp. 2-6.

Collins, Douglas. *Sartre as Biographer.* Cambridge: Harvard University Press, 1980.

Craib, Ian. *Existentialism and Sociology: A Study of Jean-Paul Sartre.* Cambridge: Cambridge University Press, 1976.

Cranston, Maurice W. "Sartre and Violence: a Philosopher's Commitment to a Pledge." *Encounter,* vol. 29, July 1967, pp. 18-24.

_____. "The Later Thought of Jean-Paul Sartre." *Modern Occasions,* vol. 29, 1966, pp. 181-201.

Cruickshank, John, ed. *The Novelist as Philosopher.* London: Oxford University Press, 1962.

Cumming, Robert D. "This Place of Violence, Obscurity, and Witchcraft." *Political Theory,* vol. 7, May 1979, pp. 181-200.

_____. The Literature of Extreme Situations" In *Aesthetics Today.* Edited by Morris Phillipson. Cleveland: Meridian Books, 1961, pp. 377-412.

_____. "Existentialist Psychology in Action." In *Scientific Psychology.* Edited by Benjamin B. Wolman. New York: Basic Books, 1965, pp. 384-401.

Dempsey, Peter. *The Psychology of Sartre.* Westminster, Maryland: Newman Press, 1950.

Desan, Wilfrid. *The Marxism of Sartre.* Garden City, New York: Doubleday Anchor Books, 1965.

Dillon, Martin. "Sartre's Inferno." *Thought,* vol. 52, June 1977, pp. 134-50.

Dilman, I. "An Examination of Sartre's Theory of Emotions." *Ratio*, vol. 5, December 1963, pp. 190–212.

Ellevitch, Bernard, "Sartre and Genet." *The Massachusetts Review*, vol. 5, Winter 1964, pp. 408–413.

Eskin, Stanley G. "The Political Themes in Sartre's Literary Works." *Midway*, vol. 9, no. 4, Spring 1969, pp. 69–98.

Fell, Joseph J. "Sartre as Existentialist and Marxist." *Bucknell Review*, vol. 13, no. 3, December 1965, pp. 63–74.

_____. *Emotion in the Thought of Sartre*. New York: Columbia University Press, 1965.

_____. "Sartre's Words: an Existential Self-analysis." *Psychoanalytic Review*, vol. 55, no. 3, 1968, pp. 426–441.

_____. "Sartre's Theory of Motivation: Some Clarifications." *Journal of the British Society for Phenomenology*, vol. 1, May 1970, pp. 27–34.

Fields, Belden. *An Examination of the Ontological Foundations of the Political Theory of Sartre*. New York, 1961.

Flynn, Thomas R. "*L'Imagination au pouvoir*: The Evolution of Sartre's Political and Social Thought." *Political Theory*, vol. 7, May 1979, pp. 157–180.

_____. "Praxis and Vision: Elements of a Sartrean Epistemology." *Philosophical Forum*, vol. 8, Fall 1976, pp. 21–43.

_____. "The Role of the Image in Sartre's Aesthetic." *The Journal of Aesthetics and Art Criticism*, vol. 33, no. 4, Summer 1975, pp. 431–442.

_____. "An End to Authority: Epistemology and Politics in the Later Sartre." *Man and World*, vol. 10, no. 4, 1977, pp. 448–465.

Forster, Kurt W. "The Image of Freedom: An Inquiry into the Aesthetics of Schiller and Sartre." *British Journal of Aesthetics,* vol. 5, June 1965, pp. 46–52.

Freeze, Donald J. "Zeus, Orestes and Sartre." *The New Scholasticism*, vol. 44, no. 2, Spring 1970, pp. 249–264.

Friedmann, Maurice. "Sex in Sartre and Buber." *Review of Existential Psychology and Psychiatry*, vol. 3, 1963, pp. 113–124.

_____. "The Atheist Existentialist: Nietzsche and Sartre." In *To Deny Our Nothingness: Contemporary Images of Man*. New York: Delacorte Press and London: Victor Gollancz, Ltd. 1967, pp. 243–261.

Furlong, E.J. *Imagination*. London: George Allen & Unwin, Ltd., and New York: The Macmillan Co., 1961.

Garaudy, Roger. "False Prophet: Jean-Paul Sartre." In *Literature Of The Graveyard*. New York: International Publishers Co., 1948. Reprinted in *Existentialism Versus Marxism*. Edited by George Novack. New York: Delta Books, 1966, pp. 154–163.

Gardiner, Patrick. "Sartre on Character and Self-Knowledge." *New Literary History*, vol. 9, Autumn 1977, no. 1, pp. 65–81.

Gelblum, Tuvia. "Samkhya and Sartre." *Journal of Indian Philosophy*, vol. 1, no. 1, October 1970, pp. 75–82.

_____. "Classical Samkhya and the Phenomenology of Sartre." *Philosophy East & West*, vol. 19, no. 1, January 1969, pp. 45–58.

Gilbert, Margaret. "Vices and Self-Knowledge." *Journal of Philosophy*, vol. 68, August 5, 1957, pp. 443–452.

Glicksberg, Charles I. "Sartrean Man." In *The Self in Modern Literature*. University Park: Penn State University Press, 1963, pp. 137–148.

_____. *Modern Literature and the Death of God*. The Hague: Nijhoff, 1966.

_____. "The Literary Struggle for Selfhood." *The Personalist*, vol. 62, pp. 52–65.

Goff, Robert. "On Sartre's Language." *Man and World*, vol. 3, no. 3-4, September-November 1970, pp. 370-374.

Gore, Keith O. *Sartre, La Nausée and Les Mouches*. (Studies in French Literature, no. 17). London: Edward Arnold, 1970.

_____. "Sartre and Flaubert: From Antipathy to Empathy." *Journal of the British Society for Phenomenology*, vol. 4, no. 2, May 1973, pp. 104-112.

Gorz, André. "Sartre: From Consciousness to Praxis." Translated by Thomas W. Busch. *Philosophy Today*, vol. 19, no. 4, Winter 1975, pp. 287-292.

_____. "Sartre and the Deaf." *Telos*, no. 33, Fall 1977, pp. 106-108.

Gotlind, Erik. *Three Theories of Emotion: Some Views on Philosophic Method*. Copenhagen: Ejnar Munksgaard, 1958.

Grene, Marjorie. "Sartre's Theory of Emotions." *Yale French Studies*, vol. 1, no. 1, 1948, pp. 97-102.

_____. "The Career of Action and Passion in Sartre's Thought." In *Philosophy In and Out of Europe*. Berkeley and Los Angeles: University of California Press, 1976, pp. 108-124.

Grossman, Morris. "How Sartre Must Be Read: An Examination of a Philosophical Method." *Bucknell Review*, vol. 16, no. 1, March 1968, pp. 18-29.

Grossvogel, David I. "Further Perils of Debate." In *The Self-conscious Stage in Modern French Drama*. New York: Columbia University Press, 1958, pp. 123-146.

_____. "Sartre: *Nausée*." In *Limits of the Novel*. Ithaca: Cornell University Press, 1967, pp. 226-255.

Halpern, Joseph. *Critical Fictions: The Literary Criticism of Jean-Paul Sartre*. New Haven: Yale University Press, 1976.

_____. "From Flaubert to Mallarmé: The Knights of Nothingness." *Diacritics*, vol. 3, no. 3, Fall 1973, pp. 14-17.

_____. "Trying to Understand '*L'Idiot*'." *Diacritics*, vol. 2, no. 4, Winter 1972, pp. 60-64.

Hamburger, Käte. *From Sophocles to Sartre*. Translated by Helen Sebba. New York: Ungar Publishing Co., 1969.

Hardré, Jacques. "Jean-Paul Sartre: Literary Critic." *Studies in Philology*, vol. 55, January 1958, pp. 98-106.

Hartmann, Klaus. "Praxis: A Ground for Social Theory." *Journal of the British Society for Phenomenology*, vol. 1, May 1970, pp. 47-58.

Hillman, James. *Emotion: A Comprehensive Phenomenology of Theories and Their Meaning for Therapy*. Evanston: Northwestern University Press, 1961.

Hochland, Janina. "A Theme in Sartre's Literary Work." *Journal of the British Society for Phenomenology*, vol. 1, May 1970, pp. 93-99.

Hook, Sidney. "Reflections on the Jewish Question." *Partisan Review*, vol. 16, no. 5, May 1949, pp. 463-482.

Horosz, William. "The Self-Transcending Totalization of Jean-Paul Sartre." *Philosophy Today*, vol. 19, no. 4, Winter 1975, pp. 293-304.

Howells, Christina M. "Sartre and the Commitment of Pure Art." *British Journal of Aesthetics*, vol. 18, no. 2, Spring 1978, pp. 172-182.

_____. "Sartre and the Language of Literature." *The Modern Language Review*, vol. 74, no. 3, July 1979, pp. 572-579.

_____. *Sartre's Theory of Literature*. London: Modern Humanities Research Association, 1979.

Huertas-Jourda, José. "The Place of *Les Mots* in Sartre's Philosophy." *Review of Metaphysics*, vol. 21, June 1968, pp. 724-744.

Jarrett-Kerr, Martin. "The Dramatic Philosophy of Sartre." *Tulane Drama Review*, vol. 1, no. 3, June 1957, pp. 41-48.

Jameson, Fredric. "Three Methods in Sartre's Literary Criticism." In *Modern French Criticism*. Edited by John K. Simon. Chicago: University of Chicago Press, 1972, pp. 193-228.

_____. *Sartre: The Origin of a Style*. New Haven: Yale University Press, 1961.

_____. "Sartre and History." In *Marxism and Form*. Princeton: Princeton University Press, 1971.

Javet, P. "Sartre: From *Being and Nothingness* to *Critique of Dialectical Reason*." *Philosophy Today*, vol. 9, Fall 1965, pp. 176-183.

Jeanson, Francis. "Moral Perspectives in Sartre's Thought." In *Contemporary European Ethics*. Edited by Joseph J. Kockelmans. New York: Anchor, 1972, pp. 270-97.

_____. "Hell and Bastardry." *Yale French Studies*, no. 30, Winter 1962-1963, pp. 5-22.

Jolivet, Regis. *Sartre or the Theology of the Absurd*. Translated by Wesley C. Piersol. New York: Newman Press, 1968.

Kaelin, Eugene F. *An Existentialist Aesthetic: The Theories of Sartre and Merleau-Ponty*. Madison: University of Wisconsin Press, 1962.

Kahn, E. "Sartre, the Philosopher and Writer." *Contemporary Review*, vol. 196, no. 1126, November 1959, pp. 243-245.

Kaufmann, Walter. "Nietzsche between Homer and Sartre: Five Treatments of the Orestes Story." *Revue Internationale de Philosophie*, vol. 18, 1964, no. 67, pp. 50-73.

Kern, Edith. "Abandon Hope, all Ye . . ." *Yale French Studies*, no. 30, 1962-1963, pp. 56-62.

_____. "The Self and the Other; a Dilemma of Existential Fiction." *Comparative Literature Studies*, vol. 5, no. 3, September 1968, pp. 329-337.

King, Thomas M. *Sartre and the Sacred*. Chicago: University of Chicago Press, 1974.

King-Farlow, John. "The Sartrean Analysis of Sexuality." *Journal of Existentialism*, vol. 2, no. 7, Winter 1962, pp. 291-302.

Klein, Maxine. "Philosopher-Dramatists." *Drama Survey*, vol. 6, Spring 1968, pp. 278-287.

Kleppner, Amy M. "Philosophy and the Literary Medium: The Existentialist Predicament." *Journal of Aesthetics and Art Criticism*, vol. 23, no. 2, Winter 1964, pp. 207-217.

Knight, Everett W. *Literature Considered as Philosophy*. Macmillan, 1958, pp. 189-218.

Kockelmans, Joseph J. "Sartre on Humanism." In *Contemporary European Ethics*. New York: Doubleday, 1972, pp. 255-269.

Krieger, Leonard. "History and Existentialism in Sartre." In *The Critical Spirit*. Edited by Boston: Beacon Press, 1967, pp. 239-266.

Laing, R.D. and Cooper, D.G. *Reason and Violence: A Decade of Sartre's Philosophy*. (With a foreword by Sartre.) London: Tavistock Publishers, 1964, and New York Vintage, 1971.

Laporte, Paul M. "Painting, Dialectics and Existentialism." *Texas Quarterly*, vol. 5, no. 4, Winter 1962, pp. 200-224.

Laufer, Roger. "Sartre as Literary Critic." *Meanjin*, vol. 18, 1959, pp. 427-434.

Lawler, James. *The Existentialist Marxism of Jean-Paul Sartre*. Amsterdam: B.R. Grüner Publishing Co., 1976.

Leland, Dorothy. "The Sartrean Cogito: A Journey Between Versions." *Research in Phenomenology*, vol. 5, 1975, pp. 129-141.

Levin, Harry. "A Literary Enormity: Sartre on Flaubert." *Journal of the History of Ideas*, vol. 23, October-December 1972, pp. 643-649.

Lycos, Kimon. "Images and the Imaginary." *Australian Journal of Philosophy*, vol. 43, no. 3, December 1965, pp. 321-338.

MacIntyre, Alasdair C. *A Short History of Ethics*. London: Routledge & Kegan Paul, 1966, pp. 249-269.

McCall, Dorothy. *The Theater of Jean-Paul Sartre*. New York: Columbia University Press, 1969.

McLeod, Ian. "Writing Biography: Sartre's Method." *The Oxford Literary Review*, vol. 3, no. 1, 1978, pp. 24-26.

McBride, William Leon. "Sartre: Man, Freedom and Praxis." In *Existential Philosophers: Kierkegaard to Merleau-Ponty*. Edited by George A. Schrader. New York: McGraw-Hill, 1967, pp. 261-330.

_____. "Sartre and the Phenomenology of Social Violence." In *New Essays in Phenomenology: Studies in the Philosophy of Experience*. Edited with an introduction by James M. Edie. Chicago: Quadrangle Books, 1969, pp. 290-313.

_____. "Sartre's Contribution to Social Theory." In *Social Theory at a Crossroads*, Pittsburgh: Duquesne University Press, 1980, pp. 41-80.

Molnar, Thomas. "The Politics of Sartre." *Commonweal*, vol. 66, 1957, pp. 439-442.

Morot-Sir, Edouard. "Sartre's Critique of Dialectical Reasoning." *Journal of the History of Ideas*, vol. 22, October 1961, pp. 573-581.

Morris, Phyllis Sutton. *Sartre's Concept of a Person*. Amherst: University of Massachusetts Press, 1976.

Morriston, Wesley. "Brute Contingency and the Principle of Sufficient Reason." *Philosophy Research Archives*, vol. 3, no. 1120, 1977.

Murdoch, Iris. "Review of *The Emotions: Outline of a Theory*." *Mind*, vol. 59, 1950, pp. 268-271.

Olson, Robert G. "The Three Theories of Motivation in the Philosophy of Jean-Paul Sartre." *Ethics*, vol. 66, April 1956, pp. 176-187.

O'Neill, John. "Situation and Temporality." *Philosophy and Phenomenological Research*, vol. 28, March 1968, pp. 413-422.

Pivčević, Edo. "Sartre's Road to Marxism." In *Husserl and Phenomenology*. London: Hutchinson University Library, 1970, pp. 133-144.

Prasad, S. "Religion and Atheistic Existentialism." *Indian Philosophical Quarterly*, vol. 4, July 1977, pp. 619-626.

Rau, Catherine. "The Aesthetic Views of Jean-Paul Sartre." *Journal of Aesthetics and Art Criticism*, vol. 9, 1950, pp. 139-147.

Robbins, C.W. "Sartre and the Moral Life." *Philosophy*, vol. 52, October 1977, pp. 409-424.

Schneider, Werner. "Sartre's Social Theory." *Dialogue*, vol. 7, June-July 1968, pp. 16-25.

Sefler, George. "Jean-Paul Sartre's A Priori Descriptions." *Philosophy Today*, vol. 19, Winter 1975, pp. 326-329.

Silverman, Hugh J. "Translating Philosophy into Sociology." *Human Studies*, vol. 1, no. 2, 1978, pp. 201-209.

_____. "Arthur C. Danto: Jean-Paul Sartre." *Man and World*, vol. 13, no. 1, Spring 1980, pp. 125-131.

_____. "Autobiographizing." *Partisan Review*, vol. 47, no. 1, 1980, pp. 142-146.

Stack, George. *Sartre's Philosophy of Social Existence*. St. Louis: Green, 1972.

St. Aubyn, F.C. "Sartre and the Essential Genet," *Symposium*, Summer 1954, pp. 82-101.

Suhl, Benjamin. *Jean-Paul Sartre: The Philosopher as a Literary Critic*. New York: Columbia University Press, 1970.

Thody, P.M.W. "Sartre's *Les Mots*: A Defense of Normality." In *Phenomenology and Education*. Edited by B. Curtis and W. Mays. London: Methuen, 1978, pp. 104-118.

Tint, Herbert. "Jean-Paul Sartre: *Critique de la raison dialectique.*" French Studies (Oxford), vol. 19, no. 2, 1965, pp. 204-206.

Ungar, Steven R. "Sartre, Ponge and the Ghost of Husserl." *Substance*, Winter 1974, pp. 139-150.

Warnock, Mary. "The Nature of the Mental Image: Phenomenology, Sartre, and Wittgenstein." In *Imagination*. Berkeley and Los Angeles: University of California Press, 1976, pp. 131-195.

Wreszin, Michael. "Jean-Paul Sartre: Philosopher as Dramatist." *Tulane Drama Review*, vol. 5, no. 3, March 1961, pp. 34-57.

Yovel, Yirmiahu. "Existentialism and Historical Dialectic." *Philosophy and Phenomenological Research*, vol. 39, no. 4, June 1979, pp. 480-497.

V. HISTORICAL AND COMPARATIVE STUDIES

(*Books and articles dealing with Sartre's relation to other major philosophers and traditions—includes not only contemporaries such as Husserl, Heidegger, Camus, Marcel, Buber, and Merleau-Ponty but also predecessors such as Parmenides, Descartes, Spinoza, Hegel, Kierkegaard, Nietzsche, and Marx.*)

Abel, Lionel. "Situating Sartre, with a Reply by Stuart Hampshire." *Partisan Review*, vol. 33, Winter 1966, pp. 152-160.

_____. "Sartre vs. Lévi-Strauss." *The Commonweal*, vol. 84, no. 13, June 17, 1966, pp. 364-368.

Adereth, Maxwell. *Commitment in Modern French Literature, Politics, and Society in Péguy, Aragon and Sartre*. New York: Schocken, 1967, pp. 127-191.

Alan, George. "Sartre's Construction of the Marxist Dialectic." *The Review of Metaphysics*, vol. 33, no. 1, September 1979, pp. 87-108.

Ames, Van Meter. "Mead and Sartre on Man." *Journal of Philosophy*, vol. 53, 1956, pp. 205-219.

Anderson, Thomas C. "Freedom as Supreme Value: The Ethics of Sartre and De Beauvoir." *Proceedings of the Catholic Philosophical Association*, vol. 50, 1976, pp. 60-71.

Aron, Raymond. "Sartre's Marxism." *Encounter*, June 1965, pp. 34-39.

_____. "Sartre's Marxism." Translated by John Weightman. In *Marxism and the Existentialists*. New York: Harper and Row, 1969, pp. 164-176. See also pp. 19-41: "Sartre and the Marxist-Leninists." Translated by Helen Weaver.

Bannan, John F. "Merleau-Ponty and Sartre." *The Philosophy of Merleau-Ponty*. New York: Harcourt, Brace and World, 1967, pp. 229-243.

Barnes, Hazel E. "Adler and Sartre: A Comment." *Journal of Individual Psychology*, vol. 21, no. 2, November 1965, pp. 163-168.

Bell, David R. "Marx, Sartre and Marxism." *Listener*, vol. 69, May 23, 1963, pp. 867-868.

Benda, Julien. "'Black' Literature and the New Philosophy." *The National Review*, vol. 127, no. 763, September 1946, pp. 249-252.

Berger, Gaston. "The Different Trends of Contemporary French Philosophy." *Philosophy and Phenomenological Research*, vol. 7, no. 1, September 1946, pp. 1-11.

Bertman, Martin A. "Existenz Politics: Camus and Sartre." *Agora*, Fall 1969, pp. 23-32.

Blair, R.G. "Imagination and Freedom in Spinoza and Sartre." *Journal of the British Society for Phenomenology*, vol. 1, May 1970, pp. 13-16.

Blakeley, Thomas J. "Sartre's *Critique de la raison dialectique* and the opacity of Marxism-Leninism." *Studies in Soviet Thought*, vol. 8, June–September 1968, pp. 122–135.

Borzaga, Reynold. *Contemporary Philosophy: Existential and Phenomenological Currents*. Milwaukee: The Bruce Publishing Company, 1966.

Brée, Germaine. *Camus and Sartre: Crisis and Commitment*. New York: Delacorte Press, 1972.

Brown, Delwin. "Sartre on the Self and Society: A Whiteheadian View of Sartre's Later Philosophy." *Southwestern Journal of Philosophy*, vol. 7, Fall 1976, pp. 65–76.

Brown, Richard H. "Dialectic and Structure in Jean-Paul Sartre and Claude Lévi-Strauss." *Dialectica*, vol. 32, 1978, pp. 165–184; also in *Human Studies*, vol. 2, no. 1, January 1979, pp. 1–19.

Burkle, Howard R. "Schaff and Sartre on the Grounds of Individual Freedom." *International Philosophical Quarterly*, vol. 5, December 1965, pp. 647–665.

Busch, Thomas W. "André Gorz on Sartre." *Philosophy Today*, vol. 19, Winter 1975, pp. 283–286.

———. "Phenomenology as Humanism: The Case of Husserl and Sartre." *Research in Phenomenology*, vol. 9, 1979, pp.

Burnier, Michel-Antoine. *Choice of Action: The French Existentialists on the Political Front Line*. Translated by B. Murchland. New York: Random House, 1968.

Carroll, O. "Sartre and Barth." *Philosophy Today*, vol. 9, 1965, pp. 101–111.

Caute, David. *Communism and the French Intellectuals 1914–1960*. London: André Deutsch, 1964.

Champigny, Robert. *Humanism and Human Racism: A Critical Study of Essays by Sartre and Camus*. The Hague: Mouton, 1972.

Charlesworth, Max. *The Existentialists and Jean-Paul Sartre*. London: George Prior Publishers, 1976.

Chiaromonte, N. "Sartre Versus Camus: A Political Quarrel." *Partisan Review*, vol. 19, November 1952, pp. 680–686.

Chiodi, Pietro. *Sartre and Marxism*. Translated by Kate Soper. Hassocks, Sussex: The Harvester Press and New York: Humanities Press, 1976.

Cohn, Robert Greer. "Sartre-Camus Resartus." *Yale French Studies*, no. 30, 1963, pp. 73–78.

Conkling, Mark. "Sartre's Refutation of the Freudian Unconscious." *Review of Existential Psychology and Psychiatry*, vol. 8, 1968, pp. 86–100.

Dillon, M.C. "Sartre and the Phenomenal Body and Merleau-Ponty's Critique." *Journal of the British Society for Phenomenology*. vol. 5, May 1974. pp. 144–157.

Donoso, Antón. "The Notion of Freedom in Sartre, Kolakowski, Marković and Kosik." *Philosophy Today*, vol. 23, no. 2, Summer 1979, pp. 113–127.

Doran, Robert M. "Sartre's Critique of the Husserlian Ego." *The Modern Schoolman*, vol. 44, May 1967, pp. 307–318.

Dufrenne, Mikel. "Existentialism and Existentialisms." *Philosophy and Phenomenological Research*, vol. 26, no. 1, September 1965, pp. 51–62.

Earle, William. "Phenomenology and Existentialism." *Journal of Philosophy*, vol. 57, no. 2, January 21, 1960, pp. 75–84.

Elkron, H. "Comment on Sartre from the Standpoint of Existential Psychotherapy." *Review of Existential Psychology and Psychiatry*, vol. 1, 1961.

Falk, Eugene H. *Types of Thematic Structures: The Nature and Function of Motifs in Gide, Camus and Sartre*. Chicago: University of Chicago Press, pp. 117–176.

Fell, Joseph J. *Heidegger and Sartre: An Essay in Being and Place*. New York: Columbia University Press, 1979.

Finklestein, Sydney. "Sartre, Existentialism and Marxism." *Political Affairs*, vol. 44, no. 10, October 1965, pp. 52–64.

_____. "Marxism and Existentialism." *Science and Society*, vol. 31, Winter 1967, pp. 58–66.

Flynn, Bernard. "The Question of Ontology: Sartre and Merleau-Ponty." *The Horizons of the Flesh: Critical Perspectives on the Thought of Merleau-Ponty*. Edited by Garth Gillan. Carbondale: Southern Illinois University Press, 1972.

Fontana, Andrea and Van de Water, Richard. "The Existential Thought of Jean-Paul Sartre and Maurice Merleau-Ponty." *Existential Sociology*. Edited by Jack D. Douglas and John M. Johnson. New York: Cambridge University Press, 1977, pp. 101–129.

Glicksberg, Charles I. "Existentialism versus Marxism." In *The Tragic Vision in Twentieth-Century Literature*. Carbondale: Southern Illinois University Press, 1963, pp. 126–136.

Gorz, André. "Sartre and Marx." *New Left Review*, no. 37, May-June 1966, pp. 29–53. Reprinted in *Western Marxism: A Critical Reader*. London: New Left Review, Verso Editions, 1978, pp. 176–200.

Grene, Marjorie. "*L'homme est une passion inutile:* Sartre and Heidegger." *Kenyon Review*, vol. 9, no. 1, Spring 1947, pp. 167–185.

_____. "Sartre and Heidegger: The Free Resolve," and "Sartre and Heidegger: The Self and Other Selves." In *Dreadful Freedom*. Chicago: Chicago University Press, 1948, 1960, pp. 41–94.

_____. "The Aesthetic Dialogue of Sartre and Merleau-Ponty." *Journal of the British Society for Phenomenology*, vol. 1, no. 2, May 1970, pp. 59–72.

Hansen, Linda. "Pain and Joy in Human Relationships: Jean-Paul Sartre and Simone de Beauvoir." *Philosophy Today*, vol. 23, no. 4, Winter 1979, pp. 338–346.

Hartmann, Klaus. *Sartre's Ontology: A Study of 'Being and Nothingness' in the Light of Hegel's Logic*. Evanston: Northwestern University Press, 1966.

_____. "Praxis: A Ground for Social Theory?" *Journal of the British Society for Phenomenology*, vol. 1, no. 2, May 1970, pp. 47–58.

Heidegger, Martin. "Letter on Humanism." Translated by Frank A. Capuzzi. In *Martin Heidegger: Basic Writings*. Edited by David Farrell Krell. New York: Harper and Row, 1974, pp. 193–242.

Heidsieck, François. "Honor and Nobility of Soul: Descartes to Sartre." *International Philosophical Quarterly*, vol. 1, 1961, pp. 569–592.

Howard, Dick. "The Rationality of the Dialectic: Jean-Paul Sartre." In *The Marxian Legacy*. New York: Urizen, 1977, pp. 153–185.

Howells, Christina M. "Sartre and Freud." *French Studies*, vol. 33, no. 2, April 1979, pp. 157–176.

Hughes, H. Stuart. *The Obstructed Path; French Social Thought in the Years of Desperation, 1930–1960*. New York: Harper & Row, 1968.

Johnson, Howard A. "On Sartre and Kierkegaard." *The American-Scandinavian Review*, September 1947, pp. 220–225.

Kern, Edith. *Existential Thought and Fictional Technique: Kierkegaard, Sartre, Beckett*. New Haven: Yale University Press, 1970.

King-Farlow, John, and Coby, Arthur. "Creation and Human Freedom: Pico's Answer to Sartre." *Darshana International*, vol. 2, no. 2, April 1962, pp. 22–28.

Kirsner, Douglas. *The Schizoid World of Jean-Paul Sartre and R.D. Laing*. St. Lucia: University of Queensland Press, 1976.

Kline, George L. "The Existentialist Rediscovery of Hegel and Marx." In *Phenomenology and Existentialism*. Edited by Edward Lee and Maurice Mandlebaum. Baltimore: The Johns Hopkins University Press, 1967, pp. 113–138.

Klinefelter, Donald. "The Sartrean Ethics of Hazel Barnes." *Philosophy Today,* vol. 19, Winter 1975, pp. 330-340.

Kvale, Steinar, and Grenness, Carl Erik. "Skinner and Sartre: Toward a Radical Phenomenology of Behavior?" *Review of Existential Psychology and Psychiatry,* vol. 7, 1967, pp. 128-150. Reprinted in *Phenomenological Psychology, Vol. 2.* Edited by A. Giorgi, C.T. Fischer, and E.L. Murray. Pittsburgh: Duquesne University Press, 1975, pp. 38-59.

Kwant, Remy C. "Merleau-Ponty and Sartre." In *The Phenomenological Philosophy of Merleau-Ponty.* Pittsburgh: Duquesne University Press, 1963, pp. 203-223.

Langan, Thomas. "Existentialism and Phenomenology in France." *Recent Philosophy, Hegel to the Present.* Edited by Etienne Gilson et al. New York: Random House, 1964, pp. 374-408.

Lapointe, François H. "The American Response to Jean-Paul Sartre." *Dialogos,* April 1975, pp. 153-157.

Larson, Curtus W.R. "Kierkegaard and Sartre." *The Personalist,* vol. 35, no. 2, Spring 1954, pp. 128-135.

Larson, Gerald J. "Classical Samkhya and the Phenomenological Ontology of Sartre." *Philosophy East & West,* vol. 19, January 1969, pp. 45-58.

Lauer, Quentin. "Four Phenomenologists." *Thought,* vol. 32, 1958, pp. 183-204.

Lessing, Arthur. "Marxist Existentialism." *Review of Metaphysics,* vol. 20, March 1967, pp. 461-482.

Levi, Albert William. "The Meaning of Existentialism for Contemporary International Relations: The Marxist Existentialism of Sartre." *Ethics,* vol. 72, no. 4, July 1962, pp. 233-249.

Lewis, John. "Marxism and Its Critics." *The Marxist Quarterly,* vol. 2, no. 4, October 1955, pp. 203-216.

Lichtheim, George. "Sartre, Marxism and History." *History and Theory,* vol. 3, 1963-1964, pp. 222-246.

Lowrie, Walter. "Existence as Understood by Kierkegaard and/or Sartre." *Sewanee Review,* vol. 58, July 1950, pp. 379-401.

Lukács, George. "Existentialism or Marxism?" In *Philosophy For The Future.* Edited by R.W. Sellars. New York: Macmillan Co., 1949. Reprinted in *Existentialism Versus Marxism.* Edited by George Novack. New York: Delta Books, 1966, pp. 134-153.

Marsh, James L. "Freedom, Receptivity and God." *International Journal of the Philosophy of Religion,* vol. 6, Winter 1975, pp. 219-233.

Martin, Vincent. *Existentialism: Kierkegaard, Sartre and Camus.* Washington, D.C.: Thomist Press, 1962.

Mazis, Glenn A. "Touch and Vision: Rethinking with Merleau-Ponty and Sartre on the Caress." *Philosophy Today,* vol. 23, no. 4, Winter 1979, pp. 321-328.

McBride, William L. *Fundamental Change in Law and Society: Hart and Sartre on Revolution.* The Hague: Mouton, 1970, and New York: Humanities Press, 1971.

Mehlman, Jeffrey. *A Structuralist Study of Autobiography: Proust, Leiris, Sartre, Lévi-Strauss.* Ithaca: Cornell University Press, 1974, pp. 151-186.

Mendoza, Esther C. "'Being-for-others' in Sartre and G. Marcel." *St. Louis Quarterly* (Baguio City, Philippines), vol. 4, 1966, pp. 5-36.

Merleau-Ponty, Maurice. "Sartre and Ultrabolshevism." In *Adventures of the Dialectic.* Translated by Joseph Bien. Evanston: Northwestern University Press, 1973, pp. 95-201.

_____. "The Battle Over Existentialism." In *Sense and Non-Sense.* Translated by Hubert L. Dreyfus and Patricia A. Dreyfus. Evanston: Northwestern University Press, 1964, pp. 71-82.

_____. "Interrogation and Dialectic." In *The Visible and the Invisible*. Translated by Alphonso Lingis. Evanston: Northwestern University Press, 1968, pp. 50-104.

Moreland, John M. "For-Itself and In-Itself in Sartre and Merleau-Ponty." *Philosophy Today*, vol. 17, no. 4, Winter 1973, pp. 311-318.

Munford, C.J. "Sartrean Existentialism and the Philosophy of History." *Journal of World History*, vol. 11, no. 3, 1968, pp. 392-404.

Murchland, Bernard. "Sartre and Camus: The Anatomy of a Quarrel." In Michel-Antoine Burnier, *Choice of Action: The French Existentialists on the Political Front Line*. Translated by B. Murchland. New York: Random House, 1968.

Natanson, Maurice. "Phenomenology and Existentialism: Husserl and Sartre on Intentionality." *The Modern Schoolman*, vol. 37, 1959, pp. 1-10. Reprinted in *Philosophy Today, No. 3*. Edited by Jerry H. Gill. New York: Macmillan, 1970, pp. 61-71.

Novack, George. "Marxism and Existentialism." *International Socialist Review*, Spring 1965. Reprinted (abridged) in *Existentialism Versus Marxism*. New York: Delta Books, 1966, pp. 317-340.

Odajnyk, Walter. "The Individual and Marxism." *Darshana International*, vol. 3, no. 3, August 1963, pp. 46-56.

_____. *Marxism and Existentialism*. New York: Doubleday and Co., Anchor Book, 1965.

Passmore, J.A. "Existentialsm and Phenomenology." In *A Hundred Years of Philosophy*. New York: Basic Books, 1966, pp. 476-516.

Patri, Aime. "Descartes, Sartre and Maritain." *Merkur*, vol. 1, 1947, pp. 615-624.

Pettit, Philip. "Parmenides and Sartre." *Philosophical Studies*, vol. 17, 1968, pp. 161-184.

Piorkowski, Henry. "The Path of Phenomenology: Husserl, Heidegger, Sartre, Merleau-Ponty." *Duns Scotus Philosophical Association*, vol. 30, 1966, pp. 177-221.

Pollman, Leo. *Sartre and Camus: Literature of Existence*. Translated by Helen Sebba and Gregor Sebba. New York: Frederick Ungar, 1970.

Poole, Roger C. "Hegel, Kierkegaard and Sartre." *New Blackfriars*, vol. 47, July 1966, pp. 532-541.

Poster, Mark. *Existential Marxism in Postwar France: From Sartre to Althusser*. Princeton: Princeton University Press, 1975.

_____. *Sartre's Marxism*. London: Pluto Press, 1979.

Prosch, Harry, "Analytic Philosophy and Existentialism." In *The Genesis of Twentieth Century Philosophy*. New York: Doubleday, 1964.

Rabil, Albert Jr. "Merleau-Ponty and Sartrian Existentialism." In *Merleau-Ponty: Existentialist of the Social World*. New York: Columbia University Press, 1967, pp. 116-140.

Rauch, Leo. "Sartre, Merleau-Ponty and the 'Hole' in Being." *Philosophical Studies* (Ireland), vol. 18, 1969, pp. 119-132.

Reinhardt, Kurt. *The Existentialist Revolt*. New York: Ungar Publishing Co., 1960.

Ricoeur, Paul. "Existential Phenomenology." In *Husserl: An Analysis Of His Phenomenology*. Translated by Edward G. Ballard and Lester E. Embree. Evanston: Northwestern University Press, 1967, pp. 202-212.

_____. *History and Truth*. Translated by Charles A. Kelbley. Evanston: Northwestern University Press, 1965, pp. 319-328.

Roberts, D.E. "Faith and Freedom in Existentialism: A Study of Kierkegaard and Sartre." *Theology Today*, vol. 8, no. 4, January 1952, pp. 469-482.

Rockmore, Tom. "Sartre and 'The Philosophy of our Time'." *Journal of the British Society for Phenomenology*, vol. 9, May 1978, pp. 92-101.

Rodriguez, Alcala H. "José Ortega y Gasset and J.-P. Sartre on Existence and Human Destiny." *Research Studies of the State College of Washington*, vol. 24, no. 3, 1956, pp. 193-211.

Sachs, Mendel. "Positivism, Realism and Existentialism in Mach's Influence on Contemporary Physics." *Philosophy and Phenomenological Research*, vol. 30, March 1970, pp. 403-420.

Salvan, Jacques L. *The Scandalous Ghost: Sartre's Existentialism as Related to Vitalism, Humanism, Mysticism and Marxism.* Detroit: Wayne State University Press, 1967.

Savage, Catherine. "Sartre and the Road to Liberty." In *Malraux, Sartre and Aragon as Political Novelists*. Gainesville: University of Florida Humanities Monographs, no. 17, 1964, pp. 17-42.

Scanlon, John D. "Consciousness, the Streetcar, and the Ego: Pro Husserl, Contra Sartre." *The Philosophical Forum*, vol. 2, no. 3, Spring 1971, pp. 332-354.

_____. "Intolerable Human Responsibility." *Research in Phenomenology*, vol. 1, 1971, pp. 75-90.

Schaff, Adam. *A Philosophy of Man.* New York: Monthly Review Press, 1963.

_____. "Stocktaking in Philosophy." *Polish Perspectives*, vol. 2, no. 11, November 1959, pp. 6-20.

Schaldenbrand, Sister Mary Aloysius. *Phenomenologies of Freedom: An Essay on the Philosophies of Jean-Paul Sartre and Gabriel Marcel.* Washington: Catholic University of America Press, 1960.

Schmidt, James. "Lordship and Bondage in Merleau-Ponty and Sartre." *Political Theory*, vol. 7, May 1979, pp. 201-227.

Silverman, Hugh J. (with David A. Dilworth). "A Cross-Cultural Approach to the De-Ontological Self-Paradigm." *The Monist*, vol. 61, no. 1, January 1978, pp. 82-95.

_____. "Jean-Paul Sartre versus Michel Foucault on Civilizational Study." *Philosophy and Social Criticism*, vol. 5, no. 2, July 1978, pp. 161-171.

_____. "Sartre and the Structuralists." *International Philosophical Quarterly*, vol. 18, no. 3, September 1978, pp. 341-358.

_____. "Biographical Situations, Cognitive Structures and Human Development: Confronting Sartre and Piaget." *Journal of Phenomenological Psychology*, vol. 10, no. 2, Fall 1979, pp.

Smith, Vincent Edward. "Existentialism and Existence." *The Thomist*, vol. 11, no. 2, April 1948, pp. 141-196, and vol. 11, no. 3, July 1948, pp. 297-329.

Smith, Colin. "Sartre and Merleau-Ponty: The Case for a Modified Essentialism." *Journal of the British Society for Phenomenology*, vol. 1, May 1970, pp. 73-79.

Spiegelberg, Herbert. "French Existentialism: Its Social Philosophies." *Kenyon Review*, vol. 16, no. 3, 1954, pp. 446-454.

_____. "Husserl's Philosophy and Sartre's Existentialism." In *Phenomenology*. Edited by Joseph J. Kockelmans. New York: Doubleday Anchor, pp. 252-266.

Stack, George R. "Dialectical Reason and Social Phenomena." *Dialogos*, April 1974, pp. 37-62.

Sukale, Michael. *Comparative Studies in Phenomenology.* The Hague: Nijhoff, 1976.

Sweeney, Leo. "Aquinas or Philosophy of Subjectivity." *The Modern Schoolman*, vol. 47, November 1969, pp. 57-70.

Thomas, Charles. "Sartre as a Critic of Camus." *New Blackfriars*, vol. 45, June 1964, pp. 269-273.

Tibbetts, Paul. "Some Recent Philosophical Contributions to the Problem of Consciousness." *Philosophy Today*, vol. 14, Spring 1970, pp. 3-22.

Tiryakian, Edward A. *Sociologism and Existentialism: Two Perspectives on the Individual and Society.* Englewood Cliffs, New Jersey: Prentice-Hall, 1962.
Ussher, Arland. *Journey Through Dread: A Study of Kierkegaard, Heidegger and Sartre.* London: Dawren-Finlayson, 1955, and New York: Devin-Adair, 1959.
Walker, Leslie J. "Gilbert Ryle and Jean-Paul Sartre." *The Month,* 1950, vol. 189, pp. 432-443.
Whitford, Margaret. "Merleau-Ponty's Critique of Sartre's Philosophy: An Interpretive Account." *French Studies,* vol. 33, no. 3, July 1979, pp. 305-318.

Notes on the Contributors

The Editors:

FREDERICK A. ELLISTON has taught at Trinity College, York University, Union College and the University of Victoria, British Columbia. He has edited several books in both ethics and continental philosophy: *Philosophy and Sex* (Prometheus, 1975), *Feminism and Philosophy* (Littlefield Adams, 1977), *Husserl: Expositions and Appraisals* (University of Notre Dame Press, 1977), *Heidegger's Existential Analytic* (Mouton, 1978), and *Husserl: Shorter Works* (University of Notre Dame Press, forthcoming). His present research, sponsored by the National Institute for Mental Health, focuses on moral and methodological issues in Criminal Justice, police ethics and principles of sentencing.

HUGH J. SILVERMAN is Assistant Professor of Philosophy and Comparative Literature at the State University of New York at Stony Brook. He taught previously at Stanford University, has been a visiting professor at Duquesne University and New York University, and has lectured in the United States, Canada, England, Germany, Italy, and Sweden. He is editor of the forthcoming *Piaget, Philosophy and the Human Sciences* (Humanities in the U.S.; Harvester in England) and has published over twenty articles in philosophical and interdisciplinary journals on recent continental thought, philosophical psychology, and aesthetics. His translations include Merleau-Ponty's *Consciousness and the Acquisition of Language)* Northwestern, 1973) and "Philosophy and Non-Philosophy since Hegel" (Telos, Fall 1976).

JOHN E. ATWELL, Associate Professor of Philosophy at Temple University, attended Franklin College (B.A. 1957), the University of Freiburg (1955-56) and the University of Wisconsin (Ph.D. 1964) where he was the recipient of the DAAD (Deutscher Akademischer Austausch-Dienst) Fellowship. His main areas of academic interest are phenomenology, existentialism, nineteenth century philosophy (especially Schopenhauer and Nietzsche), Kant and ethics.

THOMAS W. BUSCH received his M.A. (1962) and his Ph.D. (1967) from Marquette University, and is presently Professor of Philosophy at Villanova University where he has taught since 1964. He is a member of the Society for Phenomenology and Existential Philosophy, the Merleau-Ponty Circle and the American Catholic Philosophical Association. In contemporary French philosophy, his field of specialization, he has published articles on Sartre and ontology, phenomenology, Marxism and alienation.

MIKEL DUFRENNE, who was born in 1910, graduated from the Ecole Normale Superieure and received his doctorate from the University of Paris. He has been professor of philosophy and aesthetics at the universities of Poitiers and Paris-Nanterre as well as visiting professor at SUNY/Buffalo, Stanford University, and the University of Montreal. He is author of some dozen books including the celebrated *Phenomenology of Aesthetic Experience.*

THOMAS ROBERT FLYNN received his Ph.D. from Columbia University in 1970, where he also taught and was twice selected as a Danforth Teacher Grantee. He has been a member of the faculty at Carroll College (Montana), Catholic University and American University. He conducts graduate seminars at Emory University on Sartre, Foucault and Historical Intelligibility, as well as courses in existentialism, phenomenology, and aesthetics. He has published numerous articles in these areas, and is currently writing a book in social philosophy dealing with collective responsibility.

LEO FRETZ teaches philosophy at the Technische Hoqeschool in Delft, The Netherlands. He wrote the introduction to the Dutch translation of *The Transcendence Of The Ego* (1978) which also includes The Dutch version of the interview offered in this volume. His essay on Sartre's concept of individuality appeared in the special issue of *Obliques* on Sartre (1979).

GARTH JACKSON GILLAN, Associate Professor of Philosophy at Southern Illinois University, is a member of the American Philosophical Association, the Society for Phenomenology and Existential Philosophy and the Merleau-Ponty Circle. He has edited and contributed to *Horizons Of The Flesh* and authored numerous articles on phenomenology, linguistics, language and semiotics.

MICHEL HAAR graduated from the Ecole Normale Superieure in 1962 and was a fellow at the Fondation Thiers from 1965 to 1968, when he became an Assistant Professor at the Sorbonne where he is now tenured. In addition to his translations of Heidegger and Nietzsche, he has published extensively on Freud, Marcuse, technology and language.

EUGENE F. KAELIN is Professor of Philosophy at Florida State University where he has taught since 1965. Previously he was a Fulbright Scholar in France, a Postdoctoral Fellow in Bordeaux, and ACLS Fellow and a Research Fellow in Freiburg. In addition to his articles on value-theory in ethics, aesthetics, education and science, he has published *An Existentialist Aesthetic* and *Art And Existence.*

INGBERT KNECHT received his doctorate of philosophy from Bonn University in 1971 and has taught at the Bonn Institute of Pedagogics since 1972. In addition to his three books and ten articles on Sartre and Marx, he has published articles on the philosophy of science and special questions of pedagogic theory.

XAVIER O. MONASTERIO received his doctorate in philosophy from the University of Paris in 1964. He has taught in Mexico, his native country, and since 1966 at the University of Dayton. He has published three books in Spanish, and his articles in the general areas of phenomenology and existentialism have appeared in American and French journals.

PHYLLIS SUTTON MORRIS received her B.A. from the University of California, Berkeley (1953) and her Ph.D. from the University of Michigan (1969). She teaches a wide variety of courses in philosophy and the humanities at Hamilton College, where she is Associate Professor of Philosophy. In addition to *Sartre's Concept Of A Person: An Analytic Approach* she has published numerous articles on existentialism, especially on issues overlapping the philosophy of mind.